MOON

DENVER, BOULDER & COLORADO SPRINGS

MINDY SINK

Contents

Discover Denver, Boulder & Colorado Springs 6
5 Top Experiences 10
Planning Your Time 14
The Best of the Front Range 17
• Welcome to Beertown 19
• Get Outside 20

Denver 24
Sights 29
Entertainment and Events 57
Shopping 82
Sports and Recreation 92
Food 99
Accommodations 114
Transportation and Services 124
Golden 127
Loveland and Winter Park 133

Boulder 136
Sights 140
Entertainment and Events 144
Shopping 150
Sports and Recreation 154
Food 159
Accommodations 165
Transportation and Services 168
Vicinity of Boulder 169
Rocky Mountain National Park 174

Fort Collins 178
Sights 180
Entertainment and Events 184
Shopping 190
Sports and Recreation 194
Food 199
Accommodations 203

Transportation and Services 204
Vicinity of Fort Collins 205

Colorado Springs **207**
Sights 209
Entertainment and Events 218
Shopping 223
Sports and Recreation 224
Food 229
Accommodations 234
Transportation and Services 237
Vicinity of Colorado Springs 238

Background **246**
The Landscape 246
History 248
Government and Economy 252

Essentials **253**
Transportation 253
Conduct and Customs 256
Travel Tips 259

Resources **264**
Suggested Reading 264
Internet Resources 265

Index **268**

List of Maps **274**

Although every effort was made to make sure the information in this book was accurate when going to press, research was impacted by the COVID-19 pandemic and things may have changed since the time of writing. Be sure to confirm specific details, like opening hours, closures, and travel guidelines and restrictions, when making your travel plans. For more detailed information, see p. 254.

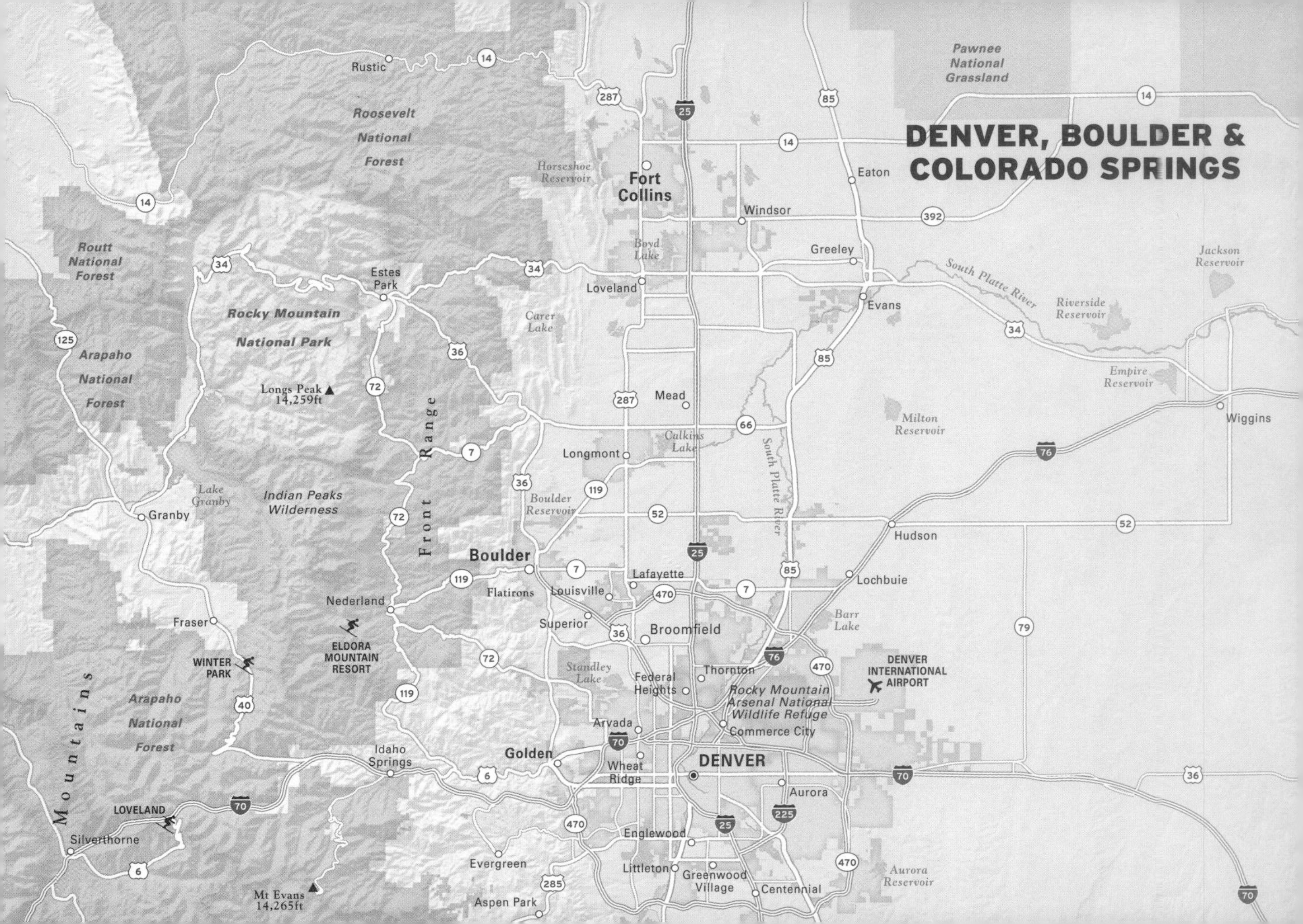
DENVER, BOULDER & COLORADO SPRINGS
Pawnee National Grassland
Roosevelt National Forest
Routt National Forest
Arapaho National Forest
Rocky Mountain National Park
Indian Peaks Wilderness
Front Range
Mountains
Longs Peak 14,259ft
Mt Evans 14,265ft
Rustic
Estes Park
Granby
Lake Granby
Fraser
WINTER PARK
LOVELAND
Silverthorne
Nederland
ELDORA MOUNTAIN RESORT
Idaho Springs
Evergreen
Aspen Park
Horseshoe Reservoir
Carer Lake
Fort Collins
Boyd Lake
Loveland
Windsor
Eaton
Greeley
Evans
South Platte River
Jackson Reservoir
Riverside Reservoir
Empire Reservoir
Milton Reservoir
Wiggins
Mead
Calkins Lake
Longmont
Boulder Reservoir
Boulder
Flatirons
Lafayette
Louisville
Superior
Broomfield
Hudson
Lochbuie
Barr Lake
DENVER INTERNATIONAL AIRPORT
Standley Lake
Federal Heights
Thornton
Rocky Mountain Arsenal National Wildlife Refuge
Arvada
Commerce City
Golden
Wheat Ridge
DENVER
Aurora
Englewood
Littleton
Greenwood Village
Centennial
Aurora Reservoir
14
287
25
85
392
34
125
36
72
7
66
287
119
52
76
470
79
70
6
40
225
285

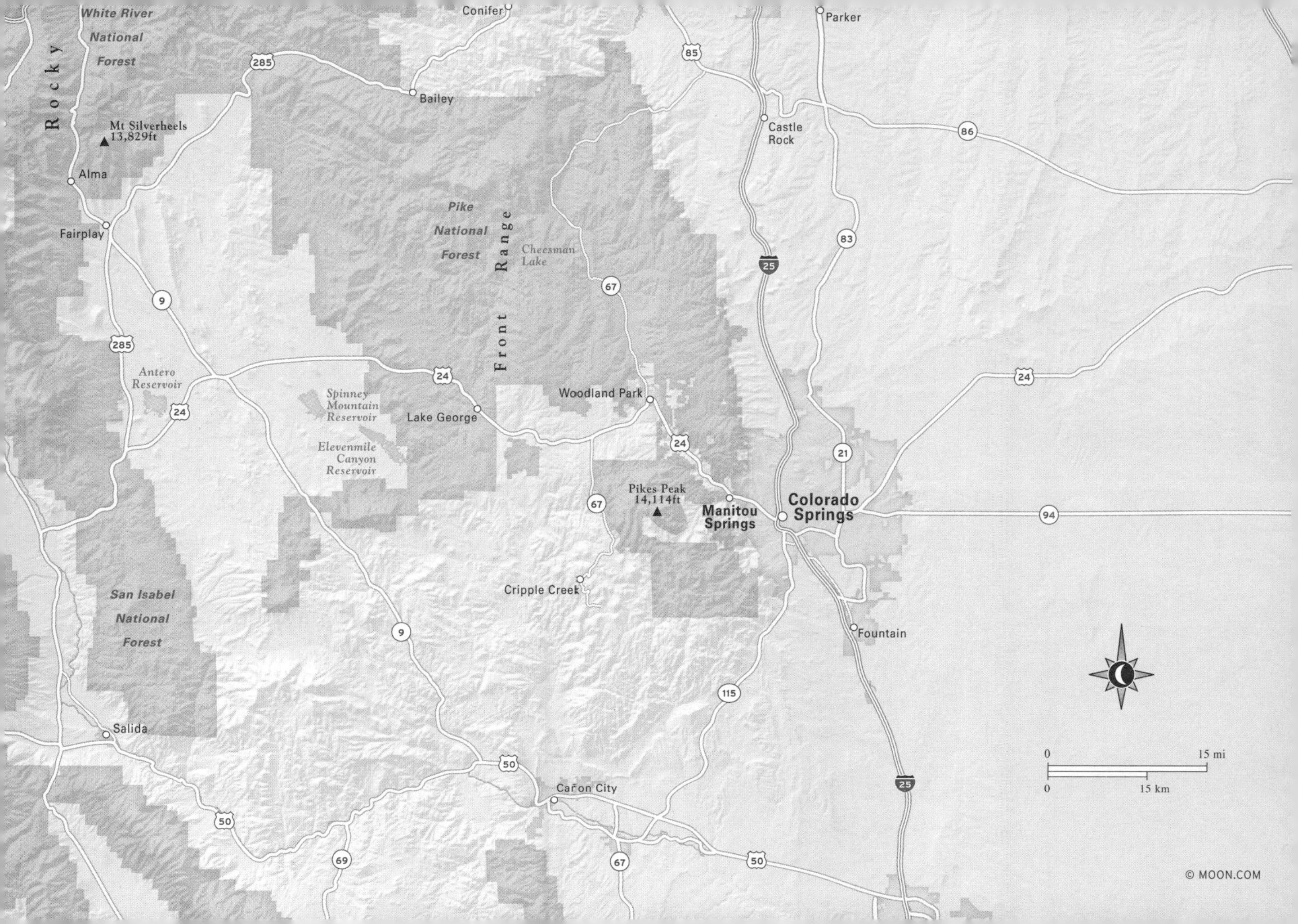
White River National Forest
Rocky
Conifer
Parker
Bailey
Castle Rock
Mt Silverheels 13,829ft
Alma
Fairplay
Pike National Forest
Front Range
Cheesman Lake
Antero Reservoir
Spinney Mountain Reservoir
Lake George
Elevenmile Canyon Reservoir
Woodland Park
Pikes Peak 14,114ft
Manitou Springs
Colorado Springs
Cripple Creek
Fountain
San Isabel National Forest
Salida
Cañon City
0
15 mi
0
15 km
© MOON.COM

DISCOVER

Denver, Boulder & Colorado Springs

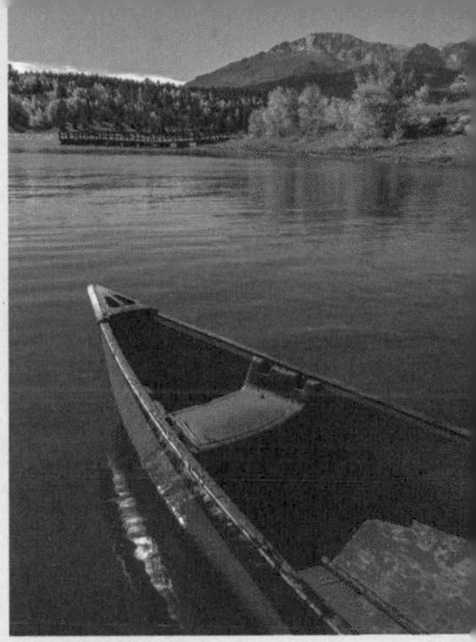

Colorado's Front Range cities straddle the space between the foothills east of the Rockies and the Great Plains—a landscape that stretches out to the horizon. While Denver, Boulder, Fort Collins, and Colorado Springs share some similarities, each has its own personality, natural appeal, and distinct history.

Denver is the Mile High City—5,280 feet (1,609 m) above sea level with a 140-mile (220-km) vista of the Rocky Mountains to the west. Recreation is a way of life here, but this diverse city also includes neighborhoods rich in ethnic and local foods, cutting-edge architecture, historical sites, packed bars and nightclubs, and an abundance of open space. Key attractions include the Denver Art Museum and the Red Rocks Amphitheatre.

Just west of Denver, the city of Boulder sits nestled up to the foothills. Home to the University of Colorado, the town offers a plethora of outdoor opportunities—visitors can hike or rock climb the Flatirons, or meander around on two wheels. Boulder is gaining recognition as a start-up hub for tech companies, but it continues to offer classic college-town appeal enhanced by sophisticated dining and nightlife.

Clockwise from top left: tulips at Boulder's Pearl Street Mall; History Colorado Center in Denver; canoeing; National Western Stock Show; Denver Zoo; Garden of the Gods.

North of Boulder is another college town with different roots to the past: Fort Collins. Its historic downtown is fueled in part by a robust craft brewing scene. Bike paths wind alongside the Cache La Poudre River as it runs through town, and cyclists can glimpse river rafters who've just hit the rapids upstream.

South of Denver, Colorado Springs was founded as a resort town, and there is still a touch of luxury here. Today it's known as home to a few notable military installations—Fort Carson, NORAD, the U.S. Air Force Academy—but the city also offers boutique shopping, world-class art, film festivals, and luxurious resorts.

On a visit to the Front Range, historic towns, distinctive architecture, mountain peaks, and funky college towns are all within easy reach.

Clockwise from top left: Rocky Mountain National Park; Denver Art Museum; the Julie Penrose Fountain in Colorado Springs; hiking near Boulder's Flatirons.

ART

5 TOP EXPERIENCES

1 **Wander the Garden of the Gods:** The striking red rocks draw visitors from all over (page 212).

2 Savor suds time: There are a lot of ways to enjoy beer along the Front Range, including Denver's Beer Spa, where you literally soak in beer and drink in the taproom (pages 19 and 65).

3 Rock out at Red Rocks Amphitheatre: This unique amphitheater is known for its phenomenal open-air acoustics and live concerts, but the scenery can be enjoyed anytime, even without music (page 53).

4 Dine in Denver: The city's food scene is alive with creativity, fresh ingredients, and some local celebrity chefs (page 99).

5 **Hike in Rocky Mountain National Park:** Waterfalls, lakes, and stellar views await (page 176).

Planning Your Time

Where to Go

Denver

Denver seems to have it all: unique history, culture, **outdoor activities,** thriving **music and sports** scenes, **world-class restaurants,** highly regarded **brewpubs,** and impressive universities. It's so easy to start the day with a **hike** in the foothills at **Red Rocks Amphitheatre,** a **bike** ride on **Cherry Creek,** a **kayak** trip on some white water in the **South Platte River**—all within the city limits or a few minutes' drive away—then rinse off, change, and find yourself savoring a gourmet meal before taking in a top show at the **Denver Performing Arts Complex.** Be sure to leave time for exploring art galleries and museums, such as the Denver Art Museum.

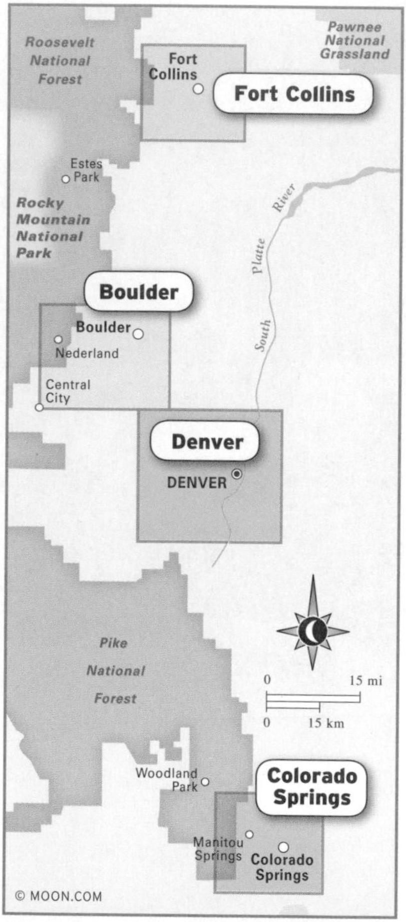

Boulder

Just 30 miles (48 km) northwest of Denver, Boulder is a small yet scenic college town with easy access to **outdoor recreation.** Wander through the **Boulder County Farmers Market** in summer, ride a **bike** along **Boulder Creek** and into the foothills, and **hike** in **Chautauqua.** For more urban adventures, enjoy an amazing meal at one of the city's many impressive **regional-fare restaurants** or amble around the **University of Colorado** campus to check out the architecture, museums, and planetarium.

Fort Collins

Fort Collins is a quiet college town about 65 miles (105 km) north of Denver. Its charming **Old Town** invites visitors to enjoy a relaxing stroll among the shops and historic buildings. Plan a day of sampling **craft beer** at some of the city's many **breweries,** and maybe **ride bikes** from one to the next to really feel like a local. The **Great Stupa of Dharmakaya** offers a scenic excursion an hour west.

Colorado Springs

Though it's Colorado's second-largest city, Colorado Springs isn't as well known as Denver or

Boulder. Situated about 70 miles (113 km) south of Denver, the city maintains a large military presence and offers a variety of sights and activities. Families will love a stay at **The Broadmoor** and a trip to the **Cheyenne Mountain Zoo.** Outdoors enthusiasts can scale **Pikes Peak** or wander the **Garden of the Gods.** The town of **Manitou Springs,** the gateway to Pikes Peak, offers historic charm and mineral springs for sampling.

When to Go

When most folks think of Colorado, they think of snow and skiing. But locals know that there is more to see and do in the warmer seasons. Denver is a draw for tourists year-round but is generally more crowded in the **summer.** This is high season, when there are music festivals and blockbuster theater and art shows, and driving into the foothills and mountains is easier. Hotel rates tend to be at their peak.

Spring is the shoulder season. Flowers are in bloom at the lower elevations in Denver, Boulder, Colorado Springs, and Fort Collins, even though it's still snowing in the mountains. There is a reverse migration of sorts as people who live in the mountains come to the lower elevations for that taste of spring. When spring fever hits, the bicycles come out to replace snowshoes and skis for a little outdoor fun.

Fall is a lovely time to visit, especially in the foothills as the trees change from green to gold and light up the hillsides. Boulder, Colorado Springs, and Fort Collins often see these fall colors sooner than Denver does.

The low season in the Front Range cities is **winter,** when hotels and attractions offer many discounts as locals and visitors alike flock to the ski slopes in the Rockies. You can combine the city and the mountains: take the Ski Train

the Flatirons above Boulder, dusted with snow

wildflowers blooming along a hiking trail

aspen trees in the fall

(aka Winter Park Express) from Union Station to Winter Park for a day. Those who don't want (or cannot get up) to the ski slopes find ways to snowshoe, cross-country ski, sled, and even snowboard at city parks to make the most of the season.

No matter what time of year you come here, you might hear a local remark, "If you don't like the weather, just wait five minutes." In a single day you might need to wear a T-shirt and shorts, a fleece coat and pants, and a sun hat or a wool cap. Or, even more likely, you'll see a guy in flip-flops, shorts, and a parka sitting outside drinking a beer when it's snowing—very Colorado!

The Best of the Front Range

Spend the week exploring Colorado's Front Range, with stops in Denver, Boulder, Fort Collins, and Colorado Springs. Following are some suggestions for where to go and what to do in each city.

Denver

DAY 1

Fly into **Denver International Airport** and check into the **Crawford Hotel** at **Union Station** after riding the light rail train into downtown. If it's summer and you've got little kids in tow, they can cool off in the splash fountain on the plaza. Do a little shopping at **Tattered Cover Book Store** and **5 Green Boxes,** then enjoy a meal at **Mercantile** or one of the station's many on-site restaurants. If it's baseball season, walk roughly two blocks north from Union Station and see if there are some cheap "rockpile" seats for the Colorado Rockies game at **Coors Field.** If the Rockies aren't in town, you can take in some greenery at **Denver Botanic Gardens,** a short drive away in the Capitol Hill neighborhood.

At night, make reservations for dinner at **The Kitchen,** or opt for relaxing pub fare at one of Denver's fine craft breweries, such as **Wynkoop Brewing Company.**

It's hard to resist those mountains, but stick to sightseeing in the city while you acclimate to the altitude (it *is* 5,280 ft/1,609 m above sea level).

DAY 2

Try alternative transportation methods to get around: If your hotel has bikes to use, ride over to the Golden Triangle neighborhood—or take the free shuttle bus down the 16th Street Mall, then walk across **Civic Center Park**—to visit the **Denver Art Museum.** You will be close to the **Colorado State Capitol,** too. Inside the Denver Art Museum, have a bite at **The Ponti,** which offers plates as sophisticated as the artwork. Then

Denver Botanic Gardens

Love This City mural by Pat Milbery, near Coors Field

head to the **History Colorado Center,** where you can learn about the entire state in an interactive way—do a virtual ski jump, visit a "mine shaft," and more. For a more budget-friendly option, head for the **Denver Public Library,** which has an art gallery and free kids' activities, and if you're heading back to LoDo, stop to see the **Big Blue Bear** in front of the Colorado Convention Center.

In the late afternoon or early evening, walk west on 16th Street over the **Millennium Bridge** for a view of the mountains at sunset. Walk through **Commons Park** and over the South Platte River into the Highlands neighborhood, where you have lots of dining options. Maybe opt for dinner at **Root Down** or just enjoy a drink at **Williams & Graham.** If the line isn't too long, top off the night with a scoop from **Little Man Ice Cream.**

Boulder

DAY 3

After breakfast at **Snooze,** you're off to Boulder for a little taste of the mountains. (You can drive to Boulder in a half hour, or take the bus from Union Station to reach downtown Boulder in an hour.) Plan your trip for a Saturday in summer or early fall to be there in time for the **Boulder County Farmers Market.** Eat lunch at one of the market vendors or stop for tea at the **Dushanbe Teahouse** by Boulder Creek.

Chautauqua is the starting point for a **hike** in the foothills, a meal, or a concert in the historic auditorium. Bonus: Kids that don't make it far on the hike will love the playground. In the evening, enjoy a top-notch dinner at **Frasca,** though families might be happier at **The Kitchen** or **Mountain Sun Pub & Brewery.**

If not visiting Boulder as a day trip from Denver, check in at the **Hotel Boulderado** downtown. Summer visitors should try to score a room or rent a cabin at **Chautauqua** for easy access to all its amenities.

DAY 4

Get up early to wait in line for chicory coffee and beignets at **Lucile's Creole Café,** just a block away from the Hotel Boulderado. Afterward,

Dushanbe Teahouse in Boulder

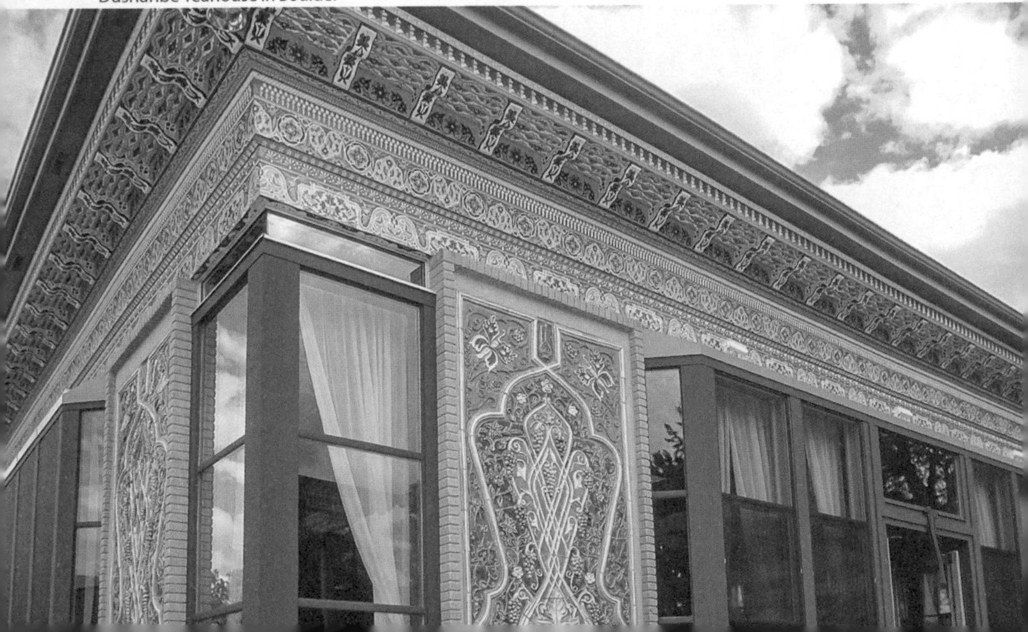

Welcome to Beertown

Denver is to beer what Napa is to wine. Forget about monikers like "Queen City of the Plains" and "Mile High City"; nowadays Denver is being called "Suds City" and "The Napa Valley of Beer."

There are scores of brewpubs and microbreweries in Denver. Whether you're just curious to find out if beer goes as well with cheese as wine does (**Great Divide Brewing Company**), or if you want a classic beer at a Colorado Rockies baseball game (**Sandlot Brewery**), you will find it here.

FESTIVALS

For serious beer lovers, fall is the time to visit. **Denver Beer Week,** usually held in mid-September or mid-October, is nine days of beer-related events. The city also hosts the three-day **Great American Beer Festival** in October. This is the Olympics of beer, where thousands of brews are sampled, and gold, silver, and bronze medals are awarded among an ever-growing array of beer styles.

BREW TOURS

If you're not visiting in fall, you can still join in on the fun. Any time of year, there are brewery tours where visitors can see how vast quantities of their favorite ales and lagers are made; then they can sample a few. In Denver, there are tours at **Wynkoop Brewing Company** and **Great Divide Brewing Company** as well as a variety of tours to various breweries. Beyond Denver, there are tours in Golden at the **Coors Brewing Company.**

Make your own sort of tour by getting a map of the **Denver Beer Trail,** featuring dozens of brewpubs, breweries, and taprooms.

BEER SPA

This town takes its beer so seriously that people are now paying to soak in it—while also drinking it. **The Beer Spa** opened in early 2021 with "Beer Bath Hydrotherapy" or a tub of hops, barley, and seasonal herbs. It's warm and considered a "wellness therapy." There's also a taproom on-site.

POUR ME ONE

For some, it's about the pour, not just the drink.

Sample Denver's beer culture.

Try **Bierstadt Lagerhaus** in the RiNo area for a Slow Pour Pils in a really tall glass. It's like foreplay with beer. In Golden, you can get a Barmen Pilsner, also a slow pour, at **Old Capitol Grill & Smokehouse.**

DENVER BEER TRIANGLE

Boulder and Fort Collins are helping turn this region into the "Denver Beer Triangle." Fort Collins is home to craft breweries such as the **New Belgium Brewing Company** and **Odell Brewing Company,** as well as industry giant Anheuser-Busch. With competition comes creative ideas to get you in the brewery door—tours, tastings, pairings, movies, and bike tours are just some of the ways you might sip a cold one. Boulder is getting into the act with local brewers such as **Avery Brewing** and **Mountain Sun Pub & Brewery.**

For those in Colorado Springs thirsty for beer, check out **Phantom Canyon Brewing Company** or **Bristol Brewery & Pub.**

Get Outside

No trip is complete without time spent basking in the Colorado sun. Fear not: Athletic skill is not required, but you must be mindful of the elevation and your body's ability to acclimate to heights thousands of feet above sea level.

Cherry Creek Bike Path

BEST HIKING

- **Red Rocks Amphitheatre** (Denver): Located in Red Rocks Park, this world-class concert venue lets you walk all over the place and take in panoramic views of Denver and the plains to the east.
- **White Ranch Open Space Park** (Denver): So close to the city but feels like you've left urban vibes behind for a day in the mountains.
- **Chautauqua** (Boulder): It's not about solitude at this popular place, but you get historical charm, views, and a variety of options.
- **Flagstaff Mountain** (Boulder): Enjoy sweeping views of Boulder and the valley.
- **Lory State Park** (Fort Collins): So much packed in—wildflower meadows, streams, a few rocks to scramble over if you choose—and hikes are not difficult.
- **Garden of the Gods** (Colorado Springs): If you love red rocks like I do, this is paradise. Hikes are easy, and it's otherworldly but popular.
- **Manitou Incline** (Colorado Springs): Not afraid of heights and like a serious workout? You'll love this hike and the feeling of accomplishment.

BEST BIKING

- **Cherry Creek Bike Path** (Denver): Slip just below the hectic pace of the city for a pleasant ride along the creek.
- **Boulder Creek Bike Path** (Boulder): It's a different climate—cooler, refreshing, often shady—along this popular path.
- **Spring Creek Trail** (Fort Collins): It's hard to explain, but this trail just feels so northern Colorado and different than bike paths in Boulder or Denver. It's paved, mostly flat, and a chance to see most of this college town.
- **Pikes Peak** via Challenge Unlimited (Colorado Springs): It's all downhill! You can ride up, but some of the best trips drive you up and let you ride down.
- **Garden of the Gods** (Colorado Springs): There are many ways to check out these natural red rock formations.

BEST ROCK CLIMBING

- **Boulder Flatirons** (Boulder): Amateurs try to climb the Flatirons, but these signature rocks require some expertise.

- **Boulder Canyon** (Boulder): It's so fun to just watch people who practice here, even if you aren't ready to climb yourself.
- **Lory State Park** (Fort Collins): It's all about Arthur's Rock when it comes to climbing, which means it's really about "bouldering" (climbing with just your hands and feet).
- **Garden of the Gods** via Front Range Climbing Company (Colorado Springs): Amazingly, climbing on these red rocks is allowed, but you'll need a guide.

BEST OUTDOOR TOURS AND EVENTS

- **Fair Winds Hot Air Balloon Flights** (Boulder): Ride a hot-air balloon while taking in views of mountain peaks and grassy plains.
- **Tour de Fat** (Fort Collins): Join the costumed bicycle parade during this one-day event in September.

BEST RAFTING AND KAYAKING

- **Clear Creek** (Denver): You'll have to put in about a half-hour drive into the mountains, but this creek also flows through Golden where you can rent inner tubes or kayak on the creek, too. Rapids range from beginner to expert levels.
- **Cache La Poudre** (Fort Collins): This designated Wild and Scenic river has everything from Class I to IV rapids.

BEST HORSEBACK RIDING

- **Sombrero Stables** (Boulder): Saddle up for a ride on the edge of a national park.
- **Academy Riding Stables** (Colorado Springs): See Garden of the Gods like early settlers did—on horseback!

BEST SNOWSHOEING

- **Brainard Lake Recreation Area** (Boulder): Snowshoe on fresh sparkling powder through a forest of trees with the goal of seeing the frozen lake.
- **Rocky Mountain National Park** (Boulder): You can snowshoe on many of the designated hiking trails to see frozen waterfalls and possibly wildlife such as elk.

BEST CROSS-COUNTRY SKIING

- **Brainard Lake Recreation Area** (Boulder): With enough snow, a paved road makes for an ideal Nordic trail that isn't too hilly.
- **Eldora Mountain Resort** (Boulder): You can rent skis, take a lesson, and choose from a variety of trails.

BEST ALPINE SKIING

- **Winter Park Resort** (Denver): Take a train from downtown to this legendary mountain known for Mary Jane, one of its seven "territories" to suit beginners to experts.
- **Eldora Mountain Resort** (Boulder): Avoid traffic and enjoy slightly cheaper lift tickets at this smaller resort close to Denver and Boulder.

a buck in Garden of the Gods

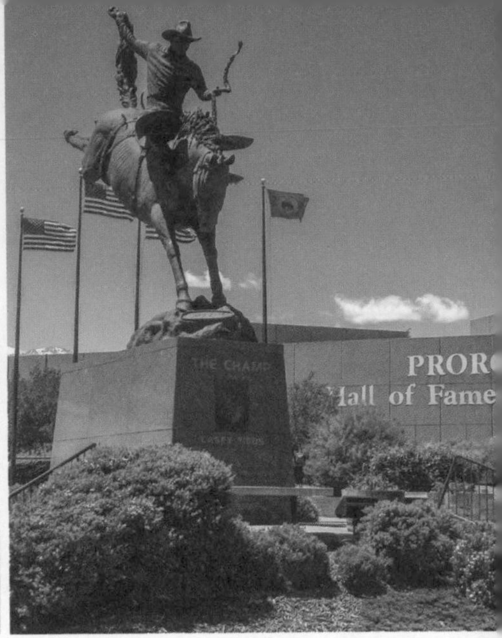

ProRodeo Hall of Fame & Museum of the American Cowboy in Colorado Springs

stroll two blocks south for some window-shopping at the **Pearl Street Mall.** A short drive south, the **University of Colorado** campus includes museums, a planetarium, art exhibits, and—if you're visiting June-August—the **Colorado Shakespeare Festival.** Or head 30 minutes west to experience the counterculture vibe in **Nederland;** if it's winter (specifically March), your visit might coincide with the town's annual **Frozen Dead Guy Days.**

At night, head back to the hotel for drinks at **The Corner Bar** or **License No. 1** before dining on-site at **Spruce Farm & Fish.**

Fort Collins

DAY 5

Begin your day by feasting on a hearty breakfast at **The Buff.** Today, we leave Boulder to explore Fort Collins, and the best way to get there is by car. Once in Fort Collins, though, you can leave the car parked and explore by foot or bicycle.

In town, rent a bicycle and take the **Spring Creek Trail** to explore the town from alongside Spring Creek. **Old Town** is a sight in itself with plenty of shops—including candy and toy shops for the little ones—to wander through. Bike over to the **Fort Collins Museum of Art** to view the public art outside, or lock up the bike to go inside and check out a current exhibit.

Brewery tours and tastings are all the rage here, and you can ride a bike or walk from one to another. Tours at the popular **New Belgium Brewing Company** include storytelling, souvenirs, and sipping samples.

Dine in at **The Emporium: An American Brasserie** at the **Elizabeth Hotel,** where there's a terrific happy hour. Later, take in a show at **Avogadro's Number** and check out the historic **Armstrong Hotel.**

Colorado Springs

DAY 6

You'll want a car for today's two-hour drive south to Colorado Springs. Enjoy the scenic route and turn off for **Garden of the Gods** to wind through the jutting red rocks. Once in Colorado Springs, one-of-a-kind museums such as the **United States Olympic and Paralympic**

Museum, ProRodeo Hall of Fame & Museum of the American Cowboy, the **World Figure Skating Museum and Hall of Fame,** and the **Peterson Air & Space Museum** offer options to fill the afternoon.

Aim to stay at **The Broadmoor,** where you can dine at some of the region's best restaurants, pamper yourself with spa treatments, golf, swim, or tour a world-class Western art collection. If this one-stop resort is booked, opt instead to stay downtown at **The Mining Exchange,** where you can walk to the **Colorado Springs Fine Arts Center** for some culture. If you're not staying at The Broadmoor, you can still dine there, or try **The Rabbit Hole** downtown.

DAY 7

The resort town of **Manitou Springs,** at the foot of Pikes Peak, beckons just a short drive away, and a visit here is truly charming. Walk along the creek and sample the **mineral springwater** that is piped through at different fountains scattered around town. In summer, 14,115-foot (4,302-m) **Pikes Peak** is within easy reach via cog railway, bus, or hiking trails. Yes, it's the rare fourteener that has a road to the top. It's breathtaking at the top in more ways than one. Seeing so much of Colorado from this great height is the perfect way to sign off on your Front Range excursion.

The Broadmoor in Colorado Springs

Denver

Sights 29
Entertainment and Events 57
Shopping 82
Sports and Recreation 92
Food 99
Accommodations 114
Transportation and Services 124
Golden 127
Loveland and Winter Park 133

Denver is a sophisticated city exploding with everything hip and desirable: outdoor recreation, farm-to-table dining, and a variety of culture and sports for intellectual stimulation and entertainment.

Denver's location at 5,280 feet (1,609 m) above sea level is an attraction in itself, with sights such as Coors Field and City Park marking mile-high spots. Touring the city's sights could mean riding a bicycle past the white-water rapids on the South Platte River in Confluence Park or meandering through the bronzed statues of Civic Center Park on the way to the Denver Art Museum's striking modern wing. Or hop onto the city's light rail and quickly zip from the Museum of Contemporary Art Denver to the Black American West Museum &

Highlights

Look for ★ to find recommended sights, activities, dining, and lodging.

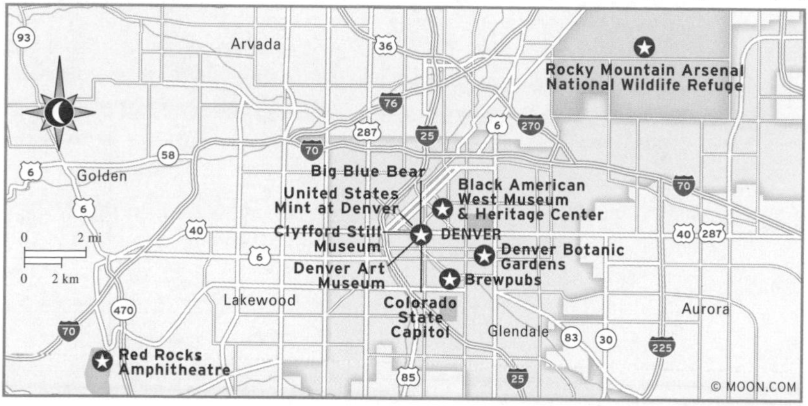

★ Take a selfie with the **Big Blue Bear,** Denver's most recognizable piece of public art (page 29).

★ Hear the stories of pioneering African Americans throughout the West at the **Black American West Museum & Heritage Center,** with a special emphasis on those who lived in Colorado (page 29).

★ Tour the **United States Mint at Denver** for a chance to see coins being made and a peek inside the elaborate interior of the original historic building (page 32).

★ See abstract expressionist art in a new light at the cool **Clyfford Still Museum,** with regularly changing exhibits drawn from its namesake's massive body of work (page 35).

★ View regional and international artworks at the **Denver Art Museum**—its architecture is a work of art in itself (page 35).

★ Take in stunning views of the city and the mountains from the dome at the **Colorado State Capitol** (page 46).

★ Relax among the beautiful plants of the **Denver Botanic Gardens,** resting amid nooks for peaceful contemplation and meandering along extensive pathways (page 47).

★ Hike the trails at the **Rocky Mountain Arsenal National Wildlife Refuge** to see more than 300 animal and bird species, including bison, eagles, and deer (page 53).

★ Go to a concert at iconic **Red Rocks Amphitheatre** or walk around anytime and enjoy the scenery, with magnificent red rocks and a view of the expansive plains to the east (page 53).

★ Sample the craft beer at Denver's **brewpubs**—the city has dozens to choose from (page 65).

Denver

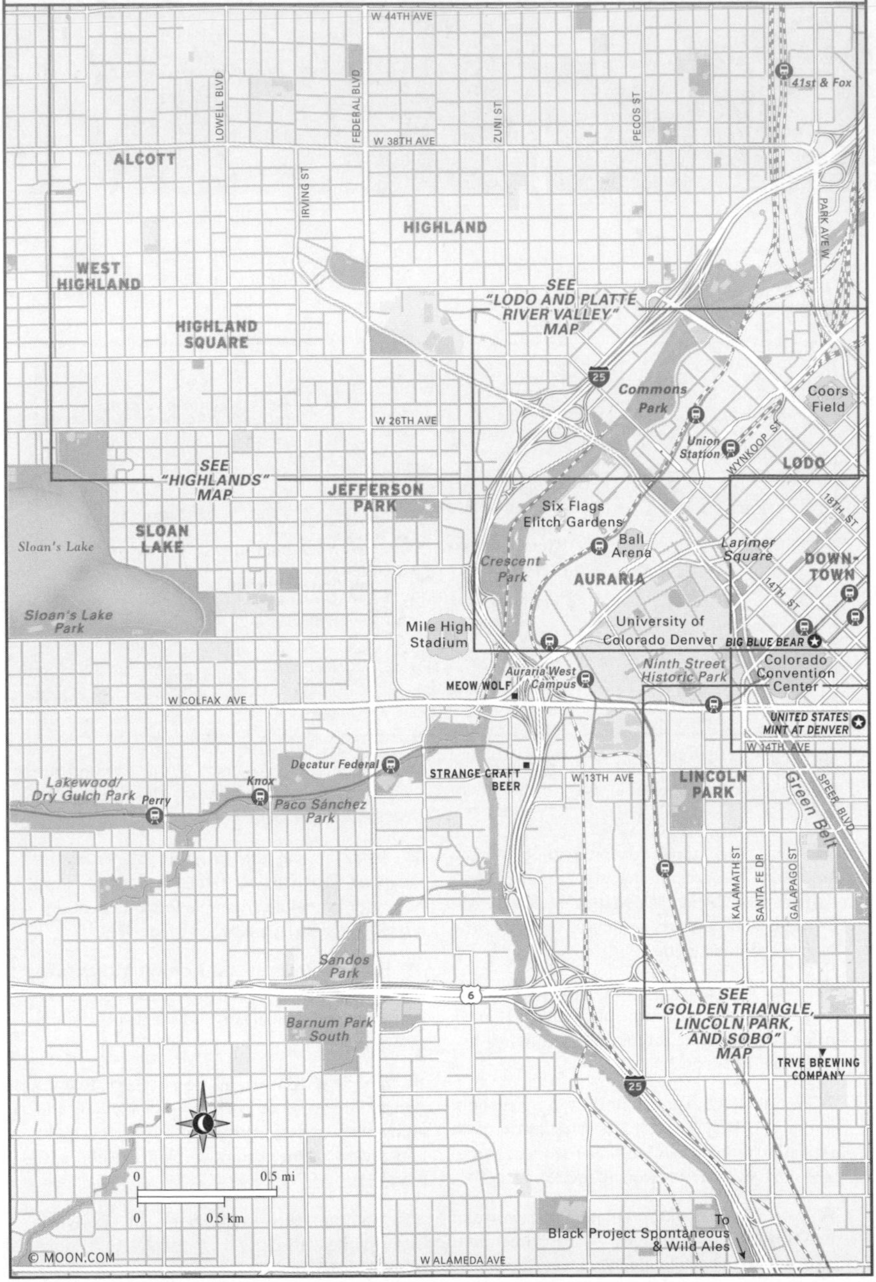
W 44TH AVE
41st & Fox
LOWELL BLVD
FEDERAL BLVD
ZUNI ST
PECOS ST
W 38TH AVE
ALCOTT
IRVING ST
PARK AVE W
HIGHLAND
WEST HIGHLAND
SEE "LODO AND PLATTE RIVER VALLEY" MAP
HIGHLAND SQUARE
25
Commons Park
Coors Field
W 26TH AVE
Union Station
WYNKOOP ST
LODO
SEE "HIGHLANDS" MAP
JEFFERSON PARK
18TH ST
Six Flags Elitch Gardens
SLOAN LAKE
Sloan's Lake
Ball Arena
Larimer Square
DOWN-TOWN
Crescent Park
AURARIA
14TH ST
Sloan's Lake Park
Mile High Stadium
University of Colorado Denver
BIG BLUE BEAR
Auraria West Campus
Ninth Street Historic Park
Colorado Convention Center
MEOW WOLF
W COLFAX AVE
UNITED STATES MINT AT DENVER
W 14TH AVE
Decatur Federal
STRANGE CRAFT BEER
W 13TH AVE
LINCOLN PARK
Green Belt
SPEER BLVD
Lakewood/ Dry Gulch Park
Knox
Perry
Paco Sánchez Park
KALAMATH ST
SANTA FE DR
GALAPAGO ST
Sandos Park
6
SEE "GOLDEN TRIANGLE, LINCOLN PARK, AND SOBO" MAP
Barnum Park South
TRVE BREWING COMPANY
25
0
0.5 mi
0
0.5 km
To Black Project Spontaneous & Wild Ales
© MOON.COM
W ALAMEDA AVE

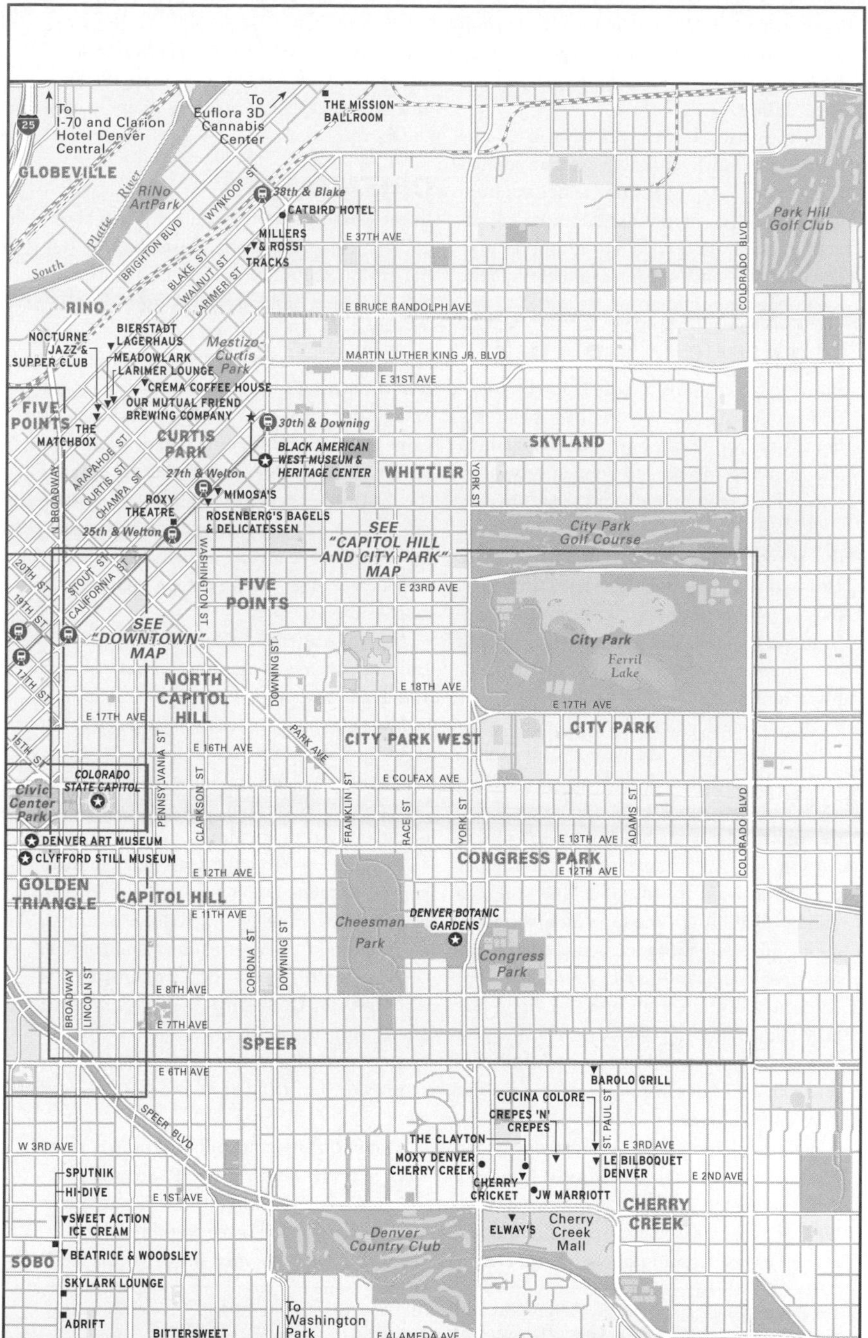
To I-70 and Clarion Hotel Denver Central
25
To Euflora 3D Cannabis Center
THE MISSION BALLROOM
GLOBEVILLE
RiNo ArtPark
South Platte River
BRIGHTON BLVD
WYNKOOP ST
38th & Blake
CATBIRD HOTEL
MILLERS & ROSSI
TRACKS
E 37TH AVE
BLAKE ST
WALNUT ST
LARIMER ST
Park Hill Golf Club
COLORADO BLVD
RINO
E BRUCE RANDOLPH AVE
NOCTURNE JAZZ & SUPPER CLUB
BIERSTADT LAGERHAUS
MEADOWLARK
LARIMER LOUNGE
CREMA COFFEE HOUSE
OUR MUTUAL FRIEND BREWING COMPANY
Mestizo-Curtis Park
MARTIN LUTHER KING JR. BLVD
E 31ST AVE
FIVE POINTS
THE MATCHBOX
CURTIS PARK
30th & Downing
BLACK AMERICAN WEST MUSEUM & HERITAGE CENTER
SKYLAND
WHITTIER
ARAPAHOE ST
CURTIS ST
CHAMPA ST
27th & Welton
MIMOSA'S
YORK ST
ROXY THEATRE
ROSENBERG'S BAGELS & DELICATESSEN
25th & Welton
N BROADWAY
SEE "CAPITOL HILL AND CITY PARK" MAP
City Park Golf Course
20TH ST
STOUT ST
CALIFORNIA ST
WASHINGTON ST
FIVE POINTS
E 23RD AVE
19TH ST
SEE "DOWNTOWN" MAP
City Park
Ferril Lake
17TH ST
NORTH CAPITOL HILL
DOWNING ST
E 18TH AVE
E 17TH AVE
E 17TH AVE
CITY PARK
15TH ST
E 16TH AVE
PARK AVE
CITY PARK WEST
COLORADO STATE CAPITOL
Civic Center Park
PENNSYLVANIA ST
CLARKSON ST
FRANKLIN ST
E COLFAX AVE
RACE ST
YORK ST
ADAMS ST
COLORADO BLVD
DENVER ART MUSEUM
E 13TH AVE
CLYFFORD STILL MUSEUM
CONGRESS PARK
E 12TH AVE
E 12TH AVE
GOLDEN TRIANGLE
CAPITOL HILL
E 11TH AVE
Cheesman Park
DENVER BOTANIC GARDENS
Congress Park
CORONA ST
DOWNING ST
BROADWAY
LINCOLN ST
E 8TH AVE
E 7TH AVE
SPEER
E 6TH AVE
BAROLO GRILL
CUCINA COLORE
CREPES 'N' CREPES
SPEER BLVD
ST. PAUL ST
THE CLAYTON
W 3RD AVE
E 3RD AVE
MOXY DENVER CHERRY CREEK
LE BILBOQUET DENVER
SPUTNIK
E 2ND AVE
HI-DIVE
E 1ST AVE
CHERRY CRICKET
JW MARRIOTT
SWEET ACTION ICE CREAM
CHERRY CREEK
Denver Country Club
ELWAY'S
Cherry Creek Mall
SOBO
BEATRICE & WOODSLEY
SKYLARK LOUNGE
ADRIFT
To Washington Park
BITTERSWEET
E ALAMEDA AVE

Heritage Center. No matter how you get from point A to point B, it's always an adventure to explore the city's rich past or discover its latest additions.

In the past, Denver was labeled a "cow town" for its stockyards and less than sophisticated vibe, but now it's known for its culture with world-class museums and theater, destination restaurants and bars, and ample parks and gardens—and, of course, its access to the Rocky Mountains.

PLANNING YOUR TIME

Plan to spend **two days** in Denver. Downtown Denver is your best bet for a home base, with transportation available to and from the airport and public transportation, rental bikes, and bike paths within easy walking distance. Once downtown—or even in a surrounding neighborhood like Capitol Hill—you can see much of what Denver has to offer without driving. It's only when you go to the foothills that you'll need a car, and even then you might be able to ride a bike or hire a tour guide.

Devote one day to exploring the city. Start with the Denver Art Museum and take in the Denver Botanic Gardens, where a pavilion with waterfalls, walkways, and tropical and subtropical plants can be enjoyed year-round. (In summer, opt for an early start to the day in order to avoid crowds, lines, and potential midday heat.) Add time for a little shopping in the LoDo neighborhood before dining out. Make reservations at Denver's iteration of The Kitchen, or explore craft brews and pub fare at Wynkoop Brewing Company. The next day, plan a quick trip into the nearby foothills and take a long bike ride or an early-morning hike.

Many of Denver's sights are family-friendly, with rooms and activities devoted to kiddos: Make art at the Denver Art Museum, cruise along the stroller-size walkways at the Denver Botanic Gardens, or dig for "bones" at the Denver Museum of Nature & Science. Downtown hotels with pools—such as the Four Seasons—will appeal to the kids in summer and will put you within walking distance (or a short drive) of theaters, museums, parks, and more.

ORIENTATION

In the **LoDo** (Lower Downtown) neighborhood is **Union Station,** a historic train station revitalized into a modern transportation hub, a stylish hotel, a dining and nightlife destination, and an urban hot spot. Also in LoDo is the **16th Street Mall,** a pedestrian-friendly strip with a large number of stores and restaurants. You can go to a baseball game at **Coors Field,** dine out, or shop—it's all here. The **Denver Art Museum** anchors the **Golden Triangle** neighborhood, with other museums and galleries to be explored. Just outside downtown is a distinctive arts district along Santa Fe Drive in the **Lincoln Park** neighborhood.

Leaving downtown, you'll find the hip galleries, diverse restaurants, eclectic shops, and dynamic dance clubs and bars that have brought vibrancy to the South Broadway corridor, popularly known as **SoBo.** If you're into handmade culture, indie rock, and vintage, don't miss the core blocks that make this neighborhood so popular.

Heading west from the heart of downtown, you cross from LoDo through the **Platte River Valley,** which has exploded as an urban neighborhood and destination. Major sights, such as the **Museum of Contemporary Art Denver, Centennial Gardens Park,** and **Commons Park,** are found in this area. Platte Street is home to a few restaurants and shops worth visiting as you make your way west.

The **Highlands** neighborhood is a short walk over the South Platte River, with historic micro-neighborhoods that have modern names like **LoHi** (Lower Highlands). In recent years, it has boomed with growth. You'll

Previous: Larimer Square; *I See What You Mean* (aka the Big Blue Bear) sculpture by artist Lawrence Argent; Great Divide Brewing Company, one of Denver's many brewpubs.

find restaurants and bars such as **Williams & Graham** and **Root Down;** the local ice cream shop, **Little Man Ice Cream,** is famous here. Lodgings are minimal in this part of town, but it's worth the walk from downtown. You can loop a visit to this area in with a **Denver Broncos** game at Mile High Stadium (formally known as Empower Field at Mile High, currently).

Instead of going west, you could easily walk from downtown to one of Denver's oldest neighborhoods—Capitol Hill or Curtis Park and Five Points. Known for being LGBTQ-friendly, **Capitol Hill** is densely packed and always lively. The neighborhood is home to some of the city's best music venues along Colfax Avenue, including the **Bluebird Theater** and **Ogden Theatre.** Expansive **City Park** is large enough to be home to the **Denver Zoo** and the **Denver Museum of Nature & Science,** plus many lakes, a golf course, and the Mile High Loop jogging path. **Five Points** and **Curtis Park** are north of downtown and now edged by the increasingly vibrant **RiNo** (River North) district.

Sights

DOWNTOWN

American Museum of Western Art

Directly across the street from The Brown Palace Hotel is the historic Navarre Building, built in 1880, which has served as a school, a hotel, a brothel (which may have once included a tunnel to bring clients over from The Brown), and a dining and jazz club. In 1997, it was bought by the Anschutz Corporation and refurbished for its private offices and to become the **American Museum of Western Art** (1727 Tremont St., 303/293-2000, www.anschutzcollection.org, tours 10am and 4:30pm Mon., Wed., and Fri., $5, advance online ticket purchase required) from the corporation's private collection. This is serious art that has been previously on loan for exhibits around the world, so viewing is limited, with no children under age 8 permitted; children under 16 must be accompanied by an adult. Artists in the collection of over 600 paintings on display include Georgia O'Keeffe, Albert Bierstadt, Thomas Moran, Ernest Blumenschein, Frederic Remington, and many more.

★ Big Blue Bear

Part whimsy, part serious artwork, with much left to personal interpretation, the 40-foot-tall **Big Blue Bear** (700 14th St., 303/228-8000, http://denverconvention.com) peering into the windows of the Colorado Convention Center has become the most popular and recognizable piece funded by the city's public art program. First installed in 2005, the sculpture is officially titled *I See What You Mean* and was designed and created by late Denver artist and art professor Lawrence Argent. It is constructed from polymer concrete and a steel frame, covered in a bright blue that is evocative of the bluish hue of the nearby Rocky Mountains.

But as with any bear you might meet in the mountains, you can't get too close. At times, the bear has been loved too much and is occasionally roped off to keep visitors at a safe distance. You can still take a fun selfie with the bear from inside the center if you can't get that shot from outside.

★ Black American West Museum & Heritage Center

A tiny house contains the **Black American West Museum & Heritage Center** (3091 California St., 720/242-7428, http://bawmhc.org, 10am-2pm Fri.-Sat., $10 adults, $9 seniors, $8 children), which shares the little-known history of the West's African Americans, particularly those who made a life in Denver

Downtown Denver

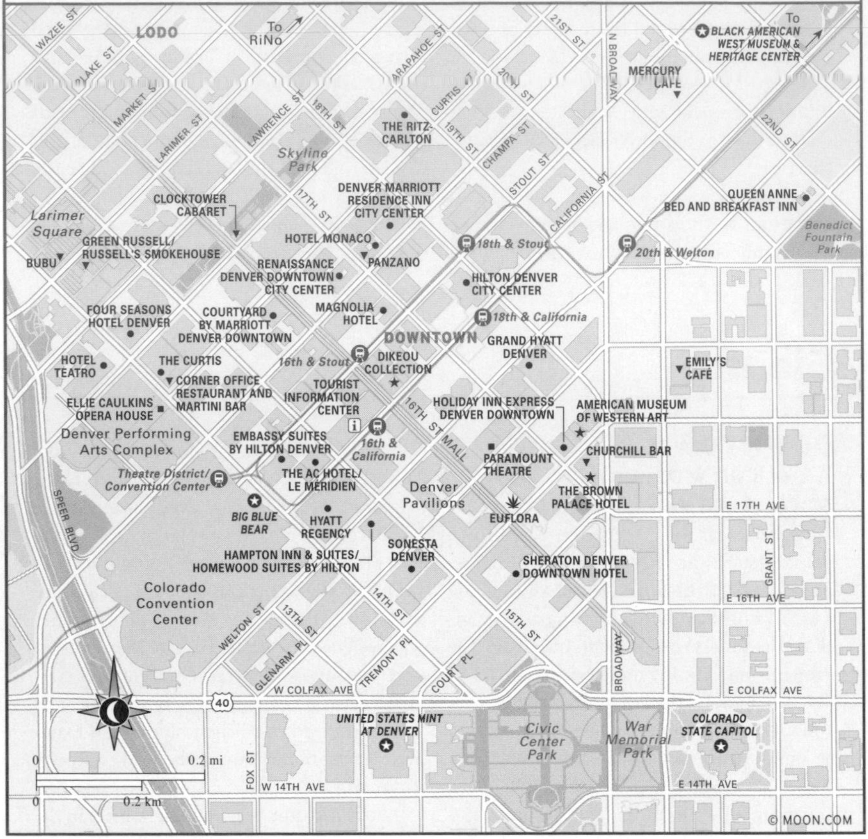

and Colorado. The building itself is the former home of Justina L. Ford, the first African American woman to be licensed as a doctor in Colorado. The house—now on the National Register of Historic Places—was saved from demolition and moved from its original location before being restored. The museum is currently closed for remodeling; check the website for the latest information on its hours and admission prices.

The museum's exhibits offer astonishing facts about African Americans in the West. For example, a third of all cowboys were Black, and the only two stained-glass portraits of African Americans hanging in a U.S. state capitol are at the Colorado State Capitol. And, formerly enslaved local businessman Barney Ford opposed statehood for the territory because Black men did not have the right to vote. The top floor of the museum has displays of Buffalo Soldier uniforms and rodeo memorabilia from the likes of Nat Love, aka "Deadwood Dick," reputed to be the greatest Black cowboy, and Bill Pickett, a rodeo cowboy who was the first Black honoree in the National Cowboy Hall of Fame.

1: Big Blue Bear **2:** Denver skyline **3:** The Brown Palace Hotel **4:** Black American West Museum & Heritage Center

1

2

3

4

The museum also owns a portion of Dearfield, Colorado, a ghost town northeast of Denver that was formerly a Black township.

The Brown Palace Hotel

Unquestionably the city's most famous hotel, **The Brown Palace Hotel** (321 17th St., 303/297-3111, www.brownpalace.com) offers enough history and architectural beauty to be visited even by those not staying the night. Ohio businessman Henry Brown came to Colorado in 1860 and bought a few acres of land, including the triangular plot where the three-sided hotel opened in 1892. Working with architect Frank Edbrooke, who also worked on the design of the state capitol, Brown opted for a grand Italian Renaissance style with a Tiffany stained-glass atrium that rises eight floors in the center of the building.

To this day, the hotel relies on its own artesian well, located beneath the building, for water. With so many famous guests over the years—from presidents to rock stars—the hotel took to naming some rooms after them. Now ordinary folks can spend a night in the Beatles or the Eisenhower suite.

In a long-held tradition, each January the hotel puts the National Western Stock Show's prize-winning steer on full display in the lobby, where anyone can be photographed with the bovine. Year-round, visitors can simply take in the ambience by dining in one of the hotel's three restaurants, sipping a **traditional English tea** (noon-4pm daily, reservations strongly recommended), or going on a 45- to 60-minute **tour** with the hotel's historian in the atrium. Public tours are available for overnight hotel guests for $10 per person; reservations are highly recommended. Nonguests can book private tours for $60 for 1-3 people ($20 pp for additional people); reservations are required.

Dikeou Collection

The **Dikeou Collection** (1615 California St., Suite 515, 303/623-3001, www.dikeoucollection.org, 11am-5pm Wed.-Fri., by appointment only, free) is an art treasure unknown even to most Denverites, but it should not be missed by anyone curious about contemporary art. This is the private art collection of Devon Dikeou, an artist who divides her time between Denver and New York, where she has published *Zing Magazine*. Not far from the architecturally famous museum buildings in downtown, the Dikeou Collection is housed on the fifth floor of a historic office building, just a few doors down from the Jamba Juice on the corner of the 16th Street Mall, with giant pink inflatable bunnies by artist Momoyo Torimitsu greeting visitors in the first of many rooms.

★ United States Mint at Denver

Perhaps inspired by the rebellious spirit of the West—or just naked entrepreneurial ambition—the **United States Mint at Denver** (320 W. Colfax Ave., 303/405-4761, www.usmint.gov, tours 8am-3:30pm Mon.-Thurs., free, reservations required) was originally founded as a private bank in the 1860s by an attorney who had the bright idea to mint coins from the gold and silver being mined in the mountains to the west. The mint was eventually sold to the government, and laws were made to prohibit private money-making. Today there are only four mints in the country, and the United States Mint at Denver is the only one with guided tours.

In 1906 the government opened the mint in this building, which is now on the National Register of Historic Places. An example of elaborate Italian Renaissance architecture, the mint appears to be two stories tall but is actually five. Starting in 1935, several additions have been made to the building to accommodate increased coin production; making billions of coins each year, the mint now occupies an entire city block.

Tours begin at the entrance to one of the building's more modern additions. Security at the mint is tighter than at any airport, and visitors cannot bring in anything larger than a wallet.

Before the official tour begins, you can

peruse *Money, Trade and Treasure,* a lobby display of primitive money and the evolution of currency. A tour guide and an armed security guard take groups into the coin production part of the plant, where you might see coins before they are pressed or as they are being sorted. It's not until the very end of the tour that you get to see the original marble hallways and unique Tiffany chandeliers of the 1906 building. Most fascinating about the tour are the facts—particularly the actual costs of making money and what materials are used to make coins. A visit here could be a last chance to see pennies being made; no one knows how much longer pennies will be produced given their low value and high cost to make.

The United States Mint at Denver can boast of never having been robbed, thanks in part to its "machine-gun nest" or sentry box that was always staffed until the 1960s. That relic is on display (now staffed by a mannequin), and current security measures are top secret.

To get a few of your own state's quarters or other collectible coins, stop in at the **gift shop** (8am-4:30pm Mon.-Thurs.), just outside the mint. Even the change from each purchase might be given in locally minted coins.

GOLDEN TRIANGLE, LINCOLN PARK, AND SOBO

Byers-Evans House

A visit to the **Byers-Evans House** (1310 Bannock St., 303/620-4933, www.cowomenshistory.org, 10:30am-3:30pm Thurs.-Sat., 1:30pm-3:30pm Sun., $8 adults, $6 seniors and students, $4 ages 6-12, free under age 6) is an opportunity to learn about Denver and Colorado history through the stories of two prominent families who once lived in this Italianate-style home. Visitors can see exactly how an upper-middle-class family lived in the early 1900s, as the house contains all original furnishings, including the family's Haviland china and Baccarat crystal, 1760 Queen Anne highboy, and original artwork. The house museum can only be seen on a 45-minute guided tour.

The house was built in 1883 for William N. Byers, who printed the *Rocky Mountain News,* the city's first newspaper. After six years, he sold the house to William Evans, son of the state's second territorial governor, John Evans. (Today there are mountain peaks named after both Byers and the elder Evans because of their significant contributions to the state; the younger Evans made his own mark as head of the Denver Tramway Company.) The daughters of William Evans lived in the home with few modern modifications until 1981, even as the neighborhood around them slowly fell away and changed. Over the years the house was expanded five times as the family grew, and it has since been restored to the 1912-1924 period; today it's worth visiting to see a well-furnished example of a World War I-era home. A tour of the house captures the history of the families who lived here and the changes each generation made to it.

Launched in 2018, the **Center for Colorado Women's History** is located inside this historic former home. It includes a gallery offering a mix of women's history topics related to Colorado, such as the state's contribution to women's suffrage.

Civic Center Park

Listed on the National Register of Historic Places, **Civic Center Park** (101 W. 14th Ave. Pkwy., 720/913-1311, www.denvergov.org, 5am-11pm daily) is today the reflection of years of input from various mayors, architects, and landscape architects. In 1904, Mayor Robert Speer was inspired by the City Beautiful movement and began to consult with planners and designers on the project, but citizens rejected his request for funding for the park, and by 1912 Speer was out of office. The next mayor hired experts to tinker with the park design, and when Speer was reelected in 1917, bits of each plan were incorporated with the new architect's design. The park was officially opened in 1919, and

Golden Triangle, Lincoln Park, and SoBo

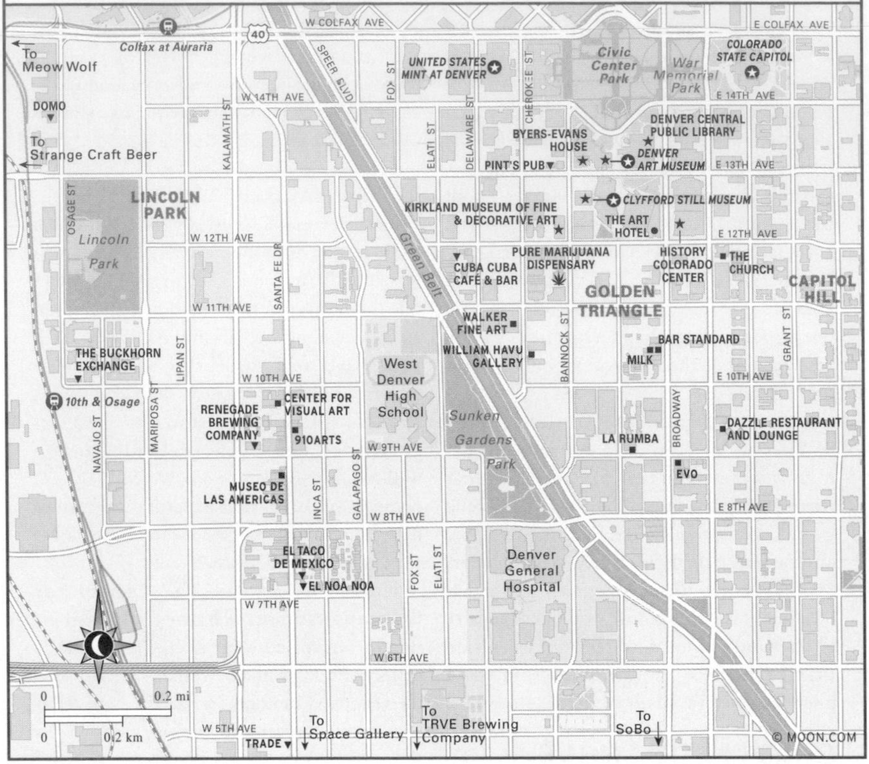

various statues and memorials have been added since.

Reflecting its name, Civic Center Park is flanked by government buildings, including the historic **City and County Building** (1437 Bannock St., 720/865-7840, www.denvergov.org), home of Denver's mayoral offices, to the west, and the **Colorado State Capitol** (200 E. Colfax Ave., 303/866-2604, www.colorado.gov) to the east. The **Greek Theater** (720/913-0700) is the most distinctive structure within the park. It hosted public concerts as far back as 1920, and in modern times it is often the staging area for cultural and political events. Two bronze sculptures in the middle of the park represent the West, portraying a cowboy and a Native American; Alexander Phimister Proctor created *Bronco Buster* in 1920 and *On the War Trail* in 1922. During protests in summer 2020, some historical statues in the Civic Center Park area were damaged or removed, so there might be new works on display during your visit.

The park extends east across Broadway, where the 45-foot-tall **Colorado Veterans Memorial** was dedicated in 1990. The memorial is made of Colorado red sandstone. The entire neighborhood around Civic Center Park has undergone tremendous growth in recent years, leading to more interest in its use and future design plans. In the spring and summer, the flowerbeds in the center of the park are filled with vivid blooms. The Greek Theater and **Voorhies Memorial** (on the north or Colfax Ave. side of the park), which features murals by the artist Allen True on the ceiling, provide welcome shade on hot days. The park is used for free public events year-round, including a Cinco de Mayo celebration and the Martin Luther King Jr. Day Parade.

★ Clyfford Still Museum

As someone who feels that abstract expressionism is, well, abstract, I have to say that my first visit to the **Clyfford Still Museum** (1250 Bannock St., 720/354-4880, www.clyffordstillmuseum.org, 10am-5pm Tues.-Sun., $10 adults, $8 seniors, $6 students and teachers, free under age 18) brought me a long way toward appreciating if not the entire genre then certainly this giant of the field. Clyfford Still is considered one of America's most influential modern artists, but he is not widely known. Still's peers, among them Jackson Pollock, Willem de Kooning, and Mark Rothko, became household names. At some point in his career, Still severed ties with commercial art galleries, and after his death in 1980 the Clyfford Still Estate was sealed off from public and scholarly view. In his will, Still stipulated that his entire estate be given to an American city willing to establish a permanent museum dedicated solely to his work. In 2004, Denver mayor John Hickenlooper was able to secure the collection with the promise of a museum.

Practically under the eaves of the Denver Art Museum, the Clyfford Still Museum attracts an audience of its own. The architecture of this building is nearly as interesting as the 2,400 drawings, paintings, and prints of the artist. Designed by Brad Cloepfil of Allied Works Architecture, the interior includes a unique waffle-like concrete ceiling that lets in natural light, which makes the paintings look slightly different at various times of the day or year. Note that the second floor consists of nine distinct galleries, each with different ceiling heights to emphasize different elements of the collection. At two points in the galleries, visitors can step onto planted patios for a breath of fresh air.

The exhibits change regularly, as only a fraction of Still's massive body of work can be displayed at one time. With the collection's proximity to the Denver Art Museum, it is possible to cram in a lot of viewing in one day, but it is recommended to set aside half a day to thoroughly experience the work of this American artist. Or plan to come during one of their events, such as the live Music in the Galleries series.

★ Denver Art Museum

The Frederic C. Hamilton Building, which houses portions of the **Denver Art Museum** (100 W. 14th Ave. Pkwy., 720/865-5000, www.denverartmuseum.org, 10am-5pm daily, $10-13 adults, $8-10 seniors and students, free under age 18) has become an attraction in itself. Designed by architect Daniel Libeskind and constructed in 2006, the 146,000-square-foot building is all sharp angles and severe points—intended as an interpretation of rock crystals and of the jagged peaks of the Rocky Mountains. The building has received its fair share of criticism, being largely panned by national art critics, with visitors complaining of vertigo inside, and questions about whether the art is enhanced or hampered by the architecture. Nonetheless, it has created a lot of exciting energy in the neighborhood and the city, leading to more development in the Golden Triangle neighborhood.

The Hamilton Building is connected to the original Denver Art Museum building, a seven-story "castle," also once controversial for its design, that has been home to the museum since it was constructed in 1971. Now called the North Building, it was designed by Italian architect Gio Ponti.

Once inside either of the museum's buildings, visitors will discover more art and activities than can be seen in one day. The museum's **Institute for Western American Art** includes works by well-known masters, including Charles Deas's *Long Jakes, The Rocky Mountain Man,* as well as the work of local contemporary artists. Like much of the museum, the Western American art rooms include interactive areas, especially for children. In this room, visitors can make their

1

2

3

4

Public Art Tours

The City of Denver has an ordinance requiring that 1 percent of any $1 million capital improvement project be spent on the acquisition of public art. As a result, the city has a considerable public art collection to show off that includes works from international artists as well as those from Colorado. The work of Dale Chihuly, Herbert Bayer, Barbara Jo Revelle, Vance Kirkland, and many more artists is exhibited both outside and inside public buildings, including Coors Field, the Denver Performing Arts Complex, and the Denver Art Museum.

Even if your visit to Denver is so short that you never leave the airport, there is a large collection of public art on display there as well—much of it permanent, but with some temporary exhibits, too. Even the little windmills along the train tunnels are a public art installation. My personal favorite is Gary Sweeney's *America, Why I Love Her,* just off the main terminal. Sweeney's wall-size map of the United States is an homage to bizarre tourist sites around the country.

Pick up a **self-guided walking tour** (720/865-4307, www.denvergov.org) of the city's public art and find out when guided tours of indoor public art are scheduled.

own postcards using ink stamps with iconic Western images and colored pencils.

Other collections at the museum include African art, American Indian art, Oceanic art, and a Modern and Contemporary collections room with thousands of pieces by artists including Andy Warhol, Man Ray, and many others. The permanent collections are exhibited on rotation, though some public art pieces, such as the Mark di Suvero sculpture *Lao-Tzu,* are always on display outdoors.

The parking garage for the museum is directly across the plaza from the Hamilton Building. The Museum Residences, also designed by Libeskind, are above the garage. The glass "walls" of these private homes are meant to complement the titanium-skinned museum that they face.

Denver Central Public Library

Denverites love their libraries; statistics show that the city is among those with the highest number of library cardholders per capita in the country. But the **Denver Central Public Library** (10 W. 14th Ave. Pkwy., 720/865-1111, www.denverlibrary.org, 10am-8pm Mon.-Tues., 10am-6pm Wed.-Sat., 9am-5pm Sun.) is no ordinary library—it holds not just books but also a large art collection, photograph archives, and genealogy data.

The Central Library was designed by well-known architect Michael Graves and opened in 1995 with 47 *miles* of books. Each section is roomy, and huge windows bring in the natural light. The fifth floor's **Western Art Gallery** and **Gates Western Reading Room** showcase the library's Western art collection. Only a fraction of the library's 400 framed pieces (including works by Albert Bierstadt, Frederic Remington, and Thomas Moran) and thousands of sculptures, etchings, lithographs, and other artifacts dating back to the mid-1800s can be on display at one time. While taking a peek at the art that is hung in an entryway hallway and set out between the stacks, you're bound to see people quietly conducting research, as this is also the **Western History and Genealogy Department;** it boasts a massive collection of digital photographs related to the history of the American West and Colorado.

The library's seventh floor has not just administrative offices but also long hallways bedecked with a bit more Western art. The **Vida Ellison Gallery** hosts exhibits of artwork made by local artists (including library staff), and the gallery provides a nice view of Civic Center Park and downtown.

The library also hosts themed film series,

1: Civic Center Park **2:** History Colorado Center **3:** United States Mint at Denver **4:** Denver Art Museum at dusk

guest lectures, book clubs, concerts, knitting and cooking classes, and more events throughout the year. Pick up the *Fresh City Life* magazine at any library for the current month's schedule.

History Colorado Center

It's been called "the first great history museum of the 21st century" by Smithsonian Affiliations director Harold Closter, and the **History Colorado Center** (1200 Broadway, 303/447-8679, www.historycoloradocenter.org, 10am-5pm Fri.-Wed., 10am-8pm Thurs., $14 adults, $12 seniors, $10 students, $8 ages 5-15, free under age 5) has permanent exhibits as well as rotating temporary exhibits. The 200,000-square-foot building was designed by Tryba Architects of Denver. The approach to history here is to feature high-tech, hands-on learning about the people and the environment that shaped the Centennial State. The experience begins with H. G. Wells-inspired "time machines" in the four-story atrium, where the mobile devices can be pushed around a terrazzo floor map of the state to learn about everything from the preservation of Mesa Verde to the tomato wars. While still in the atrium, look up to see a two-story media presentation. This six-minute video gives a taste of the historic places, first peoples, and traditions in Colorado. Step from this futuristic display into the past, where parts of the town of Keota, Colorado—inspiration for James Michener's novel *Centennial*—are recreated and others have been salvaged. Inside this former agricultural town on the Eastern Plains, kids can gather eggs, slide in the barn, and "meet" town residents. Then it's time to head upstairs for a virtual ski jump, a mine tour, and a step inside an old fort in the *Destination Colorado* exhibit, where eight stories about the state are told.

A sometimes humorous exhibit is *Denver A-Z;* on the more serious side is an exhibit about how the harsh, dry environment shaped life in Colorado. **Café Rendezvous** (8am-4pm Mon.-Fri., 10am-4pm Sat.-Sun.) and the **History Colorado Museum Store** (10am-5pm daily) are on the first floor.

Kirkland Museum of Fine & Decorative Art

The **Kirkland Museum of Fine & Decorative Art** (1201 Bannock St., 303/832-8576, www.kirklandmuseum.org, 11am-5pm Tues.-Sat., noon-5pm Sun., $10 adults, $8 seniors and students) is one of Denver's cultural gems. It began in Capitol Hill as the studio of artist Vance Kirkland, which has been preserved as if the man himself might reenter and hang from his special harness to begin another dot painting. The museum was established after his death and took over the building next door in 2002, displaying the collection of over 3,000 examples of arts and crafts, art nouveau, pop art, art deco, and more.

Eventually outgrowing its space, the museum relocated to the Golden Triangle neighborhood, reopening in a custom-designed building in 2018; the studio was moved from Capitol Hill to join the new building. In addition to the modernist decorative works that date from 1880 to 1980, Kirkland's impressive body of work and rotating exhibits of Colorado artists are on display. Children under 13 are not allowed, and ages 13-17 must be accompanied by an adult.

LODO AND PLATTE RIVER VALLEY

Auraria Campus

The **Auraria Campus** (900 Auraria Pkwy., 303/556-3291, www.ahec.edu) on the outlying rim of LoDo is Colorado's largest educational campus, with about 42,000 students, and is home to three separate institutions: the Community College of Denver, the Metropolitan State University of Denver, and the University of Colorado at Denver. One addition to this commuter campus is the teaching hotel—a Springhill Suites that is mostly operated by students as part of the hospitality program. As the campus was once a town of its own before merging with Denver in the

1860s, there are several historic sights worth visiting.

The Ninth Street Historic Park is the oldest restored block in the city and includes 13 Victorian homes (now administrative offices) and a turn-of-the-20th-century grocery store (now a bagel and coffee shop). It's free to stroll along the block and read the small signs in front of each home, which tell a bit about the architecture and the people who originally lived here.

Not far from the historic park is the relocated and restored **Golda Meir House,** one-time home of the former Israeli prime minister. When she was a girl, Meir left her parents' home in Milwaukee to live with her sister and brother-in-law in Denver in their tiny duplex. She went to high school in the city and worked in the family laundry business. In literature describing Meir's time in Denver, she is quoted as saying, "It was in Denver that my real education began." One side of the duplex contains artifacts from Meir's life, while the other side is used for small conferences. Tours (303/556-3292) are available.

The city's oldest church structure is now the **Emmanuel Gallery** (303/556-8337, www.emmanuelgallery.org, hours vary), serving as an art gallery for the campus. The little stone chapel was built in 1876 for Episcopalians, then was converted into a synagogue in 1903; it eventually became an artist's studio, a purpose it served until 1973. The gallery displays artwork by faculty and students in changing exhibits.

Still an active Catholic parish, **St. Elizabeth's Church** (also called St. Elizabeth of Hungary, 1060 St. Francis Way, 303/534-4014, http://stelizabethdenver.org) was founded by German immigrants in 1878. When the congregation grew too large for the original church, the building was torn down and the current one constructed in 1898. The monastery was added in the 1930s. Historians have uncovered the sometimes bizarre history of the church—a murdered priest, panhandling nuns, and more.

St. Cajetan's (1190 9th St., 303/556-2755, www.ahec.edu), a Spanish colonial church, was built in 1925 for the Latino community. The parish relocated in 1973 and the church is now used for campus functions. Call ahead to schedule guided tours of these historic buildings (720/556-3291).

The most distinctive building on campus is the **Tivoli Student Union** (900 Auraria Pkwy., 303/556-6330, www.tivoli.org), which started out in 1866 as one of Denver's earliest breweries. There are no tours offered of the Tivoli building; it is open to the public as a student union and holds various eateries and campus offices.

Centennial Gardens Park

In theory, it seems, this park is open to the public but is often closed for special events. I recommend taking a chance and stopping by to see if the gates are open. The gardens can still easily be viewed when the gates are closed, even if you can't walk through them.

Centennial Gardens Park (1101 Little Raven St., 720/913-1311, www.denvergov.org/parks, by permit only) is a lovely little example of the transformation of the entire South Platte Valley from urban wasteland to dynamic neighborhood. People jogging, bicycling, or sauntering along the paths parallel to the South Platte River can detour into the gardens (when open) and view dozens of carefully pruned topiary trees, smell the lavender plants, listen to the fountains trickling, or watch birds flit from trees to birdbaths.

Centennial Gardens Park is a formal garden, inspired by the gardens of Versailles in France. In the 1990s, former Denver mayor Wellington Webb and his wife, Wilma, visited Versailles and were inspired to create a formal public garden in Denver. What makes this small garden unique is the use of only native plant species and drought-tolerant plants in the neatly patterned five-acre space. There is always a spot of brilliant color among the tidy green hedges; in the spring, yellow, purple, and white crocuses push up through native buffalo grass just before miniature irises and daffodils appear around deciduous trees

LoDo and Platte River Valley

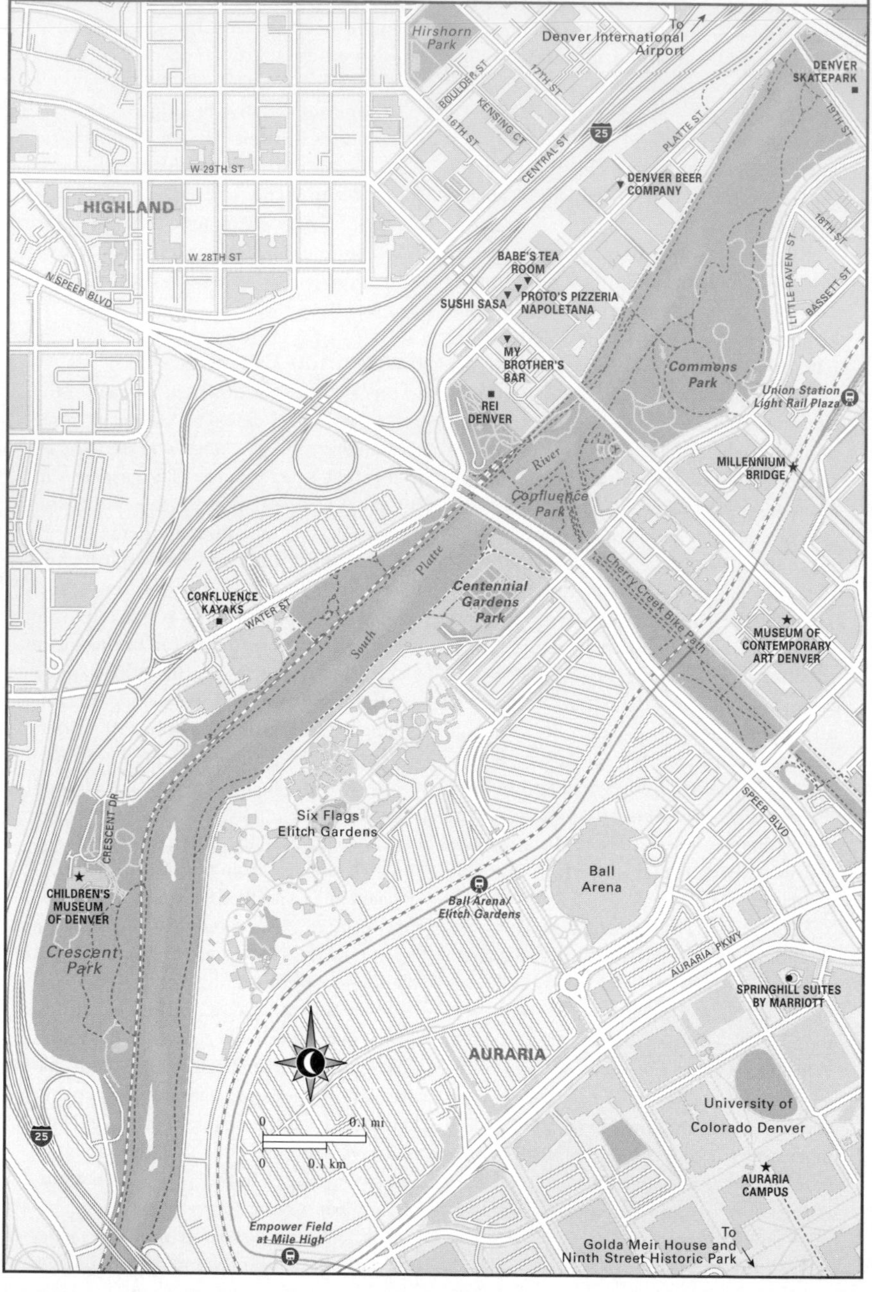
Hirshorn Park
To Denver International Airport
DENVER SKATEPARK
BOULDER ST
17TH ST
16TH ST
KENSING CT
CENTRAL ST
PLATTE ST
19TH ST
25
W 29TH ST
DENVER BEER COMPANY
HIGHLAND
18TH ST
LITTLE RAVEN ST
BASSETT ST
W 28TH ST
BABE'S TEA ROOM
SUSHI SASA
PROTO'S PIZZERIA NAPOLETANA
N SPEER BLVD
MY BROTHER'S BAR
Commons Park
REI DENVER
Union Station Light Rail Plaza
MILLENNIUM BRIDGE
River
Confluence Park
Cherry Creek Bike Path
South Platte
Centennial Gardens Park
CONFLUENCE KAYAKS
WATER ST
MUSEUM OF CONTEMPORARY ART DENVER
SPEER BLVD
CRESCENT DR
Six Flags Elitch Gardens
Ball Arena
Ball Arena/ Elitch Gardens
CHILDREN'S MUSEUM OF DENVER
Crescent Park
AURARIA PKWY
SPRINGHILL SUITES BY MARRIOTT
AURARIA
University of Colorado Denver
0 0.1 mi
0 0.1 km
AURARIA CAMPUS
Empower Field at Mile High
To Golda Meir House and Ninth Street Historic Park

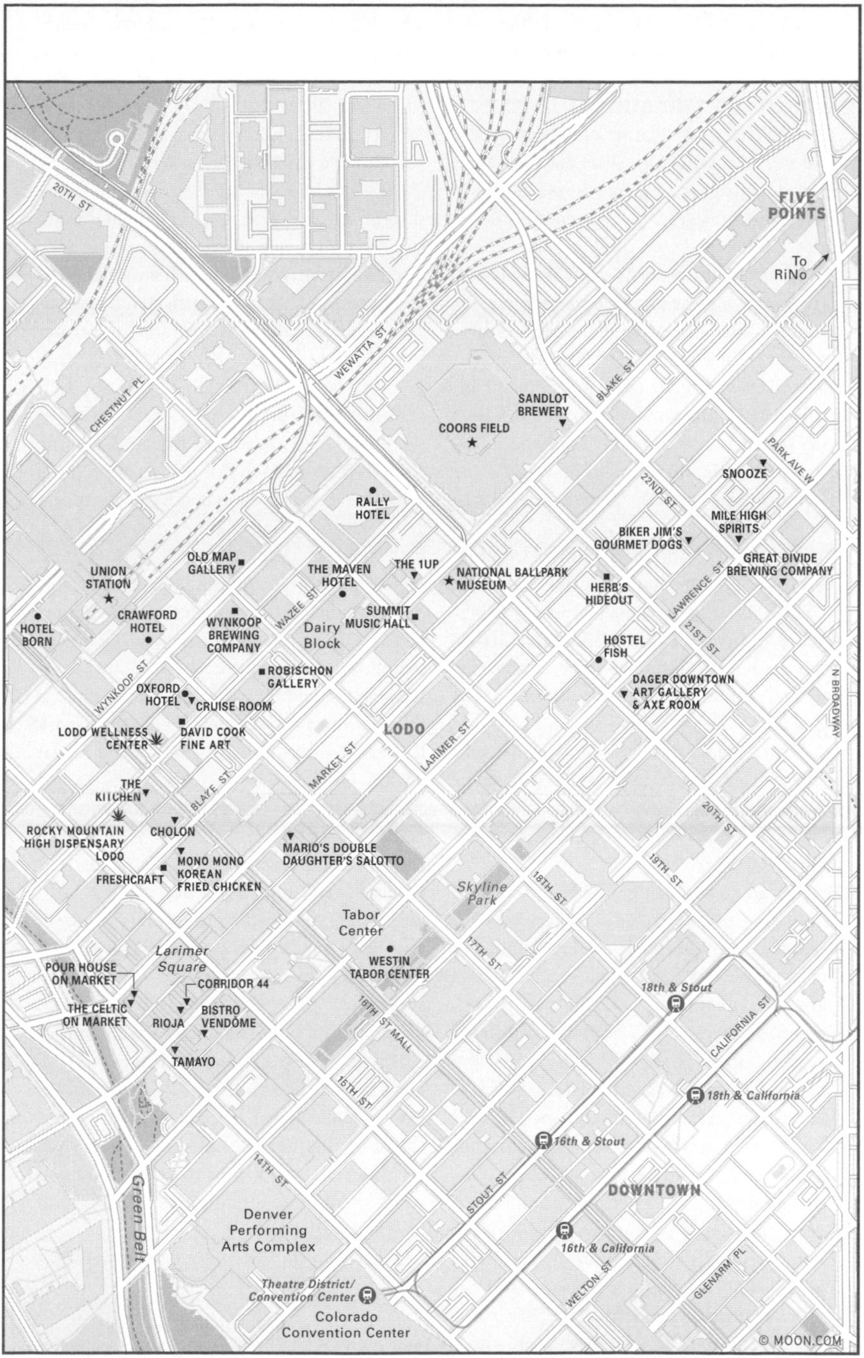
FIVE POINTS
To RiNo
20TH ST
CHESTNUT PL
WEWATTA ST
BLAKE ST
SANDLOT BREWERY
COORS FIELD
PARK AVE W
SNOOZE
22ND ST
RALLY HOTEL
MILE HIGH SPIRITS
BIKER JIM'S GOURMET DOGS
GREAT DIVIDE BREWING COMPANY
OLD MAP GALLERY
UNION STATION
THE MAVEN HOTEL
THE 1UP
NATIONAL BALLPARK MUSEUM
HERB'S HIDEOUT
LAWRENCE ST
CRAWFORD HOTEL
WAZEE ST
SUMMIT MUSIC HALL
HOTEL BORN
WYNKOOP BREWING COMPANY
Dairy Block
21ST ST
HOSTEL FISH
N BROADWAY
ROBISCHON GALLERY
WYNKOOP ST
OXFORD HOTEL
CRUISE ROOM
DAGER DOWNTOWN ART GALLERY & AXE ROOM
LODO WELLNESS CENTER
DAVID COOK FINE ART
LODO
LARIMER ST
MARKET ST
BLAKE ST
THE KITCHEN
20TH ST
ROCKY MOUNTAIN HIGH DISPENSARY LODO
CHOLON
MARIO'S DOUBLE DAUGHTER'S SALOTTO
MONO MONO KOREAN FRIED CHICKEN
FRESHCRAFT
19TH ST
18TH ST
Skyline Park
Tabor Center
17TH ST
Larimer Square
POUR HOUSE ON MARKET
WESTIN TABOR CENTER
CORRIDOR 44
18th & Stout
THE CELTIC ON MARKET
RIOJA
BISTRO VENDÔME
16TH ST MALL
CALIFORNIA ST
TAMAYO
15TH ST
18th & California
16th & Stout
14TH ST
Green Belt
STOUT ST
DOWNTOWN
Denver Performing Arts Complex
16th & California
WELTON ST
GLENARM PL
Theatre District/ Convention Center
Colorado Convention Center
© MOON.COM

and rows of junipers. A small pavilion with benches provides shade on warm days.

Children's Museum of Denver

The **Children's Museum of Denver** (2121 Children's Museum Dr., 303/433-7444, www.mychildsmuseum.org, by reservation only Wed.-Sun., $15 ages 2-59, $13 seniors and age 1, free under age 1) is a good place to explore for all ages and interests—but it's ideal for little kids who want a place to get messy or dive into their curiosity. The museum offers several exhibits divided into different themes (create, investigate, imagine, and explore), including My Market and Ready Vet Go, which offer hands-on playtime with pretend items. The simplest play areas are the best: a painting room, a small puppet theater, a mirrored wall to dress up and dance in front of, a real fire engine to "drive," and the outdoor playground near the bike path and the South Platte River.

The museum also hosts temporary exhibits and shows such as the Blue Man Group. They also offer additional games and events for Easter, Halloween, and other holidays. The Museum Café has grown-up and kid food with little tables and chairs for sitting inside. There are also picnic tables outside near the playground.

Commons Park

The broad and winding waters of the South Platte River have attracted dreamers since the earliest days of the city. In the late 1800s, this land was used for a castle and an amusement park, among other delights. As years passed, this broad expanse of land that sits roughly between LoDo's Union Station to the east and the South Platte River to the west was lost to the ravages of time and nature, and the river started being used as a dumping ground for old cars, refrigerators, and other debris. A severe flood along the river in 1965, in which lives, homes, and businesses were lost, led to long-needed changes all along the South Platte: a dam was built upstream, and the water was no longer used as an illegal garbage dump. Still, it took decades for new dreams to take shape and remake the land into a recreation area once again.

The **Commons Park** (15th St. and Little Raven St., 720/913-1311, www.denvergov.org, 5am-11pm daily) that people visit today was years in the making. A 20-acre park along the east side of the South Platte River tells the story of this land. One portion was designed to recreate how it would have looked before the settlers arrived, complete with native grasses, trees, and sand. Atop an artificial hill—popular for sledding in the winter and, in warmer weather, flying kites—there is a sunken black granite east-west directional sculpture that can't be seen from below. There are views of the Rocky Mountains and the city's skyline from the hilltop. One side of the park follows a street and looks up at condominiums and apartments, while the other drops down to foot- and bike paths along the river. Bridges on either side of Commons Park lead to shopping and dining districts in historic neighborhoods. On any given day, depending on the season, you will see fitness classes, sports contests, skiers, sledders, and dog walkers or dogs in obedience classes. Public art inside the park is user-friendly—it can all be walked in, sat on, and touched.

Coors Field

Even in the off-season, there's a chance to tour **Coors Field** (2001 Blake St., 303/762-5437, www.mlb.com/rockies, tours 10am, noon, and 2pm nongame days, 10am and noon evening game days Mon.-Sat. Apr.-Sept., noon and 2pm Mon., Wed., and Fri.-Sat. Oct.-Mar.; $12 adults, $9 seniors and children), home of the Colorado Rockies baseball team, and see parts of the field that are off-limits during games. The ballpark has been a major part of the redevelopment of LoDo from neglected warehouse district to hip urban neighborhood with expensive condominiums and dozens of bars and restaurants.

Since opening in 1995, Coors Field has

1: Children's Museum of Denver **2:** artist Lonnie Hanzon's *The Evolution of the Ball*, greeting visitors as they enter Coors Field

1

2

been noted for its modern yet classic architecture. The 75-minute tours include the field; the upper deck, where a row of purple seats marks 5,280 feet above sea level; the guest clubhouse; and suites. The upper seats have a great view of the Central Platte Valley and the Rocky Mountains.

After the tour, you can walk around the stadium and check out some of the public art on display, including Erick C. Johnson's *Bottom of the Ninth,* which shows a neon baseball figure sliding into home plate, to the north. There is a large gift and souvenir shop on the Blake Street side of Coors Field, where just about anything in the team's purple and black can be found—blankets, hats, jackets, T-shirts, and more.

Larimer Square

Larimer Square (Larimer St. between 14th St. and 15th St., 720/805-1973, www.larimersquare.com) is not really a square, but a preserved city block—the historic buildings along each side are now used for offices, restaurants, and shops. The history of this place goes back to the city's earliest days, when the area was inundated with people who wanted to strike it rich from gold found in the nearby creek. General William H. Larimer Jr. arrived in 1858 and built a cabin on what is now Larimer Square. The city quickly grew, and by the 1880s, there were 25 buildings on Larimer Street, including a bank, a drugstore, and a bookstore.

Over time, saloons and bars prospered, and this block became known as Denver's skid row. In the 1960s, officials were ready to start anew, but preservationists gathered support to save the block from the wrecking ball. With its 1870s and 1880s buildings fully restored, the block was listed on the National Register of Historic Places.

Millennium Bridge

The **Millennium Bridge** (16th St. at Chestnut St.) became an instant landmark in Denver when it was erected in 2003 and an important part of the redevelopment of the Central Platte Valley. The 16th Street Mall used to end at Wynkoop Street, where railroad tracks emanating from behind Union Station dominated the landscape. Now 16th Street has extended beyond its old boundary in LoDo, and the Millennium Bridge brings people up and over the railroad tracks into the Platte Valley, the bustling Riverfront Park development area, and Commons Park. Up out of the flat prairie floor rises a 200-foot white mast held in place on a wide deck by multiple steel cables. The bridge has stairs on either side as well as elevators, and is the most scenic walk from downtown to parks and the South Platte River. Additional bridges on the other side of Commons Park lead to restaurants and shops on Platte Street and then to the eastern edge of the Highlands neighborhood, which has a growing number of popular restaurants.

With its dramatic backdrop of the city's skyline and its distinctive architecture, the bridge has become a favorite spot for fashion shoots, selfies, and family portraits. As coal trains rattle below night and day, there are typically tourists and art students taking in the view from the bridge and trying to get a good shot of the mast. A popular photo spot is at the red and orange sculpture on the west side of the bridge, next to the bottom of the stairs.

Museum of Contemporary Art Denver

Not quite as talked about as the Denver Art Museum, but still an important aspect of the culture here, the **Museum of Contemporary Art Denver** (1485 Delgany St., 303/298-7554, www.mcadenver.org, noon-7pm Tues.-Thurs., noon-9pm Fri., 10am-5pm Sat.-Sun., $10 adults, $5 after 5pm, free under age 19) also has a building designed by an internationally known architect.

The museum had humble beginnings in 1996 in a former fish market at downtown's Sakura Square block. Incredible success clashed with space limitations, and the museum had to relocate. After hiring London-based architect David Adjaye, the museum reopened in a black glass box of a building perched on the corner of 15th Street. At first glance, the minimalist modern building can seem as challenging as contemporary art itself—and the hidden front door adds to this perplexity—but inside it is full of welcome surprises for cultural dates and artistic family interaction. Recent exhibitions include the works of Keith Haring, Francesca Woodman, Tara Donovan, Clark Richert, and others.

The museum strives to reduce its carbon footprint with its environmentally sustainable building and by offering locally grown food and drinks in the café as well as by encouraging volunteers and staff to commute to work in an eco-friendly manner. Atop the building is the **MCA Café** (noon-7pm Tues.-Thurs., 1pm-9pm Fri., 10am-5pm Sat.-Sun.), which includes an outdoor bar. There is also a rooftop garden, itself an artwork, designed by Colorado landscape architect Karla Dakin. Ceramic sculptures inside the café were made by Kim Dickey, a Colorado artist.

Children and families will find a small library with a selection of art books and the "Idea Box," where small tables and art supplies invite kids of all ages to get creative. Or, for a more laid-back experience, simply lounge in a room full of beanbag chairs.

National Ballpark Museum

Enhance your ballpark experience by visiting the **National Ballpark Museum** (1940 Blake St., 303/974-5835, www.ballparkmuseum.com, 11am-5pm Tues.-Sat., $10 adults, $5 seniors, free under age 13) before you see the game. This is an impressive private collection that goes beyond the Colorado Rockies. Did you know there was a Denver baseball team before the Rockies? Come see what the team was called and when it played. Bits and pieces of other stadiums are part of the collection—bricks, light fixtures, pieces of bats, a telephone, uniforms, and lots more.

Union Station

Union Station (1701 Wynkoop St., 303/592-6712, http://unionstationindenver.com) is the perfect representation of how far Denver has come in a relatively short time. The regal historic building has been renovated into a hotel, transportation hub, nightlife hot spot, and urban playground for all. Yet the old charm of the train station remains, with the high-backed wooden benches and soaring high ceilings setting the stage for a weekend of fun in the city.

Outside on the plaza of the station is a splash park with intermittent fountains shooting up sprays of water for kids (and grown-ups) to run through or soak themselves during summer. Diners on the various restaurant patios can enjoy the squeals of joy as kids cool off and dare each other to run through. In the winter, people come here to take holiday card photos next to the enormous and impeccably decorated Christmas tree.

It's almost easy to forget that this is still a working station, where you can walk in and buy tickets from the Amtrak window and catch a train to Chicago or Los Angeles. In addition, you can walk out the back door and down some steps into a shiny new bus station, where regional buses regularly take people to Boulder and other cities in the area. On the other side of the bus terminal is the light rail station, with trains that take passengers west to Golden, south to the suburbs, and throughout the metro area.

CAPITOL HILL AND CITY PARK

Cathedral Basilica of the Immaculate Conception

The **Cathedral Basilica of the Immaculate Conception** (1530 Logan St., 303/831-7010, www.denvercathedral.org), situated on a slight hill with its twin 210-foot bell-tower spires poking into the sky above, looks as if it reaches into the heavens. This Catholic church has both captivating history and architecture.

J. J. Brown, husband of Molly Brown, joined with a few investors to buy the land for the cathedral, and in 1902 ground was broken to start the new building. The French Gothic structure is made from limestone and granite, while Italian marble was used for the altar, communion rail, statuary, and bishop's chair. The stunning interior features a 68-foot vaulted ceiling and 75 German-made stained-glass windows—more than any other Catholic church in the country. In 1912, lightning struck one of the church's spires and toppled 25 feet off the top of the bell tower. Repairs were made before the church's dedication later that year. In 1993, Pope John Paul II read mass here during World Youth Day.

This grand church is on the corner of busy Colfax Avenue and Logan Street, just a stone's throw from the state capitol. A small garden on the north side of the building offers statues and benches.

There are three masses held each day during the week (6am, 12:10pm, and 5:30pm Mon.-Fri.) and six total on weekends (7am and 4:30pm Sat.; 8:30am, 10:30am, 12:30pm, and 6:30pm Sun.). Visitor hours are 4pm-5:15pm and 6:15pm-7pm Monday and Wednesday-Friday, 1:30pm-2:30pm and 7:30pm-8pm Sunday.

City Park

The city's largest park, at 370 acres and 1 mile (1.6 km) long, is **City Park** (3300 E. 17th Ave., 303/331-4113, www.denvergov.org, 5am-11pm daily), east of downtown. Denver's answer to New York's Central Park, City Park offers pretty much anything you could ask for in a park, sometimes in multiples: lakes, playgrounds, athletic fields, historic statues and fountains, running and cycling paths, a golf course, the **Denver Zoo,** and the **Denver Museum of Nature & Science.**

When the park was laid out in 1882, there was no surrounding neighborhood, and downtown trolleys took people to this large patch of green. But it didn't take long for the city to grow around the park and beyond. The best time to visit is in summer, when paddleboats are rented by the hour on Ferril Lake and free jazz concerts are held in the park's historic pavilion.

The park is easily traversed by paved roads—some more like paths—but note that from May through September, the roads are closed on Sunday. The park includes the Mile High Loop, a contour that is 5,280 feet (1,609 m) above sea level, and a multiuse path that goes right by the Denver Museum of Nature & Science. Walk around during spring and enjoy a lilac garden, blooming trees, rows of tulips, and more greenery. Be sure to visit all the public art in this park, including the statue of Martin Luther King Jr., by artist Ed Dwight.

★ Colorado State Capitol

A visit to the **Colorado State Capitol** (200 Colfax Ave., 303/866-2604, http://leg.colorado.gov/tour-information, tours 10am, 11am, 1pm, and 2pm daily, free) is a history lesson in the making, especially when the legislature is in session (Jan.-May) and the governor and lawmakers are hard at work. Quiet visitors can watch the legislators in action from just outside their respective chambers during sessions.

The story of the capitol building began in 1868, when Henry C. Brown, who also had The Brown Palace built a few blocks away, donated the land to the state of Colorado. Brown later tried to take it back, even going so far as to return grazing animals to the site, because he was not pleased with construction delays. After a court battle, the state was able to keep the land. Two architects and 22 years later, the capitol was completed.

Tours (reservations recommended) of the building highlight the use of native materials: marble, granite, sandstone, onyx, and gold. The original gold leaf used on the dome was a gift from Colorado miners. When standing on the first floor of the capitol, look 150 feet up to the rotunda ceiling. High up inside the rotunda is the stained-glass "Hall of Fame" that features portraits of 16 people who made remarkable contributions to the state. Other stained-glass portraits are seen on the tour as well. Before ascending the 77 marble steps of the Grand Staircase, you'll learn about the Water Murals; added in 1940, these murals are an artistic interpretation of the story of one of the state's most precious resources.

The true highlight of touring the capitol is the view from the dome's observation gallery. Like the hike up the 99 steps to the dome's interior, the views of the city and the mountains to the west are breathtaking. About halfway to the dome there is a small museum, Mr. Brown's Attic, in honor of Henry C. Brown's donation of the land. The museum includes a pop art replica of the capitol made from old soup cans by local engineering students.

On the west-side steps of the capitol, you'll find the mile-high markers that indicate the point at which the city reaches 5,280 feet (1,609 m) above sea level. This is a popular spot for tourist photos.

★ Denver Botanic Gardens

Denver Botanic Gardens (1005 York St., 720/865-3500, www.botanicgardens.org, 9am-8pm daily May-Sept., 9am-5pm daily Sept.-Apr., $15 adults, $11.50 seniors, $11 students and ages 3-15, free under age 3) was designed with all types of weather in mind, making it enjoyable year-round, regardless of snow or blazing sun. The 23-acre gardens sit at the back side of Cheesman Park and are on the outer edge of the Capitol Hill neighborhood. Each summer has brought a new sculpture show with artists like Dale Chihuly or Colorado artists, with accompanying artist-led tours and events at the gardens.

When the gardens' original site in City Park was repeatedly damaged by people who came to steal plants, the city and local gardening enthusiasts agreed to transform an old cemetery into the new gardens. The 1960s addition of the Boettcher Memorial Tropical Conservatory, which houses tropical plants in a steamy hot dome, made the gardens more than a summer attraction. While in recent years there has been a design emphasis and financial investment on making at least a portion of the gardens friendly to special events such as weddings, the original mission to highlight thriving native plants remains obvious. The Rock Alpine Garden, Water-Smart Garden, and Dryland Mesa in particular are a reminder of the arid climate of the region, and they show off what grows so well with so little water. Also check out the "green" roof of the gift shop as a progressive idea for environmental design. The Science Pyramid is where visitors can learn more about the science of the plants here.

Throughout the gardens, there are shaded benches and tables and chairs set up for enjoying a picnic—there is a small snack bar within the gardens—or taking a relaxing, pleasantly scented rest.

The Mordecai Children's Garden is atop the parking garage across the street from the main gardens. With its own gift shop at the entrance, the garden includes various water features, bridges, caves, and, of course, plants.

During the summer, Denver Botanic Gardens hosts a summer concert series with big-name bands, and tickets can be hard to come by. Membership to the gardens has many advantages, including discounts on those concert tickets and members-only hours, when the gardens have the ambience of a lovely backyard party.

Denver Museum of Nature & Science

It is difficult to imagine the humble beginnings of the **Denver Museum of Nature & Science** (2001 Colorado Blvd., 303/322-7009, www.dmns.org, 9am-5pm Sat.-Thurs., 9am-9pm Fri., $18.95-19.95 adults, $15.95-16.95 seniors, $13.95-14.95 ages 3-18, free under age 3, additional fees for special exhibitions, planetarium, and IMAX) as an oversized collection of treasured fauna specimens in the log cabin home of naturalist Edwin Carter. Today, features such as the Gates Planetarium, the Phipps IMAX Theater, and the Morgridge Family Exploration Center (which added another 126,000 square feet and five levels of exhibit and activity space) combine to make the museum a top-notch destination.

In 1908, the original Colorado Museum of Natural History opened in a stately building on a hilltop on the eastern side of City Park. The building has been expanded considerably since then, and the variety and type of

Capitol Hill and City Park

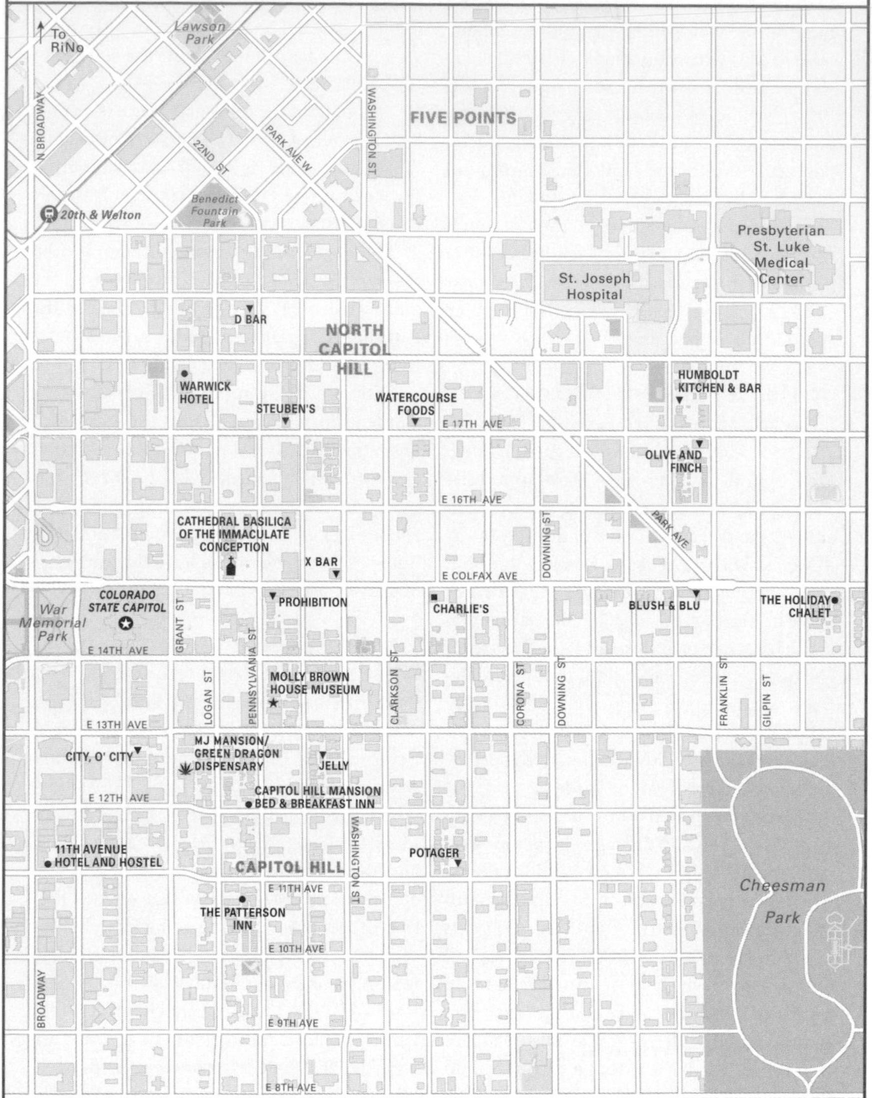
To RiNo
Lawson Park
N BROADWAY
22ND ST
PARK AVE W
WASHINGTON ST
FIVE POINTS
Benedict Fountain Park
20th & Welton
Presbyterian St. Luke Medical Center
St. Joseph Hospital
D BAR
NORTH CAPITOL HILL
WARWICK HOTEL
STEUBEN'S
WATERCOURSE FOODS
E 17TH AVE
HUMBOLDT KITCHEN & BAR
OLIVE AND FINCH
E 16TH AVE
CATHEDRAL BASILICA OF THE IMMACULATE CONCEPTION
X BAR
DOWNING ST
PARK AVE
E COLFAX AVE
War Memorial Park
COLORADO STATE CAPITOL
PROHIBITION
CHARLIE'S
BLUSH & BLU
THE HOLIDAY CHALET
E 14TH AVE
GRANT ST
LOGAN ST
PENNSYLVANIA ST
MOLLY BROWN HOUSE MUSEUM
CLARKSON ST
CORONA ST
DOWNING ST
FRANKLIN ST
GILPIN ST
E 13TH AVE
CITY, O' CITY
MJ MANSION/ GREEN DRAGON DISPENSARY
JELLY
E 12TH AVE
CAPITOL HILL MANSION BED & BREAKFAST INN
11TH AVENUE HOTEL AND HOSTEL
CAPITOL HILL
WASHINGTON ST
POTAGER
E 11TH AVE
THE PATTERSON INN
Cheesman Park
E 10TH AVE
BROADWAY
E 9TH AVE
E 8TH AVE
Governors Park
MIZUNA
VESPER LOUNGE
E 7TH AVE
DON'S CLUB TAVERN
SPEER
FRUITION
E 6TH AVE

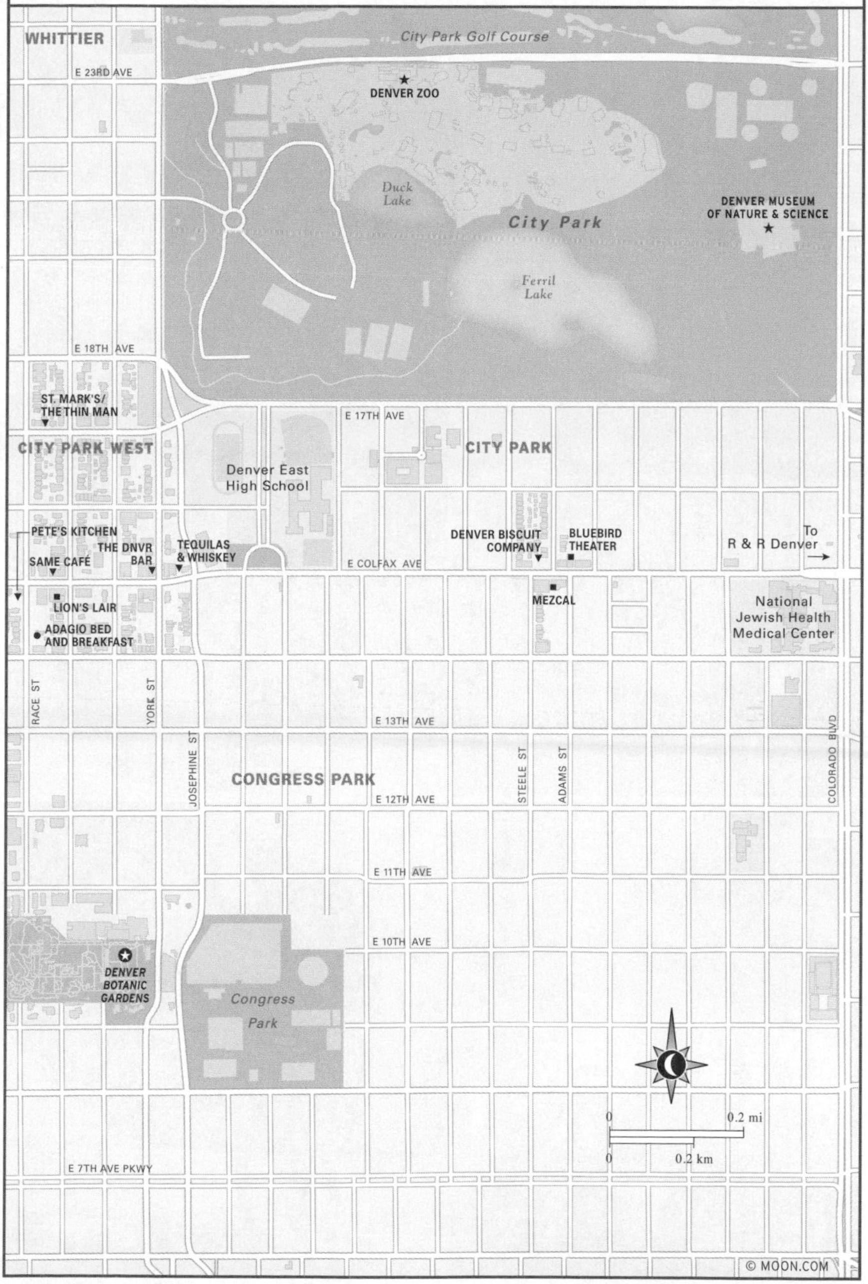
WHITTIER
City Park Golf Course
E 23RD AVE
DENVER ZOO
Duck Lake
City Park
DENVER MUSEUM OF NATURE & SCIENCE
Ferril Lake
E 18TH AVE
ST. MARK'S/ THE THIN MAN
E 17TH AVE
CITY PARK WEST
CITY PARK
Denver East High School
PETE'S KITCHEN
THE DNVR BAR
SAME CAFÉ
TEQUILAS & WHISKEY
DENVER BISCUIT COMPANY
BLUEBIRD THEATER
To R & R Denver
E COLFAX AVE
LION'S LAIR
ADAGIO BED AND BREAKFAST
MEZCAL
National Jewish Health Medical Center
RACE ST
YORK ST
E 13TH AVE
JOSEPHINE ST
CONGRESS PARK
STEELE ST
ADAMS ST
COLORADO BLVD
E 12TH AVE
E 11TH AVE
E 10TH AVE
DENVER BOTANIC GARDENS
Congress Park
0
0.2 mi
0
0.2 km
E 7TH AVE PKWY
© MOON.COM

1

2

3

4

Free Admission Days

In Denver, taxation equals free admission on specified days at many of the city's most popular sights. During a downturn in the economy in the 1980s, the state legislature eliminated funding for several of the city's main attractions, including the Denver Art Museum and the Denver Botanic Gardens. New admission fees did not provide enough financial support for these institutions, so a small sales and use tax of 0.1 percent (or $0.01 on every $10 purchase) was implemented in the surrounding seven-county area. The small tax adds up to millions, and that money is then distributed to scientific and cultural institutions throughout these seven counties. It's enough that the institutions can now afford to offer limited periods of free admission.

While the city's five largest facilities—the Denver Performing Arts Complex, Denver Art Museum, Denver Zoo, Denver Botanic Gardens, and the Denver Museum of Nature & Science—get the lion's share of the $40 million in funds annually, much smaller theaters, art museums, and nature and science centers receive funding as well. Studies have shown that these millions invested in the city's cultural facilities equal billions spent in Denver in return.

The number of free days per year varies from one place to the next, but they are generally scattered so that not every institution has a free day on the same date. And free days are not a secret—show up early because each of these places fills up quickly, and it's first-come, first-served where seating is limited at the Ricketson Theatre and Stage Theatre in the Denver Performing Arts Complex. Free days differ each calendar year. Go to www.scfd.org or pick up a bookmark listing the year's free days at any of the five major facilities.

exhibits have increased. Some of the museum's oldest displays are of animals prepared by taxidermists and staged in large naturalistic settings behind glass windows—it's like a really quiet, clean zoo. Kids enjoy running through these wide halls and pushing the buttons to hear the sounds of cougars, buffalo, and other wildlife. Head to the third level to learn about Colorado's variety of ecosystems and the plants and animals that thrive in them. The *Prehistoric Journey* exhibit in the Explore Colorado section offers plenty of huge dinosaur skeletons, and it's the only place in the museum where visitors can watch the behind-the-scenes work of preparing fossils for display. A family favorite is *Expedition Health*, where people of all ages can learn about their own health by riding bikes, taking walks, breathing, and other seemingly ordinary things. Each gadget has a fun way to measure one's ability. While the museum is one hands-on activity after another, particularly for children, educational programs are also offered off-site.

With its perch on the hill over City Park, the museum also offers two places to catch the best view of the city—the Leprino Family Atrium and the Anschutz Family Sky Terrace, both on the building's west side.

Timed entry tickets are required for admission to the museum and are slightly cheaper when purchased in advance online. Note that admission to the museum does not include tickets to special traveling exhibits or to the IMAX or Gates Planetarium shows (several daily); again, timed entry tickets are required. The museum can be especially crowded during morning school field trips; lines at the ticket windows are often much shorter in the afternoon.

The **T-Rex Café** (11am-2pm daily) and **Grab & Go** (9am-5pm daily) make it possible to spend the day here with the family as you break for lunch, then head back into the museum. The **Museum Shop** (10am-5pm daily) is a wonderful place to get a souvenir, and many of the temporary exhibits also have gift shops.

1: Denver Botanic Gardens **2:** City Park with Denver skyline **3:** Colorado State Capitol **4:** Denver Museum of Nature & Science

Denver Zoo

The **Denver Zoo** (2300 Steele St., 303/376-4800, www.denverzoo.org, zoo opens at 10am daily with varying closure times, online timed entry tickets required, $20 adults, $17 seniors, $14 ages 3-11, free under age 3) is insanely popular with tourists and residents alike. Like many modern-day zoos, the Denver Zoo is trying to make its animal habitats look and feel more natural and its residents look less like caged wild animals. One example of this is the $50 million **Toyota Elephant Passage,** which takes up 10 acres and is home not only to elephants but also rhinos, tapirs, leopards, birds, and reptiles.

There are 29 primates in the seven-acre **Primate Panorama,** and **Predator Ridge** offers 14 animal species from Africa, including lions and hyenas. The **Lorikeet Adventure** is an interactive animal exhibit where visitors can feed the birds.

In addition to the 4,000 animals packed into this 80-acre space within City Park, the zoo is pulling in crowds with features beyond its residents and habitats. A huge annual draw during the holidays is **Zoo Lights,** when nearly half the zoo is illuminated with sparkling and colorful lights. Zoo-goers are treated to a glimpse of whatever nocturnal animals are out, as well as the sounds of choirs singing, a Kwanzaa performance, live ice-sculpture carving, and fire dancers.

The best time to visit the zoo is generally midafternoon, after school groups have come and gone. In winter, plan for time inside the hot and humid **Tropical Discovery,** where there are fish, turtles, snakes, bats, and Komodo dragons.

For a relaxing break from animal viewing, take a nostalgic ride on the zoo's **Endangered Species Carousel** ($3). Children and adults can choose from 48 hand-carved zoo animals or chariots. Look for the mother polar bear and two bear cubs, which were made specially for the zoo in honor of its most famous animal residents, Klondike and Snow, two infant cubs that were hand-fed and raised by zoo staff and have since moved.

Molly Brown House Museum

For being one of Denver's better-known residents, Molly Brown's fascinating life story isn't very well known. "The Unsinkable Molly Brown" is of course best known for surviving the 1912 sinking of the *Titanic,* but the tale of how she made it off the ship while valiantly trying to help others is just the tip of the iceberg.

In 1886, at age 19, Molly married 31-year-old miner J. J. Brown—*before* he struck it rich. After the Browns became wealthy from a gold mine, they moved to Denver in 1894 and eventually bought the Pennsylvania Street house that is now the museum. The Browns' renovations on the house are still evident today. Even during Molly Brown's lifetime, the house was rented out and eventually became a run-down boardinghouse. By the 1970s, it was barely saved from demolition and then painstakingly restored to its Victorian period of glamour.

The **Molly Brown House Museum** (1340 Pennsylvania St., 303/832-4092, www.mollybrown.org, 10am-4pm Thurs.-Sun. general hours, 10am-4pm Tues.-Sun. in summer, $14 adults, $12 seniors, $10 ages 6-18, free under age 6) can only be viewed during guided tours, which are 30 minutes long and run on the hour and half hour. Visitors sign up for tours in the carriage house out back, which is also the museum's large gift shop, filled with books and movies about Molly Brown and other Victorian-era items. On the tours, visitors are led through the first floor, where rooms have been decorated to match photographs from when the Browns lived in the house. The tour then goes up to the second floor and back through the kitchen before ending on the home's back porch. Save time to watch a short movie about Molly Brown (included in the cost of the tour) and view artifacts on display on the porch.

Throughout her life, Molly Brown worked as a progressive social activist and was a tireless fund-raiser and philanthropist. As visitors learn on the guided tours, the details of her full life are more than could be squeezed into a Broadway musical or a Hollywood movie.

Tours do not include the home's third floor, but formal teas are held there regularly. Check the website for details on annual teas such as the Mother's Day Full Tea in May. Note that you get a more comprehensive tour that includes additional interesting history about Molly Brown's life.

GREATER DENVER

★ Rocky Mountain Arsenal National Wildlife Refuge

It's an odd combination—nerve gas, natural beauty, and tourists—but somehow it works, and less than 15 miles (24 km) northeast of downtown, the **Rocky Mountain Arsenal National Wildlife Refuge** (Havana St. and E. 56th Ave., Commerce City, 303/289-0930, www.fws.gov, visitors center 9am-4pm Wed.-Sun., refuge 6am-6pm daily, tour times vary, free) has become one of Denver's gems.

It's easy to spend the better part of a day at this oasis on a guided bus tour or walking through the miles of trails that traverse woodlands, wetlands, and prairie. Every season there is a chance to see some of the 300-plus species that call this place home, and it has become a destination for bird-watchers. Summer is the best time to see burrowing owls and Swainson's hawks, while fall brings an opportunity to see deer with their full antler racks. In winter, the bald eagles are more visible, and in spring, the migratory songbirds and pelicans fly in. At any time of the year, you might spy coyotes, raptors, prairie dogs, and waterfowl. More than 20 bison (which were brought from Montana in 2007) live at the refuge and can easily be seen on most tours.

As the name suggests, this was not always a wildlife refuge. In the 1940s, the U.S. Army took possession of family farms to create a 27-square-mile chemical weapons facility, Rocky Mountain Arsenal. Mustard gas and napalm were manufactured here before the site was used to make agricultural pesticides. While the center of the arsenal has been described as one of the most polluted square miles on earth, the buffer zone has been attracting wildlife for decades; a 1989 headline in *The New York Times* about the Rocky Mountain Arsenal reads, "Nature Sows Life Where Man Brewed Death." In the 1990s, the 15,000-acre area was fenced in to protect wildlife, and work began to turn the arsenal into a refuge. Optimists talk of how nature has triumphed here, while skeptics point out soil contamination concerns.

The arsenal is closed sporadically for months at a time for ongoing cleanup efforts and federal holidays.

TOP EXPERIENCE

★ Red Rocks Amphitheatre

Given its worldwide reputation as a premier outdoor concert venue, **Red Rocks Amphitheatre** (18300 W. Alameda Pkwy., Morrison, 303/697-4939, www.redrocksonline.com, 8am-7pm daily May-Sept., 9am-4pm daily Oct.-Apr., check website for events) hardly needs any introduction. The Beatles, U2, the Grateful Dead, and many more big names in music have played here over the years, even immortalizing the shows in concert movies. Red Rocks has a summer concert lineup that includes some annual events, such as Reggae on the Rocks and 1964: The Beatles Tribute Band, as well as whoever is touring this year, such as David Byrne, the Avett Brothers, Yo-Yo Ma, Jackson Browne, and more. Plan to come early on concert days to be able to park and walk around a bit.

Red Rocks is known for its phenomenal open-air acoustics and live concerts, but the scenery can be enjoyed anytime, even without music. This nearly upright ring of red sandstone cliffs 16 miles (26 km) west of Denver is surprisingly close to the city and offers more than just great concerts. The amphitheater is in **Red Rocks Park,** which is part of the city of Denver's mountain park system. Depending on the weather, visitors can either choose a hiking trail around the red rocks, where wildlife such as deer can be seen wandering about, or check out the visitors center at the top of the amphitheater to see photos of previous concerts. This is also a popular

Greater Denver

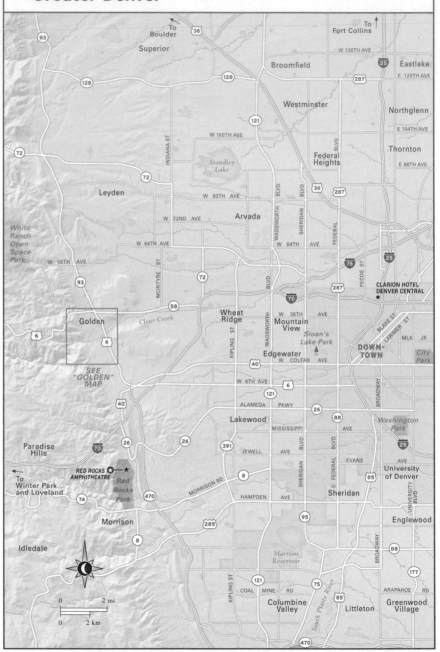

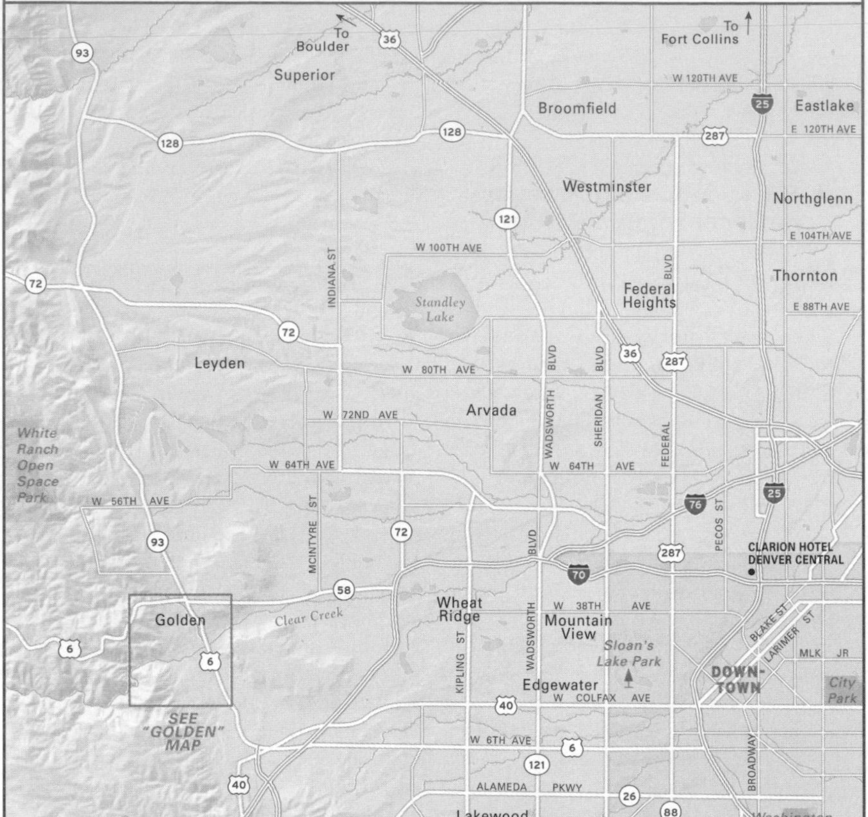

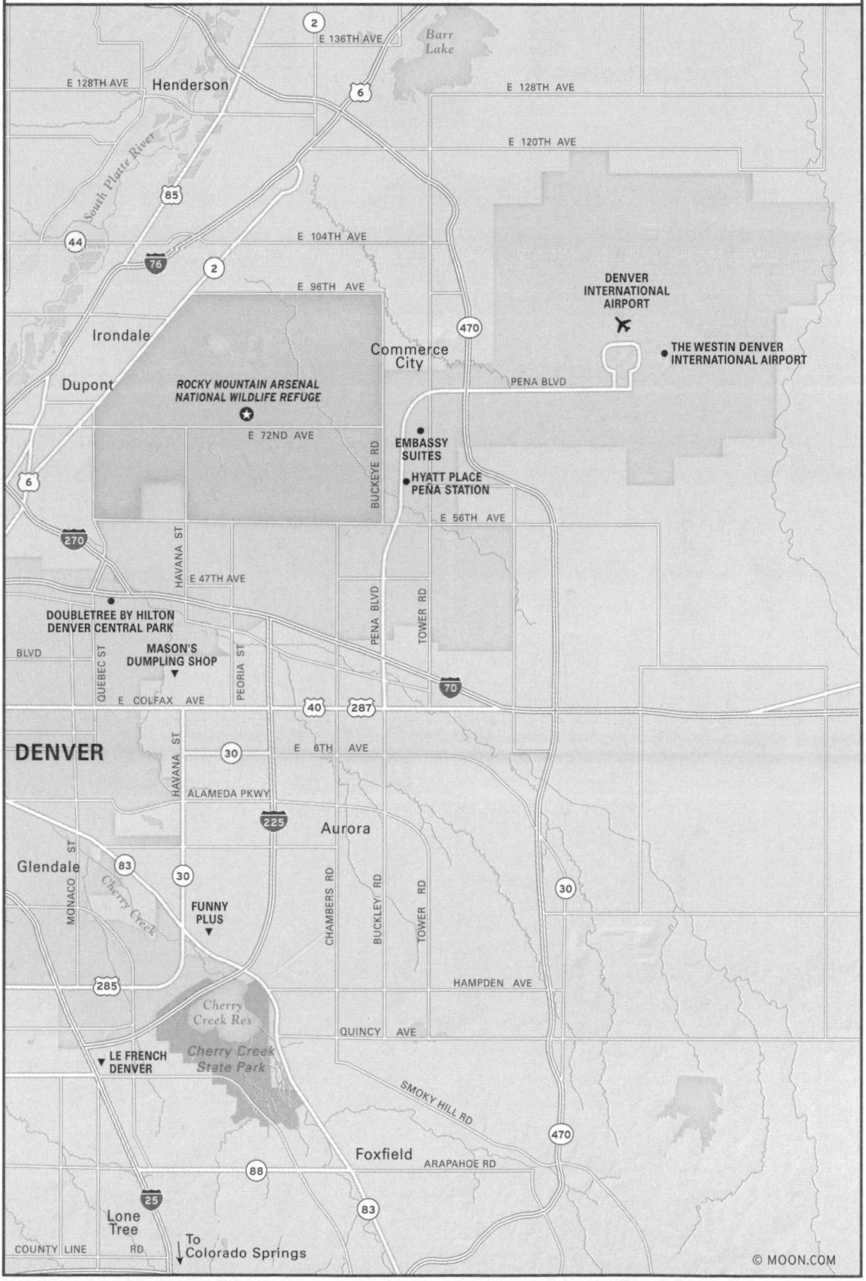
E 136TH AVE
Barr Lake
E 128TH AVE
Henderson
E 128TH AVE
E 120TH AVE
South Platte River
E 104TH AVE
E 96TH AVE
DENVER INTERNATIONAL AIRPORT
Irondale
Commerce City
THE WESTIN DENVER INTERNATIONAL AIRPORT
Dupont
ROCKY MOUNTAIN ARSENAL NATIONAL WILDLIFE REFUGE
PENA BLVD
E 72ND AVE
EMBASSY SUITES
BUCKEYE RD
HYATT PLACE PEÑA STATION
E 56TH AVE
HAVANA ST
E 47TH AVE
DOUBLETREE BY HILTON DENVER CENTRAL PARK
PENA BLVD
TOWER RD
BLVD
QUEBEC ST
MASON'S DUMPLING SHOP
PEORIA ST
E COLFAX AVE
DENVER
E 6TH AVE
ALAMEDA PKWY
Aurora
Glendale
Cherry Creek
MONACO ST
FUNNY PLUS
CHAMBERS RD
BUCKLEY RD
HAMPDEN AVE
Cherry Creek Res
QUINCY AVE
LE FRENCH DENVER
Cherry Creek State Park
SMOKY HILL RD
Foxfield
ARAPAHOE RD
Lone Tree
COUNTY LINE RD
To Colorado Springs
© MOON.COM

1

2

3

4

place for mountain biking and cycling. On days when there are no shows scheduled, visitors are allowed to roam the amphitheater for free. Climbing is not allowed on the rocks anywhere in the park, however, as they can be slippery and fragile.

Entertainment and Events

NIGHTLIFE

Given that a saloon was reportedly Denver's first building, the city has long had a rich nightlife to offer and the options just keep growing. Whether it's for music, drinks, or dancing, Denver has impressive credentials. Most bars and clubs close at 2am or earlier, but you can find a few after-hours spots, too.

In 2020, as businesses struggled to survive by mostly offering takeout, bars were granted permission to sell drinks to go. This custom was extended into 2025 at least, thanks to a law signed by the governor in 2021.

Downtown

BARS

State law prohibits smoking in bars and restaurants, and about the only place it is legal to smoke inside is a cigar bar, such as the **Churchill Bar** (321 17th St., 303/297-3111, www.brownpalace.com, 4pm-11pm Mon.-Thurs., 2pm-11pm Fri.-Sun.) in The Brown Palace Hotel. The Churchill Bar has the feel of an old gentlemen's club, with large brown leather chairs in a quiet room tucked away from the bustle of the hotel lobby and other restaurants. They offer a selection of 60 cigars as well as scotches, bourbons, and cocktails.

The Curtis Hotel is hooked on themes, and that includes the decor and everything else at its **Corner Office Restaurant and Martini Bar** (1401 Curtis St., 303/825-6500, www.thecornerofficedenver.com, 7am-1pm Mon.-Tues., 7am-1pm and 5pm-9pm Wed.-Fri., 9am-3pm and 5pm-9pm Sat., 9am-3pm Sun.). While it bills itself as a martini bar for after work (and it is that, too), it's also a daily breakfast and brunch spot where you can have wine, beer, or cocktails, too.

One of Denver phenom Frank Bonanno's handful of adored eateries, **Green Russell** (1422 Larimer St., 303/893-6505, www.greenrussell.com, 5pm-10pm Sun.-Thurs., 5pm-midnight Fri.-Sat.) is actually known more for its bar scene. To get here, walk down a stairway in mid-Larimer Square to enter what looks like a bakery (it is; Wednesday's Pie is another gem by the same owner). Upon being greeted by the host, it all clicks—this is a speakeasy. Lucky for you, there's no password other than trust in your bartender, who may be persuaded to make you something not on the menu. That's half the fun, although the listed cocktails are great, too.

On the edge of what has become known as the River North Art District (or RiNo) is **The Matchbox** (2625 Larimer St., 720/437-9100, www.matchboxdenver.com, 4pm-2am Mon.-Fri., noon-2am Sat.-Sun.). The name was inspired in part by a fire that gutted the building in 2009. Now it has been reborn, with an open-air beer garden and bocce ball court out back, and a narrow but large interior with exposed brick that reveals a mural of historical signs. This is a place for drinking, not eating, but local food trucks make a stop on special nights.

LOUNGES

Millers & Rossi (3542 Walnut St., 720/257-5342, www.millersandrossi.com, 4pm-1am Mon. and Fri., 5pm-midnight Tues.-Thurs., 1pm-1am Sat., 10am-4pm Sun.) is a speakeasy-style bar, cleverly hidden by a RiNo art gallery. Inside it really feels like you're in some cool guy's basement bar, where you can get a smoked old-fashioned or Hamm's beer from

1: Kirkland Museum of Fine & Decorative Art
2: Denver Zoo **3:** Rocky Mountain Arsenal National Wildlife Refuge **4:** Red Rocks Amphitheatre

Wisconsin. A menu of small plates like French fries and caprese skewers means you can linger without getting too drunk or hungry.

LIVE MUSIC

Clocktower Cabaret (1601 Arapahoe St., 303/293-0075, www.clocktowercabaret.com, check calendar for events) is in the basement of the landmark D & F Clocktower on the 16th Street Mall. This purple, red, and gold room hosts a wide range of entertainers, including drag queens, burlesque performers, nationally known bands, and singers.

A popular stop for indie bands, the **Larimer Lounge** (2721 Larimer St., 303/291-1007, www.larimerlounge.com, 4pm-11pm Mon.-Wed., 4pm-midnight Thurs., 2pm-2am Fri., noon-2am Sat-Sun.) is a good blend of hip and gritty. The space is intimate, which can also mean pretty loud. Bands usually don't go on until 9pm or later. Past shows have included Thurston Moore, ManCub, Saint Motel, Lukas Nelson and Promise of the Real, So-Gnar, and many others.

If you like your live music up close and personal, almost as if you are getting a private concert in your basement, then welcome to **Meadowlark** (2701 Larimer St., 303/293-0251, www.meadowlarkbar.com, 4pm-2am daily), a basement space of cellar proportions but with stylish ambience. *Westword* has dubbed Meadowlark Denver's "best place to learn to be a rock star," among other accolades. In summer an outdoor patio and performance space makes the bar twice as appealing (and twice the size).

The **Mercury Cafe** (2199 California St., 303/294-9281, www.mercurycafe.com, 5pm-midnight Wed.-Fri., 9am-midnight Sat.-Sun.) has a little something for everyone, depending on the night of the week. Their all-ages shows range from blues and swing to tango and acoustic, and dancing classes are offered as well. The entertainment doesn't stop with these specialty bands though—there's also "open stage" Wednesday for magicians, comics, and musicians, and poetry readings on Friday. The Mercury revels in its reputation as a hippie hangout for bohemian types, but anyone who enjoys dancing and live music will feel at home. No credit cards are accepted, but there is an ATM on-site. In 2021, the original owner sold the business and the building to members of Itchy-O, a local avant-garde performance group, who have kept it going the same as always.

If you're looking for a night on the town, consider **Nocturne Jazz & Supper Club** (1330 27th St., 303/295-3333, www.nocturnejazz.com, 6pm-10pm Wed.-Thurs., 6pm-10:30pm Fri.-Sat., 6pm-9pm Sun.) in the heart of Denver's RiNo district. You'll enter through an unassuming warehouse door between Larimer and Walnut and then find yourself in a renovated space that recalls old Hollywood glamour. Move beyond the velvet curtains, order a Manhattan at the bar, and find your seat while the musicians warm up. Stay for a bite and a drink, or plan ahead to enjoy a "Renditions" dinner—special five- to eight-course meals created to pair with the sounds of visiting jazz musicians.

The historic **Roxy Theatre** (2549 Welton St., 720/429-9782, www.theroxydenver.com, check calendar for events) in the Five Points neighborhood has owners intent on making it a hip place once again. The 500-seat theater was once a movie house, and it has changed hands over the years in its life as a music venue. Although there is an emphasis on hip-hop music, there is a wider variety than that on the calendar. The history of the theater is explored down the street at the **Blair-Caldwell African American Research Library** (2401 Welton St., 720/865-2401).

Golden Triangle, Lincoln Park, and SoBo

BARS

I often hear people say that Denver would be perfect if it only had a beach. Good news! **Adrift** (218 S. Broadway, 303/778-8454, www.adriftbar.com, 5pm-11pm Tues.-Thurs., 5pm-midnight Fri.-Sat.) is Denver's tiki bar, with Polynesian island decor (puffer fish lanterns, for one thing), cocktails, staff attire, and menu. The drink names alone are worth a visit—Zombie, Missionary Downfall, and Suffering Bastard, in addition to daiquiris and mai tais. The patios are perfect for playing beach "staycation" in the summer.

Sputnik (3 S. Broadway, 720/570-4503, www.sputnikdenver.com, 11am-2am daily) is the satellite bar right next door to the concert venue Hi-Dive. Sputnik features DJs six nights a week, playing everything from 1960s garage rock to punk to the latest releases by bands that have played or will play at Hi-Dive. The bar also has a rather wild bingo night on Monday. In addition to a menu of eclectic comfort food, Sputnik has a full espresso and liquor bar. The music and clientele match the Hi-Dive for the most part—loud, young, a bit grunge, and up for a very late night.

LOUNGES

For something a bit more laid-back than the many dance clubs and live music venues along Broadway, step into **Milk** (1037 Broadway, 303/832-8628, www.coclubs.com, 9pm-2am Tues.-Sat., 5pm-2am Sun.). Downstairs from Bar Standard, the pillow-festooned seating invites patrons to sit and sip while listening to DJs play everything from Goth to 1980s to industrial music. Milk-white booths with sheer curtains allow a bit more privacy than the main room. The club attracts a young and trendy crowd.

LGBTQ VENUES

Trade (475 Santa Fe Dr., 720/627-5905, www.facebook.com/Tradedenver, 3pm-2am Mon.-Thurs., 1pm-2am Fri.-Sun.) goes beyond the LGBTQ community by also welcoming those in the "kink community" as well. Check their Facebook page for upcoming themed events—like Kaftan Beer Bust and Karaoke.

DANCE CLUBS

What sets **Bar Standard** (1037 Broadway, 303/832-8628, www.coclubs.com, 9pm-2am Wed.-Sat.) apart from many Denver clubs is its retro art deco decor and ambience. The music ranges from underground house to Romanian techno with a Goth night and throwback night. While the music and dancing are great at Bar Standard, comfy booths and a reasonable volume make this a place for chatting with friends and hanging out for the evening. This is a 21-and-over club.

The name of this Denver nightclub is literal: **The Church** (1160 Lincoln St., 303/832-2383, www.coclubs.com, 9pm-2am Thurs.-Sat., no cover) is a beautiful historic church that has been transformed into a nightclub that highlights the original architecture with colorful lights illuminating the Gothic windows and immense ceilings. The Church has three dance floors, each with different reverberating dance music, along with several bars scattered throughout three floors. The Church is a bit of a singles scene for young urban professionals, but fun for anyone in the mood to dance.

This local institution for salsa dancing has a loyal fan base because it offers dependable music from both DJs and live salsa bands rocking the house. You don't have to be a pro—**La Rumba** (99 W. 9th Ave., 303/572-8006, http://larumbadenver.com, 8pm-2am Thurs.-Sat., 7pm-12:30am Sun.) is for rookie salsa dancers as well as the experts. It's all about sensuous dancing to beautiful and fun music.

LIVE MUSIC

Consistently chosen as a Denver favorite for jazz in local surveys and by music magazines, **Dazzle Restaurant and Lounge** (930 Lincoln St., 303/839-5100, www.dazzlejazz.com, 6pm-9pm Tues., 6pm-11pm Wed., 6pm-10pm Thurs., 6pm-11:30pm Fri., 5pm-11:30pm Sat.) offers live music from local, national, and international musicians. Dazzle has two rooms, the Dazzle Showroom and the Dizzy Room, each featuring a different band or event each night. The lineup changes—one night might be a mix of Latin jazz, the next night a CD release party, followed by torch singers—and each act is locally or nationally recognized. In 2021, after barely surviving as a business through the pandemic, Dazzle began Bread & Jam on Wednesdays, during which struggling musicians could come in and play music to maintain their sense of purpose and also enjoy a free meal. A food pantry was created for musicians who need assistance.

Hi-Dive (7 S. Broadway, 720/570-4500, www.hi-dive.com, 4pm-2am daily) is one of Denver's best punk and indie rock dive bars to see bands like the Thermals, Why?, the Ya-Ya's, and many more nationally known and local acts. The venue holds fewer than 300 people, so it gets packed quickly for the really popular shows. Hi-Dive offers both 16-and-over and 21-and-over shows. The club is connected to Sputnik, where they serve food and drinks.

LoDo and Platte River Valley

BARS

Denver's only champagne bar offers a small-plates menu to complement the selection of bubbly. Located in historic Larimer Square next to Rioja, **Corridor 44** (1433 Larimer St., 303/893-0044, www.corridor44.com, 3pm-midnight Sun.-Wed., 3pm-2am Thurs.-Sat.) is cleverly named after the 44-foot-long hallway that links the bustling front bar to the more intimate dining room in the rear. The small plates range from oyster shooters to mini sandwiches and salads to a caviar tasting plate. Champagnes are available by the glass or full or half bottle.

Step back in time to the 1930s in the pink-hued, art deco **Cruise Room** (1600 17th St., 303/825-1107, www.theoxfordhotel.com, 4pm-10pm Wed.-Sun.), on the first floor of the historic Oxford Hotel in LoDo. It's hard to get up and leave the Cruise Room once you've settled into one of their cushy booths and ordered a few of their fabulous martinis from the excellent bartenders. The Cruise Room, which opened the day after Prohibition ended in 1933, is modeled after a cruise ship lounge on the *Queen Mary*. The bar is great for a romantic date night or just a casual night out for drinks with friends.

Ax-throwing and drinking is a thing now, and I'm here to tell you that it's surprisingly fun. Head over to **Dagar Downtown Art Gallery & Axe Room** (2000 Lawrence St., 720/389-8699, www.downtownaxeroom.com, 5pm-11pm daily) for beer or a hard cider and to try this sport. Dagar is veteran owned, and I can say that knowing that the people teaching me how to use a tool/weapon had military training was appealing. The art gallery part is less thrilling but adds another element to the overall experience.

In the heart of LoDo, **Freshcraft** (1530 Blake St., 303/758-9608, www.freshcraft.com, 11am-10pm Tues.-Sun.) serves upscale comfort food in a buzzing urban bar setting. Guests socialize over food, beer, and spirits during a quick lunch, relaxing dinner, happy hour, or late-night snack. Fresh quality ingredients take center stage in craveable items like the Whiskey Barbecue Chicken and the Turkey Pretzel Baja. With 20 taps and 100 bottled options, there's a beer for everyone. Not into beer? The signature cocktails are no slouch either.

In the mix with LoDo's mega sports bars and brewpubs, all walking distance from Coors Field, is **Herb's Hideout** (2057 Larimer St., 303/299-9555, www.herbsbar.com, 5pm-close Mon.-Sat., 3pm-close Sun.), a classic drinking bar. The result of location and history is an intriguing mix of committed barflies and hipsters either lost or looking for something off the beaten track. There is live jazz and blues music at Herb's regularly. Reasonable prices, decent barbecue, and friendly bartenders keep people coming back for more. The sign outside reads "Herb's," but locals know it as Herb's Hideout.

My Brother's Bar (2376 15th St., 303/455-9991, www.mybrothersbar.com, 11am-10pm Mon.-Sat.) is best known for being a one-time hangout of writer Jack Kerouac's Denver buddy, Neal Cassady, a well-known barfly. It is one of Denver's oldest bars, and not much seems to change year after year. The patio out back is a great place to spend a summer evening drinking a cold beer before or after a football or baseball game nearby. The main menu items are the hamburgers, but also try the vegetarian Nina (a cheese sandwich named after a former waitress). Brother's does not have any kind of sign out front, but you can't miss it: It's right on the corner of Platte and 15th Streets, and there is always classical music playing on its outdoor speakers.

Games and drinking go together like salt and pepper, yet **The 1Up** (1925 Blake St., 303/779-6444, www.the-1up.com, 3pm-1am Mon.-Thurs., 11am-1am Fri.-Sun.) was a fairly unique concept for Denver when it first opened: Classic arcade games such as *Pac-Man, Donkey Kong, Tron,* and lots more line the walls, and there are also pinball machines, Skee-Ball, and Giant Jenga to play while drinking beer or cocktails. To complete the time-machine feel, hit the jukebox for some classic tunes. There is another location on Colfax Avenue.

LOUNGES

With Tim Burton-esque decor in dimly lit reds, blacks, and purples, **Mario's Double Daughter's Salotto** (1632 Market St., 303/623-3505, www.doubledaughters.net, 5pm-11pm Wed.-Thurs., 5pm-1am Fri.-Sat.) is typically described as LoDo's only Goth bar. Named after fictitious conjoined twins, the Double Daughter's Salotto embraces all things freakish, with drinks named Six-Toed Kitten and Rabid Monkey. There is always a DJ playing the best hip-hop and electronica music, and excellent pizza is available from Two-Fisted Mario's Pizzeria next door. The crowd is a mix of young and old, tattooed and buttoned-up, and it can be hard to snag one of their curvy red booths on a busy weekend night.

LGBTQ VENUES

In the 1980s, **Tracks** (3500 Walnut St., 303/863-7326, www.tracksdenver.com, 8pm-2am Wed.-Sat., women only 9pm-2am 1st Fri. of the month, $5-7 cover) was Denver's premier gay and lesbian nightclub, where a mixed crowd mingled for sweaty, fun-filled nights on the dance floor. But when the land was sold in 2001 to make way for new development along the old railroad tracks, the club was shuttered. In 2005, Tracks reopened in a new location and resumed its status as one of the city's best dance clubs for all. Check the calendar for event prices and age restrictions (most nights 21 and over).

LIVE MUSIC

The **Summit Music Hall** (1902 Blake St., 303/487-0111, www.thesummitmusichall.com, box office 11am-5pm Mon.-Fri. show

outside Tracks

nights) is a 12,500-square-foot space for punk, metal, hip-hop, and industrial music shows. When the former dance club isn't filled up with concertgoers for these big acts, the venue can shrink to host local bands still building an audience. Many of the shows are all-ages, but some are for 18 and over only. You never know who might be playing here—The Charlie Daniels Band? Check. Collective Soul? Check. Suicide Girls Blackheart Burlesque? Them, too. All shows are general admission.

Capitol Hill and City Park

BARS

Don's Club Tavern (723 E. 6th Ave., 303/831-0218, www.donsclubtavern.com, 3pm-2am Mon.-Fri., 1pm-2am Sat.-Sun.) has been around since 1947, and nobody wants it to change. It is routinely named the city's best dive bar for its simple qualities: a few pool tables, worn-out booths, threadbare carpet, and beer and cocktails without pretension.

The hundreds of tequilas to choose from at **Mezcal** (3230 E. Colfax Ave., 303/322-5219, www.mezcalcolorado.com, 11am-9pm Sun.-Mon. and Wed.-Thurs., 11am-10pm Tues. and Fri.-Sat.) make it the place to come for margaritas or shots. The place is done up in a Mexican movie madness theme, with posters of bodacious Latinas on the walls and Mexican church candles flickering. Across the street from the Bluebird Theater, Mezcal attracts concertgoers as well as neighborhood locals. Parking can be very limited on nearby side streets and along Colfax Avenue.

Think back to a time when drinking was not almost universally accepted and celebrated, but unlawful and unacceptable—a time of prohibition. At **Prohibition** (504 E. Colfax Ave., 303/832-4840, www.prohibitiondenver.com, 4pm-2am Wed.-Fri., 2pm-2am Sat., 2pm-10pm Sun.) in the Capitol Hill neighborhood, prohibition seems kind of stylish, with an ancient bar anchoring a refurbished space that includes banquettes and tables with framed, vintage newspaper headlines about the real time of Prohibition. Some cocktails of the era are even served in tin cups. The food is a mix of burgers, salads, pot pie, and bar snacks. In this still-rough patch of Colfax Avenue, Prohibition is aiming for a more upscale and trendy crowd.

This neighborhood dive has a rich history. Before it was **Vesper Lounge** (233 E. 7th Ave., 720/328-0314, www.vesperdenver.com, 4pm-2am Mon.-Fri., 2pm-2am Sat.-Sun.), it drew locals to its watering hole for years. Now this Frank Bonanno gem—sandwiched between two of the acclaimed chef's other successful restaurants, Bones and Mizuna—serves up surprisingly great Greek-style pub food alongside cocktails on tap. Sit at the bar, in a booth, or at one of the low tables and share a trio of hummus dips with your pals. If you're really hungry, order a Colorado shaved lamb gyro. And for the full experience, sip a house vesper cocktail, based on James Bond's signature martini.

This narrow bar with dark red lighting is a decent place to start an evening or grab a drink while waiting for a table at a nearby restaurant. The only drawback to **The Thin Man** (2015 E. 17th Ave., 303/320-7814, www.thinmantavern.com, 3pm-2am daily) is its success as the anti-LoDo place to be—it can be challenging to find a barstool or table in the packed bar, especially on the weekend, and it's also very loud. But the terrific bartenders and tasty appetizers keep regulars happily squeezed in.

LGBTQ VENUES

If you're looking for a family atmosphere, try **Blush & Blu** (1526 E. Colfax Ave., 303/484-8548, http://blushbludenver.com, 3pm-2am Tues.-Sat., 10am-11pm Sun.), which describes itself as one of the few lesbian bars left in the country, as a bar where "all humans are welcome," and also as a "relaxed LGBTQ bar." Take your pick! Drinking, dancing, food, it's all here.

Before there was *Brokeback Mountain*, there were many gay cowboys and cowgirls looking for a dance partner, even in the wilds of Denver. **Charlie's** (900 E. Colfax Ave., 303/839-8890, www.charliesdenver.com,

11am-2am daily) in Capitol Hill is the city's LGBTQ country-and-western dance club. There are free dance lessons, and for those not into the country scene, a separate dance floor with a DJ playing house and disco music creates a different vibe. Charlie's is the home of the Colorado Gay Rodeo Association.

Still keeping things on the down-low like the old days, **R & R Denver** (4958 E. Colfax Ave., 303/320-9337, 3pm-11pm Mon.-Thurs., 1pm-11pm Fri., 11am-11pm Sat., 11am-11pm Sun.) is one of the city's oldest gay bars. It has a simple neon sign out front and might be described as a dive bar, but the staff is friendly and the drinks are cheap. The bar draws a predominantly male crowd but is also welcoming to others.

Put on your dancing shoes for a fun night at **X Bar** (629 E. Colfax Ave., 303/832-2687, www.xbardenver.com, 3pm-2am Mon.-Sat., noon-2am Sun.) or make reservations for a delicious drag brunch on weekends. This is a 21-and-over club, so bring your ID too. X Bar is known for being inclusive of all communities, and also for its pink flamingo decor during Pride Month and the city's annual Pride parade and celebrations—you can't miss the giant inflatable pink flamingo atop the bar.

LIVE MUSIC

The **Bluebird Theater** (3317 E. Colfax Ave., 303/377-1666, www.bluebirdtheater.net) was originally built in 1913 and used as a movie house. After many incarnations and a bit of neglect, it was turned into one of Denver's most popular concert venues in 1994. All shows at the Bluebird are 16 and over, though anyone under 21 is restricted to the balcony during a concert while alcohol is served on another level. A wide range of acts play at the Bluebird—from popular rock stars to less-well-known groups still getting their start.

Live music at the **Lion's Lair** (2022 E. Colfax Ave., http://lionslairco.com, 303/320-9200, 3pm-2am Mon.-Fri., 2pm-2am Sat.-Sun.) can be extremely loud, with the band right in the center of the small room. The bands tend to be punk and hard rock, and sometimes alt-rock. Drinks are always reasonably priced, and seating at the bar is the best in the house. This hole-in-the-wall is a great little place to stop in for a cold beer, with no worries about style or who's who.

Highlands

BARS

At the place where the Highlands neighborhood begins on 15th Street is **Forest Room 5**

Bluebird Theater

Highlands

To I-70 and Denver International Airport
41st & Fox
Coors Field
LODO
Union Station
Union Station Light Rail Plaza
Commons Park
Platte River
South Platte
Ciancio Park
Chaffee Park
Highland Park
Viking Park
North Denver High School
SUNNYSIDE
HIGHLAND
HIGHLAND SQUARE
WEST HIGHLAND
ALCOTT
LIFE HOUSE, LOWER HIGHLANDS
ROOT DOWN
WILLIAMS & GRAHAM
LITTLE MAN ICE CREAM
ALE HOUSE
THE TRUFFLE TABLE
FOREST ROOM 5
LINGER
UNCLE
ZIO ROMOLO'S ALLEY BAR
HAMPTON INN & SUITES
DUO RESTAURANT
LUMBER BARON INN & GARDENS
WOODEN SPOON CAFE & BAKERY
RESIDENCE INN DENVER DOWNTOWN
PARK BURGER HIGHLANDS
SPUNTINO
PATZCUARO'S
CAFE BRAZIL
RAGIN' HOG BBQ
HAI BAR
NOVA COFFEE
THE PERFECT PETAL
LOCAL 46
SWING THAI
BOOKBAR
PARISI
BRAZEN DENVER
0.25 mi
0.25 km
© MOON.COM

(2532 15th St., 303/433-7001, 4pm-midnight Tues.-Thurs., 4pm-1am Fri.-Sat., 2pm-12:30am Sun.), where patio seats offer a view of the city lights. With flickering candles and large windows in the front room, Forest Room 5 is a hip little neighborhood bar that offers more than a few drinks and tapas. Forest Room 5's back room features dance music and is perfect for private parties.

Past the busy sushi chefs working near the entrance of Sushi Hai and past diners seated on black leather banquettes, stairs lead to the **Hai Bar** (3600 W. 32nd Ave., Suite D, 720/855-0888, www.sushihai.com, 4pm-9:30pm Sun.-Thurs., 4pm-10:30pm Fri.-Sat.), a cool underground room with exposed rock walls and mellow lighting. Named in reference to its home, the Highlands (Hai-lands, get it?), the Hai Bar is an inviting place for late-night sushi and specialty martinis and sake. Kick back and watch some TV or a pool game from the cushy lounge seating.

Tennyson Street is being revitalized, and that means new businesses are bringing spark to the neighborhood's commercial strip. **Local 46** (94586 Tennyson St., 720/524-3792, www.local46bar.com, 3pm-1am Tues.-Thurs., 3pm-2am Fri.-Sat., 1pm-midnight Sun.) is in a building that has been a beauty salon, a convenience store, and, more recently, the Music Bar (until rent shot up with the revitalization underway). Check the Entertainment page of Local 46's website to find out if it's karaoke night, game night, a battle of the bands, open mic, or some other live music playing.

People have not been this excited about a speakeasy since there were, well, speakeasies. Praised by *Esquire* and named the best cocktail bar in America at the Spirited Awards in 2015, **Williams & Graham** (3160 Tejon St., 303/997-8886, www.williamsandgraham.com, 5pm-1am daily) was quickly welcomed by Highlands locals for its unique faux-bookstore entrance, which cleverly hides the bar behind a velvet curtain. Staff members are dressed for the era in 1920s garb, but it's not costume-y. The extensive liquor selection and tasty small plates have led this bar to the top of many lists. Reservations are required.

Down what used to be a working alley is the art deco **Zio Romolo's Alley Bar** (2400 W. 32nd Ave., next to Tony P's Pizza, 303/477-0395, http://tonypspizza.com, 7pm-midnight Wed., 7pm-2am Thurs., 5pm-2am Fri.-Sat.). The bar includes an "exterior" wall with the original Coca-Cola sign painted on it. The 1950s-style neon signs and pressed-tin ceiling make Zio Romolo's a place to see as well as stop for a drink. Located in the evolving LoHi section of Highlands, Zio's is a friendly place for both locals and visitors. Stop in on Wednesday night 8pm-10pm for Geeks Who Drink Trivia or for live music on Friday and Saturday nights.

TOP EXPERIENCE

★ BREWPUBS

Denver is known for its beer, thanks to the sheer number of brewpubs in the Mile High City and its history as the birthplace of some innovative breweries. Having a beer is part of the experience when visiting Denver, with options ranging from the classic to the unusual (watermelon, anyone?). Plus, it just tastes darn good to have an ice-cold beer after a full day of sightseeing. Don't miss the **Denver Beer Trail** (www.denver.org/restaurants/denver-bars-clubs/denver-beer-trail), basically a map of the city's many brewpubs with 40 stops.

Downtown

No Denver neighborhood is complete without a craft brewery, and RiNo has **Our Mutual Friend Brewing Company** (2810 Larimer St., 720/722-2810, www.omfbeer.com, 4pm-10pm Mon.-Wed., 11am-10pm Thurs.-Sun.), also called OMF Brewery for short. Tasting flights are offered. In summer, step outside on the patio and sit on the bench while sipping your ale. There's no kitchen, but there is usually a food truck parked outside. You can bring your dog when out on the patio.

Also in RiNo, **Bierstadt Lagerhaus** (2875 Blake St., 720/570-7824, https://bierstadtlager.

The Beer Spa

Can you drink beer while soaking in it? Yes, yes you can. **The Beer Spa** (3004 N. Downing St., 720/810-1484, www.thebeerspa.com, 8:30am-10:30pm daily), opened in 2021, offers private Beer Therapy rooms where guests can take a bubbly beer bath infused with herbs, then hop out (see what I did there?) for a refreshing sip from the self-serve beer wall in the spa's taproom. Note that the beer you soak in is warm and the beer you drink is cold.

com, 2pm-10pm Mon.-Thurs., noon-midnight Fri.-Sat., noon-9pm Sun.) is all about being authentically German and is known for a Slow Pour Pils. This is not the place for a kooky beer flavor or seasonal pumpkin ale—no, this is a place where pride is in simplicity. They use a German kettle and a "strict Reinheitsgebot process" for their lager.

Golden Triangle, Lincoln Park, and SoBo

Pints Pub (221 W. 13th Ave., 303/534-7543, www.pintspub.com, 11am-10pm Mon.-Thurs., 11am-10pm Fri.-Sat., 11am-8pm Sun.) is a traditional British pub with cheery, old-fashioned red telephone booths and the flag of Britain flying (or emblazoned) on the sign. Just down the street from the Denver Art Museum and Byers-Evans House museum, Pints is a welcoming place to stop in for a pint and fish-and-chips for lunch or dinner. The pub is known for its cask-conditioned ales and single-malt whiskeys.

You know a neighborhood has reached a tipping point from up-and-coming to found when it gets its own brewery. Now the Santa Fe Arts District has the **Renegade Brewing Company** (925 W. 9th Ave., 720/401-4089, http://renegadebrewing.com, 3pm-9pm Tues.-Wed., 1pm-10pm Thurs., noon-11pm Fri.-Sat., 1pm-9pm Sun.) for craft beer among the arts and crafts of the area. Renegade partners with local food-truck vendors, so if you're hungry as well as thirsty, check the website to find out which truck is there on each day of the week.

With so much craft beer competition, a start-up has to stand out, and **Black Project Spontaneous & Wild Ales** (1290 S. Broadway, 303/441-4253, www.blackprojectbeer.com, 2pm-8pm Wed.-Thurs. and Sun., 2pm-9pm Fri.-Sat.) does so with kooky flavors. The decor is just as clever as the brews: tables made from reclaimed wood and a bar top made from repurposed airplane wings. They serve snacks, or you can order from Maria's Empanadas next door.

Niche breweries are a thing now, and **TRVE Brewing Company** (227 Broadway, Suite 101, 303/351-1021, www.trvebrewing.com, 3pm-11pm Mon.-Wed., noon-midnight Thurs.-Sat., noon-10pm Sun.) is a heavy-metal brewery, so get ready for some headbanging tunes to set the tone for your tasting. The entrance is somewhat hidden, and the dark decor may be off-putting to some, but the bartenders are friendly and the beer is good.

You have to mean to end up at **Strange Craft Beer** (1330 Zuni St., 720/985-2337, www.strangecraft.com, 3pm-9pm Mon.-Thurs., 2pm-9pm Fri.-Sat., noon-7pm Sun.), as it's not quite in a pedestrian-friendly zone near much else of interest. However, it's worth the stop to see what they mean by "strange." Cherry, grapefruit, and watermelon are some of the highlights in the brews here. In summer, you can play horseshoes in their patio area and enjoy the evening outside.

LoDo and Platte River Valley

The Celtic on Market (1400 Market St., 303/308-1795, www.thecelticotavern.com, 11am-2am Sun.-Thurs., 10:30am-2am

1: Renegade Brewing Company **2:** Denver Beer Company **3:** The Beer Spa taproom **4:** Wynkoop Brewing Company

offensively delicious
PANCAKES
MAPLE PORTER
RENEGADE
BREWING COMPANY
RENEGADE
BREWING COMPANY

1

DENVER BEER CO
DENVER BEER CO.

2

3

ON TAP?
Honesty Bar
Menu

4

ESTD
88

Fri.-Sat.) is a classic Irish pub where the bartenders pour Guinness (of course), Murphy's Irish Stout (which is brewed in Ireland), and a long list of other beers brewed nowhere near Ireland. The tavern also has an impressive selection of single-malt scotch and whiskeys. The scene is a mix of regulars who enjoy the leather easy chairs and volumes of books, and LoDo barhoppers. This is also an off-track betting location that is partnered with Fanduel. Check to see if they are open early for specific games.

The **Denver Beer Company** (1695 Platte St., 303/433-2739, http://denverbeerco.com, 11am-10pm Mon.-Thurs., 11am-11pm Fri.-Sat., 11am-9pm Sun.) has a bit of the essence of some guys coming up with new brews in their garage—just like the founders once did. The beers change seasonally, and this constant reinvention has led to some award-winning brews. As a result, this is the place to try something new, not necessarily tried and true. This Platte Street location is the original and there are others in the metro area.

At the **Great Divide Brewing Company** (2201 Arapahoe St., 303/296-9460, www.greatdivide.com, noon-8pm Sun.-Tues., noon-10pm Wed.-Sat.), beer is celebrated, not just consumed. Choose between seasonal, year-round, or barrel-aged brews. Plan to come for a beer-and-cheese pairing night or a Hop Disciples night (to discuss "all things beer related"), or take a tour of the place. Don't forget to shop! They have clothing and bottle openers adorned with the company logo and, of course, beer to go. There is another location in RiNo—look for the yeti! Or, visit them at Denver International Airport.

Looking for a bar atmosphere downtown? **Mile High Spirits** (2201 Lawrence St., 303/296-2226, www.drinkmilehighspirits.com, 3pm-11pm Thurs.-Fri., noon-11pm Sat.-Sun.)—a distillery and bar combined—is worth a shot. With a giant outdoor patio, distillery tours, and award-winning spirits to its name, Mile High Spirits offers something more than the typical bar experience. Try the Punching Mule—a Moscow mule in a can. Plan to spend the whole evening here with games and live music.

In the midst of the swanky nightclubs and lounges of LoDo is a comfy pub with the feel of a neighborhood bar. The barstools are the best seats in the house at the **Pour House on Market** (1410 Market St., 303/623-7687, www.pourhousedenver.com, 2pm-2am Mon.-Thurs., noon-2am Fri.-Sun.), formerly Pourhouse Pub, but also check out the heated roof deck, a great spot year-round. The music at the Pour House does not drown out conversations, and the bartenders are friendly and fun to talk to. While not a typical sports bar, Pour House does have TVs tuned to sports channels.

Coors didn't just put their name on the Colorado Rockies' home field; they also set up a brewery and restaurant at Coors Field. **Sandlot Brewery** (2161 Blake St., www.sandlotbrewery.com, 303/298-1587) features the Coors Brewing Company's Blue Moon label and other award-winning beers. The atmosphere at Sandlot is family-friendly, with a kids' menu, too. The brewery is only open on Colorado Rockies game days, and a ticket is required for access.

Denver's first brewpub remains one of the city's favorites. At the corner of 18th and Wynkoop Streets, the **Wynkoop Brewing Company** (1634 18th St., 303/297-2700, www.wynkoop.com, 11am-midnight Sun.-Thurs., 11am-2am Fri.-Sat.) was one of the pioneer businesses in transforming the LoDo neighborhood. One of the cofounders of the Wynkoop is John Hickenlooper, who went on to be the Denver mayor and Colorado governor and who was elected to the U.S. Senate in 2020. Reserve a free tour to watch the signature line of beers being made on-site. On the first floor of this historic mercantile building is the main bar and restaurant with a traditional pub menu and patio seating. The second floor has a bar, 22 pool tables, and a few dart lanes.

Capitol Hill and City Park

What is now **The DNVR Bar** (2239 E. Colfax

Ave., 303/997-6886, 4pm-midnight Mon.-Thurs., 4pm-2am Fri.-Sat., 2pm-midnight Sun.) has been many different sports bars over the years, but this newest one is truly unique: The owner is a former sports journalist who started DNVR (a digital sports network—a podcast, really) and who took his business to the real world with this bar. Not only can you watch games while having a drink, but also you can observe the making of the podcasts.

Highlands

Ale House (2501 16th St., 303/433-9734, http://alehousedenver.com, 11am-10pm daily, $11-24), one of the Breckenridge Brewery restaurants, serves more than 42 craft beers on tap that change daily. The Ale House (formerly Amato's Ale House) has developed a steady stream of regulars, with a menu of salads, burgers, and generous appetizers that can fill you up before the entrée arrives. Parking is a challenge, so take advantage of the restaurant's location next to the 16th Street pedestrian and bicycle bridge and walk, ride, or scooter over from downtown.

CANNABIS DISPENSARIES

Cannabis dispensaries are as common as . . . weeds (pun intended) around Denver and throughout Colorado. Included are a few of the better establishments for buying marijuana in Denver. Remember that most, if not all, dispensaries have a cash-only policy and therefore usually an ATM on-site. You need to be 21 to enter these facilities, with an ID to prove it.

Downtown

The only cannabis outlet right on the 16th Street Mall, **Euflora** (403 16th St., 303/534-6255, www.eufloracolorado.com, 10am-6:45pm daily) boasts a visitor-friendly atmosphere to match its prime location. The modern and spacious 6,000-square-foot basement-level shop features slick display tables decked out with aroma jars and tablet computers so customers can see, smell, and learn about each strain before making their purchase. No wonder the owner refers to the store as an "Apple Store of weed." While some visitors grumble about the quality of the herb available, consider Euflora akin to one of the many souvenir shops that line the pedestrian mall: While you might not find one-of-a-kind treasures among its product lines, it's a great way to get a taste of everything the state has to offer.

Just off the pedestrian-friendly strip that is the 16th Street Mall, you'll find **LoDo Wellness Center** (1617 Wazee St., 303/534-5020, http://lodowellnesscenter.com, 10am-7pm daily), offering "small batch craft growing" that is "trimmed by hand." Friendly staff make this a perfect stop for first-time buyers.

Golden Triangle, Lincoln Park, and SoBo

Just south of the Denver Art Museum, **Pure Marijuana Dispensary** (1133 Bannock St., 303/534-7873, www.puremmj.com, 8am-10pm daily) is known as a great all-around marijuana shop. It has an airy, friendly location, true "weed nerds" behind the counter, and the sort of product selection that gets online reviewers raving. Thanks to the fact that Pure boasts its own extracts operation, Colorado Cannabis Company, it's also a great place to sample marijuana concentrates, oil cartridges for vape pens, and topical lotions. They have five locations around town.

LoDo and Platte River Valley

Rocky Mountain High Dispensary LoDo (1538 Wazee St., 303/623-7427, https://rockymountainhigh.co, 10am-10pm Sun.-Wed., 10am-midnight Thurs.-Sat.) has several locations throughout Colorado, with this one being conveniently placed near bustling Union Station. Traveling here by train? You can stop in when you arrive or during a late night out at the station's restaurants and bars.

Capitol Hill and City Park

Opened in 2021, the **MJ Mansion** (1244

420-Friendly

Of course Denver would offer cannabis-friendly yoga classes. Every Friday evening and Sunday morning, **Twisted Sister Yoga** (3835 Elm St., Capitol Hill and City Park, 303/523-5891, www.twistedsister.yoga) offers sessions designed to heighten the effects of cannabis. Trust us, your "Oms" will have never sounded so profound. There are also retreats offered outside of Denver.

Sure, you've had a massage, but have you ever had a *marijuana* massage? That's the promise of **Primal Therapeutics** (719/429-7651, http://cannabismassagecolorado.com), which comes to your home or hotel room and offers deep-tissue rubs, sports massages, full-body scrubs, and other therapies featuring cannabis-infused lotions. While the psychoactive components of cannabis can't be absorbed through the skin, rubdowns like this are still quite the trip. Many massage treatments around town now offer a cannabis-infused option, but this claims to be the only one listed with the Better Business Bureau and an A+ rating.

Puff, Pass & Paint (2087 S. Grant St., www.puffpassandpaint.com, $50) is an inspired way to cash in on Denver's culture and cannabis. Bring your own cannabis to this marijuana-friendly art class, where you'll be artistically inspired by the two hours of formal instruction, not to mention all the joints your fellow classmates are passing around. If Van Gogh had options like this, he might have skipped his whole "Blue Period." Check out their cooking classes, too.

Grant St., 720/446-5433, https://mjmansion.com, 1pm-9pm Tues.-Sun., tours $35-60) has a connection to Amendment 64, which legalized recreational marijuana in Colorado—it's where the bill was written. You have to be 18 to go on a tour—there are several to choose from—and you have to be 21 to schedule a photo shoot on location here. The mansion is described as an "immersive art experience," so photos are encouraged. Note that you cannot smoke on the tours or during the photo shoots, but there is a giant green dispensary building out back where those 21 and older can buy cannabis in various forms: **Green Dragon Dispensary** (1250 Grant St., 720/505-5887, https://greendragon.com, 8:30am-11:45pm daily). They do not take cash.

Greater Denver

The "3D" in **Euflora 3D Cannabis Center** (4305 Brighton Blvd., 303/297-1657, www.eufloracolorado.com, 10am-8pm daily) originally stood for "Denver Discreet Dispensary," but these days the cannabis shop just off I-70 in north Denver has shed its modest roots, proudly celebrating the fact that on January 1, 2014, the operation was the first in the state to complete a legal recreational marijuana sale. The shop's historical significance isn't the only reason 3D is a good option for first-timers; the waiting area features a viewing corridor with windows into an adjoining growing facility, so shoppers can see exactly where their product is coming from. Consider it as immersive a cannabis experience as you can get without donning 3-D glasses.

With 11 locations in the Denver metro area and beyond, **The Green Solution** (2601 W. Alameda Ave., 303/990-9723, www.tgscolorado.com, 8am-11:45pm daily) is a prime example of the consolidation that's taking place throughout the state's cannabis industry, with large operations snapping up and rebranding mom-and-pops that struggled to navigate Colorado's complicated regulations and pricey licensing fees, not to mention a lack of banking options available to marijuana businesses. Still, once you walk into The Green Solution's main Denver location, on West Alameda south of downtown, and check out its clean, professional atmosphere, you'll be asking yourself if being the McDonald's of marijuana is really such a bad thing.

Proudly calling itself the largest marijuana dispensary in Denver, **Medicine Man** (4750 Nome St., 303/373-0752, www.medicinemandenver.com, 8am-midnight daily) is a family-run operation in an industrial part of north Denver that tends to draw attention; the store was the focus of international media coverage when Colorado first legalized retail marijuana, and for a while there was talk of a reality show based on its owners. Thankfully, there's substance behind the hype: Expertly trained budtenders are on hand to carefully guide you through the store's dizzying array of strains and marijuana-infused products, making sure you take home just the right medicine.

Cannabis Tours

Talk about a unique service: **420 Airport Pickup** (720/369-6292, www.420friendlyairportpickup.com, $79) is a private shuttle company that will pick you up at the airport, drive you to a retail marijuana shop, then drop you off at your hotel. Sure, the price tag is a bit more than your standard airport pickup, but what a way to start your trip.

Colorado Cannabis Tours (303/420-8687, www.coloradocannabistours.com, $39-750) offers a marijuana-friendly party bus that takes riders on an odyssey featuring stops at several Denver dispensaries, a live glass-blowing demonstration, a tour of a 40,000-square-foot indoor marijuana grow, and a lunch break at Cheba Hut Toasted Subs (yes, the restaurant's name is a cannabis reference). It's a trip you won't soon forget—or rather, depending on how many samples you try, maybe you will. There are various grow tours, industry insider tours, and more to choose from.

There's a reason **My 420 Tours** (855/694-2086, www.my420tours.com, $59-79) has garnered international media attention. The tourism company offers several tours each week of dispensaries, grow facilities, and glass galleries; customized cannabis tours for bachelor parties and other events; and even all-inclusive marijuana vacation packages. Not only that, but the company also hosts marijuana cooking classes every Sunday morning—and yes, you get to sample the treats.

THE ARTS

If you fly into Denver International Airport, you'll immediately catch a glimpse of the Denver arts scene—many permanent exhibits by local artists are on view in the main terminal. Once downtown, you will begin to notice even more public art on display in the most unexpected spaces.

Known for sunshine, outdoor activities, and a touch of the Old West, Denver has also drawn notice for its role as a regional arts powerhouse. Beyond the established Denver Art Museum and Museum of Contemporary Art Denver, Denver museums are diverse, boasting eclectic art collections such as the Kirkland Museum of Fine & Decorative Art and the one-of-a-kind Clyfford Still Museum. Every two years, the city hosts the Biennial of the Americas in the fall, with an international roster of the art world's who's who. There are museums here dedicated to single artists, whose work you may not see anywhere else in the world. A healthy art gallery scene means that artists can have actual careers here, patrons can get to know local artists, and visitors can spend their time seeing art that is only on display here—whether that's a cleverly curated traveling exhibit of Cartier jewels exclusive to the Denver Art Museum or student art at the Metropolitan State University's Center for Visual Art. This is no up-and-coming art scene—it has arrived and it's thriving.

Downtown

MEOW WOLF

How do you categorize Meow Wolf? Is it performance art? A living science fiction story? A gallery? What started as a local art installation in Santa Fe, New Mexico, has grown like Cirque du Soleil, with outposts in Las Vegas and now Denver. **Meow Wolf** (1338 1st St., 720/792-1200, https://meowwolf.com, 10am-10pm Sun.-Thurs., 10am-midnight Fri.-Sat., $45 adults, $40 seniors/military/children ages 5-13) had an entirely new building made for its "immersive psychedelic, mind-bending art" in the Mile High City, featuring the work of Colorado artists. In addition to the art experience the site offers a live music venue, café, and gift shop. Discounted admission is available to Colorado residents ($10 off per ticket).

THEATER

The **Denver Performing Arts Complex (DPAC)** (www.artscomplex.com) is the second-largest performing arts center in the United States, with 10 venues connected by an 80-foot-tall glass canopy. **Tours** (303/893-4100 or 303/446-4829) of the complex and various theater spaces are offered regularly. The DPAC is the building area, but locals also refer to this as the **Denver Center for the Performing Arts (DCPA)** (www.denvercenter.org), which is actually the name of the nonprofit theater organization. (Yes, it is a bit confusing!)

The **Ellie Caulkins Opera House** (14th St. and Curtis St., 303/357-2787, www.denvercenter.org, box office 10am-6pm Mon.-Fri.) has been called the jewel in the crown of the DPAC. The 1908 grand theater, formerly called the Auditorium Theatre, was completely renovated and can seat 2,268 for opera or other musical performances. The "Ellie," as it is called locally, is home to **Opera Colorado** (303/778-1500 or 303/468-2030, http://operacolorado.org). The Colorado Ballet also performs here. The theater is included on tours of the DPAC when performance schedules allow.

Within the DPAC is the 210-seat **Garner Galleria Theatre** (14th St. and Champa St., 303/893-4000, www.denvercenter.org, box office 10am-6pm Mon.-Fri.), which hosts cabaret-style shows. The Galleria was home to Denver's longest-running musical, *I Love You, You're Perfect, Now Change,* and continues to fill the house with hilarious parodies and zany spoofs. Shows typically run 4-6 months at the Galleria, and if you're just passing through or spontaneously going out on the town, it's the best place at the complex to get a last-minute ticket any time of year. There is a bar in the theater, so drinks are served during the show, too.

The **Helen Bonfils Theatre Complex** (1101 13th St., 303/893-4000 or 303/893-4100, www.denvercenter.org, box office 10am-6pm Mon.-Fri.) is part of the larger, city-owned DPAC at 13th and Arapahoe Streets. There are four separate theaters in the Bonfils complex—the **Wolf Theatre,** with 610 seats; the **Kilstrom Theatre,** a theater-in-the-round with over 380 seats; the **Singleton Theatre,** with 200 seats; and the **Jones Theatre,** with

Meow Wolf

just 196 seats. It's in one of these theaters that patrons are likely to see an original production by the Denver Center Theatre Company.

The **Temple Hoyne Buell Theatre** (1101 13th St., 303/893-4000, www.denvercenter.org, box office 10am-6pm Mon.-Fri.) at the DPAC has 2,830 seats and is typically the venue for big traveling Broadway shows and the crowds they draw. The theater is acoustically designed for musicals, but it also hosts dramatic plays and comedies. The city-owned and -run Buell is a former sports arena that was gutted and renovated to become the theater it is today. It is the second-highest-grossing theater in North America with fewer than 5,000 seats.

DANCE

Led by its namesake founder, artistic director, and choreographer, **Cleo Parker Robinson Dance** (119 Park Ave. W., 303/295-1759, www.cleoparkerdance.org) is known for its cross-cultural programs with African American traditions. The company is based in Five Points at the historic Shorter AME Church, but it performs at other locations in the city and around the world. This is also home to a dance school and various dance classes for children and adults. Like the performances, classes offered include a huge variety of styles, from ballet to tap to West African dance.

CONCERT VENUES

Located in the Denver Performing Arts Complex, **Boettcher Concert Hall** (1000 14th St., 303/623-7876, www.coloradosymphony.org) is the home of the **Colorado Symphony Orchestra.** When it was built in 1978, Boettcher was the first symphony-hall-in-the-round in the United States. About 80 percent of the hall's 2,634 seats are within 65 feet of the stage. There are no true vertical or horizontal surfaces in Boettcher, so that the sound is evenly dispersed.

Right off the 16th Street Mall in downtown is the historic **Paramount Theatre** (1621 Glenarm Place, 303/825-4904, www.paramountdenver.com), a relatively small 1,870-seat venue. Listed on the National Register of Historic Places, the Paramount was originally a movie theater in the 1930s and still has original art deco touches. The original Wurlitzer organ that was installed to accompany silent movies is still played; it and a sister organ at Radio City Music Hall are among the last remaining such organs in the country. The Paramount has a somewhat sporadic schedule and hosts a wide variety of entertainment, including comedy, ballet, and music.

The Mission Ballroom (4242 Wynkoop St., 720/577-6884, www.missionballroom.com) opened in the RiNo neighborhood in 2019. The 4,000-person venue has hosted Bob Dylan, The Lumineers, Steve Miller Band, the Black Pumas, Zed's Dead, The Flaming Lips, and many more.

CINEMA

UA Denver Pavilions 15 (500 16th St., Suite 10, 303/454-9086, www.denverpavilions.com), on the top level of the 16th Street Mall, is a multiplex theater that shows all the latest blockbuster movies several times each day. There are 15 screens in rooms of various sizes and seating capacities. The lobby itself is an entertainment zone, with video games and snacks galore at the immense concession stand. You can't beat the variety of showtimes here, including weekday matinees.

Golden Triangle, Lincoln Park, and SoBo

MUSEO DE LAS AMERICAS

In the heart of the Santa Fe Arts District is the **Museo de las Americas** (861 Santa Fe Dr., 303/571-4401, www.museo.org, noon-6pm Tues.-Fri., noon-5pm Sat., $8 adults, $5 seniors, free under age 13), the first museum in the Rocky Mountain states devoted to the art, history, and culture of Latin America. The mission of the Museo de las Americas is to share the diverse art and culture of Latin America, from ancient to contemporary. While its changing exhibits and artists makes it seem more like a gallery than a museum, it offers art education and community programs in conjunction with each exhibition. Artists whose work is on display give talks about their art on special nights during the exhibit. There are also hands-on workshops and customized art tours for children. Be sure to visit the unique gift shop before leaving.

GALLERIES

The Metropolitan State University's **Center for Visual Art** (965 Santa Fe Dr., 303/294-5207, www.msudenver.edu/cva, 11am-6pm Tues.-Fri., noon-5pm Sat.) is a reminder that downtown Denver is home to a large college campus. (Metro State is on the Auraria Campus, which can be seen from Larimer Square.) The off-campus facility fits right in with the high-end galleries along Santa Fe Drive, with its expansive exhibit space and crisp white walls. This nonprofit is not just a place for students; it also hosts unique contemporary art exhibits, such as an exhibition of prints and objects by Christo and Jeanne-Claude and a group show of female Vietnamese artists.

The gallery **910Arts** (910 Santa Fe Dr., 303/815-1779, www.910arts.com) is part of an artist colony along Santa Fe Drive where the green-built and colorfully painted building provides live-work space, artist studios, a coffeehouse, and a small courtyard garden. The gallery showcases visual as well as performing arts, often by 910Arts studio artists. Stop by during First or Third Friday exhibits each month. A mission of 910Arts is to foster discussion about art, so, in conjunction with exhibits, there are gallery talks scheduled each month.

In addition to the large interior exhibit space at the **Space Gallery** (400 Santa Fe Dr., 720/904-1088, https://spacegallery.org, 11am-5pm Wed.-Fri., 10am-3pm Sat.), there is also an outdoor sculpture garden and second-floor mezzanine gallery that overlooks the main floor. *Westword* art critic Michael Paglia described the building as so perfect that "the interior has just the right amount of drama to attract events—in fact, you could say that it's just about the best place in town to hold a pot-friendly same-sex wedding—or even a liquor-friendly regular one."

Given the loft-style space of **Walker Fine Art** (300 W. 11th Ave., 303/355-8955, www.walkerfineart.com, 11am-5pm Tues.-Sat., 6pm-8pm 1st Fri.), local artists such as Roland Bernier, Robert Delaney, and Munson Hunt are given ample room to display their two-dimensional and three-dimensional sculptures and large canvas works. The gallery is on the ground floor of a modern condominium building in the Golden Triangle, just four blocks from the Denver Art Museum. Even if you miss an opening or First Friday Art Walk, there is always an exhibit of new work in the rear of the gallery.

Among the handful of art galleries in the Golden Triangle, within walking distance of the Denver Art Museum, the **William Havu Gallery** (1040 Cherokee St., 303/893-2360, www.williamhavugallery.com, 10am-6pm Tues.-Fri., 11am-5pm Sat., 6pm-9pm 1st Fri.) stands out as one of the best for contemporary art. Havu represents a significant number of well-known Denver artists, many of whom choose to paint or photograph or sculpt the city and surrounding landscape. Artists include Tracy Felix, Homare Ikeda, and Stephen Dinsmore.

THEATER

The third-oldest Chicano theater in the country was started in the 1970s as a student group for those interested in the Chicano civil rights movement. Today, the **Su Teatro Cultural and Performing Arts Center** (721 Santa Fe Dr., 303/296-0219, www.suteatro.org) remains a community-based Chicano-Latino cultural arts center where visual and performing arts can be seen as well as learned in workshops.

The **Buntport Theater** (717 Lipan St., 720/946-1388, www.buntport.com) started many years ago when a group of college students moved to Denver and started their own theater company—just like that! They are hilarious and talented. Some of their shows are for all ages, and they have partnered with the Denver Art Museum to put on performances in their spaces. During the pandemic in 2020, they showed their creative side with drive-in shows in their parking lot!

DANCE

The **Colorado Ballet** (1075 Santa Fe Dr., 303/837-8888, www.coloradoballet.org) has the dependable annual performance of *The Nutcracker* during the holidays that reliably draws sold-out crowds. Otherwise, each season is a surprise, with a small handful of other dances running for limited engagements. The company performs at the Ellie Caulkins Opera House, as well as doing onetime performances at other venues. Some students at the Academy of Colorado Ballet become principal dancers who perform regularly with this company.

To say **Wonderbound** (3824 Dahlia St., 303/292-4700, www.wonderbound.com) is innovative doesn't quite capture the creativity behind this unique dance company. Wonderbound has put on shows that include a local mentalist magician and scents by a local essential oils lab. Housed in a former post office garage, this very urban space allows for some degree of interaction between dancers and audience members during performances. Whether it's a rock ballet or a customized take on a fairy tale, this is one dance you won't forget.

CINEMA

The theater itself is worth a visit at the unique art deco-style **Mayan Theatre** (110 Broadway, 303/744-6799, www.landmarktheatres.com), which has three screens—one large theater on the main level, and two smaller theaters upstairs. When the glorious building was saved from the wrecking ball in the 1980s, there wasn't much of a scene on this strip of Broadway. Now this neighborhood has its own trendy moniker, SoBo (as in South Broadway), and there are many wonderful restaurants, bars, and shops within walking distance of this neighborhood hot spot. Fans of foreign and independent cinema love the Mayan.

LoDo and Platte River Valley

GALLERIES

The emphasis at **David Cook Fine Art** (1637 Wazee St., 303/623-8181, www.davidcookfineart.com, 10am-6pm Tues.-Sun.) is on American regional art, including Native American pieces such as drums, jewelry, sculptures, fetishes, and other items. Certainly the West and Southwest are well represented here, but artifacts from tribes all over can be found, too. Gustave Baumann, Vance Kirkland, George Biddle, and dozens of other familiar and lesser-known artists' works are for sale at David Cook. The gallery is around the corner from the historic Oxford Hotel in LoDo.

The only problem with the exhibits at the **Robischon Gallery** (1740 Wazee St., 303/298-7788, www.robischongallery.com, 11am-6pm Tues.-Fri., noon-5pm Sat.) in LoDo is that they do not stay up long enough. Jim Robischon and his wife, Jennifer Doran, select such exquisite artists that it is tempting to visit more than once. The gallery hosts about seven shows per year in a variety of media—photography, painting, prints, and installations. Well-known artists whose work has been shown here include Richard Serra, Robert Motherwell, and Judy Pfaff, to name just a few. Other artists include Colorado's Jack Balas, Wes Hempel, Jae Ko, and Manuel Neri, as well as group shows of contemporary Chinese art.

COMEDY

Roseanne Barr is perhaps more famous than this club, where she got her start, but **Comedy Works** (1226 15th St., 303/595-3637, www.comedyworks.com, $15-40) is still the best-known comedy place in town, often with lines out the door. Comedy Works is where you are likely to see big-name comedians—the ones who have made it to TV, like Wanda Sykes and George Lopez. On Tuesday night, it's a chance to try out or catch up-and-coming jokesters on New Talent Night. The seating can be a bit cramped in this basement space, and there is a two-drink minimum. Parking can be found at the Larimer Square Parking Garage on Market Street or at metered spots on the street. Note that there are two locations for Comedy Works, and its online calendar lists both locations. Shows are 18 and over and 21 and over.

Sometimes the funniest comedy teams aren't found in a comedy club. Denver's own **The Grawlix** (https://adamcaytonholland.com/the-grawlix) performs at places like the **Bug Theatre** (3654 Navajo St., 303/477-9984, www.bugtheatre.org) when in town.

CONCERT VENUES

Home to two of Denver's major league sports teams—the Colorado Avalanche hockey team and the Denver Nuggets basketball team—the **Ball Arena** (1000 Chopper Circle, 303/405-1100, www.ballarena.com), formerly Pepsi Center, is also a concert venue for big-name acts like Madonna, Bruce Springsteen, Coldplay, and Céline Dion. When Red Rocks Amphitheatre is closed for the season, the Pepsi Center is the place for big concerts.

It's not quite in the Platte Valley, but the **Levitt Pavilion Denver** (1380 W. Florida Ave., 303/578-0488, www.levittdenver.org) is close enough to mention. This amphitheater is in Ruby Hill Park, 6 miles (9.6 km) south of downtown. What makes it unique is that it's a nonprofit and it offers 50 free concerts each summer. Bring a chair, a blanket, a picnic (or not—there might be food trucks), and kick back on the lawn while listening to music. There are also "ticketed" events (read: not free) from artists like Thievery Corporation, Melissa Etheridge, and many others.

CINEMA

The **Lowenstein Theatre Complex** (2510 E. Colfax Ave., 303/595-3456, www.denverfilm.org) has become a miniature cultural hub on East Colfax Avenue, with the Tattered Cover Book Store in the historic theater building and the Denver Film Society setting up in the addition next door. The Denver Film Center/Colfax is home to the annual Denver Film Festival, which has screenings at other locations around town, too. There are three main screens, plus a café seating area in the lobby.

Capitol Hill's art house movie theater has two screens devoted to independent and foreign-language films. The **Esquire** (590 Downing St., 303/352-1992, www.landmarktheatres.com), the Mayan, and the Chez Artiste theaters are all operated by the Landmark Theatres Company, which runs historic movie houses throughout the country. This is the kind of theater where you can get herbal tea with your popcorn. There is a small parking lot adjacent to the theater, but otherwise, on-street parking in this residential neighborhood can be difficult to find.

For thrilling, really-big-screen movie adventures, go to the **IMAX Theater at the Denver Museum of Nature & Science** (2001 Colorado Blvd., 303/322-7009, www.dmns.org, $6-7). Perhaps it's just the nature of IMAX films, or the fact that the theater is part of the museum, but the movies shown at this IMAX seem to always have a connection to the museum's theme. Viewers can visually explore coral reefs, beavers building dams, or humans scaling mountain peaks. Admission to the museum or planetarium is not included in IMAX ticket prices.

Capitol Hill and City Park

CONCERT VENUES

The **Fillmore Auditorium** (1510 Clarkson St., 303/837-1482, www.fillmoreauditorium.org) is a wonderfully refurbished former ice rink that hosts national touring acts such as Erykah Badu, Widespread Panic, George Clinton, and Rufus Wainwright. Located on the corner of Clarkson Street and Colfax Avenue in Capitol Hill, the Fillmore is walking distance from downtown. With a seating capacity of about 3,000, the Fillmore is the ideal space for audiences slightly smaller than those hosted at larger venues like Red Rocks Amphitheatre.

One of Denver's premier concert venues for small to midsize shows is the **Ogden**

Theatre (935 E. Colfax Ave., 303/830-2525, www.ogdentheatre.com). The Ogden is on the National Register of Historic Places, and ornate detail and interesting architectural touches can be seen throughout the building. With a capacity of about 1,200 people, the theater hosts smaller shows than the Fillmore down the street. The Smashing Pumpkins, The Hives, Jimmy Cliff, and the Goo Goo Dolls have all played at the Ogden.

Highlands

THEATER

The corner of 37th and Navajo Streets is a little arts colony of mostly visual arts galleries, as well as the **Bug Theatre** (3654 Navajo St., 303/477-9984, www.bugtheatre.org), where emerging filmmakers are showcased and original or little-seen plays are produced. The Bug started out in 1912 as a nickelodeon theater and went through many other uses before it fell into neglect; it was rescued by local artists who renovated it and found it easy to fill with popular productions like the annual *Santaland Diaries* or amateur night with *Freak Train*. It's always an affordable night out at the Bug.

FESTIVALS AND EVENTS

The arts are routinely celebrated throughout Denver. There are monthly First Friday events when galleries around the city open their doors for a casual evening of browsing and cocktails, the city boasts a full Arts Week in the fall, and the Cherry Creek Arts Festival is one of the city's biggest annual events.

Spring

The **Denver March Powwow** is Denver's largest powwow and one of the largest in the nation. Held for three days every March at the Coliseum (4600 Humboldt St., 303/934-8045, www.denvermarchpowwow.org, 10am-10pm daily), this gathering of Native Americans focuses on dance performances in elaborate costumes to the beat of live drums. To watch any of the dances—men's or women's, fancy or traditional—is to learn about a particular nation, region, or history. Vendors sell Native American jewelry, food, artwork, and religious objects. Different activities and performances take place daily.

It's not like events in Chicago or Boston, but Denver's **St. Patrick's Day Parade** (starts at 27th St. and Blake St., www.denverstpatricksdayparade.com) is huge and very popular. The parade winds its way through a portion of LoDo—where, conveniently, there are many brewpubs and bars—with a variety of things Irish or not, like bagpipers and beauty queens riding in convertibles and little dogs doing tricks. The weather can sometimes be downright wintry in March, but people still dye their hair green to match their outfits and come out for a day of celebration. The parade is held on the weekend closest to March 17.

One of the largest **Cinco de Mayo** celebrations (Civic Center Park, 100 W. 14th Ave. Pkwy., 303/534-8342, www.cincodemayodenver.com) in the United States is held in Denver every spring in a two-day event. It's a chance to eat Mexican food and enjoy Mexican music while learning more about the culture. Festivities include a parade, live music, dancing, and a green chili cook-off. The organized festival takes place at Civic Center Park, but the Highlands neighborhood, where there is a significant Latin American population, is also a hot spot for the weekend of or near May 5 every year. This often translates to streets clogged with cruisers waving Mexican and American flags.

What makes the Tesoro Foundation's **Indian Market and Ceremonial Dance** (The Fort Restaurant, 19192 Hwy. 8, Morrison, 303/839-1671, www.tesoroculturalcenter.org) worth the drive up to Morrison is the location. The market is held on the outdoor patios of The Fort Restaurant, where artisans display their wares in individual tents and booths. The powwow takes place in an open field behind the restaurant. The setting, combined with the sounds of Native American drumming and chanting, transports visitors to another time and place to truly absorb the unique experience that is a celebration of the West, Southwest, and Native American cultures. This is usually a two-day event in mid-May or early June, with performances scheduled at different times each day.

From its beginnings as a small neighborhood fair in the 1980s, the **Highlands Square Street Fair** (32nd Ave. and Lowell St., 303/777-6887, https://highlandsstreetfair.com, free) has exploded into one of the bigger annual festivals, with several blocks around Highlands Square closed off for a full day, typically in mid-June. The fair features live music on three stages, more than 100 vendors set up on the blacktop, and parking lots filled with kids' games and activities.

Summer

Just beyond the bars and nightclubs of LoDo is a relatively small high-rise building and shopping complex, Sakura Square. This quiet, serene city block stands out with its little bonsai garden and Japanese public art on display. While one can go to the Asian food market or restaurants at the square year-round, the best time to come is during the **Cherry Blossom Festival** (Sakura Square, bounded by Lawrence St., Larimer St., 19th St., and 20th St., www.cherryblossomdenver.org) in June, to celebrate Japanese American culture and hear traditional music, watch dancers, tour the temple, and sample authentic Japanese food.

Just before the heat of summer settles in, Larimer Square transforms its blacktop into a sort of piazza for one weekend in June. At the **Denver Chalk Art Festival** (Larimer Square, Larimer St. between 14th St. and 15th St., 303/685-8143, www.facebook.com/denverchalkart), amateur and professional artists use chalk to make beautiful and detailed murals on the city street. There's even a special spot for kids to practice their chalk expertise. By Sunday night, all of the art is washed away and Larimer Square returns to normal.

Sunday evening in the summer (June-early Aug.) is the perfect time to mellow out with some live jazz music and a few thousand people in **City Park** (3300 E. 17th Ave., 303/744-1004, www.cityparkjazz.org). There are 10 concerts in all, featuring local jazz musicians playing in the bandstand near Ferril Lake or closer to the Denver Museum of Nature & Science in the Meadows. The concerts are free; blankets and chairs are not provided, but some food is available for sale on-site. Parking is limited, so biking or walking to the weekly concerts is encouraged. Concerts are held rain or shine.

A lot has changed in the Five Points neighborhood over the years as the community has been gentrified. Much of its intriguing past—soul food restaurants, jazz clubs—is on display in the galleries of the Blair-Caldwell African American Research Library (2401 Welton St., 720/865-2401). The two-day **Juneteenth** festival (Welton St. between 24th St. and 28th St., 720/276-3693, www.juneteenthmusicfestival.com), which celebrates the end of slavery in the United States, includes a parade, live music, and food. The festival takes place in Five Points in June every year, but the dates change annually.

The Gay, Lesbian, Bisexual, and Transgender Community Center of Colorado hosts the annual **Pridefest** (Civic Center Park, 100 W. 14th Ave. Pkwy., http://denverpride.org) each June. The two-day event includes a parade (in a sign of how far this community has come, it is now called the Coors Light Pridefest Parade) that starts in Capitol Hill's Cheesman Park and is the highlight of the festival, with outrageous floats and costumes. Civic Center Park hosts a dance stage and booths with everything from food to crafts to health-awareness information. There is always a huge turnout for the festival, so plan accordingly when it comes to parking. This has become the third-largest pride festival in the country.

The **Cherry Creek Arts Festival** (Cherry

1: Denver March Powwow **2:** Cinco de Mayo **3:** Juneteenth **4:** Pridefest

SCFD
521
FD
3
12

1

2

THIS IS WHAT

3

REFRESHINGLY
PROUD
BEST
PLACES TO WORK

4

Creek North, bounded by 1st Ave., 3rd Ave., Clayton St., and Steele St., 303/355-2787, www.cherryarts.org) takes over the Cherry Creek North shopping district for three days, typically over Fourth of July weekend, in a huge outdoor celebration. The emphasis is on the artwork to be sure, but there is also live music and a whole street devoted to culinary creations. Wander the various booths until something catches your eye, then duck inside the tent, where you might find yourself having a one-on-one chat with one of the artists. The free festival includes local artists as well as those who have come from around the world to participate.

Boat racing meets cultural recognition and celebration at the annual **Dragon Boat Festival** (Sloan's Lake Park, Stuart St. and 23rd Ave., 303/722-6852, www.cdbf.org). This has become the largest Pan-Asian festival in the region, with crowds of 100,000 gathered to learn more about Asian American and Pacific Islander communities. The main draw at this two-day event in July is the boat racing across the lake—and the competition gets more fierce every year, as racers learn from the previous year and more types of races are offered. "Explore Asia" is one aspect of the festival, where local ethnic groups—Hmong, Filipino, Mongolian, and others—can demonstrate cultural traditions. Admission to the festival is free; it's best to consider the shuttle service options for getting there.

For four days, usually in July, the SoBo business district is taken over by the **Underground Music Showcase** (720/570-4500, www.undergroundmusicshowcase.com), with hundreds of bands performing in different venues. This is a chance to discover new favorite bands, check out live music venues, stroll along South Broadway, and just have a lot of fun. Diehards plan ahead when deciding which bands they want to see, while others just wing it and look forward to the surprises.

Labor Day weekend in Denver is a chance to sample various Colorado culinary specialties and gourmet favorites in a three-day eating extravaganza called **A Taste of Colorado** (Civic Center Park, 100 W. 14th Ave. Pkwy., 303/295-6330, www.atasteofcolorado.com). Chefs do demonstrations, and attendees can enjoy a full meal or just snack throughout the day at every little booth. Over the years, the food has become just one part of the festival; there's also live music, arts and crafts, and other special exhibits. At this time of year, be on the lookout for fresh melons and peaches, though any kind of barbecue always seems to be the favorite. Parking can be a problem, so be prepared to walk off whatever you eat on the way back to the car.

Fall

Learn about and experience the rugged life in this part of the world before it was Colorado at the **1830s Rendezvous and Spanish Colonial Art Market** (The Fort Restaurant, 19192 Hwy. 8, Morrison, 303/839-1671, www.tesoroculturalcenter.org), where mountain men and women posted in historically accurate camps and trading posts are ready to answer questions about "their" life. It's not so much "cowboys and Indians" as it is frontier folks and Native Americans, with Spanish heritage to boot. During the two-day annual event in late September, sit inside tepees, chat with fur trappers, and check out Spanish colonial artwork.

Presented by Visit Denver and the Colorado Brewers Guild, **Denver Beer Week** (www.denver.org) offers nine days of over 100 beer-related events around the Mile High City, usually in mid-September or mid-October. Think rare beer tappings, beer and food pairings, meet-the-brewer experiences, and more.

There's an event for architecture and history enthusiasts with **Doors Open Denver** (http://denverarchitecture.org). Over a span of weekends in late September through mid-October, people can sign up for guided tours (fee-based) of many of the city's historic and new buildings or take self-guided tours (free), usually of places not typically open to the public.

Thirsty? Check out the three-day **Great**

American Beer Festival (Colorado Convention Center, 700 14th St., 303/477-0816, www.greatamericanbeerfestival.com), where a ticket to just a single day of the event is a pass to try as many one-ounce samples of over 2,200 beers as possible in one evening. It might sound like a bad frat-party idea, but this is a truly serious beer competition held every October. It's basically the Beer Olympics, and the brewers and tasters mean business. Though the festival is only three days, there is a whole week of related activities around town. The festival, which takes place at the Colorado Convention Center, is now featured in the book *1,000 Places to See Before You Die.*

Just hope it doesn't snow when it comes times for the **Colfax Marathon** (starts and finishes at City Park, www.runcolfax.org). Held in mid-October, the event includes a half marathon and a marathon. This Boston Marathon qualifier race is a sightseer's delight, with a route through cultural and historical spots and views of the Rocky Mountains.

Denver Arts Week (www.denver.org/denver-arts-week) is a way for the entire city to celebrate its culture, supersized for one week each year in early November. The week usually starts off on a Friday, with free admission to all museums, which have extended hours and shuttle service between each facility. Art galleries host the First Friday Art Walk, and there are special artistic activities for kids at the Denver Zoo and Denver Botanic Gardens. The week usually also overlaps with the Denver International Film Festival, and it's not just about visual art, but also performance art and more.

Yes, the stars do come out to walk the red carpet at the annual **Denver International Film Festival** (303/595-3456, www.denverfilm.org), with famous directors and actors in attendance and giving special talks. The big gala nights are typically held at the Denver Performing Arts Complex, with the majority of films shown at the Sie FilmCenter in early November. Be sure to check the schedule for any local filmmakers who might be showcasing their latest work. It's wise to buy tickets in advance instead of at the door, as shows can sell out fast.

Every two years, the **Biennial of the Americas** (www.biennialoftheamericas.org) is hosted in Denver for a month-long celebration of the arts in mid-fall. There are exhibits sprinkled around the city in connection with the event to celebrate the diversity of the Americas, showcasing art, culture,

National Western Stock Show

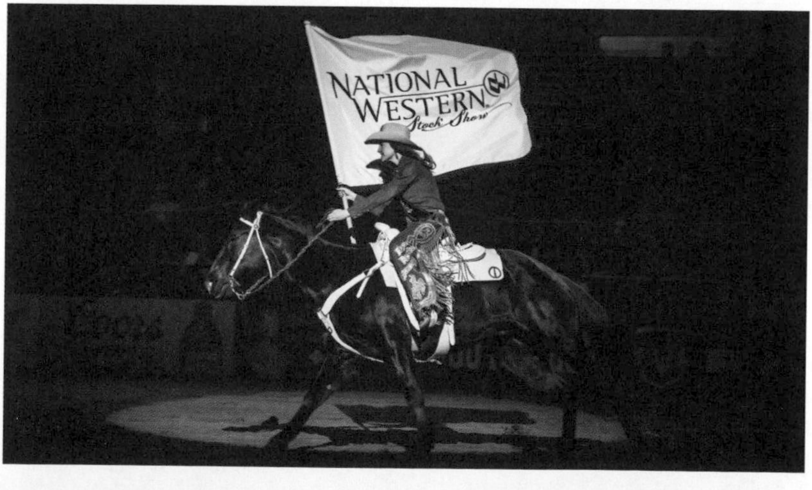

music, and food from South, North, and Central America and the Caribbean.

Winter

Beginning with one festive night every year, downtown streets and buildings are brightly lit with thousands of colorful holiday lights. Downtown Denver's **Grand Illumination** (Union Station, 16th St. Mall, and Larimer Square, 303/534-6161, www.downtowndenver.com) kicks off at Union Station in LoDo, where carolers sing and officials count down to the flip of the switch, when a large tree made of strings of lights and the building itself suddenly glow. The 16th Street Mall (where energy-efficient LED lights are used), Larimer Square, and the Denver City and County Building all turn on their yellow, red, green, and blue lights as huge crowds gather to watch and take part in the festivities. This usually takes place around Thanksgiving in late November.

Usually, the Denver Zoo is a quiet place at night as most of the animals slumber, but during the holiday **Zoo Lights** (2300 Steele St., 303/376-4800, www.denverzoo.org, 5:30pm-9pm daily, $13 adults, $9 children, $11 seniors, free under age 2) it becomes a festive gathering place for people and animals, with lights blazing through about half the zoo. It's more than just lights shaped like zoo animals and sparkling trees, though—there are ice sculptures made on-site, a Kwanzaa celebration, dances, and carolers. It's a busy time as families enjoy being outside in the crisp winter air and take the chance to see the zoo at a different time of day. The event begins in late November and ends just after the new year in January.

When the gardens are sleeping for the winter and most of the color is evergreen shrubs, brown dirt, or brilliant-white fresh snowfall, the annual holiday **Blossoms of Light** (1005 York St., 720/865-3585, www.botanicgardens.org) is a welcome burst of color. For about six weeks through December and part of January, Denver Botanic Gardens puts up over one million lights (with energy-efficient bulbs), draped across evergreen trees or shaped into luminescent flowers. On select nights there are carolers or other special events. The exact dates, times, and costs vary each year.

Denver becomes a cow town each January when the **National Western Stock Show** (National Western Complex, 4655 Humboldt St., 303/297-1166, www.nationalwestern.com, $4-25) is held over three weeks. One major highlight is the cattle drive right through the middle of downtown, in which longhorn steers are guided up 17th Street from Union Station to The Brown Palace. The event schedule at the complex is packed with 4-H competitions, horse shows, bull riding, and other rodeo shows, as well as an array of special performances like the popular Mexican Rodeo Extravaganza and Martin Luther King Jr. African American Heritage Rodeo. Construction is underway on a new National Western Center complex to host not only this annual event but more year-round celebrations of the state's "ag" communities.

Shopping

Shopping in Denver can be an all-day outing that includes a leisurely lunch and plenty of easy strolling. Whether you are looking for antiques, Western attire, a sexy dress, or the perfect shoes, there are a number of stores to check out. Heading out to do a little shopping is one of the best ways to experience Denver like a local.

Denver certainly has large malls with all the familiar stores, such as Cherry Creek Mall and the Denver Pavilions on the 16th Street Mall, but sprinkled around Denver's best neighborhoods are some even more appealing shopping districts, including posh Cherry Creek North, hip Highlands Square, and funky South Broadway. Each of these neighborhoods has a mixture of cafés and shops so people can wander from store to store browsing the goods, then grab a bite to eat and, once fortified, go back to spending.

In each neighborhood, the shops tend to represent the character of the area. On South Broadway near Ellsworth, it's about being original at FM, where up-and-coming designers sell their latest creations, or finding a mix of vintage and new duds at Decade. In Cherry Creek North, you can find beautiful clothes at Max, Garbarini, or Lawrence Covell that allow you to dress to impress. The best cowboy boots, shirts, and other Western-style clothing and accessories are mostly found in LoDo at Rockmount Ranch Wear. The Highlands area has a mix of shops, with stunning flowers at The Perfect Petal; toys, gear, and clothes for the wee ones at Real Baby; and accessories to accent an outfit in any season at Luna and Jasper. Even the museums in Golden Triangle, Capitol Hill, and along Santa Fe Drive offer great shopping opportunities in their gift shops.

DOWNTOWN

Right in the heart of downtown, **Denver Pavilions** (500 16th St., 303/260-6000, www.denverpavilions.com, 10am-9pm Mon.-Sat., 11am-6pm Sun.) is an open-air mall with all of the usual stores and restaurants, including a Banana Republic, The Gap, and Hard Rock Café. On the third level is a United Artists movie theater and a Lucky Strike Lanes.

Gift and Home

When I first heard about this shop, I could not figure out where it was because I did not believe it was in a mall. A store all about the local in a place all about the franchise? The **I Heart Denver Store** (500 16th St., 303/720-9069, www.iheartdenverstore.com, 10am-7pm Mon.-Sat., 11am-6pm Sun.) is almost like an art gallery that celebrates the city, with locally made and designed crafts and clothes. The goal is to support creative entrepreneurs through sales at the store. Even for window shoppers and browsers, it's an impressive selection of what's made in Denver.

Outdoor Gear and Apparel

I wonder how many times I walked right by **M. W. Reynolds** (1616 Stout St., 303/761-0021, http://mwreynolds.com, 10am-6pm Mon.-Fri., 10am-5pm Sat.) before I finally noticed it. Yet it's right in the middle of downtown, off the beaten path of the 16th Street Mall. This is what I might call a classic sporting goods store with gear for fly fishing, shooting, and motorcycle riding as well as apparel so you can look darn good doing any of it.

GOLDEN TRIANGLE, LINCOLN PARK, AND SOBO

Hipster alert! **SoBo** (along S. Broadway from Ellsworth Ave. to Bayaud Ave.) is short for South Broadway, part of what was once Denver's own Miracle Mile of commerce. While the neighborhood has had some ups and downs in its history, things are on the upswing with a new energy and thriving businesses of all kinds that attract a mostly young and hip crowd.

Arts and Crafts

Sewing one's own clothes is fashionable again, and it doesn't get any more hip than **Fancy Tiger Crafts** (59 Broadway, 303/733-3855, www.fancytiger.com, 10am-7pm Mon.-Sat., 10am-9pm Tues., 11am-6pm Sun.), where adults and children can take classes to learn about knitting, sewing, felting, fashion design, and a lot more creative stuff. The raw materials for sale include organic cotton fabrics by the yard, and organic yarn made from hemp, llama, and cotton.

Clothing and Accessories

One of Denver's oldest vintage apparel stores, **Boss Unlimited** (10 S. Broadway, 303/871-0373, www.bossvintage.com, 11am-6pm Mon.-Sat., noon-5pm Sun.) could dress the entire family with clothes for Mom, Dad, and the kids. Boss is pretty much a traditional vintage store, with racks stuffed with clothes from every decade, some more costumey than others. There are also shoes, handbags, and the store's own line, Daredevil, with a rockabilly theme on screen-printed T-shirts and jackets.

Wander past the retro home decor items, tempting toiletries, adorable baby gifts, and the fat store cat at **Decade** (56 S. Broadway, 303/733-2288, www.facebook.com/decadedenver, 11am-6pm Mon.-Sat., 11am-5pm Sun.) to find a women's boutique. This is a mix of new and used clothing with lacy to modern styles in jeans, T-shirts, skirts, and lingerie. There is a small section for men, but Decade is really all about femininity. Locally made jewelry is for sale at the front counter. Decade is the perfect place to find a little something girly to wear out for a casual evening—and not at an astronomical price.

From the minds of Fancy Tiger Crafts there is **FM** (55 N. Broadway, 303/282-6590, www.youarefm.com, noon-7pm Mon.-Sat., noon-6pm Sun.), which used to just be called Fancy Tiger Clothing. The idea is a groovy place—sometimes there is a DJ playing tunes—where you can shop for clothes for men and women that are made by "small" designers (some local). They offer on-site hemming, too.

It's a treasure hunter's paradise at **Goldmine Vintage** (227 N. Broadway, 303/447-0065, 11am-7pm daily) if you like searching for retro garb. It's also a place to sell your oldies but goodies. Think jeans, T-shirts, and the occasional crazy sweater or coat, all at reasonable prices.

Opened in 2021, the resale shop **Scout Dry Goods & Trade** (51 N. Broadway, 303/733-2968, www.ilovescout.com, 11am-7pm daily) not only accepts (for cash or store credit) your in-good-condition seasonal men's and women's clothing, they also work with local makers so they can sell original designer creations, too.

Maybe the tiniest of the vintage stores along Broadway is **La Lovely Vintage** (42 N. Broadway, 720/749-4452, www.lalovelyvintage.com, 11am-6pm Mon.-Sat., noon-6pm Sun.), with an emphasis on denim. It's just so inviting here with a collection of denim pants, jackets, overalls, and T-shirts and sweatshirts.

The sign out front simply reads **SEWN** (18 S. Broadway, 303/832-1493, www.sewndenver.com, 11am-6pm Mon.-Sat., noon-5pm Sun.) in large, colorful letters, and inside you'll find handmade items from local designers and artisans. Check out Jil Cappuccio's dresses and pajamas, which are all roomy and colorful pieces, with a few little ones for children; she makes men's shirts, too. The shop also carries very lovely knitwear by Pearl and other locally made items, from soap to pillows.

If you're looking for vintage clothing or albums from anytime between the 1940s and 1990s, stop in at **The Ten Penny Store** (250 N. Broadway, 720-432-4274, www.tenpennystore.com, 11am-6pm daily) to see if they have that cool '90s band T-shirt, a groovy poster, or some blast from the past for your next '50s-themed party.

Gift and Home

It's always so tempting to flop into one of the overstuffed sofas or chairs at **Djuna** (1824 S. Broadway, 303/355-3522, www.djuna.com, 10am-5pm Tues.-Sat.) and just hang out, taking in the richly hued variety of rugs, mirrors, pillows, throws, and other furnishings artfully crammed together in the store. Many of the beds and other furniture are custom-made for Djuna. On the one hand, Djuna is a store for people with large homes to decorate right down to the last detail; on the other hand, there are some wonderful linens and fabrics that appeal to smaller budgets and spaces.

Part art gallery, part jewelry and curio shop, the **Native American Trading Company** (213 W. 13th Ave., 303/534-0771, www.nativeamericantradingco.com, by appointment only) is a place to find unique Southwestern and Native American wares. Only one block from the Denver Art Museum and across the street from the Byers-Evans House museum, the store is in a 1906 mission-style townhome. It's easy to walk into the Trading Company for a quick visit and end up staying an hour or more looking at artwork and listening to the owners' stories of their relationships with the various artists and artisans whom they represent.

Pop into **Sacred Thistle** (1110 Acoma St., 720/598-6957, https://sacredthistle.com, 11am-6pm Mon.-Sat., noon-5pm Sun.) for some unexpected items that suddenly become must-haves for you or a friend: beautiful blankets, wooden bowls, candles, books, and plants.

Toys

As much for adults as kids, the **Wizard's Chest** (451 Broadway, 303/321-4304, www.wizardschest.com, 11am-7pm Mon.-Fri., 10am-7pm Sat.-Sun.) is a year-round toy store, but it is *the* place to go for Halloween costumes every fall. With its faux castle storefront, the Wizard's Chest practically screams "playful" to passersby. The name is also a clue to the many magic tricks available here—cards, prankster items, kits, and DVDs. Ask any of the helpful sales staff to point you in the direction of the toy you seek, whether it be stuffed animals or dolls, novelty items, action figures, science experiments, or those wacky costumes.

LODO AND PLATTE RIVER VALLEY

When it comes to shopping in **LoDo** (bounded by Wynkoop St. to the west, 14th Ave. to the south, Lawrence St. to the east, and 20th St. to the north), **Larimer Square** is the indisputable center of the universe, with restaurants and shops tightly packed into this historic block. These are mostly locally owned boutiques with distinctly Denver style.

Clothing and Accessories

Looking for something new, but don't want to spend more than $50? Go straight to **Common Era** (1543 Platte St., 303/433-4633, www.mycommonera.com, 11am-6pm Mon.-Sat., 11am-5pm Sun.), where there are racks of colorful simple-but-sexy dresses, tops, and tees to choose from, at very reasonable prices. The styles are so versatile that they can appeal to both a teenage girl and her mother. Don't be scared off if you happen by in October, when the store gets a bit over-the-top for Halloween, with crazy platform shoes, wigs, and other themed attire—by Thanksgiving they are back to normal.

Mostly full of teen to 30-something males, **Emage** (1620 Platte St., 720/855-8297, www.emagenetwork.com, 11am-8pm Mon.-Sat., 11am-6pm Sun.) is just a couple of blocks from the Denver Skatepark, with the purpose of outfitting anyone who likes to skateboard and snowboard. It also sells skateboards, snowboards, and all the parts and accessories needed for either sport. Emage has a good selection of shoes for the complete look, with Adidas, Nike, and Vans.

There was a time when a man got fitted for a shirt and there was no small, medium, large in a rainbow of colors. Now that concept has returned, with made-in-the-USA shirts for men that are custom fitted by appointment only. The secret is out about **Ratio** (2559 16th St., 720/515-4348, www.ratioclothing.com, 10am-5pm Tues.-Sat.)—they've appeared on CNN and in *Men's Journal*.

Rockmount Ranch Wear (91626 Wazee St., 303/629-7777, www.rockmount.com, 8am-5pm Mon.-Fri., 10am-6pm Sat., 11am-4pm Sun.) is famous for a lot of things: the founder and owner, affectionately called "Papa Jack," who worked daily at the store until he died in 2008 at 107 years old; the original snap-front cowboy shirts; the celebrities and rock stars who have bought many of Rockmount's ornate Western shirts; and the legacy of being in business in the same historic building since 1946. This is part office, part store, part museum. Don't think you can pull off a Western shirt? No problem, as one of Denver's best souvenirs is a Rockmount T-shirt featuring a bucking bronco rider in men's, women's, and children's sizes and styles.

1

2

Gift and Home

The **Old Map Gallery** (1801 Wynkoop St., 303/296-7725, www.oldmapgallery.com, 10am-5pm Mon.-Sat.) caters to serious map collectors and experts, and for the rest of us, it's a fascinating peek into the world of cartography and a place to find a unique piece of artwork or a gift for someone obsessed with a specific place. Along with antique maps featuring countries, oceans, celestial bodies, and food and wine, there are very affordable current maps for sale.

Outdoor Gear and Apparel

REI Denver (1416 Platte St., 303/756-3100, www.rei.com, 9am-9pm Mon.-Sat., 9am-7pm Sun.) is the flagship store, and it definitely stands out from other locations. REI occupies a historic tramway building right along the South Platte River. The enormous space has a 37-foot climbing pinnacle and there are multiple levels selling clothing, gear, shoes, and outdoor equipment. There is also a small bookstore and a huge map selection. Up on the children's level, parents can let kids romp in the indoor playground near the sale merchandise. Equipment rental is also available.

Outdoor-gear bargain hunters head to the **Wilderness Exchange Unlimited** (2401 15th St., 303/964-0708, www.wildernessx.com, 11am-8pm Mon.-Fri., 10am-7pm Sat., 10am-6pm Sun.), about one block from the REI flagship store, near Confluence Park. The store has a small but regularly refreshed inventory of men's and women's clothing, tents, sleeping bags, and shoes, which are all appropriate to the current season. The Wilderness Exchange buys and trades used outdoor gear at this location, and merchandise includes those used items as well as manufacturer's overstock, discontinued items, and slightly damaged items.

Specialty Foods

It's a genius idea: packaging spices in an appealing and original way. The spices and blends at **Savory Spice** (1537 Platte St., 720/283-2232, www.savoryspiceshop.com, 10am-6pm Mon.-Fri., 10am-5pm Sat., 11am-4pm Sun.) are cleverly named after local geographical highlights, such as rivers, canyons, 14,000-foot peaks, and even neighborhoods. Of course, there are also familiar herbs and spices, such as cinnamon, ginger, paprika, and so much more, but within each of these, there are several choices: origin, organic or not, whole or ground. It's hard to resist this shop when the spice scents waft out the door for half a block or so. Now a successful franchise business in at least seven different states, it all started here in this cute little shop.

CAPITOL HILL AND CITY PARK

Arts and Crafts

Sure, you'll end up paying three times what you would if you just bought a mug or a plate already painted, but it's so fun to personalize one! **Ceramics in the City** (5214 Colfax Ave., 303/200-0461, www.ceramicsinthecity.com, 11am-7pm Mon.-Fri., 10am-7pm Sat., 11am-5pm Sun.) is so popular that sometimes you have to make reservations to get a table. (No, there is no alcohol or food served here.) Adults and children come to make keepsakes and special gifts. The staff is friendly and patient with people of all ages and ability levels. Plan ahead—it can take several days before your piece gets fired and is available for pickup.

Books and Music

Capitol Hill Books (300 E. Colfax Ave., 303/837-0700, www.capitolhillbooks.com, 10am-5pm Mon.-Thurs., 10am-6pm Fri.-Sun.) is a simple, old-fashioned bookstore with that musty smell and overflowing bookshelves stuffed with a wide variety of books. Though there are few rare and antique books for sale, this is a general bookstore with various paperbacks and hardbacks available. Located on the block just behind the Colorado State Capitol, Capitol Hill Books is within easy walking distance from anywhere in downtown or Capitol

1: shopping area on 16th Street Mall **2:** Rockmount Ranch Wear

Hill. This is a mellow place to spend a few hours just browsing the stacks.

Denver's beloved independent bookstore has three large locations: LoDo, Colfax Avenue, and the suburb of Littleton. The layout of this **Tattered Cover Book Store** (2526 E. Colfax Ave., 303/322-7727, www.tatteredcover.com, 9am-9pm Mon.-Sat., 10am-6pm Sun.), within the historic Lowenstein Theater on Colfax Avenue, is unique—with bookshelves where theater seats used to be—and takes some getting used to. Each store has thousands of books and periodicals, as well as a coffee shop and event space for book readings and signings. Check the Tattered Cover website or get on the mailing list to stay up-to-date on visiting authors, book signings, and more. The McGregor Square location can be found at 1991 Wazee Street (303/436-1070), and the Littleton store is in the Aspen Grove Center (7301 S. Santa Fe Dr., 303/470-7050).

Hands down, **Twist & Shout** (2508 E. Colfax Ave., 303/722-1943, www.twistandshout.com, 10am-7pm Mon.-Sat., 10am-6pm Sun.) is Denver's favorite independent music store. The store has joined the Tattered Cover Book Store at the Lowenstein Theater Complex on Colfax Avenue, and it's better than ever. Shoppers can hang out and comfortably listen to tunes before purchasing, and the sales staff is always helpful and knowledgeable, or can find someone who knows even more. There are frequently free live music performances at the store, so check the website often to see if your favorite band is playing.

For anyone who still has a record player and not enough music to play on it, **Wax Trax** (638 E. 13th Ave., 303/831-7246, www.waxtraxrecords.com, 11am-8pm Mon.-Fri., 10am-8pm Sat.-Sun.) is the place to go for rare 45s and LPs. That's right, records—as in vinyl. The stock is not completely vintage; the shop carries CDs and DVDs to round out more recent decades of music. This is the original Wax Trax—started by the owners of the more famous Chicago store and then bought and basically preserved by new owners way back in the 1970s.

Clothing and Accessories

Talulah Jones (1122 E. 17th Ave., 303/832-1230, www.talulahjones.com, 10am-6pm Mon.-Fri., 10am-5pm Sat., 11am-4pm Sun.) is a little shop of girly and kids' treasures. The well-stocked inventory of stationery, soaps, jewelry, handbags, scarves, toys, books, and children's clothing takes some patient digging through to find that just-right item. The largest area of the two-room store is devoted to kids, with a few things set out for playing with as moms burrow through a basket of musical instruments or wiggle toys.

HIGHLANDS

The heart of the greater Highlands neighborhood is **Highlands Square** (from Julian St. to Meade St. along 32nd Ave.). Just as with Larimer Square in LoDo, there is no actual square, but rather a cluster of businesses spread over a few blocks. There's also a bustling scene of shops, restaurants, and a park with a playground on **Tennyson Street** (streets are alphabetical so that's seven blocks west of Meade St.) to explore. Either one of these spots is where I usually find myself when gift shopping for friends and family. These areas are walking distance from one another.

Books

It's hard to decide if this should be under bars or bookstores—because it's both. You can just stop by for a small plate and a glass of wine, or run in for a gift, or plan to have your book club meet here and do both. You're doing good on so many levels when you patronize **BookBar** (4280 Tennyson St., 303/284-0194, www.bookbardenver.com, 10am-10pm Mon.-Sat., 10am-8pm Sun.): supporting literacy, supporting an independent business, supporting local food and beverage makers. Be sure to check out their backyard and patio.

Children's Clothing

Founded and owned by parents in the

Highlands neighborhood, **Real Baby** (4315 Tennyson St., 303/477-2229, www.realbabyinc.com, 10am-5pm Thurs.-Sat., 10am-4pm Sun.-Wed.) is the real deal when looking for everything from hip and casual maternity clothes to baby clothes and toddler furniture, toys, and books. A Thomas the Tank Engine table set up in the book and toy area makes it easy for parents to keep shopping while junior is busy playing nearby. Don't rush through here; there are books for grown ups about babies and kids, CDs for the whole family to enjoy, and body-care products for moms and babes, all tucked into cubby shelves lining the wall.

Clothing and Accessories

The most casual of the local men's boutiques, **Berkeley Supply** (4317 Tennyson St., http://berkeleysupply.com, 303/433-6331, 11am-6pm Tues.-Sat., noon-5pm Sun.) is geared toward the man who likes a sturdy pair of jeans or casual pants and a hip T-shirt; the emphasis is on American-made products. Brands include Filson, Stitch, Red Wing, and Rogue Territory.

Here is cute and affordable women's clothing: The concept at this boutique is to keep prices under $50 as much as possible. The emphasis at **Inspyre Boutique** (4170 Tennyson St., 303/718-2645, www.inspyreboutique.com, 10am-8pm Mon.-Sat., 11am-6pm Sun.) is on women, and the window displays of sexy and colorful dresses make it appear as if the boutique is just for the fairer sex, but men are welcome and might find jeans or a hip T-shirt. These are not household brand names, but when you find that perfect summer dress or sexy top, who cares? It's always better to wear something more original.

Looking for that perfect colorful scarf, a stylish summer hat (or winter one), or just some unique jewelry? **Luna and Jasper** (3640 W. 32nd Ave., 303/477-3378, www.kismetandtrueboutiques.com, 10am-5pm Tues.-Sat., 11am-5pm Sun.-Mon.) is my personal fave for these items, but they also have sweet little dresses, tops, handbags, belts, and shoes. In the heart of Highlands Square, Luna and Jasper is a must-do part of the shopping experience in the neighborhood. The store has other locations in the metro area; check the website for details.

I'm of the belief that you can't have too many boutiques for sexy jeans, feminine tops, and shiny accessories. **Ruby Jane** (3616 32nd Ave., 720/855-7067, http://rubyjane.com, 10am-7pm Mon.-Sat., 11am-6pm Sun.) seems to agree with me because this is just one of their five Colorado locations. They've got a great mix of skinny jeans, floral summer dresses, casual shoes, and outerwear for every season.

Looking for that shoe that you can't find anywhere else in Denver? **Strut** (3611 W. 32nd Ave., 303/477-3361, www.strutdenver.com, 10am-7pm Mon.-Sat., 10am-5pm Sun.) probably has it. Miss Sixty, Butter, Ted Baker, and a dozen more brands can be found at Strut, with styles ranging from elegant sandals and flats to knockout heels. Strut is a handbag and accessories store to boot—find Rebecca Norman hoops, Foxy Originals matching necklaces and earrings, and other jeweled surprises. The knowledgeable sales staff can help find a great-looking but still comfortable pair of women's shoes.

Gift and Home

Considered one of Denver's top floral shops, **The Perfect Petal** (3600 W. 32nd Ave., 303/480-0966, www.theperfectpetal.com, 9am-7pm Mon.-Sat., 10am-5pm Sun.) is also a charming boutique in the heart of Highlands Square. It's really one of those very girly shops with cute stationery, antique jewelry, cookbooks, candles, and other sweet-smelling and looking goods. The flowers are up some steps in the rear of the store and can be bought by the stem or made into creative and unusual arrangements.

Health and Beauty

There is a growing school of thought that we should all be just as careful with the products we put *on* our bodies as we are with what we put *in* our bodies. **Vert Beauty** (3442 W. 32nd Ave., 303/623-8378, www.vertbeauty.

com, 11am-6pm Mon.-Sat., 11am-6pm Sun.) celebrates "green beauty practices" with makeup and skin-care products made from pure and organic ingredients using environmentally sustainable means. Feel good about looking good.

Specialty Foods

The selection at **St. Kilian's Cheese Shop** (3211 Lowell Blvd., 303/477-0374, www.stkilianscheeseshop.com, noon-6pm Mon.-Sat., noon-5pm Sun.) keeps growing, though the shop has remained the same size. Choosing cheese can be as daunting as finding the right wine—it requires a bit of knowledge and expertise. It's the perfect place to pick up a picnic lunch with salamis and cheese, along with bread from **The Denver Bread Company** (3200 Irving St., 303/455-7194, http://thedenverbreadcompany.com, 10am-5pm daily) down the street. Pick up a bottle of wine next door at **Mondo Vino** (3601 W. 32nd Ave., 303/458-3858, www.mondovinodenver.com, 10:30am-9pm Mon.-Sat., noon-8pm Sun.), and it's a meal.

WASHINGTON PARK AND CHERRY CREEK

Cherry Creek is also a shopping district, not just an actual creek winding through Denver. You'll find a large and appealing mall adjacent to Cherry Creek North, a neighborhood of boutiques, cafés, and galleries. Many of these boutiques cater to an elite clientele, but don't let it deter you—there are always bargains to be found.

The greater Washington Park neighborhood offers mini shopping districts with South Gaylord Street, walking distance from the park, and South Pearl Street, south of the park by car or a short walk from a light-rail stop.

Books and Music

For those in search of first editions and rare books, the **Hermitage Bookshop** (290 Fillmore St., 303/388-6811, www.hermitagebooks.com, 10am-5:30pm Mon.-Sat.) is the best place to go in search of everything from military history to children's books to Western Americana. Just below the sidewalk-level storefronts of Cherry Creek North, the Hermitage is designed for comfortable study of its many texts, with sofas, leather chairs, and coffee tables set up between the bookshelves. It's best to settle in and leisurely browse the inventory of 35,000 titles.

Clothing and Accessories

In a first for Goodwill Industries of Denver, **Déjà Blue** (303 University Blvd., 303/996-5668, www.goodwilldenver.org/dejablue, 10am-6pm daily) is a boutique that features only gently used high-end fashions and accessories. Your wallet and your conscience will like shopping here. The store is not a donation site, but the proceeds from sales go to Goodwill programs. Déjà Blue also features repurposed fixtures and displays.

Many years ago, Terri Garbarini started a small shoe store that has since expanded to a one-stop shop for women's fashion. While there are still very fine shoes, there are also heaps of women's fashions to choose from. **Garbarini** (239 Detroit St., 303/333-8686, www.garbarinishop.com, 10am-6pm Mon.-Sat., noon-5pm Sun.) stays on the cutting edge of the latest styles, and the store is always crammed full of options—from flirty Nicole Miller dresses to sexy Rebecca Beeson T-shirts. The sales staff is knowledgeable, helpful, and honest when it comes to helping you put together an outfit or find that perfect-fitting pair of jeans.

What started as a custom leather goods shop in nearby Boulder in the 1960s has evolved into one of the country's best shops for a sophisticated and discriminating clientele. While **Lawrence Covell** (225 Steele St., 303/320-1023, www.lawrencecovell.com, 10am-5pm Mon.-Sat.) sells both men's and women's clothing, this is the place for men who can afford to shop in style but aren't sure what that style is. Personal shopping and wardrobe consultation are available, with the owners as experts to help the most fashion-challenged. What man doesn't look his best in a Kiton suit and necktie or a Jil Sander shirt?

Long considered a high-water mark of women's fashion in Denver, **Max** (264 Detroit St., 303/321-4949, http://maxfashioncolorado.com, 11am-6pm Mon.-Sat., noon-5pm Sun.) is the store to visit for the woman who needs an extra-special dress, skirt, or outfit. At any one of Max's stores, a customer may be helped by the owner himself, Max Martinez. Max and his staff know women and how to dress them properly in the best styles. Look for Stella McCartney, Chloé, Prada, Thakoon, Versace, and many other fabulous designers.

Finding a good bra-fitting expert like those at **SOL** (3010 E. 6th Ave., 303/394-1060, www.sollingerie.com, 10am-6pm Mon.-Sat., by appointment)—which is short for "Store of Lingerie"—is just as important as finding a good hairdresser. Once a woman has been properly fitted for a bra, there's no going back to guessing sizes on her own. Sexy, lacy, comfortable, and practical are all found at SOL in the form of thongs, panties, bras, camisoles, and pajamas, including slinky sleepwear and loungewear from SOL's own line.

Men's casual sportswear lines are found at **Trout's American Sportswear** (1077 S. Gaylord St., 303/733-3983, https://troutsflyfishing.com, 10:30am-5pm Mon.-Sat., 10am-5:30pm Sun.), among the shops and restaurants on Old South Gaylord Street in the Washington Park neighborhood. Men who like Cole Haan footwear and the colorful prints and simple khakis of designers like Tommy Bahama and Bills Khakis will enjoy outfitting themselves at Trout's. Imagine a well-dressed man on a long vacation—that's the idea for Trout's clientele.

Gift and Home

The **Artisan Center** (2757 E. 3rd Ave., 303/333-1201, www.artisancenterdenver.com, 10am-5pm daily) is a can't-miss store for people who like precious gifty items or are looking for the perfect present. Outside the store there are colorful wind chimes and garden items, and inside it's a plethora of trinkets. There are baby clothes, soaps, candles, jewelry, dishes, scarves, rugs, cards, and little bowls of even tinier things, like matchbox shrines. It seems like there is never a season when this store is not busy with customers carefully selecting just the right treasure—and they've been doing it since 1977. The Artisan Center also offers free and lovely gift wrapping.

Really two stores, the **5 Green Boxes** locations are one block apart and have slightly different concepts. The original, what is called the "Little Store" (1596 S. Pearl St., 303/777-2331, www.5greenboxes.com, 10am-6pm Mon.-Sat., 10am-8pm Fri., noon-5pm Sun.), is chock-full of knickknacks that include pretty little shoes, colorful scarves, jewelry, and more. The "Big Store" (1570 S. Pearl St., 303/282-5481) offers home decor items, including its own line of upholstered chairs (very shabby chic) and footstools. Need a wool three-tiered wedding cake? This is the place. They also have a location in Union Station.

At first glance, **HW Home** (199 Clayton Lane, 303/394-9222, www.hwhome.com, 10am-6pm Mon.-Sat., 10am-5pm Sun.) appears to be an upscale chain furniture store, but in fact it is a locally owned shop with three locations in Colorado. What makes this store fabulous is its ability to put it all together so it looks meant to be, and maybe even like you did it yourself. It's not straight from a catalog cookie-cutter style, and it emphasizes top-notch designs for living rooms, bedrooms, and dining rooms.

Beyond eco-friendly and green shopping is recycled, or **Revampt** (2601 E. 3rd Ave., 720/536-5644, www.revamptgoods.com, 10am-5pm Mon.-Sat.)—goods that have found a second life as some useful home furnishing or decor. Skateboards are now earrings, cabins are now trunks, bike rims and sprockets are now side tables, silverware has become napkin rings, barrels are turned into one-of-a-kind chairs, and the list of seemingly improbable transformations goes on.

Open-Air Markets

The **Cherry Creek Fresh Market** (N. Cherry Creek Dr. and University Blvd., 303/442-1837, www.coloradofreshmarkets.com, 9am-1pm Sat. May-Oct., 9am-1pm Wed. June-Sept.) is very popular on Saturday mornings in summer, when fresh produce and flowers are available weekly from farms around the state. It's a chance to meet the people growing your food and hear their stories of farm life. Check out the website to see what's in season and expected soon at the market. Colorado specialties include apples, peaches, and Rocky Ford melons.

Smaller than the Cherry Creek Fresh Market, the **Old South Pearl Street Farmers Market** (S. Pearl St. between E. Florida Ave. and Iowa Ave., http://southpearlstreet.com, 9am-1pm Sun. May-Nov.) is utterly charming. The market is set right on the blocked-off street, which is lined with restaurants open for breakfast and brunch, and shops set to open shortly. Because this tends to be a quieter event, it's easy to chat with the farmers and learn more about where the produce is grown and maybe even how to best prepare it.

Shopping Centers and Districts

Cherry Creek Mall (3000 E. 1st Ave., 303/388-3900, www.shopcherrycreek.com, 10am-8pm Mon.-Sat., 11am-6pm Sun.) is the counterpoint to Cherry Creek North, drawing lots of shoppers to its anchor stores like Nordstrom, Neiman Marcus, and Macy's. The other 160-plus stores include Tiffany & Co., Burberry, and more. There is a movie theater on the second level, and the restaurants inside the mall tend to be fast food, with pizza, ice cream, and cookies. The most popular place in the mall is a free play area with giant foam pieces of cartoon characters for babies and young children to climb on. At Christmastime, the lines for Santa Claus are some of the longest in the city. Outside of the mall are additional stores and restaurants generally considered part of the mall, such as **Elway's** (2500 E. 1st Ave., 303/399-5353, www.elways.com).

Cherry Creek North (bounded by 1st Ave., 3rd Ave., Adams St., and Josephine St.) has long had a reputation for being a shopping district for the well-to-do, and it does not disappoint in this regard. Located across from the Cherry Creek Mall, the Cherry Creek North shopping district is known for the locally owned shops that have been here for decades. As boutiques have become vogue again in contrast to malls, national stores have begun to rent space in Cherry Creek North rather than in the mall, and some have the appearance of being one of the local shops. Around every corner is another shop for every occasion—menswear, womenswear, gifts, art, and more.

Sports and Recreation

Recreation is part of everything Denverites do. Rather than inhibit activity, the thinner air at 5,280 feet (1,609 m) above sea level encourages it, since the body is working that much harder and burning calories much more efficiently. Plus, it's easy to get motivated when there are more sunny days here than in Miami. Nearby parks in the foothills mean that city dwellers can get their mountain fix by driving 30 minutes or less to a trailhead for a day hike amid forests and wildflowers.

DOWNTOWN

Biking

You can rent a bike or sign up for a bike tour from downtown. Try **Mile High Bike Tours** (2301 Champa St., 303/801-1766, www.milehighbiketours.com, 9am-6pm daily) for either a rental bike ($45 half day, $65 full day) or one of their themed tours, including Bike & Brew or a City Tour for $60 per person.

Health Clubs

The **Denver Athletic Club** (1325 Glenarm Place, 303/534-1211, www.denverathleticclub.cc) is as much a social club as a place to work out, and it is also home to the Denver Petroleum Club, which was established in 1948 for members of the oil and gas industries to schmooze. Founded in 1884, the Denver Athletic Club is one of the oldest private clubs in the country. It is walking distance from the Colorado Convention Center and many hotels. Situated in a landmark historic building, the interior of the club is completely modern, with a swimming pool, racquetball and squash courts, volleyball and basketball courts, exercise studios, and a bowling alley. The 125,000-square-foot club has the latest fitness equipment and is open 24 hours daily every day of the year.

The **YMCA** (25 E. 16th Ave., 303/861-8300, www.denverymca.org), just off the end of the 16th Street Mall, is a nice affordable place to work out for people who live or work downtown. The only downside is that there is no pool at this location, though a membership at this YMCA location is valid at other locations in the city with pools. At the downtown location, there are treadmills, indoor cycling, weight machines, and fitness classes. There is a chance to relax in the sauna or steam room, or with a massage. The YMCA charges $10-15 per day for individual passes for those aged 18 and over; it also offers a three-day "Try the Y" free pass for Colorado residents only.

Ice-Skating

Sponsored by Southwest Airlines, the Southwest Rink at **Skyline Park** (1701 Arapahoe St., mid-Nov.-mid.-Feb., free, skate rentals $2) has become an annual holiday tradition for many Denver families (including mine!). Skating downtown from about Thanksgiving through Valentine's Day is a great way to enjoy seeing the city all dressed up for the season. The rink is at the base of the D&F tower, where there is a small outdoor pizza restaurant and bar. Families, couples, experts, and novices all come out to slip, slide, and glide around the small rink during winter.

Spas

An affordable facial and friendly service, what more could you want? **Jalan Facial Spa** (801 E. 17th Ave., 720/476-5593, www.jalanspa.com, 9am-7:30pm Thurs.-Mon.) has more than facials for men and women. Before a massage, body wrap, or other treatment, arrive early to take advantage of amenities like a foot soak or to sit in the Zen Garden Room.

GOLDEN TRIANGLE, LINCOLN PARK, AND SOBO

Biking

Bikes need regular maintenance just like automobiles. Schedule a tune-up at **evo** (860 Broadway, 303/831-7228, www.evo.com, 10am-7pm Mon.-Fri., 10am-6pm Sat.-Sun.), formerly Bicycle Doctor, and get the wheels aligned and the tires checked, along with other advice on fixing up your bike. The shop also sells lots of cycling gear, and it offers a large selection of quality bikes to rent with a friendly staffer to offer advice and tips on where to go and the best routes for bikes.

LODO AND PLATTE RIVER VALLEY

Parks

The point where Cherry Creek merges with the South Platte River is the approximate spot where gold was discovered by prospectors in 1858, leading to the founding of Denver. The confluence is now a mecca for outdoor enthusiasts. Rushing water carries kayakers through chutes and under bridges, while runners and cyclists whir past on riverside paths and families relax on the grassy knolls and sandy beaches throughout **Confluence Park** (15th St. between Platte St. and Little Raven St., 720/913-1311, www.denvergov.org, 5am-11pm daily). A large deck on the side of the

REI store in the enormous former Denver Tramway Building invites people to sit and rest from all the activity or contemplate their next move while having a bite to eat.

Don't miss the historical signs posted along pedestrian paths in the park that tell the tragic story of the Native Americans who first called this spot home. Nearby Little Raven Street is named in honor of the Arapaho chief who struggled to coexist with white settlers.

Biking

The **Cherry Creek Bike Path** (Confluence Park to University Blvd.) is one of the most popular off-street recreation paths in the city. A concrete path along either side of Cherry Creek has one side designated for wheels and the other for pedestrians. Starting at Confluence Park, the creek and paths run below the street level of busy Speer Boulevard all the way to the Cherry Creek shopping district, where Speer Boulevard intersects with University Boulevard. There are ramps at intervals on the paths to climb up to street level and see the nearby sights. Down below the streets, it's a world away from traffic and urban life, with greenery and the sounds of the water to listen to instead. It's 4.4 miles (7.1 km) from Cherry Creek to University Boulevard, but the trail continues on to the Cherry Creek Reservoir, another 9 miles (14.5 km) from University Boulevard.

The bike paths along the **Platte River Greenway** (Confluence Park to Bear Creek Trail) are truly appealing, with lots of cottonwood trees and other greenery along the way. Leaving from Confluence Park in either direction, there are some stretches through industrial sites that are less attractive. Heading south from the park, the concrete path goes out to the nearby suburbs and affords views of the Front Range at different intervals. To go all the way to Bear Creek Trail is an easy ride of 8.6 miles (13.8 km).

The Cherry Creek Bike Path and Platte River Greenway are the main activity paths within the city, but each extends beyond the county lines with offshoots to many other popular paths for bicycling, running, and other sports.

Climbing

The **REI Denver Flagship Pinnacle** (1416 Platte St., 303/756-3100, www.rei.com, noon-8pm Fri., 10am-6pm Sat.-Sun., $20 nonmembers, $5 members) is a 47-foot imitation of the actual sandstone climbing rocks west of town. The pinnacle is a 6,400-square-foot surface of hand-sculpted formations, including hand- and footholds instead of bolts. REI offers classes for beginners, women, kids, and more with a schedule that changes monthly. (Classes are for REI members, but it's easy to join.) While most of the people who scale this monolith are serious about climbing, it has become a favorite snapshot spot with people paying to climb just high enough for that "Look at me!" moment.

Kayaking

The South Platte River through **Confluence Park** (15th St. between Platte St. and Little Raven St., www.denvergov.org) has been slightly manipulated to create an exciting white-water park with Class II-III rapids, depending on the flow. From behind REI to just below 20th Street, there are 13 drops in 1.5 miles of river. Don't be shy about your kayaking skills here, though, because bridges hover right over the chutes, making this as popular a spot to watch boaters as it is to boat. Also be careful with those rollovers, as the water quality is highly questionable.

Whether you're looking for advice and gear to head up to the white water of the mountains, or just interested in a quick lesson steps away on the South Platte River, **Confluence Kayaks** (2301 7th St., 303/433-3676, www.confluencekayaks.com, 10am-7pm Mon.-Fri., 10am-6pm Sat., noon-5pm Sun.) is the place to go. If you are in Commons Park or Confluence Park during the warm months, chances are you will spot a few kayakers either in the chutes or dripping wet as they walk back to Confluence Kayaks to return their rented boat. Pool and lake lessons are taught at other locations, and private instruction is also available.

Skateboarding

One of the largest free public skate parks in the country is the **Denver Skatepark** (2205 19th St., www.denverskatepark.com, 5am-11pm daily, free), on the northern edge of Commons Park just off the South Platte River. Its three acres (or 50,000 square feet) of concrete are meant to mimic an urban skate environment. The park includes a half-pipe, a 10-foot-deep "dog bowl," handrails, and a lot more features. Although helmets and pads are always recommended, they are not required by law at the skate park. Check out the website to see photos of the park and find links to other skate parks around the state.

Sledding

Depending on your perspective, Denver has been either blessed or cursed with some blizzards in recent years. Sure, the roads were a nightmare of icy potholes, but it made for great urban sledding conditions and a chance for residents to sample what's within walking distance of their homes. One of the more popular sled slides is in **Commons Park** (15th St. and Little Raven St., 720/913-1311, www.denvergov.org, 5am-11pm daily), where different sides of the hill provide a variety of speeds and chutes for all ages. For those who aren't close enough to walk and don't want to drive on winter roads, Commons Park is just a short walk from the light-rail station behind Union Station.

Spectator Sports

Even amid a recent run of losing seasons, the **Colorado Rockies** (Coors Field, 2001 Blake St., 303/762-5437, www.mlb.com/rockies) continue to attract committed fans to home games at Coors Field. The team played its first game in 1993 at the original Mile High Stadium (most recently dubbed Empower Field at Mile High, previously Invesco at Mile High, and rebuilt) to such huge success that architects working on the new Coors Field expanded the seating capacity to over 50,000 for the 1995 opening game. The "rockpile" cheap seats and attractive stadium keep the fans donning the purple-and-black team colors, even when the Rockies aren't winning a lot of games. An on-site playground and the Buckaroo snack bar make the baseball field popular with families. There are 75-minute tours of Coors Field offered throughout the year. Call ahead to join a tour that goes down into the clubhouses and up to the "mile high" seats.

Certainly a number of big-name basketball players have been on the **Denver Nuggets** team (Ball Arena, 1000 Chopper Circle, 303/405-1100, www.nba.com/nuggets) over the years, but that hasn't translated into titles. A championship win still eludes the Nuggets despite regular playoff appearances. The Nuggets' home games are almost more entertaining during breaks in the game itself, with performances by the cheerleaders and various contests. This National Basketball Association team plays at the Ball Arena (formerly the Pepsi Center).

The **Denver Broncos** (Empower Field at Mile High, 1701 Bryant St., 720/258-3333, www.denverbroncos.com) continue to have a serious fan base year after year. Once the team's Super Bowl-winning quarterback, John Elway is now president of the team. This is a football kind of town, and Broncos fans will brave the coldest weather to cheer on their team in orange and blue.

After relocating from Canada, the **Colorado Avalanche** (Ball Arena, 1000 Chopper Circle, 303/405-7646, http://avalanche.nhl.com) was the team to beat in the National Hockey League. The 1996 and 2001 Stanley Cup dream team has changed as players have retired, but a recent influx of young talent has again made the Avalanche a team that is exciting to watch. Some former star players, such as Joe Sakic, have become team executives to help oversee this next generation. The Avalanche plays home games at the Ball Arena.

1

2

3

4

CAPITOL HILL AND CITY PARK

Parks

Where the Capitol Hill neighborhood blends into the Congress Park neighborhood is **Cheesman Park** (Franklin St. and 8th St., 720/913-1311, www.denvergov.org, 5:30am-11pm daily), which abuts the south end of the Denver Botanic Gardens. The large Parthenon-like pavilion in Cheesman Park is popular for wedding pictures, with a stunning view of the Rocky Mountains serving as a backdrop. Many high-rise apartment buildings overlook the park, an oasis of green in the densely packed neighborhood. Features include a large playground and a gravel running path. Due to the sizable gay and lesbian population in Capitol Hill, Cheesman is known as an LGBTQ hangout and is the place where the annual Pridefest parade begins.

Boating and Fishing

At 25 acres, **Ferril Lake** (City Park, 3300 E. 17th Ave., www.denvergov.org/parks, 5am-11pm daily) is the largest lake in City Park. It allows fishing in a fairly serene setting, considering that it is in the middle of the city and walking distance from downtown. Ferril Lake has yellow perch, sunfish, and carp stocked in the fall, and rainbow trout stocked in the spring. Only rented novelty paddleboats are allowed in Ferril Lake, and fishing is only permitted from piers or platforms.

Golf

The location of the 18-hole regulation **City Park Golf Course** (2500 York St., 303/295-2096, www.denvergov.org/denvergolf) is pretty great, given its proximity to downtown and views of the skyline and mountain peaks beyond. Tree-lined fairways can make the course a little challenging. The course features a pro shop, a driving range, and the pleasant Bogey's on the Park restaurant. The golf course is part of City Park, but a road separates it from the main park and attractions, such as the Denver Zoo and the Denver Museum of Nature & Science.

HIGHLANDS

Parks

Though the greater Highlands neighborhood has numerous small parks and is also close to downtown parks (such as Commons Park), the gem in this part of town is **Sloan's Lake Park** (Sheridan Blvd. and W. 26th Ave., www.denvergov.org, 5am-11pm daily). The park is primarily the lake itself, which is encircled by a mile-or-so-long running and biking path. There are two playgrounds, tennis and basketball courts, and athletic fields. Boating, waterskiing, and fishing are all permitted on the lake. It rarely feels crowded at Sloan's Lake, except during the very popular **Dragon Boat Festival** each summer.

Fishing

While downtown Denver may seem a long way from a perfect fly-fishing spot, it's just a couple of hours' drive from some great rivers ideal for hooking a big one. **Trout's Fly Fishing** (1025 Zuni St., 303/733-1434, www.troutsflyfishing.com, 10am-6pm Mon.-Wed., 10am-7pm Thurs.-Fri., 9am-5pm Sat., 10am-5pm Sun.) not only sells gear and flies but also teaches the necessary skills in its outfitting and education center. Visit the store or the website to find out about fishing events in the area and to get local fishing reports, along with a list of the best places in Colorado to fish.

WASHINGTON PARK AND CHERRY CREEK

Parks

With two lakes, tennis courts, jogging and bicycle paths, playgrounds, a soccer field, a recreation center, flower gardens, and more within its 165 acres, **Washington Park** (S. Downing St. and E. Louisiana Ave., 303/698-4962, www.denvergov.org, 5am-11pm daily) is one of the city's most popular parks. People are drawn to this neighborhood for

---

1: Cheesman Park **2:** Cherry Creek Bike Path
3: Washington Park **4:** kayaking at Confluence Park

the historic bungalows that surround the park as much as for the active lifestyle of the park. Poet and journalist Eugene Field lived in Denver for two years in the late 1800s and is remembered in Washington Park with a statue titled *Wynken, Blynken, and Nod,* after his best-known poem. Rent a boat or go fishing in the summer to get a different perspective from the water in this park. Views of the mountains can be had from various spots in the park, too.

Smith Lake is one of three lakes at Washington Park that offer many recreational options, including fishing. The 19-acre Smith Lake is stocked with carp, catfish, largemouth bass, and rainbow trout. Smith Lake also allows sailboats, canoes, kayaks, and rowboats, and it has a fishing pier. Willow trees provide a bit of shade on hot days, and a boathouse at the lake can be rented out for private parties. **Grasmere Lake** is also 19 acres with a similar selection of fish to catch, but the difference is that this lake is a little less busy than Smith, which has the boathouse on one side. **Lily Pond** is a mere one acre and is designated for children under 16 to practice their fishing skills.

Spas

Just a block or so away from the busy sidewalks of the Cherry Creek North shopping district is the calm oasis of fabulous skin care at **Edit Euro Spa** (159 Adams St., 303/377-1617, www.editeurospa.com, 9am-5:30pm Mon.-Sat.). In a two-story Victorian house, rooms have been transformed into miniature day spas where the city's best facials and waxing are done. One look at the owner's gorgeous skin and anyone will be sold on the services and products at Edit. To combat Colorado's dry climate and harsh sunshine, be sure to check out the hydrating treatments and skin care line.

Tennis

Located just beyond the shops and mall of Cherry Creek is **Gates Tennis Center** (3300 E. Bayaud Ave., 303/355-4461, www.gatestenniscenter.info, 7am-10pm Mon.-Thurs., 7am-9pm Fri., 7am-8pm Sat.-Sun., $6-8), a 20-court outdoor tennis center with an indoor pro shop and lounge. The center is open in the winter, but it's hit-or-miss based on current weather conditions for outdoor courts. There are private lessons, group programs, adult mixers, and peewee classes, all taught by professionals.

GREATER DENVER

Parks

Red Rocks Park (18300 W. Alameda Pkwy., 720/865-2494 or 720/865-0900, www.denvergov.org or www.redrocksonline.com) is best known for its amphitheater—a world-class concert venue—but it's also part of the city of Denver's mountain park system, even at 16 miles (26 km) west of downtown. This 640-acre park offers opportunities to hike and mountain bike (and climb the stairs of the amphitheater, or take a yoga class in the amphitheater) with views of the giant red rocks. One thing that's not allowed is rock climbing, so pay attention to the signs and resist the temptation.

Food

TOP EXPERIENCE

I don't know which is hotter—the restaurant scene or the real estate business in Denver. Trying to keep up with the incredible food scene in the Mile High City is like trying to hold Jell-O. Here is my best representation of the current dining options—alive with creativity, fresh ingredients, and some local celebrity chefs—plus the old favorites.

DOWNTOWN

Coffee and Tea

With coffee shops on almost every corner in downtown, does it really matter where you stop for a cup of joe? Yes! **Emily's Café** (1860 Lincoln St., 720/423-4797, www.emilygriffith.edu/emilys-cafe, 8:30am-9:30am and 11am-1pm Mon.-Wed.) is part of the Emily Griffith Technical College (formerly Emily Griffith Opportunity School), where immigrants and refugees learn job skills. The shop also serves really good espresso. The pastries are baked by students in the school's baking program, and the coffee beans are locally roasted by Kaladi Brothers Coffee Company. Even the aprons worn here were made by women at the local African Community Center. Each cup of coffee bought will have a community ripple effect.

Named for the thick, silky layer of umber-hued foam—the hallmark of a well-crafted espresso—**Crema Coffee House** (2862 Larimer St., 720/284-9648, www.cremacoffeehouse.net, 7am-5pm daily, $4-8) sees no shortage of bean connoisseurs. Even the website has espresso-tasting instructions. Did you know that so much of tasting espresso is in the nose? Order a shot, swirl it around, and give it a whiff as you check out this minimalist urban shop. If you're hungry, order a hearty breakfast burrito, quiche, or a sandwich. You'll find this place in the RiNo neighborhood on the north edge of downtown.

Breakfast and Brunch

Just off the beaten path downtown, the **Mercury Cafe** (2199 California St., 303/294-9258, www.mercurycafe.com, 5pm-midnight Wed.-Fri., 9am-midnight Sat.-Sun., $7-16) is one of the city's most popular brunch hangouts. With an emphasis on organic and locally sourced ingredients, the menu offers a selection of hearty egg dishes, some with Colorado elk meat, as well as stuffed burritos—the No More War Burrito is a house favorite, with green chili, polenta, and cheese. The café is also a nightclub with live music ranging from folk to swing bands and a variety of dance lessons offered, including tango, salsa, and belly dancing.

Visitors from the East Coast will find carb-y comfort in **Rosenberg's Bagels & Delicatessen** (725 E. 26th Ave., 720/440-9880, http://rosenbergsbagels.com, 6am-3pm Tues.-Sun., $1.25-11), owned by former Jersey resident Joshua Pollack. He's so dedicated to creating the perfect New York-style bagel that he figured out how to replicate NYC water in the Mile High City, a key ingredient in his soft, chewy, oven-fresh bagels. Order yours with house-smoked and -cured lox, a crisp salad, a cup of coffee—even a pastry. I recommend The Frenchie: a toasted cinnamon raisin bagel with scrambled egg, sausage, cheddar cheese, and maple syrup. There is a location in Boulder and one in the Stanley Marketplace in Aurora, east of Denver.

If you want something for a special occasion, try **Mimosa's** (2752 Welton St., 720/372-7572, https://mimosasdenver.com, 8am-4pm Tues.-Sun., $13-22), where you can start your meal with beignets or fried green tomatoes before moving on to hearty egg dishes. And, of course, champagne and mimosas, too!

Barbecue

Attached to Green Russell is **Russell's Smokehouse** (1422 Larimer St.,

303/893-6505, www.russellssmokehouse.com, 5pm-9pm Mon.-Thurs., noon-10pm Fri., 11am-10pm Sat., 11am-9pm Sun., $12-25), a barbecue restaurant beneath trendy Larimer Square. The creative craft cocktails and home-cooked goodness of smoked and barbecued meats draw those looking for something a little more rustic, but still encapsulated in an upscale space. Adorned in leather and wood, this place is cowboy-chic. Look up from your smoked pork shoulder with cheddar grits, okra, and cornbread, and notice the green ceiling and stained-glass decor.

Wine Bar

Sophisticated but chill, **Sunday Vinyl** (1803 16th St., 720/738-1803, www.sundayvinyl.com, 4:30pm-10pm Wed.-Sat., 10am-8pm Sun., $18-28) is as much about the ambience as the food and drink menus. Happy hour is 4:30pm-6:30pm Wednesday-Sunday, and Wednesday evenings are Flight Nights. It's the kind of place for a special night out—a birthday or anniversary—where the music will be spot on while you dine on croque monsieur, lobster toast with caviar, or smoked trout. You can plan your night here around pre-scheduled music selections such as a David Bowie night on the turntable.

Asian

Chef Troy Guard is best known for his renowned TAG restaurant on Larimer Square, but **Bubu** (1423 Larimer St., Suite 010, 303/996-2685, www.bubu-denver.com, 11am-4pm Mon.-Fri., $4-14)—his fast-casual, healthy Asian-fusion concept—also draws the lunchtime crowds. Pop in and choose a bowl of fresh, flavorful goodness, like the Hawaii Five-O bowl with hearts of palm, soybeans, crispy puffed rice, shiitake mushrooms, raw fennel, and soy onion dressing. Add rice, noodles, or salad, top it all off with your choice of protein, and you have yourself a quick and satisfying meal. There are two more Denver locations of this eatery.

Continental

For that extra-special dining-out experience in downtown Denver, make a reservation at the **Palace Arms** (321 17th St., 303/294-3659, www.brownpalace.com, 5pm-9:30pm Tues.-Sat., $32-40) in the iconic Brown Palace Hotel. Start with caviared eggs and then opt for seafood or a 48-hour sous vide brisket. Leave room for dessert as you will be choosing between items like a raspberry mousse and champagne Napoleon cake or walnut flourless cake with roasted grapes.

Italian

At **Attimo Winery** (2246 Larimer St., 720/287-4988, www.attimowine.com, 3pm-8pm Wed.-Thurs., 3pm-9pm Fri.-Sat., 3pm-7pm Sun., $11-16) the food is secondary to the wine. In short, the owner of the wildly popular Snooze restaurants moved to Italy and worked on a vineyard, then came back to Denver with a new concept. There are tours of the cellar and a tasting room. The menu features traditional antipasti appetizers and handmade pastas.

Panzano (909 17th St., 303/296-3525, www.panzano-denver.com, 5pm-9pm Tues.-Sat., $25-32) has been called not only one of Denver's best restaurants but one of the best in the United States, and it has won numerous awards. Located adjacent to the Hotel Monaco in downtown, Panzano offers a taste of the northern Italian countryside. In addition to the fine food, diners are made aware of the sustainable practices behind the scenes so that they can make true the saying, "*chi manga bene, vive bene*" (those who eat well, live well). And if you think Italian food is synonymous with pasta, think again—chef Elise Wiggins has created gluten-free menus.

You may have heard about restaurants built into shipping containers, but you won't believe it until you actually have a meal in one. **Cart-Driver** (2500 Larimer St., 303/292-3553, www.cart-driver.com, 3pm-10pm Tues.-Thurs., noon-11pm Fri.-Sat., noon-10pm Sun., $8-16) is one of Denver's first shipping container restaurants, serving wood-fired pizza, fresh oysters, prosecco on tap, and as much warm hospitality as you can fit into 640 square feet. The Italian inspiration is rooted in the *carrettiere,* a horse-drawn cart driver who delivers food to Italian villagers. Step up to the bar and order the namesake pizza with sausage, kale, mozz, and chili flakes. If it's nice, stretch your legs a bit on one of the two patios.

Latin American

Traditional Mexican food is delicious, but the masterminds behind **Los Chingones** (2461 Larimer St., Suite 102, 303/295-0686, www.loschingonesmexican.com, noon-9pm Wed.-Thurs. and Sun., noon-10pm Fri.-Sat., $5-15) wanted to amp up the experience with adventurous proteins, sassy service, and plenty of excitement from brunch until late. Try the Mexican sashimi with hibiscus and jalapeño, or the Colorado empanadas with antelope, venison, elk, wild boar, *and* buffalo topped with *crema* and corn *pico.* Wash it down with a T&T—that's code for a tequila, lime, Tang, and orange soda cocktail. There are four other locations, including one in Fort Collins.

Work & Class (2500 Larimer St., 303/292-0700, www.workandclassdenver.com, 4pm-10pm Sun.-Thurs., 4pm-11pm Fri.-Sat., $6-28) is the brainchild of owner-chef Dana Rodriguez, who wanted an approachable, fun restaurant that offered affordable plates in a trendy atmosphere. Her dream came true, and it's housed in an intimate space—shipping containers form the walls—where the motto is "food for people who can eat." Visit for no-fuss Latin and American-style dishes that change seasonally but might include red chili-braised pork, coriander-roasted Colorado lamb, and blue corn empanadas.

GOLDEN TRIANGLE, LINCOLN PARK, AND SOBO

Contemporary

After an environmental cleanup of this former gas and service station, **Bittersweet** (500 E. Alameda Ave., 303/942-0320, http://bittersweetdenver.com, 5pm-9pm Tues.-Sat., $11-42) has become one of Denver's hottest restaurants, garnering rave reviews from local and national media. The concept is a seasonally influenced menu of traditional foods with a modern twist. Think pork with rhubarb *gastrique* sauce in the spring, for example. Given the word-of-mouth and terrific press, it's best to make reservations, as the small space can only accommodate so many diners on a busy night.

Beatrice & Woodsley (38 S. Broadway, 303/777-3505, http://beatriceandwoodsley.com, 5pm-10pm Mon.-Thurs., 5pm-11pm Fri., 9am-2pm and 5pm-11pm Sat., 9am-2pm and 5pm-10pm Sun., $9-33) emphasizes the woods in its decor. It is meant to be an indoor wilderness with an inspired use of wood throughout the restaurant. (This can make for unexpected bumps in the dining tables, but the restroom area is really a hoot.) And the ever-changing menu is for the adventurous eater, with choices such as turtle dumplings in a rabbit *ragù* sauce (The Tortoise and The Hare) and crawfish beignets. A friend and I have plans to return soon for the brunch and share the grapefruit crisp and Monkey Brains—actually gooey cinnamon rolls.

Inside the Denver Art Museum, **The Ponti** (100 W. 14th Ave., 720/913-2761, www.denverartmuseum.org/en/dining, 11am-2pm Wed.-Mon., 11am-2pm and 5pm-close Tues.) is named after the building's original architect, Gio Ponti. Local chef and James Beard award winner Jen Jasinski is behind this restaurant concept with sophisticated dishes that focus primarily on Colorado vegetables, paired with fish and meats. Reservations are recommended.

Steakhouse

Founded by one of frontiersman Buffalo Bill Cody's scouts, ★ **The Buckhorn Exchange** (1000 Osage St., 303/534-9505, www.buckhornexchange.com, 11am-2pm and 5pm-9pm Mon.-Thurs., 11am-2pm and 5pm-10pm Fri.-Sat., 5pm-9pm Sun., $24-56) has been open for business since 1893, serving all variety of beef and game meats. Over time, the walls of The Buckhorn were filled with a menagerie of hundreds of taxidermied animals to reflect some of the menu selections, such as bison and elk. The kitschy decor of taxidermy trophies is done with a sense of humor—such as the "herd" of antelope heads near the front door. To round out the Old West feel, there is cowboy music in the upstairs lounge on weekends. With a light-rail stop practically at the front door, The Buckhorn is more accessible from downtown than ever.

Asian

Authentic Japanese peasant food is a rarity in Denver. Not far from the edge of downtown is ★ **Domo** (1365 Osage St., 303/595-3666, www.domorestaurant.com, 11am-8:30pm Tues.-Sun., $17-25), a Japanese garden oasis of small ponds, burbling fountains, blossoming trees, and a unique menu of fresh seafood and "sea vegetables," along with a menu of artisanal sake. On one side of the garden is a folk art museum that draws schoolchildren on field trips. Domo also has a tea menu for anyone who just wants to get away from the city and sip tea in this little garden. The restaurant's sushi presentations are works of art, and the goal is to give customers a very authentic experience (so forget about special orders or having soy sauce on your table to season your food).

Latin American

Before stepping inside **Cuba Cuba Café & Bar** (1173 Delaware St., 303/605-2822, www.cubacubacafe.com, 5pm-10pm Mon.-Thurs., 5pm-10:30pm Fri.-Sat., $13-26), you get a sense of the colorful and playful Caribbean vibe. The restaurant occupies two little Victorian houses joined together and painted blue with yellow trim. It's mellow and even cozy inside, where the night gets off to a perfect start with a smooth mojito and a bowl of plantain chips while listening to some live music. The entrées at Cuba Cuba are traditional Cuban favorites done to perfection, such as a Cubano sandwich or *ropa vieja* (Cuban beef stew). In the summer, the back patio is adorned with lanterns and it feels like an island vacation in the city.

Drawing repeat customers long before the bustling Santa Fe Arts District developed along this strip, **El Noa Noa** (722 Santa Fe Dr., 303/623-9968, http://denvermexicanrestaurants.net, 10am-9pm Mon.-Thurs., 10am-10pm Fri.-Sat., 10am-8pm Sun., $10-15) has been serving icy margaritas and smothered burritos for decades. On weekends in the summer, a mariachi band plays music on the patio, where umbrella-sheltered tables make this the ideal place to nosh on reasonably priced chiles rellenos, fajitas, enchiladas, or tacos during the First Friday Art Walk. Although the patio is popular and fills up in nice weather, there is rarely a wait for a table inside. There is live music on Thursday nights.

Next door to El Noa Noa is **El Taco de Mexico** (714 Santa Fe Dr., 303/623-3926, http://eltacodemexicodenver.com, 11am-8pm Tues.-Sun., $4-9, cash only), an almost roadside stand of a restaurant. The average customer at El Taco orders a traditional shredded beef taco and a *horchata* (cinnamon-flavored rice milk) for a quick, satisfying meal, but those in search of "authentic" Mexican food are thrilled to find tongue and brain on the menu as well.

Dessert

Making the SoBo neighborhood just that much more hip is ★ **Sweet Action Ice Cream** (52 Broadway, 303/282-4645, www.sweetactionicecream.com, noon-midnight daily), with its creative flavors, vegan options, and locally sourced ingredients. Try the molasses cornbread, Stranahan's whiskey brickle, or Thai iced tea—or better yet, try them in an enormous ice cream sandwich. The flavors change daily, so you might find something surprising as well as cool and refreshing.

LODO AND PLATTE RIVER VALLEY

Coffee and Tea

With a focus on all things British, **Babe's Tea Room** (2401 15th St., 303/455-4832, https://

babestearoom.com, 10am-6pm Mon.-Thurs., 10am-8pm Fri.-Sun., $8-11), formerly The House of Commons, fills a niche for tea lovers and those who want something more original than a biscotti and cup of coffee. There are over 60 teas to choose from and a large menu of savory bites and sweets in this low-key and modern setting on the first floor of a historic building. When I've stopped by, the place is always full, apparently with groups celebrating an occasion.

Breakfast and Brunch

It's no wonder that the pancakes at **Snooze** (2262 Larimer St., 303/297-0700, www.snoozeeatery.com, 6:30am-2:30pm Mon.-Fri., 6:30am-4pm Sat.-Sun., $8-13) have developed a loyal following: With options such as caramel glazes and shameless amounts of chocolate, they are somewhere between breakfast and dessert. There's even a pineapple upside-down pancake. The menu also features savory egg dishes and sandwiches on the lunch side, though breakfast is served all day. The colorful and unique *Jetsons*-meets-*Happy Days* decor makes Snooze fun, too. There are several Snooze locations around Denver and Colorado. No reservations are accepted, but you can come in early and put your name in to be texted when there is a table available. It is always busy, so plan ahead.

Bistro

★ **The Kitchen** (1530 16th St., 303/623-3127, www.thekitchen.com, 4pm-9pm Mon.-Thurs., 10am-3pm and 4pm-10pm Fri.-Sat., 10am-3pm and 4pm-9pm Sun., $17-38) started in Boulder and now has locations in other Colorado cities. The menu is slightly different than the Boulder original, with a large selection of seafood. The ample starters can make for a fun sampling with friends before selecting an entrée. Save room for dessert: the sticky toffee pudding is so good that people seem to favor it over the *pot au chocolat*. Dinner at this posh restaurant makes for a special night out.

Hot Dogs

Biker Jim's Gourmet Dogs (2148 Larimer St., 720/746-9355, www.bikerjimsdogs.com, 11am-10pm daily, $6.50-10) is the story of the quintessential American Dream, if that dream involves a jalapeño cheddar elk dog in a bun. Once a car repo man, Biker Jim fulfilled his dream of making gourmet hot dogs with exotic and unusual meats, like elk, Alaskan reindeer, rattlesnake, wild boar, pheasant, and duck. It's a place where a buffalo dog seems

breakfast pot pie at Snooze

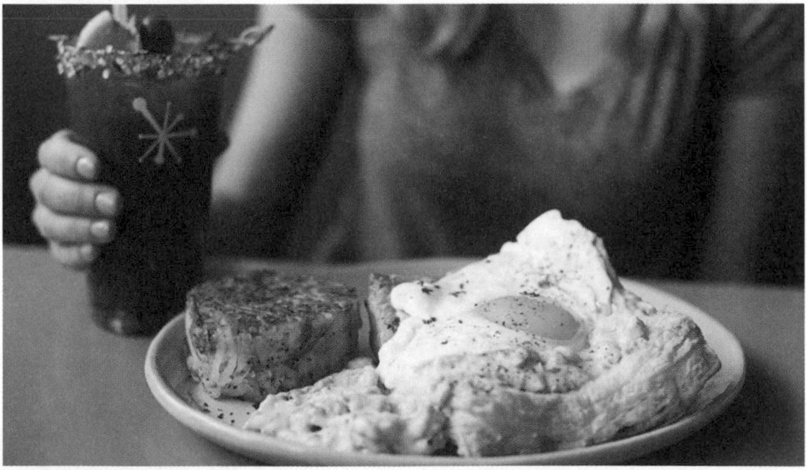

Union Station Dining Spots

Revitalization completely transformed the city's iconic **Union Station** (1701 Wynkoop St.). The once dimly lit Great Hall now buzzes with business diners, stylish travelers, children and families, first dates, and late-night revelers. Grand dining options abound from morning until night. Following are some top picks.

- **Cooper Lounge** (720/460-3738, www.cooperlounge.com, 4pm-midnight daily, $7-23): The high-end cocktails will give you a taste of 1930s Hollywood glamour, a chance to rub elbows with local power brokers, and a sophisticated menu by local chef Lon Symensma.
- **Stoic & Genuine** (303/640-3474, www.stoicandgenuine.com, 11am-10pm Sun.-Thurs., 11am-11pm Fri.-Sat., $17-38): Owner-chef Jennifer Jasinski serves a creative selection of seafood-focused dishes and cocktails that includes signature granitas and house soda.
- **Mercantile** (720/460-3733, www.mercantiledenver.com, 11am-2pm and 5pm-9pm Tues.-Sat., $15-32): This restaurant and marketplace offers everything from spices and cheeses to a full-service coffee bar with tasting flights.
- **Pigtrain Coffee** (720/460-3708, www.pigtraincoffee.com, 7am-7pm Mon.-Thurs., 7am-8pm Fri.-Sun.): Pick up local coffee from Denver's family-owned Novo coffee, with sensuous pastries and freshly squeezed juice.
- **Snooze** (303/825-3536, www.snoozeeatery.com, 6:30am-2:30pm Mon.-Fri., 6:30am-4pm Sat.-Sun., $8-13): One of Denver's most loved breakfast diners dishes up creative pancake dishes amid sunny decor.
- **Next Door** (720/460-3730, www.thekitchen.com, 11am-9pm daily, $10-17): From the owners of The Kitchen, this is a perfect spot for lunch or a relaxed dinner on the expansive patio.
- **Milkbox Ice Creamery** (720/460-3707, www.milkboxicecream.com, noon-7pm Mon.-Fri., noon-8pm Sat.-Sun.): Options range from ice cream by the scoop to boozy shakes.

like the most normal item on the menu. The toppings are equally outrageous, as in harissa-roasted cactus. Jim's dogs have been featured on shows like Anthony Bourdain's *No Reservations*. The restaurant's offerings include a kids' menu and beer. There's a second location at Coors Field as well as a food truck.

Asian

Ask anyone if they have eaten at **ChoLon** (1555 Blake St., 303/353-5223, www.cholon.com/denver, 5pm-9:30pm Tues.-Thurs., 5pm-10pm Fri.-Sat., $15-37), a modern Asian bistro, and the answer is invariably, "Yes—I had the onion soup dumplings." This explosion of flavor is just one example of the exciting tastes found at ChoLon, where the presentation is just as thrilling as the food itself. Try a dish with an Egg Cloud (kind of like French toast, it is a spicy custard-like egg mixture on toast points) or Chow Fun (a noodle bowl with fresh, house-made tapioca rice noodles, shrimp, lobster, and black bean sauce). Those on a dining budget might come for the happy-hour menu (3pm-5pm Tues.-Fri., 2pm-5pm Sat.), with small plates ranging $4-12 each.

Mono Mono Korean Fried Chicken (1550 Blake St., 720/379-6567, https://monomonokfc.com, 11am-10pm Mon.-Thurs., 11am-11pm Fri.-Sun., $11-33) is a new kind of chicken wings joint, prepared Korean style to be extra crispy. You can get other parts of the chicken too, not just the wings, and with a selection of sauces.

It would be pretty hard to just stumble across **Sushi Sasa** (2401 15th St., 303/433-7272, www.sushisasa.com, 11:30am-2:30pm and 5pm-9:30pm daily, $11-28) while out looking for a bite to eat. The acclaimed sushi restaurant's entrance is practically the back door of a large historic building, just as the sidewalk ends before 15th Street heads over I-25. But inside, it is calm serenity, with bamboo and white decor and a perfectly balanced menu of Japanese dishes beyond just sushi. Noodle bowls, tempura, vegetarian plates, and salads with or without seafood—all are on offer alongside the extensive sushi list.

French

Tucked in behind the shops of Larimer Square in the historic Sussex building is the charming **Bistro Vendôme** (1416 Larimer St., Suite H, 303/825-3232, www.bistrovendome.com, 4pm-10pm Mon.-Sat., 4pm-9pm Sun., brunch 10am-2pm Sat.-Sun., $17-27), which has the feel of being off the beaten path in Paris or New York. Owned by the same women who started the restaurant Rioja across the street—chef-owner Jennifer Jasinski and manager-owner Beth Gruitch—Bistro Vendôme is one of Denver's most romantic date restaurants, with seating inside or outside on the small patio, and complimentary champagne for anyone celebrating a special event. Their weekend brunch features fresh croissants and crêpes.

Italian

For an evening of sophisticated dining, visit ★ **Rioja** (1433 Larimer St., 303/820-2282, www.riojadenver.com, 11am-2:30pm and 4pm-10pm Mon.-Thurs., 11am-2:30pm and 4pm-11pm Fri., 10am-2:30pm and 4pm-11pm Sat., 10am-2:30pm and 4pm-10pm Sun., $12-32) in Larimer Square to try some delectable Mediterranean-inspired seasonal cuisine. The muted earth tones and copper-topped bar set off against exposed brick are reminiscent of the colors of the Spanish wine country, La Rioja. The wine list, of course, features wine from the Rioja region. The dinner menu includes a memorable artichoke tortellini, unexpectedly light gnocchi, and hearty entrées, some made with handmade pastas.

After moving to Colorado, Pam Proto craved the thin-crust Italian-style pizza of her childhood—in Connecticut. She opened her first pizzeria in Longmont, Colorado, and now has five locations of **Proto's Pizzeria Napoletana** (2401 15th St., 720/855-9400, www.protospizza.com, 11am-9pm Sun.-Thurs., 11am-9:30pm Fri.-Sat., $6-24). A few months after starting her business, Proto visited Italy for the first time and was thrilled to discover that she was serving authentic Italian pizza in Colorado. Proto's does not have delivery but does offer takeout. Friday nights are all about clam pizza, a surprisingly popular pie.

Latin American

On the southeast corner of Larimer Square, **Tamayo** (1400 Larimer St., 720/946-1433, www.richardsandoval.com, 11am-3pm and 5pm-9pm Sun.-Thurs., 11am-2pm and 5pm-10pm Fri., 11am-3pm and 5pm-10pm Sat., $13-29) has great views of the mountains from inside the main restaurant or, better yet, up on their rooftop deck. Tamayo is part of Richard Sandoval Restaurants, which has several different establishments in Denver, all with a similar theme of sophisticated Latin American food. The best way to experience Tamayo is from the rooftop, watching the sun set over the mountains.

CAPITOL HILL AND CITY PARK

Coffee and Tea

The theme at **St. Mark's** (2019 E. 17th Ave., 303/322-8384, www.stmarkscoffeehouse.com, 6:30am-10pm daily) is Venetian—from name to artwork—while the vibe is urban and original. St. Mark's offers Espresso Roma coffee from the San Francisco Bay Area and a selection of teas, tasty sandwiches, and too many yummy cookies, pastries, and desserts. An old garage door is yanked open on warm days, making the coffee shop feel even larger. With late hours and The Thin Man tavern located right next door, St. Mark's can be a decent place to chill out before calling it a night.

Breakfast and Brunch

What makes biscuits so darn good is that they can be turned into a breakfast, lunch,

Food Halls Everywhere

outdoor dining at The Source

For a minute, it was news when a food hall opened in the Denver, but now everyone is using this concept. It's actually an ideal setup with various diets (gluten-free, dairy-free, nut-free, meat-free) so that large groups can dine together but from different restaurants at the same time. Here's a list of some of the city's best food halls—some attached to hotels.

- Once an 1880s-era foundry building, the gourmet marketplace **The Source** (3350 Brighton Blvd., 720/443-1135, www.thesourcedenver.com) became a trendy spot for food and beverages—from artisanal breads to freshly butchered meats—as well as an industrial-chic date-night destination. In the marketplace building, you'll find **Grabowski's Pizzeria** (11am-9pm Tues.-Thurs., 11am-10pm Fri., noon-10pm Sat., noon-9pm Sun.) and several other places to get a drink or a bite to eat. Next door is the Source Hotel as well as **Safta Restaurant** (720/408-2444, www.eatwithsafta.com, 4:30pm-9:15pm Tues.-Thurs., 4:30pm-9:30pm Fri., 11am-2:30pm and 4:30pm-9:30pm Sat., 11am-2:30pm and 4:30pm-9:15pm Sun., $13-17), with a tasty Middle Eastern menu and shared plates.

- **Zeppelin Station** (3501 Wazee St., https://zeppelinstation.com, 11am-11pm Sun.-Thurs., 11am-1am Fri.-Sat.) is brought to you by the same people behind The Source. The vibe here is more experimental and international with Filipino food, Colombian food, Japanese street food, Thai street food, and more.

- **Milk Market** (1800 Wazee St., 303/792-8242, www.denvermilkmarket.com, 7am-10pm Mon.-Thurs., 7am-midnight Fri.-Sat., 7am-9pm Sun.) is chef Frank Bonanno's latest creation, and he's often seen in one of the kitchens. It's like a mini-version of each of his Denver restaurants here with pasta, pizza, seafood, poke, and so much more. This is part of the Maven Hotel and the Dairy Block, a block of historic buildings that were once a dairy and are now connected by an alleyway filled with public art and outdoor dining space.

- East of downtown in Aurora is **Stanley Marketplace** (2501 Dallas St., Aurora, 720/990-6743, www.stanleymarketplace.com, 7am-9pm Sun.-Wed., 7am-10pm Thurs.-Sat.), which is part food hall and modern mall with shops and event space. Among the food stalls of tacos, sushi, empanadas, and more is the award-winning restaurant **Annette,** with James Beard-nominated seasonal fare.

- Also in Aurora is **Mango House** (10180 E. Colfax Ave., Aurora, 303/900-8639, http://ardasclinic.com/mangohouse.htm, 8am-7pm Mon., 8am-8pm Tues.-Sat., 9am-7pm Sun.), a refugee and medical center as well as a food hall. You can sample Burmese, Syrian, and Nepalese food.

or dessert with a few simple toppings. The **Denver Biscuit Company** (3237 E. Colfax Ave., 303/377-7900, www.denbisco.com, 8am-2pm Mon.-Fri., 8am-3pm Sat.-Sun., $10-13) has it covered with the basic biscuits and gravy (a platter, no less!) and strawberry shortcake biscuits; then it goes to the next level with over-the-top biscuit sandwiches, a biscuit cinnamon roll, and the requisite Southern side dishes for mopping up a selection of jams, butters, and honey, or eggs and grits.

Olive & Finch (1552 E. 17th Ave., 303/832-8663, www.oliveandfincheatery.com, 7am-7pm Mon.-Fri., 7am-5pm Sat.-Sun., $6-12.50) is a quaint and cozy café and bakery that brings all the joy and warmth of a countryside kitchen to the heart of Denver. This neighborhood spot serves freshly baked pastries, frothy cappuccino, vibrant juices, and a selection of sandwiches, salads, and soups every day. In good weather, the patio is lovely—and dog-friendly! They have more than just breakfast, but they are known for this morning meal. There is also a location in the Uptown neighborhood near downtown.

Comfort Food

Steuben's (523 E. 17th Ave., 303/830-1001, www.steubens.com, 11am-10pm Mon.-Fri., 9am-10pm Sat.-Sun., $4-19) is an homage to 1950s style and food. The menu is all comfort food: mac and cheese, fried cheese, fried chicken with mashed potatoes and gravy, root beer floats, cheeseburgers, and hot dogs. Booth seating inside adds to the nostalgic feel, and the patio on the side of the restaurant is modern and delightful.

Contemporary

When ★ **D Bar** (494 E. 19th Ave., 303/861-4710, www.dbardesserts.com, 11:30am-9pm Wed.-Thurs., 11:30am-10pm Fri., 10:30am-10pm Sat., 10:30am-9pm Sun., $11-20) first opened, people were drawn by the celebrity owner, Keeghan Gerhard from *Food Network Challenge*. Gerhard opened D Bar with his wife, Lisa Bailey, who is also a pastry chef. Now people come for the food first, whether it's the crazy-good desserts or the savory small(ish) plates. Reservations are recommended; just know that it's always worth the wait when the Southern Fried Belgian 2.0 (fried chicken and waffles) arrives. Leave room for the liquid-center chocolate cake (aka Molten Cake Thingy). This is a fun dining experience, with friendly service, a couple of TVs tuned to the *Food Network*, and lots of natural light from the large windows that surround the dining room.

Fruition (1313 E. 6th Ave., 303/831-1962, www.fruitionrestaurant.com, 5pm-9pm Tues.-Thurs., 5pm-9:30pm Fri.-Sat., $25-29) annually garners local and national awards for best chef, best farm-to-table cuisine, traveler's choice, and many more. Foodies can't stop raving about chef Alex Seidel's contemporary take on comfort food that emphasizes locally grown and seasonal ingredients. This small and cozy restaurant, where meals are paired with the perfect wine, is ideal for a special date night. In winter, there's fanciful chicken noodle soup; in summer, there are crisp, flavorful salads plus more extravagant entrées that include duck breast, pork belly, and pastas. Reservations are recommended.

Mizuna (225 E. 7th Ave., 303/832-4778, http://mizunadenver.com, 5pm-9pm Tues.-Sat., $28-45) is a must for anyone serious about food and gourmet dining. It has been voted Denver's number one restaurant by *Zagat*, and chef-owner Frank Bonanno has received nods from many other publications. Mizuna is known for delectable lobster mac and cheese, as well as artfully presented ostrich loin and beef tenderloin. The seasonal menu is changed monthly, and the service is as impeccable as the food, with servers attending to every need but not aggressively so. Reservations are strongly recommended.

★ **Potager** (1109 Ogden St., 303/832-5788, www.potagerrestaurant.com, 5pm-9pm Tues.-Sat., $10-29) was on the cutting edge of seasonal, locally grown ingredients long before those ideas became mainstream. Across the street from a laundry and a grocery store in the thick of the Capitol Hill neighborhood,

Potager stands out as a simply elegant restaurant in the clatter of the city. There are tables out back, where the chef grows a few herbs and small vegetables, while inside crisp white tablecloths stand out against the pockmarked concrete walls. The menu changes frequently to keep up with what is seasonally available; some examples include spinach and nettle soup in spring, Colorado lamb and beef, fresh garden salads, and summer desserts with Colorado-grown peaches, rhubarb, and strawberries. No reservations are accepted; the best time to come is early or on a weeknight. There is limited free parking behind the restaurant.

Diners

There are very few places open 24 hours in Denver, and **Pete's Kitchen** (1962 E. Colfax Ave., 303/321-3139, www.petesrestaurants.com, 7am-9pm Mon.-Thurs., 24 hours Fri.-Sat., noon-9pm Sun., $5-25) has folks lined up out the door and waiting in any weather on weekends after the bars have closed and for breakfast. The food and ambience is classic diner with a Greek flair. Breakfast basics like eggs, pancakes, and hash browns are always available, as are gyros and souvlaki and burgers and burritos. Driving along East Colfax, look for the neon sign of a chubby chef flipping burgers.

The idea at **SAME Café** (2023 E. Colfax Ave., 720/530-6853, www.soallmayeat.org, 11am-2:30pm Mon.-Sat.) is simple: There are no prices, but the food is not free. Customers are expected to pay what they can, or what they feel their meal is worth, by dropping cash in a can by the door. The goal is in the name: So All May Eat (SAME). And not eat just any food, but food made from fresh, organic ingredients. The menu changes daily, based on the availability of what's in season, but it generally includes soups, salads, pizzas, and desserts. If people cannot afford to pay anything for their meal, they are asked to do work at the restaurant as payment.

Latin American

At ★ **Tequila & Whiskey** (1514 York St., 720/475-1337, http://tacostequilawhiskey.com, 3pm-9pm Thurs., 4pm-10pm Fri., 11am-10pm Sat., 11am-9pm Sun., $3-11), formerly Pinche Tacos, order one taco at a time or order them like doughnuts—by the dozen—depending on your favorite. Just be sure to order *quesa a la plancha* (a fried salty cheese with a dollop of tomatillo salsa), *rajas con crema y maiz* (a creamy corn dish with green chiles), and the *carnitas* (pork with pickled red onions) as well. The restaurant also has a dizzying selection of tequilas. The vibe is almost like a food-truck dining experience, with tight quarters and loud music—but it's all about the food and not the conversation anyway.

Vegetarian

City, O' City (210 E. 13th Ave., 303/318-9844, www.cityocitydenver.com, 10am-10pm daily, $6-25) is a pizza place, a coffee shop, a sandwich shop, and a bar all in one, where any eating and drinking needs throughout the day and into the night can be met. Its central location on the southern edge of the Capitol Hill neighborhood makes it walking distance from downtown and the Golden Triangle, and it attracts everyone from lawmakers to tattooed hipsters who call the neighborhood home.

Denver's premier vegan restaurant, ★ **WaterCourse Foods** (837 E. 17th Ave., 303/832-7313, www.watercoursefoods.com, 11am-9pm Mon.-Thurs., 10am-10pm Fri.-Sun., $10-14), has an all-day menu that specializes in creative ways to eat tofu, salad, tempeh, pasta, and, of course, vegetables. Try the tamales for breakfast or dinner and design your own salad. There's also a wine and beer list, a variety of teas, and fresh smoothies. The spacious and comfortable setting make this a place where you want to stay and savor your meal.

HIGHLANDS

Coffee and Tea

Novo Coffee (3617 W. 32nd Ave., 303/749-0100, www.novocoffee.com, 6:30am-4pm Mon.-Fri., 7am-5pm Sat.-Sun.) has multiple cafés in Denver. The family-owned business sources beans from all over the world and roasts them in its local Denver roasting facility. Pop into the café for an espresso—and be prepared to share a table with the laptop brigade—or make a reservation at the roastery for an educational "cupping" session (coffee tasting).

Breakfast and Brunch

After being open for about two seconds, the ★ **Wooden Spoon Café & Bakery** (2418 W. 32nd Ave., 303/999-0327, www.woodenspoondenver.com, 8am-1pm Wed.-Sun., $7-11) became a neighborhood favorite for its scrumptious breakfast pastries (apple tarts, blueberry scones, croissants, and more) and hearty sandwiches. Located in a historic building amid a block filled with restaurants, the Wooden Spoon feels like a European shop. Or perhaps it's the strict rules on no screens—no laptops or phones allowed—that make it feel old-fashioned.

Barbecue

Westerners love good barbecue. Luckily, there are several great places to find it in Denver. **Ragin' Hog BBQ** (4361 Lowell Blvd., 303/859-6003, http://raginhogbbq.com, 11am-7pm Tues.-Sat., $13-25) offers pork, chicken, hot links, and ribs, all smoked daily and served with sides like collards, potato salad, and mac and cheese. Sauces are decidedly Southern (no Kansas City-style 'cue here), and meats are available by the pound for catered parties and backyard barbecues. This cash-only spot will close early if they sell out, so don't dally!

Burgers

Craving a basic meal? Look no farther than **Park Burger Highlands** (2643 W. 32nd Ave., 303/862-8461, http://parkburger.com, 11:30am-9pm daily, $7-11) for a burger, hot dog, and fries. What makes Park Burger worth a stop is the fact that the burgers are not that basic. Along with never-frozen beef burgers, options include a turkey burger, a veggie burger, and a buffalo burger; turn one of those into a specialty burger with cheese, onions, egg, guacamole, and more. Then wash it all down with a milkshake, beer, wine, or cocktail.

Contemporary

Brazen Denver (4450 W. 38th Ave., Suite 130, 720/638-1242, www.brazendenver.com, 5pm-10pm Mon.-Sat., $5-27) boldly opens its doors to local and visiting diners, offering a warm, authentic dining experience in a rustic-chic space. Try the deviled eggs, braised meatballs, and roast chicken. Sitting outside? Stay after dark to enjoy a cocktail around the fire pit.

Duo Restaurant (2413 W. 32nd Ave., 303/477-4141, www.duorestaurants.com, 5pm-9pm Mon.-Thurs., 5pm-10pm Fri., 10am-2pm and 5pm-10pm Sat., 10am-2pm Sun., $19-28) is on the ground floor of a large historic building that has been renovated and filled with shops and restaurants. Pick a seat next to one of the large windows and watch the people stroll by, or sit at one of the tables along the exposed brick walls for a more intimate evening while you dine on farm-to-table entrées featuring Colorado specialties. Note that they have a 22 percent "service and hospitality" fee rather than a tipping system.

Linger (2030 W. 30th Ave., 303/993-3120, www.lingerdenver.com, 5pm-9pm Tues.-Thurs., 5pm-11pm Fri., 10am-2:30pm and 5pm-10pm Sat., 10am-2:30pm and 5pm-9pm Sun., $7-33) found a way to turn a piece of the historic Olinger mortuary into a hot spot. Chef Justin Cucci created a menu of eclectic world tastes. Translation: Come here with a group of friends and order lots of small plates to sample dishes evocative of Asia, Africa, the Middle East, America, Europe, and Eurasia. The drink menu is nearly as extensive, with beers from as far as China, wines from Colorado and Austria, and cocktails with curious names like Corpse Reviver. There is even a kids' menu (American-style with chicken tenders and mac and cheese). Reservations are advised.

Playing off the theme of the building's

1

2

3

former incarnation as a car repair garage, staffers at **Root Down** (1600 W. 33rd Ave., 303/993-4200, www.rootdowndenver.com, 5pm-9pm Mon.-Thurs., 11am-2pm and 5pm-10pm Fri., 10am-2:30pm and 5pm-10pm Sat., 10am-2:30pm and 5pm-9pm Sun., $13-32) don mechanics' shirts, and some of the old signs (like one reading Tires) remain. The theme of the food is global, inspired by local ingredients. Root Down strives to please the customer with options to make some entrées gluten-free or vegan, and a promise that a majority of the ingredients are organic. My fave is the veggie burger sliders with scrumptious sweet potato fries on the side.

There's so much to love about **The Truffle Table** (2556 15th St., 303/455-9463, www.truffletable.net, 2pm-9pm Tues.-Thurs. and Sun., 2pm-10pm Fri.-Sat., $7-27) in the LoHi area. The place is quiet enough to have lengthy conversations with your friends over dinner, and shared small plates make the meal part of the conversation as you dip into fondue and select meats and cheeses. Come on a Wednesday for all-you-can-eat raclette night.

Asian

Come hungry but patient for the flavorful, savory ramen that **Uncle** (2215 W. 32nd Ave., 303/433-3263, www.uncleramen.com, 5pm-10pm Mon.-Sat., $3-16) is known for. A seat at the bar affords a great view of the kitchen, where airy *bao* buns and rich pots of broth steam and bubble away. Start with an order of pork belly buns before diving into a hot bowl of the good stuff. Order the duck ramen with a soft egg over curly noodles and shoyu broth, or add an "umami bomb" of miso bacon jam or spicy seven-pepper for even more yum factor.

Italian

Parisi (4401 Tennyson St., 303/561-0234, www.parisidenver.com, 11am-8pm Mon.-Sat., noon-8pm Sun., $10-19) is a modern take on a traditional neighborhood pizzeria and market, with wonderful sandwiches, wood-oven-baked pizzas, and salads for lunch or dinner. Customers line up to place their orders, then take their number to a table. While waiting for their food, they can browse the Italian market and deli or get gelato and other pastry desserts for something to take home. Downstairs is **Parisi's Firenze a Tavola** (Florence at Your Table, 303/561-0234, 5:30pm-10pm Wed.-Sat.), a more formal restaurant with a full bar that is perfect for a private party or special date night.

Latin American

Off the beaten path of Highlands hot spots, **Cafe Brazil** (4408 Lowell Blvd., 303/480-1877, www.cafebrazildenver.com, 5pm-9pm Wed.-Sat., $16-24) remains a perennial favorite for South American fare. With orange walls and blue tablecloths, it has a playful and casual feel. My personal favorites here include *palmito* (hearts of palm in a white wine cream sauce) and the *feijoada completa,* a Brazilian black bean stew with fried bananas, collard greens, sausages, and oranges. House-made desserts change daily. Reservations are recommended.

As Denver's Highlands neighborhood has changed, it has lost some of the Mexican restaurants that filled the storefronts for years. But **Patzcuaro's** (2616 W. 32nd Ave., 303/455-4389, www.patzcuaros.com, 11am-8pm Mon.-Thurs., 11am-9pm Fri.-Sun., $8-17) has held its ground and remains a favorite for locals still craving pork smothered with green chili and platters of enchiladas or burritos. Menudo is served on weekends only. The favorite drink here is a *liquado,* a very sweet fruit juice loved by adults and children.

Thai

Denver has a fair number of Thai restaurants to choose from, but **Swing Thai** (4370 Tennyson St., 303/477-1994, www.swingthai.com, 11am-8pm Sun.-Thurs., 11am-9pm Fri.-Sat., $10-14) stands out for their dependably good food, appealing decor, and fast service. This location is one of their largest, with a

1: Rioja **2:** Linger **3:** Little Man Ice Cream

bar, banquette, and tables inside as well as a patio out back. In an effort to be more health-conscious, Swing Thai offers gluten-free and vegan menu items, as well as all-natural beef and chicken and organic tofu. Takeout and delivery are available.

Dessert

You would think people had never tasted ice cream before **Little Man Ice Cream** (2620 16th St., 303/455-3811, www.littlemanicecream.com, 11am-midnight daily in summer, check for winter hours) came along. Built on the site of the Olinger Mortuary in the Lower Highlands neighborhood, Little Man is a giant replica of a silver milk can, and named after its founder's nickname. People gaze at the Denver skyline as they wait in the line that stretches up the block all summer. Little Man Ice Cream runs out of the favorite flavors early every day, but cross your fingers for the salted Oreo because it is the best.

WASHINGTON PARK AND CHERRY CREEK

Breakfast and Brunch

It's crepes for breakfast, lunch, and dinner at **Crêpes 'N' Crêpes** (2816 E. 3rd Ave., 303/320-4184, http://crepencrepe.online, 8am-3pm Sun.-Mon., 8am-9pm Tues.-Sat., $9-15), and still people can't seem to get enough of them. Perhaps it's because this is a true French *crêperie,* with French sweet or savory ingredients filling the thin pancakes cooked on hot French griddles—even the menu is in French (with English translations).

Cafés

It started out as a place for sweets and just kept growing until **Devil's Food Bakery & Cookery** (1024 S. Gaylord St., 303/777-9555, www.devilsfooddenver.com, 7am-5pm daily; 1020 S. Gaylord St., 303/733-7448, 7am-2:30pm daily; $10-17) turned into two side-by-side restaurants. Whether you're in the mood for a full breakfast, lunch, brunch, or supper, or simply tea, coffee, or just something sinfully sweet, Devil's Food Bakery & Cookery can fill your craving. Try the grapefruit tart, vanilla-bean cream puffs, or double-chocolate "doughnut." There can be a wait for brunch on weekends.

Burgers

What people like about the **Cherry Cricket** (2641 E. 2nd Ave., 303/322-7666, www.cherrycricket.com, 11am-2am daily, $6-9) is that it hasn't changed much, if at all, with the rest of the neighborhood. Year after year, this is the place to go in Denver for a green chili burger—or any burger. They also serve Mexican food, sandwiches, and salads. There is free parking in the lot behind the building. There's now a location at 2220 Blake Street, near Coors Field.

Steakhouse

A former Super Bowl-winning quarterback for the Denver Broncos, John Elway is one of Denver's biggest celebrities. For years he put his name on car dealerships, but now he has switched to restaurants. **Elway's** (2500 E. 1st Ave., 303/399-5353, www.elways.com, 4pm-9pm Tues.-Sat., $16-78) is a brightly lit modern steakhouse with lots of windows and a piano bar that offers seafood, steak, and a few surprises, like tacos for an appetizer and s'mores for dessert. Certainly the restaurant draws a lot of sports fans hoping for a glimpse of Elway himself as well as other celebrities. Other locations are downtown at the Ritz-Carlton Hotel (1881 Curtis St., 303/312-3107), at Denver International Airport (Concourse B, 303/342-7777), and in Vail.

Asian

★ **Sushi Den** (1487 S. Pearl St., 303/777-0826, www.sushiden.net, 4:30pm-9pm Sun.-Thurs., 4:30pm-10pm Fri.-Sat., $8-17) has a consistently long wait, but no one is complaining—it's see and be seen here among a young good-looking clientele in the cramped waiting area and bar. Pull up a chair to watch and listen as the sushi chefs make their beautiful creations, or grab a table and start ordering sushi or another of the house specialties. Then sink your teeth into what many consider to be the city's best sushi. The chefs also take custom orders.

An offshoot of Sushi Den comes in the form of **Izakaya Den** (1518 S. Pearl St., 303/777-0691, www.izakayaden.net, 4:30pm-9pm Sun.-Thurs., 4:30pm-10pm Fri.-Sat., $12-16). Certainly this serene restaurant benefits from the overflow crowd at Sushi Den across the street, but Izakaya Den has a reputation of its own for its delicate and flavorful small plates. In addition to sushi and sashimi, Izakaya has a Japanese-Mediterranean fusion tapas menu featuring combinations like Kobe beef with edamame and watermelon.

French

Owned by Philippe Delgrange and Rick Wahlstedt, **Le Bilboquet Denver** (299 St. Paul St., 303/835-9999, www.lebilboquetdenver.com, 11:30am-9pm Mon.-Thurs., 11:30am-10pm Fri., 11am-10pm Sat., 10:30am-9pm Sun., $16-32) opened in 2019 as an outpost of New York's Le Bilboquet. Open for brunch, lunch, and dinner, this restaurant has a solid reputation for serving authentic Parisian food.

Italian

Everyone who works at **Barolo Grill** (3030 E. 6th Ave., 303/393-1040, www.barologrilldenver.com, 5pm-9:30pm Tues.-Thurs., 5pm-10pm Fri.-Sat., $20-34) is an expert on northern Italy, since the owner takes the entire staff there each year to experience the inspiration for the restaurant's food and wine. This firsthand knowledge equals first-class service that matches the excellent menu, which changes seasonally with the exception of a single dish: the braised duckling with kalamata olives. Barolo also offers a five-course tasting menu with optional wine pairing. The grill has a warm and inviting atmosphere year-round, but a table next to the fireplace is especially cozy in winter. Reservations are recommended on weekends.

On the corner of a quiet block in Cherry Creek North is one of the neighborhood's best restaurants. **Cucina Colore** (3041 E. 3rd Ave., 303/393-6917, www.cucinacolore.com, 11:30am-10pm Mon.-Sat., 11:30am-9pm Sun., $13-34) offers upscale contemporary Italian food and a pleasant wine list for lunch and dinner. Try the *pollo e orzo* salad or a crisp pizza with the house sangria for lunch. Patio seating at umbrella-sheltered tables is available on both sides of the restaurant, and indoor tables are bathed in natural light from the many windows.

Occupying a busy corner near Washington Park on Old South Gaylord Street, **Homegrown Tap & Dough** (1001 S. Gaylord St., 720/459-8736, www.tapanddough.com, 11:30am-9pm daily, $5-15) is a lively, friendly bar and restaurant with a fun outdoor patio and expansive bar seating. This is primarily a pizza joint, with chewy, charred wood-fired pies of all toppings and sauces. And since Homegrown comes from the owners of legendary Park Burger, they have a killer burger on the menu. It's family-friendly and often crowded, with a reliable draft list of local suds.

GREATER DENVER

Many of the city's ethnic restaurants are found beyond downtown and surrounding neighborhoods. You might need to take the light rail train or drive for one of these culinary adventures.

Dim Sum

East of downtown in Aurora, **Mason's Dumpling Shop** (9655 E. Montview Blvd., Aurora, 303/600-8998, https://masonsdumplingshop.com, 11am-2pm and 4:30pm-8pm Wed.-Mon.) has steamed, boiled, and pan-fried dumplings, as well as noodle bowls, rice bowls, and buns. What you don't see at other restaurants though are the sweet and sour lotus roots you can try as an appetizer—so pretty!

French

South of downtown in the Tech Center area, **Le French Denver** (4901 S. Newport St.,

Wild West Dining

For a one-of-a-kind dining experience in the West, **The Fort** (19192 Hwy. 8, Morrison, 303/697-4771, www.thefort.com, 4:30pm-7:45pm Sun. and Tues.-Thurs., 4:30pm-8:45pm Fri.-Sat., $28-59) is the place to go. Inspired by a drawing of a historic fort, Sam Arnold bought the land in the 1960s and hired a crew to build (or recreate) a true 1840s fort. When it wasn't feasible as a private home, Arnold decided to make it a restaurant and studied cooking so that he could provide only the best ingredients and menu. Today, with Arnold's daughter Holly Arnold Kinney at the helm, The Fort offers what can only be described as exotic Western, with a large variety of game meats, trout, Rocky Mountain oysters, Southwestern spices, and other unexpected culinary delights. A gift shop is on-site, and annual Western-themed events such as a powwow are held here. Reservations required for indoor dining.

720/710-8963, https://lefrenchdenver.com, 11am-9pm Tues.-Thurs., 11am-10pm Fri., 8am-10pm Sat., 8am-2:30pm Sun., $15-42) is special because it is both true French cuisine while also offering some dishes that are Senegalese French. Entrées include *gniiri* (Senegalese creamed cornmeal with peanuts and black-eyed peas), a selection of savory and sweet crepes, *moules frites* (mussels and fries), and much more.

Korean

For truly authentic Korean food, try **Funny Plus** (2779 S. Parker Rd., Aurora, 303/745-3477, www.funnyplus.us, 4pm-midnight Sun.-Thurs., 4pm-1am Fri.-Sat., $12-30), where you can sample Korean fried chicken, Korean barbecue, and Army Stew *(budae jjigae)*, made with kimchi, Spam, and ramen noodles.

Accommodations

Most of Denver's accommodations are within walking distance of recommended sights, shops, restaurants, bars, nightclubs, and recreation areas. Not only are many of these wonderful places to stay, they are also home to some of the city's top-notch restaurants and bars.

Budget travelers will have the toughest time finding a decent, affordable room that is very close to the action of the city's sports venues, bars, restaurants, and nightclubs. Options include hostels and a couple of hotels that overlook downtown from the eastern edge of the Highlands neighborhood. Bed-and-breakfasts in the Capitol Hill neighborhood give visitors the best chance to experience life like a local in an area of historic homes and a few apartment buildings. Capitol Hill is also close enough to downtown to walk. East of the city center, there is a strip of hotels along Quebec Street. While this is not walking distance from downtown, there are parks and restaurants nearby.

Some Denver hotels condone cannabis consumption but don't openly advertise. For links to these and marijuana-friendly rental properties, visit **Colorado Pot Guide** (www.coloradopotguide.com) or **Visit Denver** (Convention and Visitors Bureau, www.denver.org/hotels).

The rates listed are based on double occupancy in the high season (summer).

DOWNTOWN

$150-250

The AC Hotel Denver Downtown (750 15th St., 303/825-2888, www.marriott.com, $175-279) and **Le Meridien Denver**

Downtown (1475 California St., 303/893-1888, www.lemeridiendenverdowntown.com, $264-304) are two hotels in one. Both hotels are stylish, but Le Meridien has a European touch throughout. Features include a rooftop bar with fireplaces and views of the city and mountains, a workspace, and a bar and dining on the ground floor, and the location is a mere block away from the Colorado Convention Center. Check out the Moet & Chandon champagne vending machine in the lobby of Le Meridien for that last-minute celebration in life.

Catbird Hotel (3770 Walnut St., 720/990-5555, www.catbirdhotel.com, $200-300) in the RiNo area is a hybrid hotel offering extended stays of 90-plus nights as well as typical short stays of a night or two. These rooms are designed for you to make yourself at home with lofted beds, full kitchens, and pleasant seating areas for lounging about. Don't miss the rooftop bar and fabulous views! You can hang out for a drink, play cornhole, or snooze in a hammock up there.

Formerly the Comfort Inn, the **Holiday Inn Express Denver Downtown** (1715 Tremont Pl., 303/296-0400 or 888/465-4329, www.ihg.com, $150-299) has the perk of a relationship with The Brown Palace luxury hotel while lodging at this more affordable hotel just across the street. The two hotels are connected by a sky bridge, which allows easy access to The Brown's restaurants, shops, and spa. Guests can also order room service from The Brown. The Holiday Inn Express is just one block from the 16th Street Mall and its shops and restaurants, and it's an easy walk from the Colorado Convention Center. While rooms are budget-size, they are designed to maximize views of downtown, with little glimpses of mountains between skyscrapers when you face west, as well as windows letting in the natural light. There is a fee for parking.

The **Courtyard by Marriott Denver Downtown** (934 16th St., 303/571-1114, www.marriott.com, $189-399) is right on the 16th Street Mall and just down the street from the Denver Performing Arts Complex. Being near the Colorado Convention Center, the hotel is ready for business travelers too, with desks and high-speed internet access included in the rates. This is a pet-free and smoke-free hotel. Parking is tricky at the Courtyard, which offers $44-per-day on-site parking.

The **Sonesta Denver** (1450 Glenarm Place, 303/573-1450 or 877/227-6963, https://sonestahotel.com, $175-260), formerly the Crowne Plaza Denver Downtown Hotel, has a key location within walking distance of the Colorado Convention Center, the Denver Art Museum, the 16th Street Mall, and many restaurants and shops. The hotel offers a rooftop pool with city views, dining and drink options at Lockwood Kitchen & Bar, and designated Quiet Zone floors.

Guests need a sense of humor and playfulness to truly enjoy **The Curtis** (1405 Curtis St., 303/571-0300, http://thecurtis.com, $159-1,000) and its whimsical touches. The pet-friendly hotel is across the street from the Denver Performing Arts Complex and one block from the Colorado Convention Center, so it caters to a spectrum of theater types and business travelers, with an emphasis on youthful attitude. The common areas are themed, from Austin Powers to Elvis (whose voices can also be ordered for wake-up calls), and they offer "hyper-themed" rooms along with simple and contemporary rooms with modern amenities. Each of the hyper-themed rooms is unique: Disco, for example, has a lava lamp, a large poster of glitter shoes, and other touches that make you want to dance the night away.

The 14-story **Denver Marriott Residence Inn City Center** (1725 Champa St., 303/296-3444 or 800/331-3131, www.marriott.com, $169-439) features 229 studio and one-bedroom guest suites that include full kitchens, with separate living areas in the one-bedroom suites. There is both wired and wireless internet access throughout the hotel, in rooms as well as in the lobby and business center. After a hectic day of meetings, head up to the eighth floor and enjoy the rooftop hot tub for a relaxing soak amid the city lights.

At Hampton/Homewood Downtown

Denver, **Hampton Inn & Suites** (550 15th St., 303/623-5900, www.hamptoninndenver.com, $249-399) and the **Homewood Suites by Hilton** (303/534-7800) form a "combo hotel." Inside this single 13-story building are two distinctly different hotels—two lobbies, two front desks, unique decor for each, different kitchens for each, and 302 rooms to choose from in total. The name says it all—it's about proximity for convention-goers. Amenities include an indoor pool, a gym, complimentary high-speed internet access, and complimentary breakfast.

Pet-friendly **Hotel Monaco** (1717 Champa St., 303/296-1717 or 800/990-1303, www.monaco-denver.com, $199-499) has a modern chic design befitting the Kimpton brand. In addition to 189 guest rooms, there is a 24-hour fitness room available to guests, a spa and salon, and **Panzano** (5pm-9pm Tues.-Sat., $25-32), a top Denver restaurant featuring Italian fare. Complimentary hotel bicycles are available to guests, as well as dog/pet-walking or -sitting services on request for guests.

With nearly half of the 600-plus rooms designed for business travelers, the **Hilton Denver City Center** (1701 California St., 303/297-1300, www.hilton.com, $179-450) definitely has a niche clientele. It is a three-block walk from the convention center and has more than 25,000 square feet of meeting space, along with a full-service business center. The hotel also attracts leisure travelers and has laundry and babysitting services available for families. There is a fitness center and pool as well as Prospect's Urban Kitchen & Bar on-site.

Between the skyscrapers of downtown and the historic homes of the Five Points neighborhood is one of the most charming blocks in Denver, home to the ★ **Queen Anne Bed and Breakfast Inn** (2147-51 Tremont Place, 303/296-6666, www.queenannebnb.com, $165-230). The inn is made up of two separate late-1800s Victorian houses, connected by a large backyard and patio area. Typically bed-and-breakfasts are not the preferred lodging of business travelers, but because the Queen Anne is so close to downtown and many restaurants and sights, it attracts business travelers as well as tourists on a romantic getaway.

The **Sheraton Denver Downtown Hotel** (1550 Court Place, 303/893-3333 or 800/325-3535, www.sheratondenverdowntown.com, $182-432) anchors the east end of the 16th Street Mall. A portion of the 1,238 rooms are in an I. M. Pei-designed building. Features include an outdoor heated pool, a fitness center, and a selection of comfortable restaurants on the ground floor with windows to watch the world go by along the mall.

Paired with the Colorado Convention Center, the **Hyatt Regency** (650 15th St., 303/436-1234, www.hyatt.com, $189-650) was built to welcome business travelers to Denver. The 1,110 spacious rooms and suites afford mountain and city views, as does the hotel's Peaks Lounge on the 27th floor. Assembly Hall Bar + Market and Former Saint Craft Kitchen and Taps on the ground floor round out the food and drink options at this property. The state-of-the-art hotel features ergonomic chairs at workstations, high-speed wireless internet access, individual climate control, and the low-tech option of being able to open the windows in guest rooms.

Over $250

Since first opening its doors in 1892, one hotel has been a symbol of lodging elegance and luxury in Denver. So it's not that ★ **The Brown Palace Hotel and Spa** (321 17th St., 303/297-3111, www.brownpalace.com, $269-1,700) needed to be improved, but that's exactly what happened with a $10.5 million renovation that has given 200 rooms a contemporary look that still respects the classic Victorian bones of the hotel. The triangular building has a beautiful eight-story stained-glass atrium where visitors can enjoy cocktails or English tea service while listening to live piano music. The 230 rooms range from standard rooms to suites and remodeled presidential suites (so named for the many presidents who stayed in them, including Eisenhower, Roosevelt, and Reagan). The Brown is just a short walk from the Colorado State Capitol, the Denver Art Museum, and many other sights. Or stay in and enjoy the hotel's spa and salon, award-winning restaurants, and cigar bar. **Ship Tavern** (11am-10:30pm daily, $26-48) has an Old World pub atmosphere and an extensive menu of burgers, prime rib, Rocky Mountain trout, seafood, pasta, and salads, as well as live music (8:30pm Wed.-Sat.). The atmosphere at the **Palace Arms** (5pm-10pm Tues.-Sat., $40-55) is one of opulence, and it has long been considered one of Denver's very best restaurants.

The Brown Palace also capitalizes on having truly local amenities: sip a Palace Pale Ale made from the hotel's own artesian well water, or sample some of the spa's Rooftop Honey Amenity Line of beauty products—made from honey produced on the hotel's rooftop, where the hotel maintains a bee colony (this is the only hotel in Denver, if not the United States, with its own beekeeper). The daily afternoon tea service also features the honey. Colorado residents can take advantage of discounted rates on summer weekends thanks to the "Local Love" program, when fabulous rooms can be had for a discount.

The 13-story **Magnolia Hotel** (818 17th St., 303/607-9000, www.magnoliahotels.com, $249-449) is in a luxuriously remodeled 1906 bank building with guest rooms and suites, some with fireplaces. With its proximity to the convention center and the city's business district, the Magnolia caters to guests who appreciate high-speed internet access and a conference room. The hotel is also pet-friendly. Harry's Bar and the billiards room offer places to wind down before calling it a night.

The **Embassy Suites by Hilton Denver-Downtown/Convention Center** (1420 Stout St., 303/592-1000, http://embassysuites1.hilton.com, $329-400) is taking full advantage of its across-the-street proximity to the Colorado Convention Center. There are 400 rooms, plus meeting and banquet space. And the best part: daily complimentary cooked-to-order breakfast and a nightly Manager's Reception in the atrium. It's not exclusive to business travelers—this hotel boasts family-friendly amenities that include a children's menu, cribs, and playpens.

Not just one of Denver's finer hotels, the **Four Seasons Hotel Denver** (1111 14th St., 303/389-3000, www.fourseasons.com/Denver, $650-1,125) is also an important piece of the city's skyline, with a distinctive spike sitting atop 45 stories of residences and guest rooms. It hosts a unique combination of travelers and locals, which means that you might be swimming next to a Denverite in the third-story pool, or mixing it up with conventioneers in the hotel's spa. The **EDGE Restaurant & Bar** (303/389-3343, www.edgerestaurantdenver.com, 7am-10pm Sun.-Thurs., 7am-10:30pm Fri.-Sat., $42-65) just off the grand lobby feels elegant for dinner and casual for lunch. What you see is what you get here—the photos on the website accurately show the terrific views of downtown and the mountains, as well as the luxurious decor.

One of the larger downtown hotels is the **Grand Hyatt Denver** (1750 Welton St., 303/295-1234, http://denver.grand.hyatt.com, $399-499), with 512 rooms. Like other downtown hotels, the Grand Hyatt is walking distance to the Colorado Convention Center, the 16th Street Mall, and numerous sights, restaurants, and other attractions. Guests can enjoy a game of tennis on the hotel's rooftop or swim in the indoor pool. You'll have access to Courier Kitchen and Bar and the Fireside Bar.

As Denver's boutique luxury hotel, the ★ **Hotel Teatro** (1100 14th St., 303/228-1100, www.hotelteatro.com, $299-519) never disappoints with its excellent service, comfortable rooms (with Frette linens), and award-winning restaurant. The hotel is named for its proximity to the Denver Performing Arts Complex across the street, and the lobby is decorated with photographs and costumes of past productions. Amenities at the 110-room Teatro include complimentary transportation in a Cadillac Escalade anywhere in downtown, Godiva chocolates with turndown service, and many perks for pets.

The historic Colorado National Bank

1

2

3

4

building has been transformed into the **Renaissance Denver Downtown City Center** (918 17th St., 303/867-8100, www.rendendowntown.com, $419-599). Of course you're here to stay in one of the 221 guest rooms and suites, but what's special about this hotel is the atrium, where white marble columns dominate the space and restored murals by renowned artist Allen Tupper True adorn the walls (other murals by True are found in the City and County Building, Civic Center Park, and the Colorado State Capitol). This lobby has ample seating, a bar, and a hip ambience for hanging out before you hit the town for the evening. The building's banking history is a bit of a theme in the decor, with an old vault that serves as a meeting room. Dining options include Range, open for breakfast, lunch, and dinner, and the Teller Bar, open for happy hour and dinner with a yummy selection of apps to go with your cocktails.

The Ritz-Carlton (1881 Curtis St., 303/312-3800, www.ritzcarlton.com, $589-3,500) is a plush place to stay, either as an extravagant stopover after a week of skiing and snowboarding or while on a business trip. The hotel's 202 rooms all have marble baths with two sinks and separate oversize bathtubs for soaking, as well as 37-inch flat-screen TVs. Guests dine at the award-winning **Elway's** (303/312-3107, 4pm-9pm Tues.-Sat., $16-78), a popular steakhouse owned by NFL Hall of Fame quarterback John Elway.

GOLDEN TRIANGLE, LINCOLN PARK, AND SOBO

Over $250

★ **The Art Hotel** (1201 Broadway, 303/572-8000, www.thearthotel.com, $309-419) immediately has its own niche thanks to its $100 million art collection on display. Located on the same block as the Hamilton wing of the Denver Art Museum, the hotel claims to be the "only hotel of its kind to showcase original works of this caliber." The in-house curator, Diane Vanderlip, former curator of the Denver Art Museum, selected contemporary art—Andy Warhol, Claes Oldenburg, Ed Ruscha—for the hotel's two galleries and other spaces. Each floor of the hotel is "inspired" by a particular artist and their style is "translated" in the rooms on that floor. With 165 rooms, that's a lot of style. Dining and cocktail options include FIRE Terrace (4th floor), with a view of the city's skyline, FIRE Lounge (next to the main restaurant) for intimate cocktails, and FIRE, which serves breakfast, lunch, and dinner. Get comfortable in the Living Room, where you can watch TV, sip an adult beverage, or just visit with friends. When selecting your room, think of what you want your window to frame: a museum view, a mountain view, or an urban view.

LODO AND PLATTE RIVER VALLEY

Under $150

I declare this Denver's most stylish hostel. The ★ **Hostel Fish** (1217 20th St., 303/954-0962, www.hostelfish.com, $45 shared bunkroom, $87-170 private room) is only a couple of blocks from Coors Field and many of the bars in LoDo. The historic building has a varied history: It was once home to a saloon, a brothel, and a peep show. On the second floor are the affordable accommodations, which include amenities like free use of iPads and a daily housekeeping. The rooms are best described as "urban rustic," with wooden floors, stylish baths—and a view of the parking lot below.

$150-250

Visitors to ★ **Springhill Suites Denver Downtown** (1190 Auraria Pkwy., 303/705-7300, www.springhillsuitesdenver.com, $189-369) can rest assured that the employees will be graded on everything they do: This is one of only 10 college student-operated hotels in the country, and the only one in an urban setting. Springhill Suites is on the Metropolitan State University of Denver campus, and

1: Hotel Teatro's lobby **2:** The Art Hotel's terrace **3:** the lobby of The Curtis **4:** Magnolia Hotel's bar

approximately 80 percent of the staff are students enrolled in the school's hospitality program. There are 150 guest rooms, meeting space, and more. Let's give them an A-plus for being Denver's first LEED Gold hotel, which means this building promotes clean, renewable energy. Hospitality students aren't the only ones represented here: All of the art you see was made by students, faculty, and alumni of MSU.

The renovated historic ★ **Oxford Hotel** (1600 17th St., 303/628-5400, www.theoxfordhotel.com, $240-500) is no longer relying on guests who are interested in Victorian charm alone; it is also meeting the needs of busy executives. The hotel had its beginnings in 1891, when Union Station was a thriving transportation hub for the Rockies and all those train travelers needed a classy place to rest. The Oxford was designed by Frank Edbrooke, who also designed The Brown Palace Hotel. The 80 rooms are still appointed with lovely antiques, but now they include high-speed internet access and dual phone lines. Stop in the **Cruise Room** (4pm-10pm Wed.-Sun.) for a cocktail and for a feel of what it was like back in the day.

Over $250

For loyal Westin clients, the **Westin Tabor Center** (1672 Lawrence St., 303/572-9100, www.westindenverdowntown.com, $250-400) will not disappoint, with its signature Heavenly Bed and Heavenly Bath, as well as some rooms with views of the Rocky Mountains. The hotel's location can't be beat: It is right off the 16th Street Mall and just a couple blocks from historic Larimer Square and several restaurants, shops, and nightclubs. In town for a baseball game? You can walk over to Coors Field from here.

There's a new micro-district in town and it's home to **The Maven Hotel** (1850 Wazee St., 720/460-2727, www.themavenhotel.com, $256-399) in the Dairy Block. A former dairy is now home to this swanky 172-room hotel filled with a curated art collection, Kachina Southwestern Grill Huckleberry Roasters, Poka Lola Social Club, and gift shops, plus **Milk Market** (303/792-8242, www.denvermilkmarket.com, 7am-10pm Mon.-Thurs., 7am-midnight Fri.-Sat., 7am-9pm Sun.), a food hall of 15 different restaurants and bars. Rooms have city views and ballpark views, some with balconies for chilling out on a warm night. The Maven was home to the crew of *Top Chef Colorado,* and it's

Hostel Fish

easy walking distance from Union Station, Coors Field, and the train to and from Denver International Airport.

Across the street from Coors Field at McGregor Square is the **Rally Hotel** (1600 20th St., 720/907-1234, www.therallyhotel.com, $250-500), with 182 rooms and a pet-friendly sensibility. There's a touch of a baseball theme, with guests "being treated like MVPs" and The Grandstand Café (where ice cream comes in a mini Colorado Rockies helmet), as well as the main restaurant, The Original, sticking to American classics (like baseball itself).

Oh là là! When friends and family come to town, the ★ **Crawford Hotel** (1701 Wynkoop St., 720/460-3700, www.thecrawfordhotel.com, $289-649) is where I suggest they stay. The transformation of **Union Station,** Denver's historic train station, into a 112-room luxury hotel is fabulous and worth a visit even if you're not staying here. The area where people once whiled away their time waiting for trains is now the Great Hall, with a flower shop, a handful of shops and restaurants, tabletop shuffleboard, and plenty of comfortable seating. You might be surprised to look up from the Great Hall and see hotel rooms, but there is minimal noise and full privacy in these Pullman rooms (evocative of train sleeping cars). All the rooms and suites—and the hallways—have artwork by Colorado artists.

Among the restaurants in Union Station are **Mercantile** (720/460-3733, www.mercantiledenver.com, 11am-2pm and 5pm-9pm Tues.-Sat., $15-32), **Snooze** (303/825-3536, www.snoozeeatery.com, 6:30am-2:30pm Mon.-Fri., 6:30am-4pm Sat.-Sun., $8-13), **Stoic & Genuine** (303/640-3474, www.stoicandgenuine.com, 11am-10pm Sun.-Thurs., 11am-11pm Fri.-Sat., $17-38), **Next Door** (720/460-3730, www.thekitchen.com, 11am-9pm daily, $10-17), and the **Milkbox Ice Creamery** (720/460-3707, www.milkboxicecream.com, noon-7pm Mon.-Fri., noon-8pm Sat.-Sun.). Bars include the **Cooper Lounge** (720/460-3738, www.cooperlounge.com, 4pm-midnight daily, $7-23), with its unique view to the west, and the Terminal Bar; both have a selection of Colorado craft brews. Shops include the **Tattered Cover Book Store** (www.tatteredcover.com, 10am-8pm daily) and **5 Green Boxes** (720/460-3705, www.5greenboxes.com, 10am-7pm Mon.-Thurs., 10am-9pm Fri.-Sat., 11am-5pm Sun.). Guests have access to the Oxford Hotel's spa, half a block away.

The Crawford is the only hotel in Denver where you can arrive at the back door by train or buy your train tickets for your next trip. The central location is ideal—mere blocks from Coors Field, the Museum of Contemporary Art Denver, Larimer Square, and the 16th Street Mall, from where a free bus will zip you a mile east to the Civic Center Park and more.

To the west of Union Station is a new urban forest of skyscrapers in which you'll find the **Hotel Born** (1600 Wewatta St., 303/323-0024, www.hotelborndenver.com, $257-357), a Kimpton property. The theme here? "Alpine modern," which conjures up images of A-frame houses for me, but of course it's very chic natural wood touches against sleek glass and metal. Speaking of wood, Citizen Rail is the on-site restaurant, offering wood-fired fare.

CAPITOL HILL AND CITY PARK

Under $150

It's a bargain at the **11th Avenue Hotel and Hostel** (1112 Broadway, 303/894-0529, www.11thavenuehotelandhostel.com, $29 dorm room, $53 private room with shared bath, $65 private room with private bath), which is just steps from the Denver Art Museum, History Center Colorado, Civic Center Park, the Colorado State Capitol, and many other local sights. All accommodations include use of the community room and Wi-Fi.

The flip side of modern accommodations is found at **The Holiday Chalet** (1820 E. Colfax

Ave., 303/437-8245, www.theholidaychalet.com, $120-210), but that's not a bad thing. This 1896 restored brownstone with 10 guest rooms has a homey style and feel, with lacy curtains, flowery bedspreads, and antiques throughout.

$150-250

Historically known as the Croke-Patterson-Campbell Mansion, **The Patterson Inn** (428 E. 11th Ave., 303/955-5142, www.pattersoninn.com, $241-347) has a reputation as a haunted house. Built in 1891 from sandstone blocks, this castle-like building has been used as offices and apartments over the years, and has now been converted into nine guest rooms that highlight many of the original features, such as the hand-carved oak stairway and stained-glass windows. The rumors of ghosts began in the 1970s and surely will be part of the allure for some guests.

While certainly not unique to Denver, the **Warwick Hotel** (91776 Grant St., 303/861-2000, www.warwickdenver.com, $189-389) has an outstanding reputation that is upheld here. The 219 large rooms and suites include marble baths and antique European furniture, with ample room for sitting on comfortable chairs and couches. Amenities include a fitness room with views of the city, a heated rooftop pool that is open year-round, and dining at the inviting Gattara restaurant, with outdoor patio seating for warmer days and indoor tables near the hearth in winter.

HIGHLANDS

$150-250

There are limited lodging options within the Highlands neighborhood. Located on the eastern edge of Highlands and perched on a hill overlooking downtown, the **Hampton Inn & Suites** (2728 Zuni St., 303/455-4588, www.hamptoninn.com, $169-209) is a relative bargain compared to many of the hotels right in downtown. The 62 guest rooms and public areas are pretty basic, with both smoking and nonsmoking options, and there's a pool. Just off the top of an I-25 exit ramp, the hotel is convenient for road-weary travelers.

The 189-room **Residence Inn Denver Downtown** (2777 Zuni St., 303/458-5318, www.marriott.com, $179-209) is also on the eastern edge of the Highlands neighborhood, within walking distance of Empower Field at Mile High, the Ball Arena, and all downtown restaurants, shops, and parks. Hemmed in by a couple of busy streets and a gas station, the hotel's location is a bit odd, but the entire property is fenced in and in a world of its own.

Over $250

Life House, Lower Highlands (3638 Navajo St., 866/466-7534, www.lifehousehotels.com, $500-750) celebrates the neighborhood's Victorian-era architecture and history with a modern flair. The guest rooms are designed for groups, with bunk beds that look like they are from another time and have thick drapes to pull across at bedtime. There are also traditional rooms with a king-size bed instead of bunks. On-site restaurant Wildflower emphasizes Colorado ingredients in a predominantly vegetarian Italian menu.

CHERRY CREEK

$150-250

Under 35? You'll probably love **MOXY Denver Cherry Creek** (240 Josephine St., 303/463-6699, http://moxy-hotels.marriott.com, $213-260), because it was designed with you in mind. Check in at a bar, play some games, and don't spend all your time in your room. Surely it's the place to be during the annual Cherry Creek Arts Festival over July 4th weekend.

Over $250

After years as a drop-in destination neighborhood, Cherry Creek has made itself into a vacation destination with the 196-room **JW Marriott** (150 Clayton Lane, 303/316-2700, www.jwmarriottdenver.com, $250-509) on the rim of the Cherry Creek North shopping district. This luxury hotel includes suites with surprising views of the Rocky Mountains to the west. The perks extend to canine guests, with special pet-friendly services available.

The Clayton (233 Clayton St., 303/551-1600, www.claytondenver.com, $300 and up for nonmembers), formerly the Inn at Cherry Creek, is a hotel as well as a members-only social club. The idea is to create a social networking place for the members, who have full access to the restaurants and bars on-site, the small outdoor pool, and the many meeting spaces. This modern boutique hotel has only seven rooms to choose from, but guests have access to all of the amenities. Nonmembers get a peek at the private club life while staying on property.

CANNABIS-FRIENDLY

Adagio Bed and Breakfast (1430 Race St., 303/370-6911, www.adagiodenverbb.com, $179-399) is all about infusing the traditional bed-and-breakfast with a touch of marijuana. Check in to one of the property's six imaginatively decorated suites and get ready for "wake and bake" themed breakfasts, a 4:20 Happy Hour celebration every day, and cannabis-infused massage therapy treatments. Talk about high hospitality. Formerly a regular bed-and-breakfast, the Victorian-era house maintains the same room names with a classical music theme (e.g., The Vivaldi).

Back in the day, when Molly Brown was in residence just a few blocks away, Capitol Hill was a neighborhood of stately mansions with views of the Rocky Mountains. While it's more crowded with apartments and office buildings now, inns like the ★ **Capitol Hill Mansion Bed and Breakfast Inn** (1207 Pennsylvania St., 800/839-9329, www.capitolhillmansion.com, $154-229) offer guests an opportunity to experience life in that bygone era, with a few modern touches. Meet your fellow guests over a gourmet breakfast each morning. Guests are free to smoke and vape on the balconies of rooms and in a designated area in the garden. Listen carefully and you might hear the ghosts of Colorado's mining barons giving their approval.

The Highlands neighborhood is brimming with exquisite turn-of-the-20th-century homes, but perhaps none more special than the 8,500-square-foot **Lumber Baron Inn & Gardens** (2555 W. 37th Ave., 303/477-8205, http://lumberbaron.com, $149-239). The inn is something of a special events center, hosting weddings and other events in the third-floor ballroom, as well as bed-and-breakfast guests. Each of the five well-appointed rooms has a whirlpool tub and free Wi-Fi. The inn is walking distance from some good restaurants and is only a mile from the sights of downtown. A spacious garden with flowering trees and seating areas make it more inviting in the spring and summer. The large bed-and-breakfast has embraced fun and quirky activities, from murder-mystery parties to casino dinners, so it's fitting that this luxury inn has turned cannabis-friendly (outside only).

A popular budget hotel in north Denver, **Clarion Hotel Denver Central** (200 W. 48th Ave., 303/296-4000, www.choicehotels.com, $119-149) is also the home of the 2015 High Times Cannabis Cup, and allows vaping in some of its rooms and marijuana smoking outside. Rooms go for less than $150 on a summer weekend.

GREATER DENVER

$150-250

When Denver International Airport (aka DIA) opened in the 1990s, the hotels across the road from the closed Stapleton Airport remained open. Eventually new hotels began popping up closer to DIA, but today, this area is an infill community; now the area is booming with malls and housing, and the old hotels are serving business travelers who don't want or need to go into downtown. Halfway between downtown and the airport, with complimentary shuttle service to DIA, the **Doubletree by Hilton Denver Central Park** (4040 Quebec St., 303/321-6666, http://doubletree3.hilton.com, $185-199) is a good bargain. Amenities include complimentary breakfast daily, an indoor pool, included Wi-Fi, and a fitness center. It should be noted that the Stapleton name came from a former mayor of Denver who was a member of the Ku Klux Klan, so in 2020, locals changed the name of their community to Central Park instead. You may see references to the former name of the airport that was once here and the original community name.

The **Embassy Suites** (7001 Yampa St., 303/574-3000, http://embassysuites1.hilton.com, $150-300) is quite close to Denver International Airport, just 6 miles (10 km) away. The hotel has 174 two-room suites spread out on six floors surrounding a six-story atrium. Amenities include a pool, a fitness center, meeting rooms, and airport shuttle service.

Hyatt Place Peña Station (6110 N. Panasonic Way, 720/405-4321, www.hyatt.com, $235-325) is a short walk from a station on the light rail system, which takes travelers to and from the airport. The lobby has a restaurant, coffee bar, games, and fun Western-themed local art. An indoor pool, fitness center, and complimentary breakfast round out the amenities. The hotel's dog greets visitors, letting you know that this place is pet-friendly. At 8 miles (13 km) from the airport, this hotel is convenient for travelers.

Over $250

The 14-story, 519-room ★ **Westin Denver International Airport** (8500 Peña Blvd., www.westindenverairport.com, 303/317-1800, $400-500) is part of the airport. The hotel mimics the airport's distinctive appearance, with glass walls in the shape of wings taking flight (though some have said it looks like a cruise ship or a mustache). Those walls offer nice views of the mountains to the west, and triple-pane windows mean no outdoor noise (like, say, a jet taking off) penetrates the rooms. Amenities include a conference center with ballrooms and boardrooms, a transit center, a pool, a fitness center, and restaurants.

Transportation and Services

GETTING THERE

Air

Denver International Airport (DEN, 8500 Peña Blvd., 303/342-2000, www.flydenver.com), known locally as DIA, is the major regional hub for domestic and international flights. This is the 5th-busiest airport in the country and the 20th-busiest in the world, with more than 69 million passengers annually (based on 2019 data). There isn't really a hometown airline anymore, but competition helps ensure sale fares are available both to and from this airport. The airport itself could be a destination, with offshoots of some of the city's best eateries, public art on display, and a hotel. The airport is about 25 miles (40 km) from downtown Denver, typically a 30-minute drive. You will exit the airport on Peña Boulevard heading west, then merge with I-70 west and continue west to I-25 south. Take the Speer Boulevard exit east to get to downtown. The traffic on I-70 can get jammed (especially during rush hour); an alternative route downtown is Quebec Street south to Martin Luther King Drive west, then left on Colorado Boulevard and right on 17th Street.

Denver International Airport is served by many international airlines, such as British Airways, Lufthansa, Aeroméxico, Icelandair, and Air Canada, and of course domestic airlines, including Southwest, United, American, and Delta. Budget carriers like JetBlue, Frontier, and Spirit also fly out of DIA.

AIRPORT TRANSPORTATION

When making your hotel reservations, ask if they have a free shuttle pickup from the airport. Several hotels that are within 10 miles of the airport have shuttle service.

You'll need to prearrange limo service, but there are plenty of companies to choose from; see the www.flydenver.com website for a full list of limo companies. When you are meeting a limo ride, go to Level 5, Island 2, outside the Jeppesen Terminal, outside doors 505-507 and 511-513 on the east side and doors 504-506 and 510-512 on the west side.

Commuter shuttles can be prearranged or are available on demand from Jeppesen Terminal, Level 5, Island 5, outside doors 505-507 (east side) and doors 510-512 (west side). **Super Shuttle** (800/258-3826, www.supershuttle.com) is one of the many companies that can get you to downtown.

Taxis have flat rates for airport transportation; it costs $55 one-way to go from DIA to downtown Denver. Taxis can be found on Level 5, Island 1, outside doors 505, 507, and 511 on the east side and 506, 510, and 512 on the west side. Call **Denver Yellow Cab** (303/777-7777) or **Metro Taxi** (303/333-3333) to schedule a ride.

Follow signs to the east end of the airport where the **RTD light rail train** (303/299-6000, www.rtd-denver.com) awaits outside at the bottom of a long escalator. The ride from here to downtown is about 35 minutes for $10 per person with a handful of stops at hotels along the way.

Car

I-25 runs north-south along the west side of downtown Denver. I-70 runs east-west and is the highway that leads into Denver from the airport. These two highways intersect just north of downtown.

If you are planning to head up I-70 to visit a mountain town, check traffic online (www.cotrip.org) because there can be significant delays for any number of reasons (snow, ice, rockslides, wildlife). I-25 has a significant amount of commuter traffic, as well as jams near downtown exits when there are sporting events and concerts. I-25 south will get you to Colorado Springs in about one hour; I-25 north will reach Fort Collins in about one hour. To drive to Boulder, you'll need to exit to Highway 36 from I-25; plan the drive to take 30 minutes or less from downtown Denver.

Train

Amtrak (www.amtrak.com) provides train service through Denver on the California Zephyr route, which goes to Chicago and San Francisco. Tickets can be bought at **Union Station** (1701 Wynkoop St., 303/592-6712), and trains pull up on the west side of the historic station. Two trains arrive and depart daily from this station—one leaves for Chicago and the other for San Francisco.

Bus

You can travel in and out of downtown Denver by **Greyhound** (800/231-2222, www.greyhound.com), which runs its service through **Union Station** (1701 Wynkoop St., 303/592-6712). Greyhound travels to Salt Lake City from Denver, with stops along the way on I-70 through the mountains. **Burlington Trailways** (800/992-4618, www.burlingtontrailways.com) provides bus service out of Union Station to points east such as Fort Morgan, Brush, and Sterling.

GETTING AROUND

The best way to get around Denver is by car, in part because you may want to get into the foothills, too, and options like bus and light rail may add considerable time to such excursions. That said, if you are flying into Denver and are planning to spend your time in the city, you can take the light rail train from the airport and easily navigate by foot, rental scooter, and local bus to see a significant number of sights, dine in excellent restaurants, and even see views of the Rocky Mountains. Union Station is a hub of bus lines and light rail options to get you beyond the city center.

Car

Two major highways run through Denver—I-70 going east to west and I-25 going north to south. Traffic can be congested, especially during rush hour, which can lengthen travel times if you need to get on the highways.

Most hotels charge a fee for parking on their property, and there is very limited parking downtown, with some metered options on streets and a few fee-based lots, so consider taking the light rail train in from the airport to avoid these extra costs.

RENTAL CARS

You'll need to take a shuttle from Denver International Airport to one of the more than 10 rental car companies located "on property" (beyond the closest airport parking lots). Rental car shuttles pick up and drop off from Jeppesen Terminal, Level 5, Island 4, outside doors 505-513 on the east side and outside doors 504-512 on the west side. You'll find **Enterprise** (800/261-7331, www.enterprise.com) and **Hertz** (800/654-3131, www.hertz.com) among the car rental agencies that also have locations in the city. Some of these rental car companies have locations close to downtown, so you can take the light rail train from the airport to downtown and rent a car as needed from the city.

Bus

The **Regional Transportation District** (RTD, 1600 Blake St., 303/299-6000, www.rtd-denver.com, $3-10.50 one-way) has daily bus service across eight counties in the Denver metro area, including service to Boulder. An underground **bus concourse** (17th St. and Wewatta St.) is found behind Union Station. RTD provides local bus service around Denver, regional bus service to Boulder, and light rail service. There are also specialty rides for sporting events, service for people with disabilities, and more.

Light Rail

The **RTD light rail system** (303/299-6000, www.rtd-denver.com, $3-10.50) is getting better and making more sense as it grows tracks to more destinations, including Denver International Airport. The C, D, E, F, H, and W lines are convenient for commuters, as well as for suburbanites coming into the city to bar-hop or attend sporting events so they don't have to pay for parking or worry about driving home tipsy. All of these lines pass through downtown, with lines C, E, and W stopping at Union Station. Fares vary depending on the number of zones your trip travels through. Service is available 24 hours a day, 365 days a year. The A, B, G, and R lines are part of the FasTracks project, with the A line going from the airport to downtown.

Rental Scooters

Dockless **Lime electric scooters** (www.li.me) are found all around town using an app. The cost is $1 to unlock and $0.15 cents per minute.

Guided and Walking Tours

It's a rare thing to see a Segway rolling along the streets of the Mile High City, where people prefer to get exercise by simply walking from point A to point B. Nonetheless, **Colorado Adventure Segway Tours** (303/449-6780 or 866/573-6749, www.coloradosegwaytours.com, $75 pp) offers the opportunity to see the city's historic high points without wearing oneself out too much. Instead of walking alongside the South Platte River through Confluence Park, you get to "glide." Tours are guided and helmets are required (and provided) for everyone. Reservations are mandatory.

There's a theme for every kind of tour, and a range of ways to tour, with **Denver History Tours** (720/234-7929, www.denverhistorytours.com, $20 adults, $10 ages 12-18, free under age 12). There are haunted-house tours, a visit to historic Littleton, and a look back at the seamy side of the city when bordellos and saloons thrived. Many of these are guided walking tours that usually last about two hours. There are also bus tours that can take an entire day and go well beyond the downtown environs to everywhere from local infill projects to Victorian towns in the foothills. Prices vary. Call ahead to make reservations; tours require a minimum of two people.

Lower Downtown (LoDo) has a rich history, from the first encampments along the South Platte River to the first buildings, including all of the colorful characters along the way. **LoDo Historic Walking Tours**

(303/534-5288, http://historicdenver.org, $18-20, free under age 2) offers three different walking tours, each departing from a different locale with a unique schedule and itinerary. The two-hour tour is a chance to learn about the businesses that first occupied many of the beautiful buildings, or that still do, such as the Oxford Hotel.

Departing from behind REI, just off of 15th and Platte Streets, the **Platte Valley Trolley** (15th St. and Platte St., 303/458-6255, www.denvertrolley.org, 11am-4pm Thurs.-Mon Memorial Day-Labor Day, $5 adults, $2 ages 4-13, free under age 4) is a quirky tour of Confluence Park and the businesses along this stretch of the South Platte River, including the Children's Museum. Perhaps more interesting is the history of this open-air car, a "breezer," and the fact that there used to be an entire trolley-car system throughout the city. The trolley serves as a shuttle ride to Broncos games during the football season. The trolley schedule has been cut back each year, so double-check the website for the most current days and times.

INFORMATION AND SERVICES

The **Denver Convention and Visitors Bureau** (303/892-1112, www.visitdenver.org) is where to begin learning about the Mile High City. There are also three Denver Tourist Information Centers: one downtown on the 16th Street Mall (1575 California St., 303/892-1505); at the airport (8500 Pena Blvd., 5th Fl., 303/317-0629); and at the Colorado Convention Center (700 14th St., 303/228-8000).

Denver Public Library has 25 branch library locations in addition to the **Central Library** (10 W. 14th Ave. Pkwy., 720/865-1111, www.denverlibrary.org, 10am-8pm Mon.-Tues., 10am-6pm Wed.-Fri., 9am-5pm Sat., 1pm-5pm Sun.), which has a robust children's library with story times, an art gallery, a Western History and Genealogy department, and of course lots of books and media. The library also hosts monthly events from musical performances to craft classes. All library locations have free unlimited Wi-Fi available.

In an emergency, dial 911 for immediate assistance. **Denver Health** (777 Bannock St., 303/436-6000, www.denverhealth.org) and **Presbyterian/St. Luke's Hospital** (PSL, 1719 E. 19th Ave., 303/839-6000, www.healthonecares.com) are both close to downtown. **Children's Hospital Uptown** (1830 Franklin St., 720/777-1360, www.childrenscolorado.org) is on the same block as PSL.

Golden

As the western suburbs have sprawled out, the town of Golden now feels like a corner of Denver and not a separate destination—it's only a 15-minute drive from downtown. However, this historic town—briefly the first capital of the Colorado Territory (1862-1867), when it was called Golden City (now it's the City of Golden)—retains a distinct identity. Home to the Colorado School of Mines, Golden has museums, restaurants, creek-side paths, and close access to the foothills. A day in Golden can feel like a little vacation from Colorado's capital.

SIGHTS

Bradford Washburn American Mountaineering Museum

The country's only museum devoted to the culture, technology, and history of mountaineering is right in downtown Golden at the **Bradford Washburn American Mountaineering Museum** (710 10th St., 303/996-2755, www.mountaineeringmuseum.org, 10am-4pm Tues., 10am-6pm Wed., 10am-4pm Thurs.-Fri., noon-5pm Sat., $7 adults, $3 ages 6-16, $1 under age 6). Inside, visitors will see a rare scale model of Mount Everest, experience interactive exhibits on Colorado's highest mountains and what it's like to sleep on a mountain face, and learn more about many famous mountain climbers.

Buffalo Bill Museum and Grave

Above Golden and with a view of both the plains and the mountains is the **Buffalo Bill Museum and Grave** (987 Lookout Mountain Rd., 303/526-0747, www.buffalobill.org, 9am-5pm daily May-Oct., 9am-5pm Tues.-Sun. Nov.-Apr., $5 adults, $4 seniors, $1 ages 6-15, free under age 6). This spot so impressed frontiersman and showman William F. "Buffalo Bill" Cody that he asked to be buried here. More than 20,000 people came to this site on Lookout Mountain in 1917 when Cody was laid to rest.

Close to the grave is a 3,000-square-foot museum where visitors learn about the thrilling life and times of Buffalo Bill Cody. He worked herding cattle and riding for the Pony Express but earned his nickname from his skills as a buffalo hunter. He truly became a legend as a magnificent performer in his Wild West shows. On display at the museum are the costumes he wore in the shows, silent and talking movies, original posters, and guns from Cody's own collection. While the memorabilia is interesting enough, what many people come for is the view. A breezy and scenic picnic spot is not far from the grave, and the **Pahaska Teepee Gift Shop** (8:30am-8:30pm daily May-Labor Day, 9am-5pm daily Labor Day-Apr., $4-10) between the museum and gravesite serves food such as buffalo burgers, buffalo chili, and ice cream.

The best route from downtown Denver is to go through Golden and follow 19th Street as it goes up into the mountains. You can also take I-70 west; just past the Lookout Mountain exit there is a buffalo herd, most visible in winter and early spring.

Clear Creek History Park

Not all museums are indoors. The **Clear Creek History Park** (11th St. and Arapahoe St., www.goldenhistory.org, sunrise-sunset daily, free), just one block off the main street in downtown, can be visited year-round. The park is made up of a reconstructed ranch that was moved here in the 1990s. It includes a schoolhouse, cabins, a blacksmith shop, and more.

Colorado School of Mines

The **Colorado School of Mines** campus

the city of Golden, first capital of the Colorado Territory

Golden

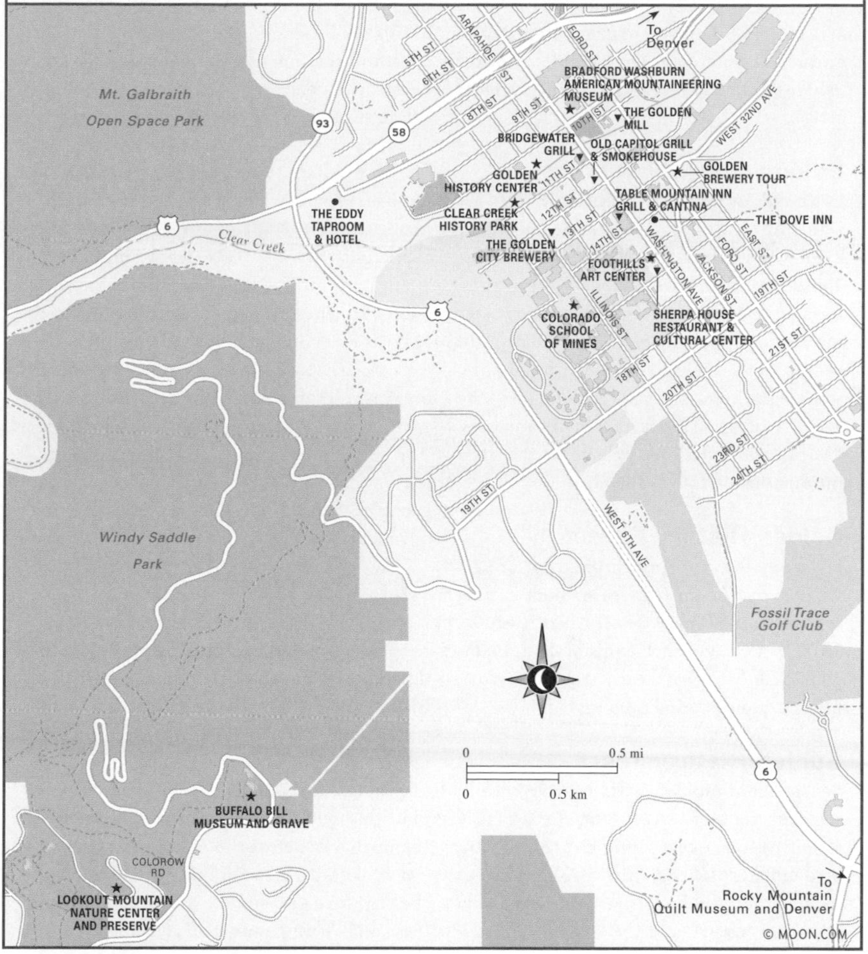

(1500 Illinois St., 303/273-3000, www.mines.edu) is relatively small, but just the right size for Golden. The campus has some attractive historic buildings, such as the Guggenheim Building, home to the school's first Geology Museum. Today, the **Mines Museum of Earth Science** (1310 Maple St., 303/273-3815, www.mines.edu, 9am-4pm Mon.-Sat., 1pm-4pm Sun., free) is two levels filled with rocks, fossils, and gemstones from all over the world—and beyond, since it has a moon rock and meteorites on display. Learn more about the mining history that helped to found this town.

Foothills Art Center

On the perimeter of the School of Mines campus are two historic buildings—a former church and a former home—that house the **Foothills Art Center** (809 15th St., 303/279-3922, www.foothillsartcenter.org, 10am-5pm Mon.-Tues. and Thurs.-Sat., noon-5pm Sun., free), which draws surprisingly big names to this small town. The center has hosted exhibits by internationally known artists like glass artist Dale Chihuly and painter Edgar Degas, and it has watercolor shows and sculpture exhibits annually that include work by local artists.

Golden Brewery Tour

Founded in 1873, the **Coors Brewing Company** (13th St. and Ford St., 303/277-2337, www.coorsbrewerytour.com, 10am-4pm Mon. and Thurs.-Sat., noon-4pm Sun., free)—now MillerCoors—has long been making beer and showing off how it's done right here in Golden. The tour ends with sampling some of the beers, so a valid ID is required. Be sure to call ahead for current hours and holiday closures. Check the website for the latest information on tour availability.

Golden History Center

For a small town, Golden has a lot of varied history, and one can learn about it all at the **Golden History Center** (923 10th St., 303/278-3557, www.goldenhistory.org, 10am-4pm Wed.-Sat., free). Learn about dinosaurs, mining, pioneers, and beer.

Golden History Tours

Learn about Golden with a guided walking tour via **Golden History Tours** (1010 Washington Ave., 720/432-1166, www.goldenhistorytours.com, $15-55). Offerings include the Wild West Short Tour, the Wild West Pub Crawl, and the Golden Ghost & Spirits Tour.

Lookout Mountain Nature Center and Preserve

Not exactly in Golden, but worth the 10-mile (16-km) drive (or bicycle ride, for the extremely fit) is the **Lookout Mountain Nature Center and Preserve** (910 Colorow Rd., 720/497-7600, http://jeffco.us/open-space, noon-4pm Fri., 11am-4pm Sat.-Sun.), with grand views of the Queen City of the Plains far below. The land was once owned by the prominent Boettcher family of Denver, and their summer home remains on the property near the nature center and along one of the hiking trails here. Check the website for the latest information on seasonal hours for the center; the preserve is open from one hour before sunrise to one hour after sunset daily.

Rocky Mountain Quilt Museum

Quilts truly are works of art, and the **Rocky Mountain Quilt Museum** (200 Violet St., Suite 140, 303/277-0377, www.rmqm.org, 10am-4pm Mon.-Sat., 11am-4pm Sun., $10 adults, $6 seniors, $5 students, free under age 6) hosts marvelous exhibits showing off quilters' skills. Moved from its longtime home on Washington Avenue, the museum is still worth a stop for those interested in textiles. The gift shop sells fabric and other items for the wannabe quilter. If you are part of a large group of 10 or more, request a guided tour in advance.

RECREATION

Golden feels like Denver's backyard, and for residents, it is. Hiking trails are very close to downtown Golden. Some popular trails for hikers are the **Matthews/Winters Park** trails (1103 Hwy. 93, 303/271-5925, http://jeffco.us/open-space). A basic understanding of geologic formations is helpful as you explore this foothills area, where the plains meet the hogbacks before the mountains rise up. For a hike with views of Red Rocks Park and the city, take a 10-minute drive from downtown on I-70 west and get off at exit 259. From the parking lot, begin the 6.5-mile (10.5-km) **Red Rocks/Dakota Ridge** loop up to the top of the hogback for the best views. The hike is moderately difficult, and the trail is used by mountain bikers as well. Bring a hat, since this trail does not provide much shade.

The **White Ranch Open Space Park** (25303 Belcher Hill Rd., 303/271-5925, http://jeffco.us/open-space) is just outside the town of Golden and has several trails to choose from. The **Rawhide Trail** is a 4.8-mile (7.7-km) loop that goes through forest and grassy plains. The moderate-level trail is shared with mountain bikers and sometimes wildlife, including deer, mountain lions, and bears.

For winter fun in the foothills, try snowshoeing or cross-country skiing at **Golden Gate Canyon State Park** (92 Crawford Gulch Rd., 303/582-3707, http://cpw.state.co.us). This park is accessible via Highway 93. All trails in Golden Gate Canyon State Park can be used for snowshoeing and cross-country skiing, and on the website is a list of the best trails and where conditions tend to be consistently good, with less wind or melt-off. The site also provides helpful detailed directions to each trailhead.

Rent a bike and explore the town on two wheels from the **Golden Bike Library** (1010 10th St., 303/597-3600, www.cityofgolden.net, 2 hours free, then $10 per day), where helmets and water bottles are included.

Right in downtown Golden is some fun for kayakers at the **Clear Creek Whitewater Park** (1201 10th St., 303/384-8133, www.cityofgolden.net). The park is designed for canoeing and kayaking. It includes a stretch of flat water, giant boulders to steer around, drop-offs, and fast-moving eddies. There are roughly seven city blocks of white-water fun. The park is used for many championship events during the year, and can also be rented for private functions. Rent a tube at **Golden River Sports** (806 Washington Ave., 303/215-9386, www.goldenriversports.net, 10am-6pm Mon.-Sat., 10am-5pm Sun., $15-37) and give it a go *if* you are a strong swimmer or wear a life vest; this is white-water tubing complete with rapids.

For those who just want to cool off, head over to **Splash Aquatics Park** (3151 Illinois St., 303/277-8700, www.splashingolden.com, 10am-6:30pm daily summer, day-use $6-11). The littlest children will enjoy the spray fountain, sandy beach area, and smaller slippery slides. Older kids and their grown-ups are sure to have a blast on the two huge curly slides and getting splashed by the giant bucket of water. Splash is about a 10-minute drive from downtown. Go early on the hottest days, as this place gets jammed. Check Splash's website for the latest information on hours and whether reservations are required.

Play a round at the **Fossil Trace Golf Club** (3050 Illinois St., 303/277-8750, www.fossiltrace.com), a stunningly beautiful golf course designed by golf course architect Jim Engh. The 18-hole course is highlighted by rocks with dinosaur fossils still visible. This course has received accolades for being a "top course for women" and having the "most fun holes," and is generally rated one of Denver's best golf courses by everyone from *Golf Digest* to *5280 Magazine*.

SHOPPING

Every one of the sights listed for Golden has a unique gift shop for finding that special item from Colorado. Along Washington Avenue is a variety of local stores in which to browse. If you're planning a hike, go to **Vital Outdoors** (1224 Washington Ave., 303/215-1644, www.vitaloutdoors.com, 10am-6pm Sun.-Thurs., 10am-7pm Fri.-Sat.) to get gear for the whole family. The store's helpful staff might also have some insider tips on hikes.

Stop in at **Red Wagon Gift Shop** (1118 Washington Ave., 303/278-3994, www.facebook.com/TheRedWagonGolden, 10am-6pm daily) for that Colorado-themed gift to take home. If you are inspired by what you see at the Rocky Mountain Quilt Museum, shop for supplies at the **Golden Quilt Company** (1108 Washington Ave., 303/277-0717, www.goldenquiltcompany.com, 10am-4:30pm Mon. and Wed.-Sat., noon-4pm Sun.).

FOOD AND DRINK

Certainly you can make a day of it in Golden and dine out for every meal at a different local place. Playing off the town's history is the **Old Capitol Grill & Smokehouse** (1122 Washington Ave., 303/279-6390, http://oldcapitolgrill-smokehouse.com, 11am-8pm Mon.-Wed., 11am-9pm Thurs.-Sun., $13-25), located in the old capitol building where the first legislature sessions were held. Come in for sandwiches at lunchtime or steak for dinner. This is the place for the rare Barmen Pilsner, known for its seven-minute pour.

To learn about a completely different history from another part of the world, walk over to the **Sherpa House Restaurant & Cultural Center** (1518 Washington Ave., 303/278-7939, www.sherpa.house, 11am-2:30pm and 5pm-9:30pm daily, $9-13). Here you can taste authentic Himalayan cuisine while learning about Sherpa culture, Tibet, and Nepal.

The **Table Mountain Inn Grill & Cantina** (1310 Washington Ave., 303/277-9898, www.tablemountaininn.com, 7am-10pm Sun.-Thurs., 7am-11pm Fri.-Sat., $12-23) serves Southwestern cuisine inspired by its Santa Fe-like architecture and decor. If the weather is cooperating, go for a creek-side patio table at the **Bridgewater Grill** (800 11th St., 303/279-2010, www.bridgewatergrill.com, 9am-9pm daily, $9-28), for breakfast, lunch, or dinner.

For dessert (or anytime), **Golden Sweets** (1299 Washington Ave., 303/271-1191, www.golden-sweets.com, 11am-9pm Sun.-Thurs., 11am-10pm Fri.-Sat.) sells ice cream, taffy, chocolates, and a key-lime bar on a stick that is divine. The **Windy Saddle Café** (1110 Washington Ave., 303/279-1905, http://windysaddle.com, 7am-5pm daily) is your go-to coffee shop.

The Golden City Brewery (920 12th St., 303/279-8092, http://gcbrewery.com, 11am-8pm daily) is the city's second largest brewery—second to Coors, that is—and it's in the backyard of the founders, two former geologists with a connection to mines. There's a limited food menu in addition to the award-winning homebrews available.

If you can't go to the Coors facility, you can look at it from the expansive decks of **The Golden Mill** (1012 Ford St., 720/405-6455, www.thegoldenmill.com, 11am-9pm Sun.-Thurs., 11am-10pm Fri.-Sat.), which opened in 2021 with its own self-pour tap wall (there's technology involved). This is a food hall with live music, awesome views, and plenty of Colorado beer. Tacos, sushi, barbecue, and, um, New Zealand ice cream are just some of the foods you can enjoy.

ACCOMMODATIONS

Being so close to Denver, it is completely practical to spend a day in Golden and rest your head back in the Mile High City. However, Golden does have some lovely hotels for those making a weekend of it. It's close to Red Rocks Park and Amphitheatre, convenient if you're in town for a concert, and closer to the foothills for various adventures like hiking, mountain biking, skiing, and more.

The Dove Inn (711 14th St., 720/608-1714, www.doveinn.com, $155-225) is a boutique hotel with luxurious rooms—picture large bathtubs, leather sofas, and velvet drapes.

The Southwestern architecture of the **Table Mountain Inn** (1310 Washington Ave., 303/277-9898, www.tablemountaininn.com, $250-400) makes it one of the most distinctive buildings in downtown. Many of the rooms have beautiful views of the mesas and foothills from the balconies.

The Golden Hotel (800 11th St., 303/279-0100, www.thegoldenhotel.com, $250-350) is right on both Clear Creek and Washington Avenues, making it possible to walk to most of Golden's major sights and the Washington Avenue shopping district.

We've reached that point in Colorado's history where hotels and taprooms are one category. This is the case with **The Eddy Taproom & Hotel** (1640 8th St., 720/442-8150, www.theeddygolden.com, $225-400), which opened in 2021 on the site of a former brick-works factory. The location is convenient whether you are walking or driving, as you can easily amble down to Clear Creek and into downtown Golden, or hop on Highway 93 to Boulder or be in downtown Denver in 15 minutes. But if you all you need is a cold beer and view, stay right here.

TRANSPORTATION AND SERVICES

To reach downtown Golden from downtown Denver, either take 6th Avenue—which turns into a highway as you drive west—and turn off at 19th Street, or take I-70 west to the exit for Highway 58 and then take the Washington Avenue exit.

For more information, contact the **Golden Visitors Center** (1010 Washington Ave., 303/279-3113, www.goldenvisitorsbureau.com, 8:30am-5pm Mon.-Fri., 10am-4pm Sat.) to learn more about other interesting things to see and do in this charming town. They also have detailed directions for a bike route to town from Denver.

Loveland and Winter Park

Yes, skiing can be a day trip when you are staying in Denver.

WINTER PARK RESORT

My personal favorite option for a ski day is **Winter Park Resort** (85 Parsenn Rd., 970/726-5514, www.winterparkresort.com, 9am-4pm Mon.-Fri., 8:30am-4pm Sat.-Sun. usually mid-Nov-early Apr., single-day lift ticket $159 adults, $104 ages 6-12 and over age 70, $10 under age 6), which is actually owned by Denver and accessible by a Ski Train from Union Station. Keep in mind, there is a distinction between the resort and the town. There is an incredible amount packed into the resort, though, so if all you want is to enjoy some outdoor activities, food, beer, and shopping, you don't need to leave the resort area. The nearby towns of Winter Park and Fraser are tiny—less than 1,000 population each—and situated at about 9,000 feet above sea level.

Recreation

Obviously, there's skiing here. Winter Park Resort is known for Mary Jane, one of the mountain's seven "territories" and loved by skiers who appreciate the bumps and love the 4.5-mile run down to the base. Keep in mind the base of the mountain is at 9,000 feet (2,750 m) above sea level and the peak is at 12,060 feet (3,675 m). There are runs for beginner and intermediate skiers, too, not just those aiming for the top. There are over 3,000 acres of skiable terrain with just more than half considered "most difficult" and only 8 percent labeled "beginner." That sounds daunting, but it really depends on which territory you're in. Beginners, stick to Winter Park. Double-black-diamond seekers, enjoy the other six territories.

Nonskiers won't be bored. There's ice skating, snowcat tours, ski bike tours, snowshoe tours and rentals, and snow tubing, for starters. And that's just in the winter! This is increasingly a year-round destination, especially for families. Hiking, swooshing down the alpine slide, mountain biking, even a ride on the chair lift are all on offer when the snow is long gone.

Nordic skiers will be delighted to find **Devil's Thumb Ranch Resort & Spa** (3530 County Rd. 83, Tabernash, 970/726-5632, www.devilsthumbranch.com), a cross-country ski resort with private cabins, a lodge, a pool, restaurants, and a spa all a short drive from Winter Park. This is a wonderful vacation destination for the whole family, with a spa, four restaurants, indoor/outdoor pool, and fat-tire bikes for rental—I even tried biathlon rifle target practice here! I've also taken advantage of the complimentary yoga class for guests, gone cross-country skiing, and look forward to horseback riding in any season. A game room and a movie theater inside offer entertainment for those cold nights.

Food and Accommodations

Check out **Sunspot Mountain Lodge** (160 Sunspot Way, 970/726-1446, www.winterparkresort.com, 11am-2pm daily in summer, check website for winter hours), reached by Zephyr Express Lift or the gondola. This restaurant sits at 10,700 feet (3,260 m) elevation and serves lunch, a three-course fixed-price menu, or fondue. Reservations for dinner are recommended. It's lunch only at **Snoasis** (daily during ski season) between the Eskimo and Prospector lifts. Down at the base and in the village, you'll find over a dozen places for everything from coffee or beer to tacos and waffles.

There is quite the mix of lodging options right at the base village—traditional hotel rooms, condos with fireplaces, and lofts. To find the one to suit your budget and taste, return again to the resort's website. Insider tip: There are package deals when you take the Ski Train.

Transportation

Winter Park Resort is a 90-minute drive from Denver. That is, when there isn't any traffic or snow and ice. Take I-70 west to Highway 40 and drive over Berthoud Pass to reach the resort.

From Union Station in downtown Denver, take the **Winter Park Express** (www.amtrak.com/winterparkexpress, Sat.-Sun., $29-59), run by Amtrak, and you won't have to worry about road conditions or parking. Also known as the **Ski Train,** it's a two-hour ride that passes through dozens of historic tunnels and gorgeous scenery, then gets you back to Denver in time for dinner.

From Denver International Airport, take the **Home James Shuttle** (800/359-7503, www.homejamestransportation.com, $37-74, reservations required) and leave the driving to someone else. It's also about a two-hour ride.

LOVELAND

Most of the ski resorts you hear about in Colorado are on the other side of the Continental Divide, or on the other side of the Eisenhower Tunnel you drive through on I-70. **Loveland Ski Area** (303/571-5580, http://skiloveland.com, 9am-4pm Mon.-Fri., 8:30am-4pm Sat.-Sun. and holidays, single-day lift ticket $94 adults, $38 ages 6-14, $75 ages 60-69, $139 season pass over age 69, free under age 5) is practically on top of the tunnel, right on the divide and only 53 miles (85 km) from Denver. This is good to reduce time spent on the road. It's also less expensive than many resorts.

The Loveland Ski Area has two areas in 1,800 skiable acres: Valley and Basin. The Valley is for beginners, whether you are skiing or snowboarding, young or old, just take it easy; the Basin is for intermediate and advanced skiers. The summit is at 13,010 feet (3,965 m) above sea level and the base is at 10,800 feet (3,290 m). Hydrate and acclimate before you come up this high! There are 94 trails, and the longest run is 2 miles (3.2 km). Expert skiers can arrange for a free snowcat ride to the very top.

On-mountain warming cabins set Loveland apart from other ski areas. Some of the cabins are basic with no restrooms, electricity, or services, while others serve food and beer.

Food

Dining at Loveland is pretty basic, with burgers, pizzas, barbecue, and beer. **Ptarmigan Roost Café** (top of Ptarmigan Lift) is at 12,050 feet (3,675 m) elevation. Enjoy the view and a bite to eat!

Transportation

Form Denver, take I-70 west to exit 216. There is free parking at the base. You can take the **Snowstang** (www.ridebustang.com/snowstang, $25) bus to Loveland on weekends from Denver's Union Station or a park-n-ride lot in Lakewood.

1: Loveland ski area **2:** skiing in Winter Park Resort

1

2

Boulder

Sights 140
Entertainment and
Events 144
Shopping 150
Sports and
Recreation 154
Food 159
Accommodations 165
Transportation and
Services 168
Vicinity of Boulder 169
Rocky Mountain National
Park 174

Sitting at the base of the purple Rocky Mountains, the breathtaking city of Boulder invites even the most committed couch potato to get outside.

While the city's 45,000 acres of open space and hundreds of miles of hiking, biking, and jogging trails are a big attraction, there is plenty more to see and do in this busy college town. Though Boulder's reputation as a home to eco-minded rock-climbing vegetarians is not totally inaccurate, there is much more going on here, with impressive regional-fare restaurants, a hip art scene, and nationally significant scientific research organizations.

Amazingly, it was on a visit to the new town of Boulder in 1908 that famed landscape architect Frederick Law Olmsted Jr. adequately

Highlights

Look for ★ to find recommended sights, activities, dining, and lodging.

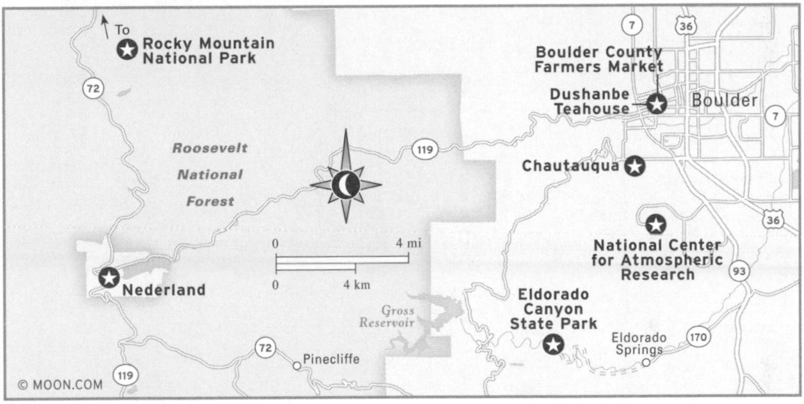

★ Sample the best of what Colorado has to eat—Western Slope peaches, corn, chickens, and more—at the weekly **Boulder County Farmers Market** (page 140).

★ Picnic on the lawn at **Chautauqua,** a historic educational and cultural summer retreat at the base of the Flatirons, with lodging, dining, hiking, concerts, and movies (page 141).

★ Savor a cup of tea at the **Dushanbe Teahouse** and appreciate the magnificent details carved by 40 artisans over a three-year period (page 143).

★ Walk the trail at the I. M. Pei-designed **National Center for Atmospheric Research** to learn about local weather and take in the view of the city below (page 143).

★ Spend a beautiful day in **Eldorado Canyon State Park,** where you can go rock climbing, hiking, mountain biking, and fishing (page 169).

★ Soak up the funky vibe in **Nederland,** a small mountain town that has long embraced a counterculture reputation (page 172).

★ Hike to waterfalls, lakes, and stellar views in **Rocky Mountain National Park,** a relatively short drive from Boulder (page 176).

Boulder

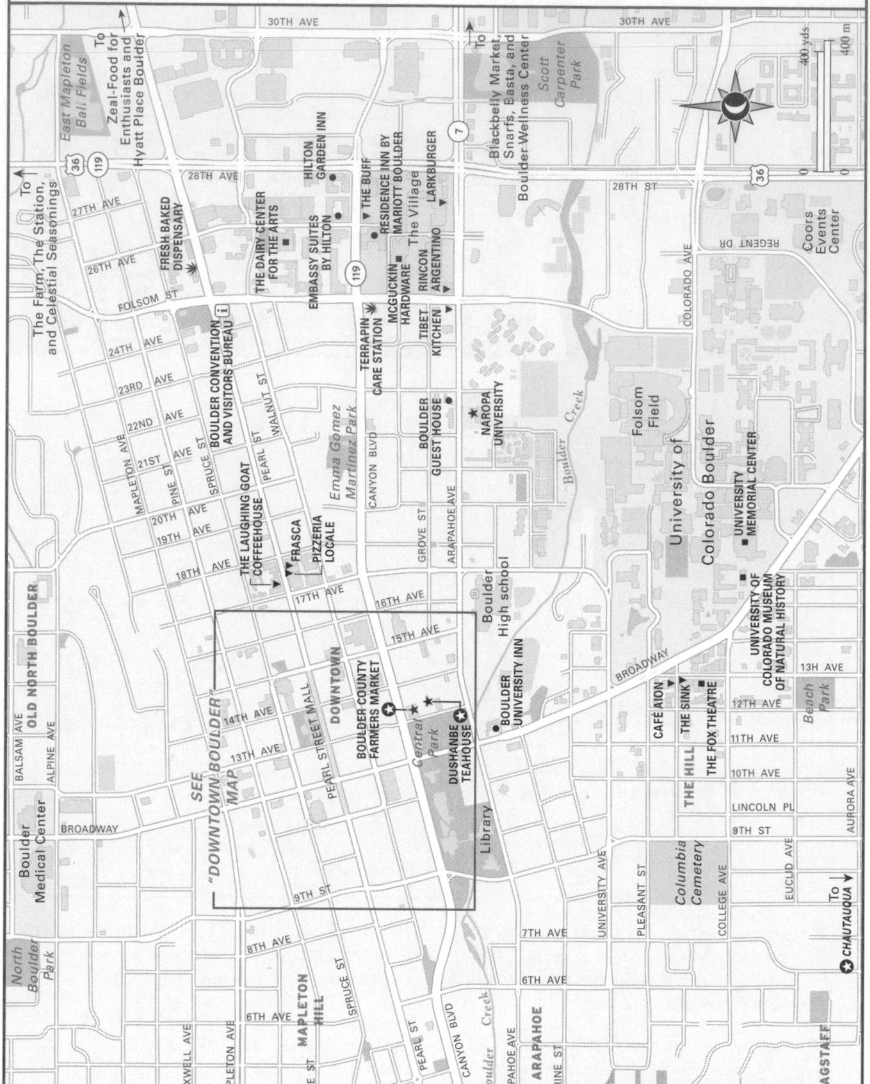

30TH AVE
28TH AVE
28TH ST
27TH AVE
26TH AVE
FOLSOM ST
24TH AVE
23RD AVE
22ND AVE
21ST AVE
20TH AVE
19TH AVE
18TH AVE
17TH AVE
16TH AVE
15TH AVE
14TH AVE
13TH AVE
13H AVE
12TH AVE
11TH AVE
10TH AVE
LINCOLN PL
9TH ST
8TH AVE
7TH AVE
6TH AVE
BROADWAY
MAPLETON AVE
PINE ST
SPRUCE ST
PEARL ST
WALNUT ST
CANYON BLVD
GROVE ST
ARAPAHOE AVE
BALSAM AVE
ALPINE AVE
MAXWELL AVE
MARINE ST
UNIVERSITY AVE
PLEASANT ST
COLLEGE AVE
EUCLID AVE
AURORA AVE
COLORADO AVE
REGENT DR
FLAGSTAFF RD
PEARL STREET MALL
36
119
7
To The Farm, The Station, and Celestial Seasonings
To Zeal-Food for Enthusiasts and Hyatt Place Boulder
To Blackbelly Market, Snarfs, Basta, and Boulder Wellness Center
East Mapleton Ball Fields
Scott Carpenter Park
FRESH BAKED DISPENSARY
THE DAIRY CENTER FOR THE ARTS
EMBASSY SUITES BY HILTON
HILTON GARDEN INN
THE BUFF
RESIDENCE INN BY MARIOTT BOULDER
The Village
LARKBURGER
MCGUCKIN HARDWARE
RINCON ARGENTINO
TERRAPIN CARE STATION
TIBET KITCHEN
BOULDER CONVENTION AND VISITORS BUREAU
BOULDER GUEST HOUSE
NAROPA UNIVERSITY
Emma Gomez Martinez Park
THE LAUGHING GOAT COFFEEHOUSE
FRASCA
PIZZERIA LOCALE
Boulder High school
Boulder Creek
Folsom Field
University of Colorado Boulder
UNIVERSITY MEMORIAL CENTER
UNIVERSITY OF COLORADO MUSEUM OF NATURAL HISTORY
Coors Events Center
OLD NORTH BOULDER
SEE "DOWNTOWN BOULDER" MAP
DOWNTOWN
BOULDER COUNTY FARMERS MARKET
Central Park
DUSHANBE TEAHOUSE
BOULDER UNIVERSITY INN
CAFÉ AION
THE SINK
THE HILL
THE FOX THEATRE
Beach Park
Library
Boulder Medical Center
Columbia Cemetery
To CHAUTAUQUA
North Boulder Park
MAPLETON HILL
LOWER ARAPAHOE
FLAGSTAFF
Boulder Open Space and Mountain Parks
MT. SANITAS TRAIL
To Boulder Adventure Lodge
Eben G. Fine Park
FOOT OF THE MOUNTAIN MOTEL
FLAGSTAFF HOUSE
0
400 yds
400 m
© MOON.COM

summed up what remains true of the place today. According to a 1992 report about Olmsted by Beverly Halpin Carrigan, "He wrote that the citizens of Boulder should not have to simply endure working in a community in order to move elsewhere for recreation and beauty. Recreation and beauty were already present if the people had the good sense to use them properly." It is this combination of living and working in a beautiful place with easy access to outdoor recreation that makes Boulder the appealing place it is today, with 45,000 acres of open space, almost 300 miles of trails, and more than 50 parks.

Despite its reputation as a foodie destination and a mecca of all things outdoors, people still ask, "So what is there to do in Boulder?" The answer to that question is: explore. Visiting Boulder is very different than spending a day in Denver. For all its sophistication and natural appeal, Boulder is refreshingly not a big city. Sights like the Pearl Street Mall allow you to take in the town's authentic flavor through street performers, shops, and a mix of locals. Or wander through the Boulder County Farmers Market in the summer, ride a bike along Boulder Creek and into the foothills, stroll a path at Chautauqua or around the University of Colorado campus, and then take in a movie under the stars.

As Denver has been striving—and arguably succeeding—at becoming a world-class city, Boulder has comfortably established itself as a world-class town. This is a place that inspires entrepreneurs, artists, and writers, and welcomes a crop of freshman students each fall. Swing by and hang out to discover the laid-back lifestyle for yourself.

PLANNING YOUR TIME

As Boulder has gained a reputation for itself in recent years as a hip place, people naturally want to come and see what all the buzz is about. While the view coming into Boulder is breathtaking, and it can seem obvious why people like it here, it can take a bit of planning and effort to really experience this college town. What do you want to get out of this visit? A great workout? To soak up local arts culture? A meal to write home about? An intellectual high? It's all here, but you have to plan.

If you come in the summer—whether solo, as a couple, or with family—you can do a little of all these things and get a real flavor for what sets Boulder apart from other destinations. On a Saturday morning, hit the Boulder County Farmers Market for a nibble and a walk. Later, go up to Chautauqua for a late-afternoon hike, to have dinner, or to take in a concert. Or maybe you planned ahead and got tickets to the Colorado Shakespeare Festival on the University of Colorado campus. If you still have some energy later that night, stop in at one of the bars in the Hotel Boulderado for a drink and a look around the historic lobby.

Boulder is a haven for runners, triathletes, and other fitness buffs, but that doesn't mean you have to be an athlete to have a great time here. The Pearl Street Mall is four long pedestrian-only blocks, with more shops and restaurants on the surrounding blocks. You can spend hours leisurely wandering from shop to shop, with a break for a bite to eat, and never leave this general neighborhood.

The University of Colorado campus includes museums, a planetarium, art exhibits, and again, with some advance planning, interesting events worth attending. Here, too, you can pack a lot into one location and easily walk from place to place.

You can see many of Boulder's highlights in just one day, but if you want to have time for longer hikes or touring the campus, consider two days to really soak up the vibes.

If you are coming from sea level, factor in the altitude before you take off for any hikes or long bike rides. You are over a mile above sea level and it can take a day or two to acclimate.

Previous: downtown Boulder and the Flatirons; hiking at Bear Lake in Rocky Mountain National Park; the historic dining hall at Chautauqua.

Sights

★ BOULDER COUNTY FARMERS MARKET

The biweekly **Boulder County Farmers Market** (www.bcfm.org, Wed. 4pm-8pm and Sat. morning Apr.-Nov.) is the best farmers market along the Front Range, if not in the entire state. My favorite time to come is in summer for fresh locally grown strawberries (June) and Colorado peaches (Aug.). This is the real deal—a farmer might still have dirt on his or her hands from digging up vegetables to display and sell. At many booths, you may overhear (or become part of) a conversation about what the farmer grows and how productive the season has been.

BOULDER HISTORY MUSEUM

Boulder is a pretty special place. To learn how it became the city it is today, visit the **Boulder History Museum** (2205 Broadway, 303/449-3464, www.museumofboulder.org, 9am-5pm Sun.-Mon. and Thurs.-Sat., 9am-8pm Wed., $10 adults, $8 seniors/students/children). The museum moved from the historic Harbeck House to a fully remodeled historic Masonic Lodge thanks to the generosity of a longtime trustee. First-floor exhibits change several times annually but tend to focus on a historical Colorado event. On the second floor are artifacts more specific to Boulder history. Programs and events range from the ongoing *Boulder Conversations with Extraordinary People* series, which features local professors, businesspeople, and civic leaders, to crafts and games for kids.

BOULDER MUSEUM OF CONTEMPORARY ART

The **Boulder Museum of Contemporary Art** (1750 13th St., 303/443-2122, www.bmoca.org, 11am-5pm Tues.-Sun., $2 adults/seniors/students, free under age 12) is in a great location next to the Dushanbe Teahouse and Boulder Creek. The museum includes three galleries and a small black-box theater where regional, national, and international contemporary visual and performing arts are showcased year-round. This is also a popular venue for special events, so be sure to check

the Boulder County Farmers Market

Downtown Boulder

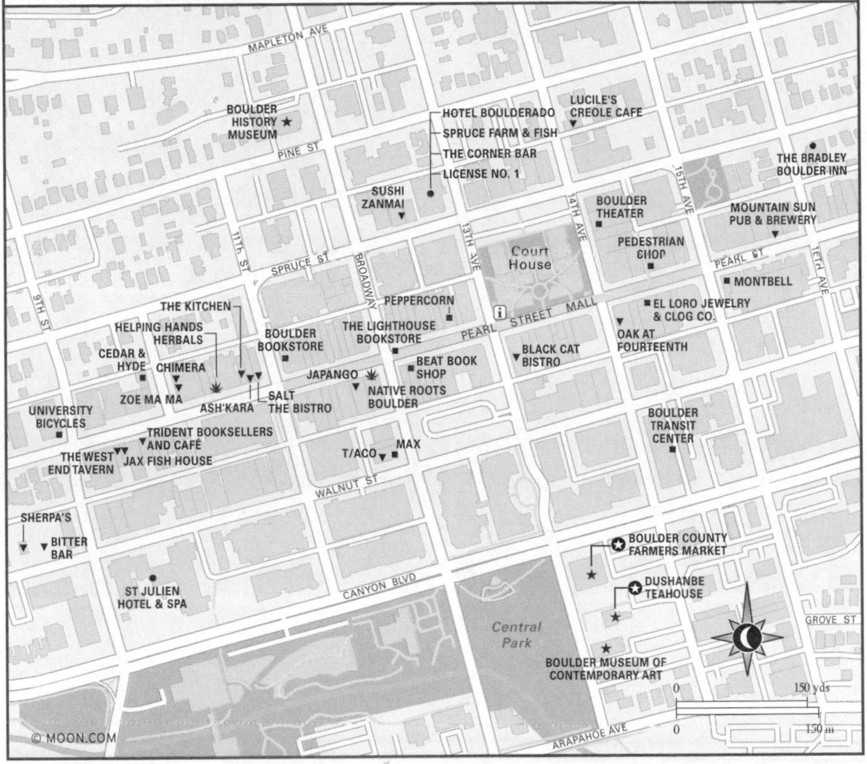

the schedule before stopping by, or make it a point to be here during the **Boulder County Farmers Market** Saturday morning or Wednesday evening (4pm-8pm) in the summer.

CELESTIAL SEASONINGS

It's hard to remember a time when herbal tea was a cutting-edge health food concept, but back in the 1960s a group of tea radicals began picking fresh herbs in the nearby Rocky Mountains and bagging them dried for sale in health food stores. Now **Celestial Seasonings** (4600 Sleepytime Dr., 303/530-5300, www.celestialseasonings.com, 9am-6pm Mon.-Sat., 10am-5pm Sun.) is a household name and visitors have flocked here to take a free factory tour, watching the millions of tea bags roll off the assembly line. Check the website for the latest information on tour availability.

★ CHAUTAUQUA

It's not just that **Chautauqua** (Colorado Chautauqua Association, 900 Baseline Rd., 303/442-3282, www.chautauqua.com) is a beautiful gateway to the broad meadow of Bluebell Shelter and other well-worn hiking trails that lead up to the Flatirons; with its historic auditorium, cabins, and dining hall (breakfast, lunch, and dinner year-round), it's also a relaxed setting for wonderful summer events like the Silent Film Festival (June-Aug.) and the Colorado Music Festival (June-Aug.). In addition to its natural attributes, the park

1

2

3

includes a large playground and grassy area perfect for playing Frisbee, enjoying a picnic, or sunbathing. Located on 26 acres leased from the city, Chautauqua was part of the nationwide Chautauqua Movement, an effort to provide cultural and educational programs in the summer.

Chautauqua is located west and south of downtown and the University of Colorado campus. There is free parking at the ranger station and near the restaurant, but it can be crowded during the summer; people often park along Baseline Road and walk in. Lodge rooms and cottages are available for nightly rental.

★ DUSHANBE TEAHOUSE

Thanks to a sister-city partnership, Boulder has the unique **Dushanbe Teahouse** (1770 13th St., 303/442-4993, www.boulderteahouse.com, 11am-8pm Tues.-Fri., 9am-9pm Sat., 9am-8pm Sun.), just a couple of blocks from the Pearl Street Mall. It took three years for artisans in Tajikistan to create the hand-carved and hand-painted ceiling, columns, and ceramic tiles of the building before it was sent to the United States in the 1990s. The rose garden out front and the creek side location complement the delicate architecture inside. It's worth stopping by just to gawk, but the teahouse is also a full-service restaurant and offers an extensive tea menu. This place can be busy—especially on weekends when the Boulder County Farmers Market is set up on the street out front—so call for a reservation if you want to eat here and not just see the architecture.

★ NATIONAL CENTER FOR ATMOSPHERIC RESEARCH

The mountains are the first thing to grab your attention if you drive into Boulder from the east—but then you begin to wonder about the distinctive building just below those magnificent rocks. It's the **National Center for Atmospheric Research** (1850 Table Mesa Dr., 303/497-1000, http://ncar.ucar.edu, 8am-5pm Mon.-Fri., 9am-4pm Sat.-Sun.), a federal research center that studies all aspects of weather. There is a lot of important and fascinating work going on daily, but the building and its surroundings have a reputation and history all their own. The center was designed by renowned architect I. M. Pei, whose 1960s design was influenced by Native American cliff dwellings in southern Colorado and the dramatic rocks above the site. The building was immortalized in Woody Allen's film *Sleeper.* Check the website (https://scied.ucar.edu/visit) for information on the availability of free guided tours. Audio tours and self-guided tours are available anytime the center is open. There's also a gift shop and art gallery inside the building. Outside, you can walk the **Walter Orr Roberts Weather Trail,** an easy 0.5-mile (0.8-km) loop, to learn about local weather and take in the view of the city below.

UNIVERSITY OF COLORADO

Most of the people at the **University of Colorado Boulder** (CU Boulder, 914 Broadway, 303/492-1411, www.colorado.edu) are either students or their visiting parents or professors. But this place is also open to the public, and it's worth a stop.

The university was founded in 1876, the same year that Colorado became a state, and there were a mere 44 students. Now the school is like a small town, with over 30,000 students arriving each fall. While the misbehavior of partying students and a few sports team members has made headlines, it is actually a very well-regarded school academically; five Nobel laureates have been on staff, and nine MacArthur fellows have called CU Boulder home. Prestigious annual events such as the **Colorado Shakespeare Festival** (http://cupresents.org) and the **Conference on World Affairs** are held on the campus.

1: intricate designs adorning the Dushanbe Teahouse **2:** the Celestial Seasonings tea factory **3:** the meadow of Bluebell Shelter at Chautauqua

To learn more about the history of the campus, start with the **Heritage Center** (Old Main, 3rd Fl., 1600 Pleasant St., 303/492-6329, www.cuheritage.org, 10am-4pm Mon.-Sat.), where you can get an overview of the school's early history, learn about "CU in Space," read the roster of distinguished alumni (most of whom have buildings named after them on the campus), and see the trophies in the CU Athletics Gallery. The **University of Colorado Museum of Natural History** (303/492-6892, www.colorado.edu/cumuseum, 9am-5pm Mon.-Sat., 10am-4pm Sun.) is very child-friendly, with permanent dinosaur collections and changing exhibits that feature everything from meteorites to Inuit culture.

The University Memorial Center is the hub of the campus, with the **Alferd Packer Grill** and other restaurants, a bowling alley, and a bookstore. The halls of the center have become like a small fair or mall, with tables often set up where you can buy sweaters, T-shirts, or phone cards.

Fiske Planetarium (303/492-5002, http://fiske.colorado.edu, matinees Sat.-Sun., evening shows Thurs.-Sat., $7-10) has star and laser shows with different themes, such as Perseus and Andromeda or Pink Floyd. Check the website for upcoming shows (and note that they are closed on CU Buffs football game dates). You can't miss the white dome of the **Sommers Bausch Observatory** (303/492-6732, www.colorado.edu/sbo); it's open to the public, with free stargazing through the telescopes on Friday night and during other special events.

Entertainment and Events

NIGHTLIFE

In a college town with a reputation for wild parties, there is no shortage of places to go for a drink after dark. The two main parts of town for nightlife are the **Pearl Street Mall** and **The Hill,** which is the small business district adjacent to the University of Colorado campus, literally up the hill from downtown.

Bars and Clubs

The West End Tavern (926 Pearl St., 303/444-3535, www.thewestendtavern.com, 11:30am-9pm daily), on the west end of the Pearl Street Mall, has a very appealing rooftop deck with a view of the mountains that is perfect for happy hour and watching the sunset. There is live music Thursday-Saturday nights.

The Corner Bar (Hotel Boulderado, 2115 13th St., 303/442-4880, www.cornerbarboulderado.com, 11am-midnight daily), on the corner of Spruce and 13th Streets, has been a Boulder favorite for 20 years—in large part due to the daily happy hour (3pm-6pm). This bar evokes an Old West saloon feel with tasteful taxidermy and tufted booths inside and a modern sunny patio outside.

Descend into the basement of the Hotel Boulderado for a taste of liquid history at **License No. 1** (2115 13th St., 303/442-4880, www.license1boulderado.com, 5pm-close Wed.-Sun.), which holds the city's first legal liquor license, issued in 1969—60 years after the hotel opened. Enjoy $4 cocktails and casual bites during happy hour (5pm-7pm daily) and be sure to take a moment to look over the ample whiskey list.

The **Bitter Bar** (835 Walnut St., at 9th St., 303/442-3050, www.thebitterbar.com, 5pm-11pm Sun.-Tues., 5pm-midnight Wed.-Sat.) serves trendy cocktails with hipster names, but at the end of the day these are craft cocktails made with sublime expertise. These aren't your ordinary bartenders—not just anyone can use "hellfire shrub" and sauvignon blanc along with some other fine ingredients to make a fancy cocktail. Small bites are also on the menu.

Brewpubs and Distilleries

Mountain Sun Pub & Brewery (1535 Pearl St., 303/546-0886, www.mountainsunpub.com, noon-8pm daily) is just east of the Pearl Street Mall. Mountain Sun has a groovy kind of reggae vibe with tasty burgers and lots of vegetarian options. Stacks of games for kids and adults make this a family-friendly place.

Meet the next hybrid in bars: a brewery distillery. **Ska Street Brewstillery** (1600 38th St., Suite 100, 720/510-9921, www.skastreet.com, noon-8pm Wed.-Sun.) has combined its two businesses from Palisade, Colorado, and Durango, Colorado, creating a combo mixology dream of drink options with Ska beers on taps alongside "ska-tails" made with freshly distilled spirits.

Uhl's Brewing (5460 Conestoga Ct., 720/542-3870, http://uhlsbrewing.com, 3pm-7pm Wed.-Thurs., noon-8pm Fri.-Sat., noon-6pm Sun.) is east of downtown Boulder, where there is room to spread out inside and outside. They offer IPAs, pale ales, stouts, Vienna-style lagers, milkshake and maltshake IPAs, and coffee-infused beers. They specialize in barrel-aged fruity ales.

Also east of downtown, **Wild Provisions Beer Project** (2209 Central Ave., 303/993-3598, www.wildprovisionbeer.com, 2pm-9pm Mon.-Fri., noon-9pm Sat.-Sun.) is known for its oak-fermented lagers and 4 Noses Beers. There is ample indoor and outdoor seating (dogs welcome outside), and food trucks park here regularly, with pizza, Mexican food, and more.

Upslope Brewing Company (1898 S. Flatiron Ct., 303/396-1898, www.upslopebrewing.comwww.upslopebrewing.com, 11am-10pm daily) is a microbrewery with two taprooms available (the other is at 1501 Lee Hill Rd., 303/449-2911, 2pm-10pm daily), featuring both year-round and seasonal beers, as well as Spiked Snowmelt hard seltzer. Come in spring for blackberry lemon sour ale, and again in fall for . . . yep, pumpkin ale. The location on Flatiron Court is just east of downtown in an industrial neighborhood, and the Lee Hill Road location is on the north edge of the city.

Avery Brewing (4910 Nautilus Ct., 303/440-4324, www.averybrewing.com, 3pm-9pm Wed.-Thurs., 11:30am-9pm Fri.-Sun.) has made a name for itself far beyond Colorado, despite the fact that it grew up in a tiny industrial space in Boulder. In 2015 it got a new home, expanding to two levels, about 150 seats, and a full dinner menu featuring Southern soul food like gumbo, pork green chili, fried rabbit and waffles, and blackened catfish. There are daily specials, barbecued dishes from the house smoker, and 30 taps of Avery beer. The brewery is in the suburb of Gunbarrel, northeast of the city off Highway 119.

CANNABIS DISPENSARIES

Boulder is home to many cannabis dispensaries—each with its own style so you can choose your buds based on the vibes of the establishment. The dispensaries are not cookie-cutter franchise businesses where you walk in and know exactly what's on the menu at each place; these places have "craft cannabis" and "award-winning strains" to choose from, along with different edibles (food made with marijuana), pipes, and other marijuana accessories.

A popular spot on the east side of town, **Boulder Wellness Center** (5420 Arapahoe Ave., Unit F, 303/442-2565, www.boulderwc.com, 9am-7pm Mon.-Wed., 9am-8pm Thurs., 9am-9pm Fri., 10am-9pm Sat., 10am-6pm Sun.) channels the sort of Eastern philosophies the community is known for, with ornate lacquered furniture and ceremonial masks on the walls. If that doesn't get you into a Zen-like state, the moderately priced buds, concentrates, and edibles certainly will.

Garnering attention from the likes of *Vogue* and *GQ*, **The Farm** (2801 Iris Ave., 303/440-1323, http://thefarmco.com, 9am-8pm Sun.-Wed., 9am-9pm Thurs.-Sat.) fashions itself the Rolls Royce of Colorado cannabis. The north Boulder operation feels like a high-end

1

2

Boulder
KT TUNSTALL
3

4

What's 420?

April 20 is known as a day to smoke weed, and it has been since long before it became legal to smoke marijuana in Colorado. The day has its origins in a pot smokers' meeting held at 4:20pm to get high together. It has since evolved into a celebration at various locales around the globe to smoke on April 20.

The University of Colorado campus has been one such location for these informal gatherings; upward of 10,000 people converge on the campus on April 20 to publicly smoke marijuana. Campus security has dealt with this in a variety of ways, whether by closing the entire campus for the day or just closing the popular meeting spot on the Norlin Quadrangle. It seems legalization has helped to spread the number of events surrounding this "pot holiday," therefore reducing the intensity of the crowds on campus.

Remember, although it is legal to buy marijuana in Colorado, it cannot be smoked in public.

fashion boutique, with polished wood accents, an endless variety of glassware, and accessories branded with The Farm's logo (a cow sporting a marijuana leaf on its hide). It's all to showcase The Farm's small-batch, pesticide-free (and slightly pricey) "craft cannabis," all of which is grown locally in Boulder. This is marijuana's response to the farm-to-table movement. There is also an "express" location (5420 Arapahoe Ave. #D, 303/443-0240) on the east side of town.

Located in a cozy single-level house on Pearl Street, east of the mall, **Fresh Baked Dispensary** (2539 Pearl St., 303/440-9393, www.freshbakedcolorado.com, 9am-9:50pm daily) feels like your neighborhood hangout, complete with old-school arcade games in the waiting area and relaxed, friendly budtenders eager to answer your burning questions. Best of all, this chill-out zone boasts a hefty selection of award-winning strains.

Tucked away behind a nondescript door on a busy stretch of the Pearl Street Mall, **Helping Hands Herbals** (1021 Pearl St., 720/476-6186, www.helpinghandsdispensary.com, 10am-7pm daily) is a cozy second-floor recreational pot shop that offers a huge variety of strains, edibles, and concentrates that belies its small size. Helping Hands is also known for in-house strains you won't find anywhere else, including Gupta Kush, named in honor of Sanjay Gupta, the CNN medical correspondent who's become a major medical marijuana advocate.

Pop into **Native Roots Boulder** (1146 Pearl St., 720/726-5126, www.nativerootsdispensary.com, 11am-6:50pm daily), a slickly designed basement-level shop in a prime location on the Pearl Street Mall, and you'd be forgiven if you thought you'd wandered into an Apple Store. However, there are no iPads for sale behind these sleek modern counters—just a healthy selection of *indica* and *sativa*. Wherever you go in Colorado, you might find one of their locations, as they have at least 20 shops.

The excellently named **Terrapin Care Station** (1795 Folsom St., 303/954-8402, ext. 2, www.terrapincarestation.com, 8am-9:45pm daily) was the first recreational shop to open in Boulder, and it scored enviable real estate just off the CU campus. The timing and location seem to have paid off. These days, this hippie-inspired joint boasts its own line of T-shirts, specially branded "TerraPen" vaporizers, and even online ordering through its own smartphone app. Just be prepared: The place can get busy, so it might not be the best option for those who are looking to browse at their leisure.

1: Avery Brewing **2:** University of Colorado Boulder **3:** Boulder Theater **4:** Colorado Shakespeare Festival

THE ARTS

Boulder has a rich arts scene throughout the year, but perhaps more so in the summer when there are concerts at Chautauqua in the historic auditorium, the Shakespeare Festival on the University of Colorado campus, and other events featuring live dancers and actors. It's a well-rounded life here with exposure to all facets of the arts, though the big traveling theater shows still require a trip to Denver.

Dance

The **Boulder Ballet** (2590 Walnut St., 303/443-0028, www.boulderballet.org) performs at different locations around town, including Macky Auditorium on the CU campus, the Boulder Theater, and the Dairy Center for the Arts. In June, they offer free performances as part of the annual "Ballet in the Park," with at least one performance in the Boulder Central Park Bandshell.

Live Music and Radio

Up on The Hill (the area near the CU campus up the hill from downtown) is **The Fox Theatre** (1135 13th St., 303/447-0095, http://foxtheatre.com), known for booking bands that appeal to its audience—the college crowd, in other words. Many shows are all-ages. Chances are, if you are over the age of 25, you've never heard of many of these bands that sell out here, including Pigeons Playing Ping Pong, Taylor McFerrin, and The Nth Power.

You might have heard of **eTown** (1535 Spruce St., 303/443-8696, www.etown.org) on the radio, and this is the place where those shows are recorded in front of a live audience—in a solar-powered studio, no less. This independent radio program features well-known live musicians as well as thought leaders answering a few questions on a variety of topics. Shows often feature the house band, the eTones. Check the website for videos of past events and to get a feel for the type of performances, as well as to view the calendar for upcoming events and to buy tickets.

Performance Spaces

The **Dairy Center for the Arts** (2590 Walnut St., 303/440-7826, www.thedairy.org, galleries 2pm-6pm Mon.-Sat., check website for performance schedule times) is home to three art galleries, two theaters, a performance space, and classrooms for ballet (and yes, once upon time it was a dairy). The place is humming with creative energy, as various art forms are practiced or displayed here throughout the year. Visit the box office (10am-6pm Mon.-Fri., noon-8pm Sat., noon-5pm Sun.); many of the events at the Dairy are free.

The **Boulder Theater** (2032 14th St., 303/786-7030, www.bouldertheater.com) is a century-old theater that started out as an opera house and has gone on to host many other types of performances. The art deco-style facade was part of a 1930s expansion to the theater, and the building has had many owners and incarnations over the years. Today there are over 250 events held annually. A peek at the calendar shows the impressive breadth of acts: Govinda and the Dub Kirtan All Stars, Marc Maron, Lyle Lovett, Joan Armatrading, Dweezil Zappa, and Bruce Cockburn.

FESTIVALS AND EVENTS

Annual events in Boulder tend to have a connection to sports or at least being outdoors. Throw on jeans, a pair of Nikes or Birkenstocks, and a T-shirt or lightweight fleece, and you'll fit in at almost any festival here.

Spring

Even nonrunners have heard of the **BolderBOULDER** (www.bolderboulder.com, May), an annual 10K that takes over the town on Memorial Day and has become one of the largest road races in the world. It's so popular that there are over 100 wave starts—otherwise it would be pandemonium for the 5,000 people who run, jog, or walk during the event each year.

Over the same weekend as the BolderBOULDER is a three-day event that seems to grow each year: the **Boulder Creek Festival** (www.bceproductions.com, May), which features multiple stages for live music, activity areas for kids, hundreds of vendors, local food, and, best of all, a huge rubber ducky race in the creek.

Each spring the Tulip Fairy parades down the Pearl Street Mall with lots of little fairies and elves trailing during the **Tulip Fairy and Elf Festival** (www.boulderdowntown.com, Apr.). Gossamer wings in a rainbow of colors fill the pedestrian mall as kids run along behind the Tulip Fairy to a main stage where this half-day festival offers face painting, live music, ballet dancers, arts and crafts, cookie decorating, and more.

Composer Gustav Mahler is celebrated during the weeklong **Colorado MahlerFest** (www.mahlerfest.org, May). Concerts take place in Macky Auditorium on the University of Colorado campus, and films are shown at the Dairy Center for the Arts. There is also a symposium about the Austrian composer and conductor who was once the director of the New York Metropolitan Opera and New York Philharmonic.

The **Conference on World Affairs** (www.colorado.edu/cwa, Apr.) is an incredible week of intellectual discussion at the University of Colorado campus. Panelists discuss everything. Yes, everything, or so it seems. The topics include immigration, economics, human rights, weapons of mass destruction, satire, politics, sex, drugs, sports, and health. The panelists are experts on these many and varied topics and come from around the world: Germany, Saudi Arabia, Uganda, Japan, and across the United States, as well as professors from CU. Panelists are not just academics but judges, storytellers, musicians, attorneys, authors, and entrepreneurs.

Summer

The annual **Colorado Shakespeare Festival** (http://cupresents.org, June-Aug.) takes place outdoors in the Mary Rippon amphitheater and indoors at the University Theatre, both on the University of Colorado campus (914 Broadway). The tradition of Shakespeare under the stars in the historic Mary Rippon Outdoor Theatre has been going on for about 60 years. In addition to the traditional plays of the bard, there are also plays *about* his most famous works; for example, *I Hate Hamlet* and *Unexpected Shaxpere!* have been performed.

The **Silent Film Festival** (Chautauqua Auditorium, 900 Baseline Rd., www.chautauqua.com, June-Aug., $12) is a special treat for film buffs and families. Weekly through the summer you can catch classics like Charlie Chaplin's *The Great Dictator* or Buster Keaton's *Steamboat Bill Jr.* and enjoy the live accompaniment of pianist Hank Troy. The audience participates just like audiences did when these films were originally shown—booing and hissing when the bad guy appears on the screen or cheering for the hero.

The **Colorado Music Festival** (Chautauqua Auditorium, 900 Baseline Rd., www.coloradomusicfestival.org, June-Aug., ticket prices vary) holds Young People's Concerts and Family Fun Concerts during the day, with full orchestra and chamber music at night, as well as a few surprises each year. It's typical for people to settle themselves outside of the theater and enjoy the beauty of both nature and music.

Fall

The **Boulder International Fringe Festival** (www.boulderfringe.com, Sept.) is about two weeks' worth of art performed and displayed throughout Boulder. This festival is in the same spirit as fringe festivals around the world, and as such attracts an international lineup of artists, musicians, and performers. Check the calendar for those arts you might not see every day—puppetry, circus arts, and poetry, in addition to dance and theater. There are workshops offered during this event.

The Pearl Street Mall is transformed into the **Downtown Boulder Fall Fest** (www.boulderdowntown.com, late Sept.) as art booths, music stages, and food vendors set up to entertain during this three-day event.

It includes a children's carnival, and grown-ups have microbrews to sample.

Get your "fat pants" out before Thanksgiving and make a reservation for **First Bite: Boulder Restaurant Week** (www.firstbiteboulder.com, mid-Nov.). More than 50 local restaurants participate with three-course menus ($34 pp). On the list are some of the most popular dining spots in town: SALT the Bistro, the Dushanbe Teahouse, The Kitchen, and dozens more.

Winter

Switch on the Holidays (www.downtownboulder.org, Dec.) with a lighting ceremony and Santa visit the weekend after Thanksgiving. The Boulder Chorale provides the sounds of the season as the Boulder County Courthouse on the Pearl Street Mall is illuminated.

Just because it's cold out doesn't mean people have given up on crazy outdoor fun in Boulder. Each New Year's Day many hardy souls take the **Polar Bear Plunge** (Jan.) into Boulder Reservoir to benefit the American Cancer Society or another health-related organization. As if freezing cold wasn't enough, there are a lot of silly—and soon frozen!—costumes worn for this event, too.

Shopping

The Pearl Street Mall is the heart of locally owned business in Boulder. There are other pockets of independent shops scattered around town, but if you're on foot you can find books; men's, women's, and children's clothes; body care products; toys; and more somewhere along this street.

PEARL STREET MALL

The **Pearl Street Mall** (Pearl St. between 10th St. and 15th St., 303/449-3774, www.boulderdowntown.org) started as a 1970s antidote to the indoor mall craze and has since become more than a shopping destination. Shops and restaurants trickle off Pearl Street for several blocks in every direction. In addition to shops like the Boulder Bookstore and Peppercorn, there are carts selling hats, sunglasses, and other items. In the summer, entertainers hang out on each block (often in front of the courthouse) to perform magic tricks, eat fire, sing songs, make balloon animals, and deliver other unexpected delights to throngs of people.

Books

A longtime staple and anchor on the west end of the mall is the **Boulder Bookstore** (1107 Pearl St., 303/447-2074, www.boulderbookstore.net, 10am-10pm Mon.-Sat., 10am-8pm Sun.), with many floors of books (children's, travel, cooking, science fiction, and much more) and magazines, as well as a popular coffee shop.

The **Beat Book Shop** (1200 Pearl St., 303/444-7111, www.beatbookshop.com, 3pm-8pm Sun.-Mon., 1pm-9pm Tues., 1pm-9:30pm Wed., 1pm-10pm Thurs.-Sat.) is a rare store. The owner is a fan of Beat Generation authors such as Jack Kerouac (author of *On the Road)* and Allen Ginsberg (poet of *Howl*) and is also locally known as a cofounder of the Jack Kerouac School of Disembodied Poets at Naropa University. You don't come here just to buy a book—you come to talk about the meaning of life, poetry, and writing.

If you are on a spiritual journey (or want to be on one), there's a book for you at **The Lighthouse Bookstore** (1201 Pearl St., www.lighthousebookstoreofboulder.com, 303/939-8355, 10am-6pm Mon.-Sat., 11am-6pm Sun.). Learn about your chakras, get a psychic reading, pick up some tarot cards, or read up on any number of New Age, religious, metaphysical, and spiritual topics.

Clothing and Shoes

Women who like Prada, Bottega Veneta, Missoni, and other high-end designers are sure to find something special and sophisticated at **Max** (1177 Walnut St., 303/449-9200, 10am-6pm Mon.-Sat., noon-5pm Sun.).

The **Pedestrian Shop** (1425 Pearl St., 303/449-5260, www.comfortableshoes.com, 10am-6pm Mon.-Sat., 11am-5pm Sun.) has been keeping men, women, and children shod in practical, durable, and comfortable shoes for more than four decades. Need Birkenstocks or Merrells? They've got them here, as well as Dansko, Ecco, Keen, and other brands.

Weekends (1200 Pearl St., 303/444-4231, http://weekendsboulder.com, 10am-6pm Mon.-Wed., 10am-7pm Thurs.-Sat., 11am-6pm Sun.) is a one-stop shop for both men and women who like to dress business-casual or just stylishly casual. Choose from a large selection of denim, including brands such as Rag & Bone and Citizens of Humanity.

Toss out your assumptions about **prAna** (1147 Pearl St., 303/449-2199, www.prana.com, 11am-6pm daily) just offering yoga-wear and step inside for your next favorite pair of jeans (both men and women), a great winter coat, or just a comfy sweater. This Boulder location is a flagship store with very friendly service in an ideal location.

Gift and Home

As the Pearl Street Mall has grown and changed over the years, the **Peppercorn** (1235 Pearl St., 303/449-5847, www.peppercorn.com, 10am-6pm Mon.-Sat., 11am-5pm Sun.) has remained and grown considerably itself. Peppercorn calls itself a "home" store, but it's largely a kitchen store with cookbooks, dishes, and flatware. In the front of the store are featured Colorado products and books.

It's really hard to categorize **Cedar & Hyde** (2015 10th St., 720/287-3900, www.cedarandhyde.com, 11am-5pm Mon.-Sat.)—it's like a modern boutique meets old-fashioned department store. In other words, those are bath towels next to that gorgeous sweater over by the shoes just to the left of the bowls. Somehow, it all goes together perfectly, like a well-styled magazine spread, and it makes sense to be shopping for kitchen, bath, and wardrobe in the same place.

El Loro Jewelry & Clog Co. (1416 Pearl St., 303/449-3162, www.ellороboulder.com, 10am-9pm Mon.-Sat., 11am-8pm Sun.) is another shop that is difficult to categorize. I just have a soft spot for this Pearl Street Mall institution that has stuck it out for nearly 40 years with the same sensibility for moccasins, clogs, and a large assortment of semiprecious stones and jewelry.

Given Boulder's connection to climbing, there is also Tibetan culture, such as **Old Tibet** (948 Pearl St., http://oldtibetboulder.com, 303/440-0323, 11am-8pm daily), which carries Buddha statues, incense, singing bowls, Tibetan music, and clothing.

Outdoor Gear

The bicycles at **Vecchio's Bicicletteria** (1833 Pearl St., 303/440-3535, www.vecchios.com, 10am-6pm Tues.-Sat.) are custom-built to order, with hand-built wheels and hand-assembled parts. Vecchio's services bikes as well. If you want to look the part, check out their many colorful bike jerseys.

One day I wandered into **Montbell** (1500 Pearl St., 303/449-5331, www.montbell.us, 11am-6pm Wed.-Fri., 10am-6pm Sat., 11am-6pm Sun.) and found the perfect winter coat for my teen, then a few weeks later we returned and found snow pants for each of us, and I returned again for a colorful pullover for hiking. Founded in Osaka, this is their flagship U.S. location with good prices and quality for basic outdoor clothes and other supplies.

Toys

Given the high winds along the Front Range, there is often a chance to go fly a kite in Boulder. Take advantage of the skies at **Into the Wind** (1408 Pearl St., 303/449-5356, www.intothewind.com, 10am-6pm daily), a kite store with a large selection of toys for all ages.

SCENIC
BOULDER
CANYON
COLORADO
1242 Pearl St
1242
1

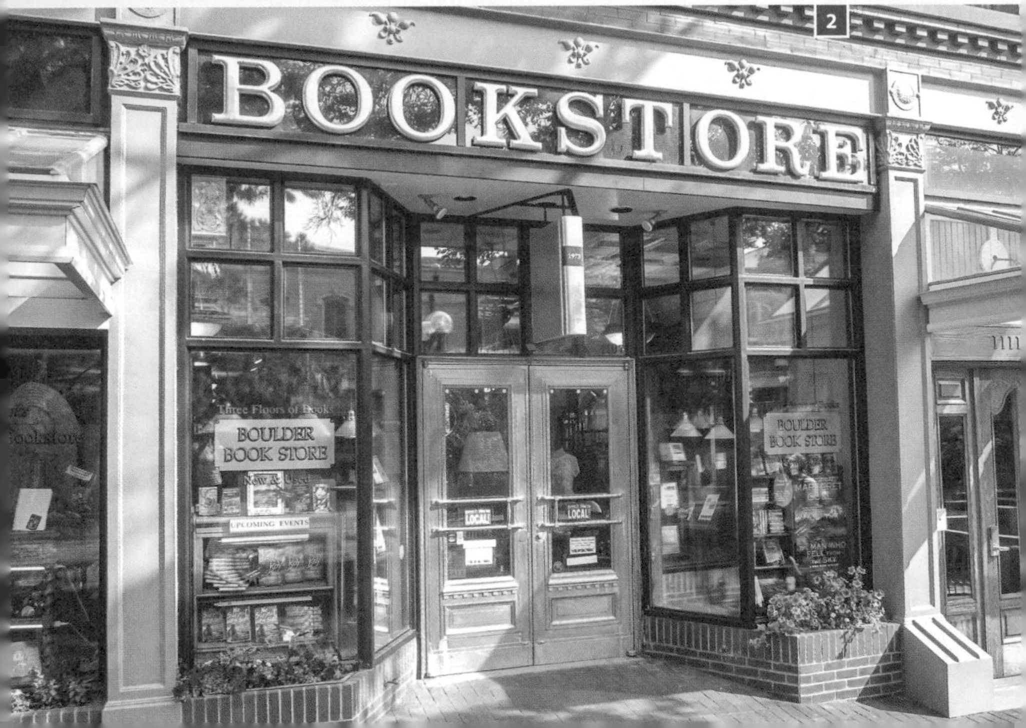
2
BOOKSTORE
Three Floors of Books
BOULDER
BOOK STORE
New & Used
UPCOMING EVENTS
LOCAL
LOCAL
BOULDER
BOOK STORE
1111

Puzzles are so much more than cardboard pieces: At **Liberty Puzzles** (1468 Pearl St., 720/524-6082, www.libertypuzzles.com, 10am-6pm Fri.-Sat., 10am-5pm Sun.), they are wooden works of art worthy of framing. Also, whimsical pieces make for treasures within each puzzle. The factory and showroom are on the east side of town (2526 49th St., 303/444-1442; call for current hours).

VILLAGE SHOPPING CENTER

Between Arapahoe Avenue and Canyon Boulevard is **The Village** (2525 Arapahoe Ave., www.villageboulder.com), a little jumble of shops and restaurants that are worth a stop.

It's something of a Boulder tradition to shop at **McGuckin Hardware** (2525 Arapahoe Ave., 303/443-1822, www.mcguckin.com, 7:30am-8pm Mon.-Fri., 8am-7pm Sat., 9am-6pm Sun.), and this giant store has much more than the name might lead you to believe. Helpful salespeople will answer all of your questions about picking out seeds for the garden or a new waffle iron, as well as give advice about actual hardware.

Another Boulder staple is **Grandrabbit's Toy Shoppe** (2525 Arapahoe St., 303/443-0780, www.grtoys.com, 9:30am-7pm Mon.-Fri., 9:30am-6pm Sat., 10am-5pm Sun.), with a big selection of books, games, and dolls. If you come with your kids, they can put a coin in the old-fashioned pony and go for a ride while you shop. Or take a seat between the bookshelves and read a little. Or chase some toy cars around. It's so fun to shop here—even if you leave the kids at home.

INDEPENDENT SHOPS

Not all retail locations are grouped together with others of their kind in Boulder. It can be worth a drive or checking pop-up market dates to shop at a few places in Boulder.

The **Firefly Handmade Market** (www.fireflyhandmade.com) is a pop-up market that occurs seasonally in different indoor and outdoor locations in Boulder. This is where hipster craftspeople come together to sell their very cool goods. You might find baby onesies, stationery, felted creatures, jewelry, ceramics, and lots of other handmade stuff that you just have to have.

If you have an interest in one-of-a-kind fragrances, make time to visit **DSH Perfumes** (4593 N. Broadway, 720/563-0344, www.dshperfumes.com, by appt. only), north of downtown. The owner combines a sense of history and knowledge about scents to create a personal perfume just for you.

So nice you want to use it twice? **The Boulder Sports Recycler** (4949 Broadway, 303/786-9940, http://bouldersportsrecycler.com, 10am-7pm daily), north of downtown, is an outdoor gear consignment store with not just gear but equipment for your next outdoor adventure, whether it's skiing or boating.

In Motion Running (1880 30th St., Unit B, 720/808-7232, http://inmotionrunning.com, 10am-6pm Mon.-Sat., 11am-4pm Sun.), east of downtown, was founded by a runner/physical therapist who is there to help with an injury or to find the best pair of running shoes for your body.

What is **Green Guru Gear** (2500 47th St., www.greengurugear.com, 303/258-1611, 9am-6pm Mon.-Fri., 10am-4pm Sat.) anyway? A bike shop? An upcycled industrial purse store? A bike maintenance place? The answer is yes (except they call them "pouches," not purses). Awareness of environmental impact of outdoor gear led to the upcycling of bicycle tire tubes and now a little empire of all these somehow related pursuits. To reach Green Guru Gear, head east on Pearl Street just past the Foothills Parkway, about 3 miles (5 km) from downtown.

Neptune Mountaineering (633 S. Broadway, www.neptunemountaineering.com, 303/499-8866, 10am-7pm Mon.-Fri., 9am-6pm Sat.-Sun.) has been around for decades, helping local climbers and athletes get the right gear before they tackle the nearby mountains. Buy a tent, a climbing

1: performer at the Pearl Street Mall **2:** Boulder Bookstore rope, a cute dress, and whatever you want or need while doing anything active. Neptune Mountaineering is found in the Table Mesa neighborhood south of downtown in a double-decker strip mall.

Sports and Recreation

What makes Boulder so appealing is its easy access to the great outdoors, where you can simply start running, biking, or hiking right out the front door. This city is often voted the fittest in America due to its low obesity rate. While the football games at Folsom Field on the University of Colorado campus are very popular, many of the popular sports such as cycling and bouldering aren't necessarily spectator sports.

Whatever sport you choose—even a casual guided walk—keep the altitude in mind. Boulder is 5,430 feet (1,655 m) above sea level, and many recreational activities will take you higher than that as you hike or bike into the foothills. Each person has a different experience as the body adjusts to a higher altitude, but difficulty breathing is the most common symptom. If possible, don't go for that 25-mile bike ride or 10-mile hike on your first day in town. Instead, drink plenty of water and acclimate with minimal physical exertion.

PARKS

If you just want to hang out with the little ones and enjoy a playground, the best options are **Chautauqua** (900 Baseline Rd.), where there is a playground and large grassy field; **Scott Carpenter Park** (30th St. and Arapahoe St., 303/441-3427, www.bouldercolorado.gov), which has a large outdoor pool, skate park, and playground; and **Eben G. Fine** (3rd St. and Arapahoe St., www.bouldercolorado.gov), with a playground, picnic spots, and a chance to wade into the creek.

BALLOONING

Fair Winds Hot Air Balloon Flights (303/939-9323, http://hotairballoonridescolorado.com, $229 per person) offers 1.5-hour flights from Boulder with your pilot-guide explaining points of interest. Go online to get $50 off during spring specials; note that prices are about $30 higher on weekends.

BIKING

Bike paths along Boulder Creek and designated bike lanes on most city streets make it easy to navigate the town on two wheels. There are about 200 miles (320 km) of bikeways and trails in Boulder; a popular portion of that is on the **Boulder Creek Bike Path** (www.bouldercolorado.gov), which stretches east of town to Cherryvale Road from its starting point in the foothills at Fourmile Canyon. The trail is very popular and there are speed-limit signs on this 7-mile (11-km) path.

The popular **Greenbelt Plateau Trail** (trailhead just east of the intersection of Hwy. 128 and Hwy. 93, www.bouldercolorado.gov), 4.5 miles (7.2 km) round-trip, offers a chance to see a bit of wildlife, some birds, and probably some equestrians. It's an easy ride on the plains below the foothills and connects to other trails.

Yes, you can ride bikes on all kinds of roads and trails around Boulder—or you can ride at the **Boulder Valley Velodrome** (303/818-5817, www.bouldervalleyvelodrome.com), 15 miles (24 km) from Boulder in the town of Erie. This track-cycling facility isn't just for athletes—anyone can take a "Taster Session" introductory lesson. While the bike is provided, check the website for a list of mandatory items you will need to bring, like a helmet, cycling shorts, socks, and more.

1: a hot-air balloon over Boulder **2:** biking, a favorite activity in and around Boulder **3:** tubing down Boulder Creek **4:** hiking near Boulder

1

2

3

4

The **Valmont Bike Park** (3160 Airport Rd., 303/413-7200, www.bouldercolorado.gov, dawn-dusk daily, weather permitting, free) has 42 acres of natural-surface cycling terrain. Given the size of the park, there is room for both families with little ones on the balance bikes and cyclocross riders practicing their skills on ramps. Dogs are not allowed on the trails. The park is accessible by bike or car. Call ahead to check trail conditions.

Bike Rentals

There are about two dozen bike stores in Boulder. That may seem like a lot for a town of this size, but there is a demand for new, used, rentals, repairs, parts—in short, everything to do with bikes for all ages and abilities. **University Bicycles** (839 Pearl St., 303/444-4196, http://ubikes.com, 10am-7pm Mon.-Fri., 10am-6pm Sat., 10am-5pm Sun.) is just west of the Pearl Street Mall and offers rentals of all kinds—kids' bikes, mountain bikes, road bikes, and more—with a really helpful staff that knows the area. **Boulder B-cycle** (http://boulder.bcycle.com) has electric bikes (e-bikes) to rent from kiosks around town, which allows you to rent a bike for a daily, weekly, or annual fee (bring your own helmet).

BIRD-WATCHING

The **Boulder Bird Club** (www.boulderbirdclub.org) meets the first Sunday of each month at Cottonwood Marsh at **Walden Ponds Wildlife Habitat** (75th St., between Jay Rd. and Valmont St., 8am and 11am May-Sept., 9am and noon Oct.-Apr.). There are additional Wednesday meetups from mid-April through September with different destinations. While these events do not require reservations (bring your own binoculars, though!), you can check the club's newsletter for information on guided field trips offered throughout the year. You might see the occasional pelican or egret, but mostly you will see and hear warblers and ducks.

FISHING

Where you fish in Boulder might depend on your age. So often activities need to be all-inclusive of ages and abilities, but here people might be able to enjoy this sport while only with others of similar ages and ability.

Cattail Ponds at the Boulder County Fairgrounds (9595 Nelson Rd., Longmont, 303/678-6200, www.bouldercounty.org) is open exclusively to kids under age 16; they do not need a fishing license. The ponds are stocked with bluegill and channel catfish. On the other end of the spectrum is **Wally Toevs at Walden Ponds** (75th St. and Valmont St., 303/678-6200, www.bouldercounty.org), which has wheelchair-accessible ramps and is for people over age 63 and people with disabilities. This pond has bluegill, rainbow trout, and largemouth bass. There is fishing allowed for all ages at other locations at Walden Ponds, too.

Stream fishing is permitted at **South Boulder Creek on Walker Ranch Open Space** (303/678-6200, www.bouldercounty.org), where the creek is regularly stocked with rainbow trout. To get here, take Baseline Road west out of town to where it becomes Flagstaff Road, and then continue 7.9 miles (12.7 km) on Flagstaff Road.

Front Range Anglers (2344 Pearl St., 303/494-1375, http://frontrangeanglers.com, 9am-6pm Mon.-Fri., 9am-5pm Sat., 10am-4pm Sun.) is probably the best place to check in on fishing conditions in the area, take a fly-fishing lesson, or get your fishing gear. They also give guided fishing trips in the area so you don't have to go it alone your first time.

HIKING

When there are numerous books written with detailed advice on where to hike in and around Boulder, it's a daunting task to select just a few to include here. Just know that this is not a comprehensive list of hikes for this area, but this author's personal favorites that will provide a taste of Boulder hiking. Also note there is wildlife—mountain lions, coyotes, foxes, deer, and more—on many of

Rock On

Those ubiquitous **Flatirons** were pushed into place some 40 million years ago; today they serve as an enticement to rock climbers and photographers who want to conquer or capture them. Images of the five slabs of rough sandstone that once made up a seafloor are everywhere in Boulder, as is the name (there are Flatirons car dealerships, churches, malls, and more).

Rock climbers have been scaling the Flatirons since 1906, and much has been written about the technical aspects of climbing each of the formations. Nesting raptors—including peregrine falcons and prairie falcons—are protected here, and therefore climbing is off-limits in mating season.

Over the years the Flatirons have been not only climbed on but also roller skated on, skied on, and unfortunately, painted on (though the giant C and U have since been covered). These gigantic rocks inspire all kinds of zany behavior (full moon hikes, hikes in "the buff," racing) as people come up with new ways to experience the climb.

Unless you have the equipment and skill, it's probably best to just enjoy the view.

these trails, as well as other natural hazards to factor in, such as lightning. The **Boulder County Open Space and Mountain Parks** website (www.bouldercolorado.gov/osmp) has detailed tips on how to mitigate these dangers and how to handle the situation if you do encounter adverse conditions or situations (there is a whole page devoted to bears and mountain lions, for example). Know the symptoms of altitude sickness and be sure to rest as needed.

CHAUTAUQUA

Chautauqua (900 Baseline Rd., www.bouldercolorado.gov), also known as Chautauqua Park, is a great place to start for hikes of varying length and difficulty. Go to the **Ranger Cottage** (9am-4pm Mon.-Fri., 8am-6pm Sat.-Sun.) near the entrance of the park for maps, brochures, and expert advice from the staff.

Royal Arch, a natural arch, can be reached via a rewarding moderate out-and-back hike (3.5 mi/5.6 km round-trip). You get views to the southwest and east showing the plains and hogbacks below from a peek through the arch. Go early to avoid crowds. This is also a starting point to reach the base of the three Flatirons, which can also be climbed.

You can climb up to the rocks on the **Flatirons #1** hike. This 2.9-mile (4.7-km) round-trip hike rewards you with views along the way. There are switchbacks and you are gaining elevation, but it's not too steep and is considered a moderate hike.

For a bit steeper climb, **Gregory Canyon** is pretty and thick with trees before opening up to beautiful views. You have options in deciding length, destination, and level of difficulty. There is a difficult 3.3-mile (5.3-km) loop that is quite popular. It offers a variety of scenery and vistas, including a historic cabin, a view of Boulder to the east from atop Green Mountain, and a creek that you cross.

FLAGSTAFF MOUNTAIN

Once you've acclimated to the altitude, go for the **Flagstaff Mountain** hike and take in the view of the valley below from 6,850 feet (2,090 m) above sea level. The **Flagstaff Nature Center** (Flagstaff Summit Rd., 303/441-3440, www.bouldercolorado.gov, 10am-4pm Sat.-Sun. Memorial Day-Labor Day) is worth a visit, especially with small children who will enjoy some of the interactive exhibits. Flagstaff Trailhead is where Baseline Road turns into Flagstaff Road; the trail is 1.5 miles (2.4 km) and gains more than 1,000 feet (300 m) of elevation.

MT. SANITAS TRAIL

The **Mt. Sanitas Trail** (0.5 mi/0.8 km west of 4th St. on Mapleton Ave., 303/441-3440, www.

bouldercolorado.gov) is very popular for day hikers and trail runners—and their dogs! Part of the appeal of this 3-mile (4.8-km) loop is that you don't necessarily need to drive here if you are already in downtown Boulder. Note that this short but difficult hike has a big elevation gain (over 1,200 feet/366 m), so you'll need plenty of water, maybe snacks, and time—but you're rewarded with views of the city of Boulder, the Flatirons, and beyond.

ANNE U. WHITE TRAIL

For something easier and with less altitude gain, try the tree-lined **Anne U. White Trail** (www.bouldercounty.org), which is 3 miles (4.8 km) round-trip. This easy-to-moderate hike is great to do with young kids and people new to Colorado for its gentle uphill gain of less than 500 feet (152 m). Take Broadway north to Lee Hill Road west. Turn left on Lee Hill Road, then take a left on Wagonwheel Gap Road and another left on Pinto Drive to reach the trailhead.

NCAR TRAILHEAD

How often do you get science and nature combined in a trail? Well, maybe more often than you realize, but it's especially the case at the **NCAR Trailhead** (1850 Table Mesa Dr., 303/441-3440, www.bouldercolorado.gov). Beginning at the National Center for Atmospheric Research's iconic Mesa Lab building, the **Walter Orr Roberts Weather Trail,** an easy 0.5-mile (0.8-km) loop, includes interesting signs about the local weather (fun for kids who might find plain old hiking dull). If you're interested in a longer hike, the trail meets up with a handful of popular easy-to-moderate hiking trails. There is a very good chance of seeing deer around the NCAR building or along the hike.

HORSEBACK RIDING

Many of Boulder's trails are multiuse, so be aware that as you walk, you might have a horse and rider come up or a mountain biker zoom by.

The **Cherryvale Trail** (66 S. Cherryvale Rd., 303/441-3440, www.bouldercolorado.gov) is on the east side of Boulder and is an easy trail. What I like about this trail is that you get to experience a different side of Boulder, and not just literally. There is different wildlife here, and you're enjoying that view of the mountains and Flatirons instead of being *in* the mountains. It can also be less crowded than the foothills.

Resources for horseback riders include the **Boulder County Horse Association** (www.boulderhorse.org), with trail information.

ROCK CLIMBING

Yep, you can climb them. The **Boulder Flatirons** are climbed regularly, but know that this is not for the inexperienced. Ill-prepared climbers are rescued here what seems like annually as they get stuck for lack of proper equipment or they start too late in the day and cannot find their way out in the dark. Contact the **Colorado Mountain School** (2829 Mapleton Ave., http://coloradomountainschool.com, 800/836-4008, ext. 3, $429) to sign up for a full-day guided climb (beginners must also take a prep course for an additional fee the night before the climb) on the 1st or 3rd Flatiron.

Climbing in **Boulder Canyon** is so legendary that there have been books written about the granite rock faces here. If you have the experience and gear, drive west on Canyon Boulevard to where it turns into Highway 119; there you'll see both groups of cars and people along the roadside. There are many different skill levels and interest levels for climbers here, so do a little more detailed research before you head into the hills. A great place to start is **Neptune Mountaineering** (633 S. Broadway, 303/499-8866, www.neptunemountaineering.com), which has all the climbing gear you might need. While you can shop online, visiting the store means you can also get advice from the people who work here—and who happen to be experienced local rock climbers. Rental gear is also available.

The country's first indoor ice climbing gym, **The Ice Coop** (2500 47th St.,

720/219/0977, https://theicecoop.com, 10am-6pm Mon. and Fri., 10am-8pm Tues.-Thurs., by appt. only Sat., $12-275) is new to Boulder, with just the right conditions for practicing this extreme sport. Gear rentals are available, or bring your own. Sign up for a day pass or take a class.

SPAS

The Spa at St. Julien (900 Walnut St., 877/303-0900, www.stjulien.com) is where I would want someone to buy me a gift certificate to enjoy a day of pampering in Boulder. Just imagine, after a strenuous hike in the foothills, getting a Sole Delight treatment here, in which reflexology and aromatherapy blend together to rejuvenate those tootsies. Or counteract the effects of the altitude and dry climate with a Canyon Rain treatment: soak in a warm bath before being thoroughly scrubbed under a Vichy shower. Bliss! Their spa menu offers dozens of possible treatments sure to bring a smile to your face.

Find your Zen at the **Dragontree Holistic Day Spa** (1521 Pearl St., 303/219-1444, www.thedragontree.com), where you can improve your sense of well-being both inside and out. The spa offers acupuncture, herbal medicine, and nutrition services in addition to the usual spa massages, skin care, and body treatments. Check out the Sangha room if you like a community atmosphere while getting a hand or foot treatment.

SWIMMING

There are a few options for cooling off in Boulder on a hot summer day. First, the **Boulder Reservoir** (5100 51st St., 303/441-3468, www.bouldercolorado.gov, $11 adults, $8.25 seniors, $6.50 ages 3-18) east of town is Boulder's version of a beach. It's a shadeless sandy park along the water, and fun in the summer for sailing, swimming, fishing, or just floating. **Boulder Creek** is used for kayaking and tubing, but be aware of the rough conditions before trying either activity. The creek is very choppy in spots and dotted with large rocks. **Scott Carpenter Park** (30th St. and Arapahoe St., 303/441-3427, www.bouldercolorado.gov, $11 adults, $8.25 seniors, $6.50 ages 3-18) has a large outdoor pool.

Food

Boulder has become a foodie town, with menus at various restaurants that feature the bounty of local produce and meats from nearby farms and ranches. The chefs and owners here have been featured on TV shows and in food and wine magazines. Some local chefs own their own farms and participate in farm-to-table dinners—you might even meet one while shopping at the Boulder County Farmers Market. The selection of Boulder restaurants includes everything from casual vegetarian options to upscale, once-in-a-lifetime meals served amid wonderful views. If you live here or are visiting in the fall, see if you can get a reservation during **First Bite: Boulder Restaurant Week** (mid.-Nov.) to sample prix fixe menus at dozens of restaurants.

COFFEE AND TEA

The **Dushanbe Teahouse** (1770 13th St., 303/442-4993, www.boulderteahouse.com, 11am-8pm Tues.-Fri., 9am-9pm Sat., 9am-8pm Sun., $12-18) is worth a visit on its own, but it's also a great place for a meal and a cup of tea. Breakfast, lunch, and dinner menus are fairly simple, but with a mix of cultures—Tajikistani *plov* (a traditional beef rice dish), Indian tikka masala, and pizza are all offered.

My go-to coffee and tea shop in Boulder is ★ **Trident Booksellers and Café** (940 Pearl St., 303/443-3133, http://tridentcafe.com, 7am-8pm daily), just west of the Pearl Street Mall. A doorway connects the separate café and bookshop spaces. On the bookstore side are new and used books on art, religion, and poetry, many of which are rare or hard-to-find titles. On the café side there is selection of coffees, teas, and pastries to choose from and a lovely back patio to visit with friends over an iced beverage in summer.

The Laughing Goat Coffeehouse (1709 Pearl St., 303/440-4628, www.thelaughinggoat.com, 6:30am-8pm Mon.-Fri., 7am-8pm Sat.-Sun.) has three locations around Boulder. This downtown branch serves Kaladi Brothers coffee (based in Denver), but it's more than just a place for a morning pick-me-up. They host regular events, serving as an evening out for poetry, jazz, and other performances, when they also serve beer and wine.

BREAKFAST AND LUNCH

The playful, bright, orange-accented interior of **Tangerine** (2777 Iris Ave., 303/443-2333, www.tangerineboulder.com, 7:30am-1:30pm Mon.-Fri., 7:30am-2:30pm Sat.-Sun., $7-16) will certainly wake you up. If not, order a velvety latte and brioche French toast to ease into the day. Owner-chef Alec Schuler is mindful of maintaining a healthy balanced lifestyle. Creative breakfast dishes like polenta and *romesco* sauce with poached eggs sure make a statement, as do the caprese frittata and trout and apple Benedict.

★ **Lucile's Creole Café** (2124 14th St., 303/442-4743, www.luciles.com, 7am-2pm Mon.-Fri., 8am-2pm Sat.-Sun., $10) started here. The original Lucile's—the iconic yellow Victorian on 14th Street—is a culinary landmark in Boulder, especially for the brunch-minded. Even if you show up early, expect to wait a while for a spot in this popular breakfast and brunch restaurant, where the chicory coffee and beignets are as good as they are in the Deep South. Don't miss the shrimp and grits or *pain perdu* (French toast), and beware—the famous home-style buttermilk biscuits are larger than life. There are six locations of Lucile's, including in Denver and Fort Collins.

What would Boulder be without its mascot? Roll into **The Buff** (2600 Canyon Blvd., 303/442-9150, www.buffrestaurant.com, 7am-2pm daily, $10) on a weekend morning, and you'll find a hungry breakfast crowd, slow-moving college kids, and tourists looking for a hearty mountain meal. You'll also find lots of local products like Ozo Coffee, Teatulia organic teas, Avery beer, and Boulder granola—plus fancy mimosas, giant Bloody Marys (ask for the Tatanka), and a chai they call The Dirty Hippie. They also serve breakfast staples like omelets and griddle cakes, as well as a few Southwestern dishes like huevos rancheros and chilaquiles (on the menu as Buffaquiles).

BISTRO

My lunch favorite (though it's also open for dinner) is ★ **The Kitchen** (1039 Pearl St., 303/544-5973, http://thekitchen.com, 11am-3pm and 5pm-9pm Mon.-Thurs., 10am-3pm and 5pm-9pm Fri.-Sun., $12-30), which made a name for itself by being "green" in a variety of ways—using wind power, recycling grease—and because of its delicious food. Check out the giant blackboard to see the list of local purveyors who grow the food you eat at this simply elegant restaurant.

SALT the Bistro (1047 Pearl St., 303/444-7258, www.saltthebistro.com, 11am-3pm and 5pm-9pm Mon.-Wed., 11am-3pm and 5pm-10pm Thurs., 11am-3pm and 5pm-close Fri.-Sat., 10am-3pm and 5pm-9pm Sun., $15-30) comes from chef-owner Bradford Heap, the man behind the countryside-chic Colterra in nearby Niwot. Walk in and marvel at the interior design, constructed completely from recycled materials by local artists. Heap is big on local farmers and non-GMOs, which you'll notice on the tempting menu, featuring produce from his own farm and countless others. For dinner, select from pastas, entrées, and small plates, as well as a lineup of creative seasonal cocktails and several local craft beers.

Black Cat Bistro (1964 Pearl St., 303/440-5500, https://blackcatboulder.com, 5:30pm-close Mon.-Sat., $16-24) doesn't have quite the

Dinners at Black Cat Farm

If you plan ahead and are here at the right time of year (May-Oct.), you can have an alfresco dinner at **Black Cat Farm** (9889 N. 51st St., Longmont, 303/440-5500, https://blackcatboulder.com). On the outskirts of Boulder to the northeast, the farm is owned by Eric and Jill Skokan, who also own Black Cat Bistro downtown. Stunning views of the mountains and meticulously prepared meals await. The cost for three-course farm prix-fixe dinners is $125 per person (not including tax, beverages, and gratuity), and the menu is "blind" in that you won't know what is being served until it's in front of you.

same buzz as The Kitchen or Frasca, but it's popular with locals who appreciate the simple organic fare made into unexpected dishes like Juxtaposition of Duck with lavender honey or Blue Crab, Hot and Cold. Black Cat offers a few tasting menus (including vegetarian or vegan) paired with wines.

BURGERS

One of the best burger restaurants in Colorado has a place in Boulder: **Larkburger** (2525 Arapahoe St., 303/444-1487, www.larkburger.com, 11am-8pm Sun.-Thurs., 11am-9pm Fri.-Sat., $2-8) has yummy burgers and to-die-for truffle parmesan fries, plus healthy sides like salads and edamame.

COMFORT FOOD

Located on The Hill (the area near the University of Colorado campus up the hill from downtown), **The Sink** (1165 13th St., 303/444-7465, www.thesink.com, 11:30am-9pm Sun.-Thurs., 11:30am-10pm Fri.-Sat., $15) boasts more than 90 years of serving casual sandwiches, pizza, burgers, and more to the hungry public. Still a family-owned eatery, The Sink caters especially to locals and University of Colorado students and alumni, whom you'll find in abundance on any given day. But celebrities know the spot, too: Guy Fieri made a stop in 2011, and President Barack Obama paid a visit in 2012. The interior is decorated with wall murals and eclectic marker art, giving you something to contemplate over your Cowboy Reuben or SinkBurger.

CONTEMPORARY

OAK at fourteenth (1400 Pearl St., 303/444-3622, www.oakatfourteenth.com, 5pm-9pm Wed.-Sun., $15-30) is where Boulder's modern style blends with Colorado's rustic environs. The food is driven by seasonal ingredients and unmatched service, and OAK centers around the restaurant's oak-fired oven and grill, the primary inspiration for chef-owner Steve Redzikowski's take on contemporary New American food. Locally sourced meats and produce, as well as sustainable seafood, top house-made pastas and crisp greens, all seasoned with that signature oak flavor.

FINE DINING

The ultimate in fine dining has long been the ★ **Flagstaff House** (1138 Flagstaff Dr., 303/442-4640, www.flagstaffhouse.com, 5:30pm-9pm Sun.-Thurs., 5pm-9:30pm Fri.-Sat., check for winter hours, $32-76). Everything will make you swoon—the view, the food, the wine. This family-owned gem is one of the country's premier dining experiences, and well worth the drive up the twisting mountain road for a classic special night out.

LOCAVORE

Zeal—Food for Enthusiasts (1710 Pearl St., 720/708-6309, www.zealfood.com, 11am-8pm Mon. and Wed.-Thurs., 9am-9pm Fri.-Sat., 9am-8pm Sun., $10-20) is committed to locally sourced, mostly organic, and regional ingredients that celebrate a true zest for life. Walk in and you'll see the list of local farms and purveyors on a chalkboard on the wall. Zeal finds most of their ingredients in and around Boulder County, serving breakfast, lunch, and dinner made from the purest food they can get their hands on. Try their fresh, cold-pressed juices (and juice cocktails), veggie bowls, and a range of fermented goodies like kimchi and house pickles.

★ **Blackbelly Market** (1606 Conestoga St., 303/247-1000, www.blackbelly.com, 7am-9pm Mon.-Fri., 4pm-9pm Sat.-Sun., $15-40) is led by award-winning chef-owner Hosea Rosenberg (winner of Bravo TV's season 5 of *Top Chef*), serving fresh and expertly butchered charcuterie, burgers, steaks, and hand-cut Kennebec fries in this sleek and social environment, where the philosophy hinges on the hyperlocal. Rosenberg raises his own lambs and pigs, supplies organic produce from his greenhouse, and even operates a catering service out of a food truck. Parking at the restaurant is plentiful, and seating includes dining room tables, the chef's counter, an intimate bar, and two outdoor patios.

SANDWICHES

Sandwiches are big business, and **Snarf's** (5340 Arapahoe Ave., 303/444-3404, www.eatsnarfs.com, 11am-8pm daily, $10) is proof of that. Snarf's opened in 1996 as a humble family-owned sandwich shop. The chain now has nearly 20 locations in Colorado, Missouri, and Texas. What makes it so good? The homemade oven-toasted bread, the house *giardiniera* peppers, and the scratch-made dressings add something special to your made-to-order 5-, 7-, or 12-inch sandwich. There are even Snarflettes—mini-sandwiches with kid-friendly ingredients—for the young'uns.

SEAFOOD

Jax Fish House (928 Pearl St., 303/444-1811, www.jaxfishhouse.com/boulder, 3:30pm-9pm Sun.-Thurs., 3:30pm-10pm Fri.-Sat., $15-20) has served the fruits of the briny sea to Boulder (and locations in Fort Collins, Denver, Colorado Springs, and Glendale) for more than 20 years. Grab a seat at the raw bar for a round of freshly shucked oysters before diving into their sustainably sourced seafood menu, guaranteed to make you feel a little less landlocked.

Spruce Farm & Fish (2115 13th St., 303/442-4880, www.sprucebboulderado.com, 7am-2pm and 5pm-10pm daily, $15-30) is the smartly outfitted eatery in the classy, historic Hotel Boulderado. Spruce holds on to its early 1900s heritage (think stained glass and black-and-white floor tiles) while entertaining contemporary guests with cozy booths, handsome wooden tables, and crowd-pleasing dishes like the smoked trout dip, stuffed *piquillo* peppers, and the show-stopping crispy whole snapper. Don't forget dessert; the rustic apple pie is worthy of a visit all on its own.

CHINESE

Right here in Boulder, Chinese street food! **Zoe Ma Ma** (2010 10th St., 303/545-6262, ext. 1, www.zoemama.com, 11am-9pm Sun.-Thurs., 11am-9:30pm Fri.-Sat., $2-14) is encouraging a new way of not only preparing Chinese food—cage-free eggs, fresh homemade organic noodles, all-natural meat—but also how you tip. They add 15 percent to provide staff with a living wage and maintain a recycling program. Eat good, do good.

Chimera (2014 10th St., 720/835-2323, http://chimera.restaurant, 11:30am-9pm Sun.-Thurs., 11:30am-9:30pm Fri.-Sat., $14-25) might not quite be categorized as Chinese cuisine, but it's the same owner as Zoe Ma Ma, this time with Pacific Rim dishes. The menu is a mix of Japanese, Chinese, and Taiwanese specialties and flavors like jasmine-tea-infused chicken, duck dumplings, and ramen.

ITALIAN

It's a special night out to dine at ★ **Frasca** (1738 Pearl St., 303/442-6966, www.frascafoodandwine.com, 5pm-9pm Tues.-Sat., $28-36), where the menu is based on the cuisine of the Fruili region of Italy. Frasca also

1: Dushanbe Teahouse **2:** Jax Fish House **3:** Japango **4:** Frasca

1

jax
HAPPY HOUR
DAILY 4:00 - 6:00
$1.50 OYSTERS
2

Japango
3

frasca
FOOD AND WINE
4

emphasizes using local sources for its Italian dishes. Dining here is a total experience—therefore reservations are recommended—which makes sense when you consider the owner has done a TEDx Talk and the restaurant has won the James Beard Foundation Award for its wine program, among many other accolades. Come with friends and linger over the wine and food to make it a really special night.

Local food lovers can't get enough of **Basta** (3601 Arapahoe Ave., 303/997-8775, www.bastaboulder.com, 5pm-8:30pm Tues.-Sat., $15-20), Boulder's hip and casual Italian concept. Chef Kelly Whitaker cooks everything in a wood-fired oven—taking the techniques he learned in Italy, sprinkling on his own innovation, and achieving a mouthwatering char on pizzas and entrées. Guests enjoy the locally grown ingredients, seasonal menus, and a creative beverage list.

From the owners of Frasca—Boulder's top spot for northern Italian fine dining, located right next door—**Pizzeria Locale** (1730 Pearl St., 303/442-3003, www.localeboulder.com, 5pm-9pm Mon.-Thurs., 11:30am-9pm Fri.-Sat., $15) offers a comfortable place to experience Neapolitan-style pizza in Boulder. Pizzas are fired in a 10,000-pound, Italian-made pizza oven, which cooks pies to chewy, charred perfection in less than two minutes. High-quality ingredients and warm service make it great for a casual date or a family dinner—especially with a pair of *aperitivos* and a shared side of meatballs.

JAPANESE

Japango (1136 Pearl St., 303/938-0330, www.boulderjapango.com, 11am-10pm daily, $17-32) has graced bustling Pearl Street for years. Japango springs into the current era with an expanded, illuminated bar, a bustling open-air patio, and (still) the largest sake collection in Boulder. A seat at the sushi counter will give you a good view into the artistry behind your *maki.* And if you stick around for the late-night, DJ-driven happy hour, you're bound to make a few new friends over a round of sake bombs.

★ **Sushi Zanmai** (1221 Spruce St., 303/440-0733, www.sushizanmai.com, 11:30am-2pm and 5pm-9pm Wed.-Thurs. and Sun., 11:30am-2pm and 5pm-9:30pm Fri.-Sat., $3-14) has long been Boulder's favorite sushi restaurant. Thirty-plus years is an impressive run in the restaurant industry! There are great deals at this casual spot during happy hours (5pm-6:30pm Wed.-Sat., all night Sun.). If you don't eat sushi, their menu has a lot of tasty entrées featuring chicken, beef, or cooked fish.

LATIN AMERICAN

Rincon Argentino (2525 Arapahoe Ave., 303/442-4133, www.rinconargentinoboulder.com, 11am-8pm Mon.-Thurs., 11am-9pm Fri.-Sat., 11am-6pm Sun., $5-10) has a menu of empanadas—South American sandwich pies, if you will, mostly savory and served with a variety of dipping sauces. This makes for a quick, affordable, and filling lunch with a little spice or a great simple meal before a movie night.

MEXICAN

T/aco (1175 Walnut St., 303/443-9468, http://tacocolorado.com, 11am-10pm Mon.-Sat., 11am-9pm Sun., $4-8) has street tacos at street food prices, plus larger entrées like Mexican pizza for bigger appetites.

MIDDLE EASTERN

If you know your Hebrew slang, you'll be saying **Ash'Kara** (1043 Pearl St., 303/993-5286, www.ashkarafood.com, 4pm-9pm Tues.-Sun., $11-21), which translates to "Right on!" Falafel, kabobs, creamy hummus, and other flavorful Israeli staples make for a hearty meal to be shared with friends.

NEPALESE

With rock and mountain climbers comes climbing food, and that means traditional Himalayan and Nepalese fare. **Sherpa's** (825 Walnut St., 303/440-7151, www.sherpas-restaurant.com, 11am-3pm and 5pm-9pm daily, $15) is more than an opportunity to sample the tastes of the Mount Everest region. This is also a cultural center with a gallery of mountain-trek photos and a library of mountaineering books—you can even sign up for a trek! But first, order some warm naan and . . . yak stew. You only live once, right? The menu is a combination of Indian, Himalayan, and Nepalese foods.

The sound of it rolling off your tongue is almost as good as the flavor: *momo.* These Tibetan dumplings served at **Tibet Kitchen** (2359 Arapahoe St., 303/440-0882, www.tibetkitchen.com, 11am-10pm Mon.-Sat., 5pm-10pm Sun., $10) make for an affordable, delicious, and filling meal. At these prices, you can experiment to find the flavors you prefer in sauces, rice, soups, and more.

SPANISH AND MOROCCAN

Exposed brick, cozy window seats, and a rustic central fireplace are doused in sunlight at **Cafe Aion** (1235 Pennsylvania Ave., 303/993-8131, www.cafeaion.com, 3pm-9pm Tues.-Sat., 11am-9pm Sun., $10-40), a convivial Spanish tapas restaurant done the Boulder way. Join a relaxed, social crowd sampling small plates of locally farmed and ranched ingredients like Moroccan-spiced pork sliders and fried cauliflower with saffron yogurt. Breakfast is practically legendary, so come in the morning and enjoy egg dishes and breakfast tapas, even better with Ozo espresso. By night, try the house-cured salt cod croquettes and Colorado lamb *merguez* sausage over flatbread, washed down with a glass of cava.

Accommodations

Always keep in mind that Boulder is a college town; when booking a hotel, do so in advance for those times when the families of the thousands of students come to visit, such as graduation in May or when school starts in late summer. There are lodging options within walking distance of the campus for those who are here to say "Farewell!" to their freshman or "Congratulations!" to their graduate.

While Boulder isn't necessarily the place for budget lodgings, chances are you will find a place that embraces that quintessential Boulder quality you desire. Meditation room? Check. Hiking trails right outside? Check. Luxurious spa? Check. Historic character? Check. Whether you are in town to visit the campus or just as a tourist, you can walk or ride a bike to many fine restaurants or trailheads, or go shopping near many of these hotels.

UNDER $150

The ★ **Boulder Adventure Lodge** (91 Four Mile Canyon Dr., 303/444-0882, www.a-lodge.com, $129-199) is popular with the rock climbers who come to the area with big dreams and little cash. It's in a very pretty setting and includes affordable options like a bunk room or camping (at much lower rates) in addition to rooms and suites. This is old school, with no a/c in the rooms, but if you are here to soak up the mountain scenery, this is for you.

Technically in Boulder, but closer to the suburb of Gunbarrel, is the **Boulder Twin Lakes Inn** (6485 Twin Lakes Rd., 303/530-2939 or 800/322-2939, www.twinlakesinnboulder.com, $145-159). Accommodations resemble short-term corporate apartments, with some level of kitchen supplies in each room. Guests have use of a communal kitchen and guest laundry, and there are running trails nearby with a view of the Flatirons. Weekly and monthly rates are available. Note that Gunbarrel is northeast of downtown Boulder, so you'll need a car for this stay.

$150-250

The **Boulder University Inn** (1632 Broadway, 303/417-1700, www.boulderuniversityinn.com, $150-225) has a very convenient location a block from Boulder Creek, just at the base of The Hill adjacent to campus, and a short stroll from the Pearl Street Mall. There's even an outdoor pool to use in the summer months. Rates are generally under $200 in high season. While this isn't the most modern or stylish accommodation in town, it makes up for that with its central location and clean rooms.

The **Boulder Guest House** (2151 Arapahoe St., 303/442-3007, www.boulderguesthouse.com, $189-250), formerly Briar Rose Inn, is a very cute property with eight rooms available between the main house and carriage house. Tea and organic breakfast are served daily and can be enjoyed outside in the sweet garden. This is one of the closest lodging options to Naropa University. The inn has a meditation room for those who need to find their Zen.

Get away from downtown just a bit at the **Foot of the Mountain Motel** (200 W. Arapahoe Ave., 303/442-5688 or 866/773-5489, www.footofthemountainmotel.com, $200-370), where it's 1930s rustic on the outside and modern and tidy on the inside. While this place is dog-friendly, they do not allow dogs in all of the rooms, so be sure to ask when making your reservation if you intend to bring your pooch. You're still easy walking and cycling distance from all downtown amenities.

To stay someplace truly unique and just-so-Boulder, book a cottage at ★ **Chautauqua** (900 Baseline Rd., 303/442-3282, www.chautauqua.com). Cottages ($185-285) range from studios to three-bedrooms with kitchens; lodge rates ($1,155-1,275) are for the entire eight-bedroom facility. From mid-June to mid-August, nightly rentals ($75-126) are available at the Columbine Lodge. There is no air-conditioning in some of the cabins, and daily housekeeping is not offered.

★ **The Bradley Boulder Inn** (2040 16th St., 303/545-5200, www.thebradleyboulder.com, $225-300) is like a home away from home, if home is just steps away from the city's shops, restaurants, and nightlife. Mingle with your fellow guests in the inn's great room, which has a fireplace and comfy sofas and chairs. Note that children under age 14 are not allowed, and there are only stairs to the second floor. This is a nonsmoking facility.

the historic Hotel Boulderado

OVER $250

The Victorian architecture and decor make the ★ **Hotel Boulderado** (2115 13th St., 303/442-4344, www.boulderado.com, $270-400) timeless and always appealing for a comfortable night's stay. It's one block off the Pearl Street Mall and walking distance to many recommended restaurants and shops. Meet friends for a drink and a nibble at **The Corner Bar** (303/442-4880, www.cornerbarboulderado.com, 11am-midnight daily) or **License No. 1** (303/442-4880, www.boulderado.com, 5pm-close Wed.-Sun.) on the ground floor of the Boulderado. The Boulderado not only has a wonderful history since its opening in 1909, but much of it *is* history by now—the distinctive red sandstone came from Fort Collins, the mosaic tile in the lobby and elsewhere is original, and you can use the white marble drinking fountain, which once piped water directly from a glacier. Go to the hotel's third floor for what they call a "living history museum" to learn more about who has stayed here and other local lore. A 2017 multimillion-dollar renovation has given guests the choice between historic rooms and modern rooms, city or mountain views, and more meeting space.

East of downtown, away from the Pearl Street Mall and the foothills, but close to some shops and restaurants and still walking distance from campus, you'll find some comfortable chain hotels. The **Embassy Suites by Hilton** (2601 Canyon Blvd., 303/443-2660, http://embassysuites3.hilton.com, $280-360) and the **Hilton Garden Inn** (2701 Canyon Blvd., 303/443-2200, http://hiltongardeninn3.hilton.com, $216-400) are known collectively as "Hiltons on Canyon." They have a combined 376 rooms, a ballroom, a saline-based rooftop pool that is open year-round, state-of-the-art fitness centers, and on-site restaurants, but what makes these hotels so distinctive are the art collections on display, featuring the work of local artists. The 1,500 pieces of unique art were curated by NINE dot ARTS. There is an additional charge for parking on the property.

Across the street from Hiltons on Canyon, the **Residence Inn by Marriott Boulder Canyon Boulevard** (2550 Canyon Blvd., 303/577-7300, www.marriott.com, $279-350) has 155 suites with public spaces so appealing you'll spend just as much time here as in your room. There's a giant hot tub, a barbecue grill, complimentary breakfast, an on-site fitness center with an indoor pool, and glass walls on the first floor letting in the Colorado sunshine. It's all across the street from the 29th Street shopping area, where there are restaurants too.

Farther east of downtown is the **Hyatt Place Boulder/Pearl Street** (2280 Junction Place, 303/442-0610, http://boulderpearlstreet.place.hyatt.com, $315-440), with 150 suites, some with kitchenettes. Complimentary breakfast and Wi-Fi, plus dine-in options 24 hours daily, are among the amenities. A fitness center and on-site parking (extra cost) are offered.

One of Boulder's swankiest hotels is the ★ **St. Julien Hotel and Spa** (900 Walnut St., 720/406-9696, www.stjulien.com, $329-489), a AAA four-diamond hotel with more than 200 rooms and suites. This place, located in the heart of downtown just off the Pearl Street Mall, evokes the mountains that can be seen from several key vantage points on the property, with liberal use of pink-red sandstone throughout the design. But it's designed to make you think not just of rocks like those stunning Flatirons you look out at, but also the entire natural world you may well be here to enjoy. The St. Julien has its own Green Committee that continually reviews how the hotel can minimize its ecological footprint. Add in the 10,000-square-foot spa and indoor pool and the result is true modern luxury in which you can feel good about your stay. On-site Jill's Restaurant and Bistro caters to the local dietary trend, leaning to vegan with vegan-only dishes every Friday and a four-course vegan dinner on Monday.

Transportation and Services

CAR

Boulder is an easy 30-mile (48-km) drive west from Denver. The most common route is to take Highway 36 north from I-25 in Denver; a handful of exits point out how to get to the University of Colorado campus or other locales. Another route is to take I-70 west for 15 miles (24 km) to Highway 6 in Golden, then head north for about 30 miles (48 km) on Highway 93 to Boulder, where the highway turns into Broadway. While this is a more scenic drive closer to the foothills—there is not much development this close to the old Rocky Flats Nuclear Weapons Facility—the road is not safe during high winds.

PUBLIC TRANSIT

The **RTD** (Regional Transportation District, www.rtd-denver.com, $6 day pass) offers regional bus service several times daily from Union Station in downtown Denver to the Boulder Transit Center. In-town buses then originate from the **Boulder Transit Center** (14th St. and Walnut St., 303/229-6000, $3). Look for the affordable around-town buses with silly names like Hop (downtown, CU campus), Skip (Broadway), and Dash (South Boulder Rd.).

Greyhound buses and Amtrak trains do not serve Boulder.

TOURS

Boulder Bike Tours (303/747-6191 or 303/570-9177, http://boulderbiketours.com, rates vary) offers mountain or road biking tours in the foothills of Boulder that last a half day or a full day. There are also two-hour rides around Boulder ($99 pp). Each tour includes a guide, snacks or lunch, water, a bike, and a helmet. You don't have to be an expert—these guides can go at a leisurely pace and roll along or get your heart racing with something more intense.

Colorado Wilderness Rides and Guides (720/242-9828, http://coloradowildernessridesandguides.com, rates vary) offers half-day, multiday, full-day, and custom trips where you can depart from Boulder or just ride around the area. Note that they consider a 7-mile (11-km) bike ride an "easy to moderate" half-day experience. Bike, helmet, water, snacks, and transport to and from hotel are included.

There are **self-guided history tours** available with downloadable guides found at https://bouldercolorado.gov/transportation/boulder-walks. Or, take a tour of Boulder's ever-growing **murals** around town and walk or ride a bike to see them all (and of course, take photos for the 'gram!). Find a map at www.streetwiseboulder.com and see what's new on the walls of the city.

INFORMATION AND SERVICES

For more information, visit the **Boulder Convention and Visitors Bureau** (2440 Pearl St., 303/442-2911, www.bouldercoloradousa.com). The city's major daily newspaper is the ***Boulder Daily Camera*** (www.dailycamera.com). There's also the ***Colorado Daily*** (www.coloradodaily.com), a free tabloid-style paper found all over town. The town's "alternative" newspaper is the ***Boulder Weekly*** (www.boulderweekly.com), with long feature stories and weekly events. The glossy ***Boulder Magazine*** (www.getboulder.com) offers lots of suggestions for fun activities in the area.

Vicinity of Boulder

ELDORADO SPRINGS

The town of Eldorado Springs, south of Boulder, provides access to wonderful outdoor recreation. You can rock climb, hike, go to a yoga class, trail run, and cool off in a natural springs pool. The road into Eldorado Springs usually has a few cyclists on it, too, so consider that as an alternative mode of transportation for getting here from Boulder. While it is possible to ride a bike from Boulder to Eldorado Springs (it's under 10 mi/16 km one-way), keep in mind the high altitude and the fact that you might be hiking or biking on a trail later. It's a short drive to Eldorado Springs, but totally worth it for a real mountain experience.

★ Eldorado Canyon State Park

Eldorado Canyon State Park (9 Kneale Rd., 303/494-3943, http://cpw.state.co.us, sunrise-sunset daily year-round, $4-10) is at the end of the road into Eldorado Springs. The park is popular with rock climbers—there are more than 500 technical climbing routes—but you can also hike in the summer or snowshoe in the winter on trails ranging from easy to difficult. Fishing is allowed for brown and rainbow trout (a Colorado fishing license is required). Golden eagles nest here, so there may be trail closures at times to protect wildlife.

Fees for park use vary depending on whether you drive in or not. If you are driving into the park, try to go on a weekday when it is less crowded with rock climbers and fellow day hikers—this is a popular place. Go all the way up the road to the visitors center for educational programs and live music on summer evenings.

Hikes include easy-to-moderate options suitable for families with young children and those who want a bit of a workout. The easy **Streamside Trail** (0.5 mi/0.8 km one-way) will stimulate your senses with the roar of South Boulder Creek, the cool creek air and the shade of nearby canyon walls, and the beautiful scenery. The **Fowler Trail** (0.7 mi/1.1 km one-way) is just a bit longer but is still an easy walk with benches for sitting and gazing up at

the view from Eldorado Canyon State Park

Vicinity of Boulder

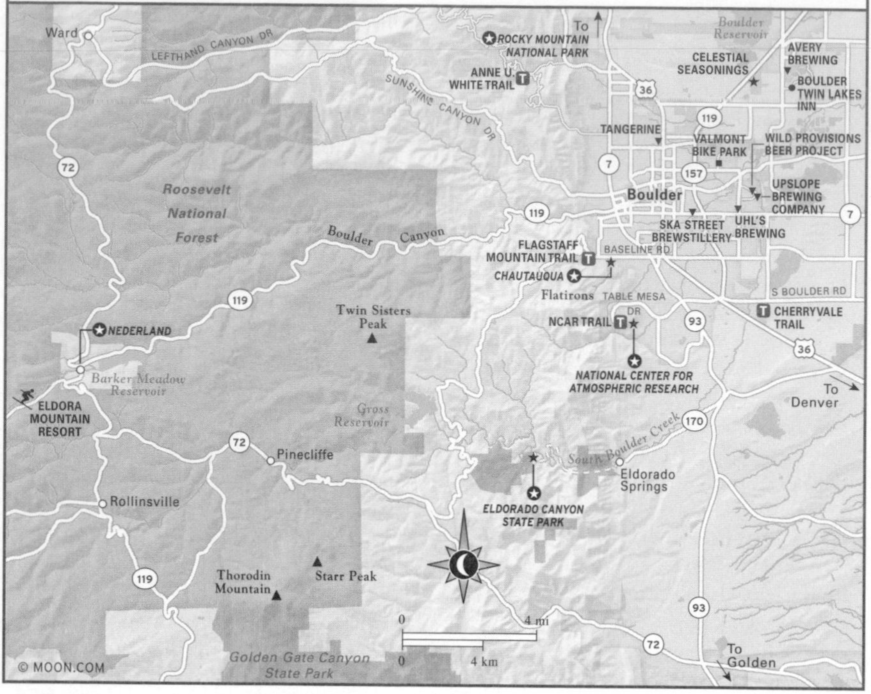

the rock climbers scaling the steep canyon walls.

The **Rattlesnake Gulch Trail** (1.4 mi/2.3 km one-way) qualifies as a moderately difficult hike, but your reward is the site of the former Crags Hotel. Once you've arrived at the viewpoint, take in the broad views from this elevation. The trail is also open to mountain biking, but this is a steep and bumpy ride with an 800-foot (245-m) elevation gain and switchbacks. Portions of this trail may close to protect wildlife; check the park website.

The **Eldorado Canyon Trail** (3.5 mi/5.6 km one-way) is the park's most challenging, but you have excellent views to look forward to. The Eldorado Canyon Trail is also a good one for horseback riders, but it's wise to opt for weekdays when there are fewer people—horse trailers may not be allowed in the parking lot on a busy weekend.

Biking

Doudy Draw (www.bouldercolorado.gov, fee for parking) is a 1.7-mile (2.7 km) one-way multiuse trail that is popular with mountain bikers. The trail passes over creeks (or creek beds, depending on the time of year) and connects with other bike-friendly trails in the area. While it's lovely to hear the songbirds in the fields as you ride along, be mindful that bears and mountain lions live here, too. (I've also been here when the University of Colorado cross-country team practically leapt off a bus for practice and barreled past me like a herd of gazelles.) The trailhead is 1.8 miles (2.9 km) west of Highway 93 on Eldorado Springs Drive (Hwy. 170).

1: snowshoers in the forest near Boulder
2: Brainard Lake Recreation Area

1

2

Hiking

Along the drive to Eldorado Canyon State Park is the **South Mesa Trail** (www.bouldercolorado.gov), which starts out as a gentle hike in grasslands and shrubs, then gets more interesting as you begin stepping "stairs" and increasing elevation. You can aim for Bear Peak, but that makes for nearly 9 miles (14.5 km) round-trip. The increasing elevation and final ascent turn this into a moderately difficult hike, but certainly you can turn around once the wide gravel trail turns into a narrow path in the trees for the steeper section. The trail is wheelchair-accessible at the start and has picnic tables, restrooms, and a fee-based parking lot. Leashed dogs are permitted, but cyclists are not. Be aware that mountain lions, bears, and other wildlife inhabit this area. The trailhead is 1.7 miles (2.7 km) west of Highway 93 on Eldorado Springs Drive (Hwy. 170).

Swimming

The **Eldorado Springs Pool** (294 Artesian Dr., 303/499-9640, www.eldoradosprings.com, 10am-6pm daily Memorial Day-Labor Day, $12 adults, $8 children and seniors) is a classic Boulder experience in the summer. Note these are not hot springs; the pool opened in 1905 and has remained true to its origins—the water is not heated. If you ride a bike here from Boulder on a hot summer day, it will feel absolutely perfect to cool off. There is a small snack shop on-site, or you can picnic at the pool. Be warned: It's a bit of a dare to use the old-fashioned slide.

Yoga

With all the hiking, biking, and climbing, one might get the impression that the only way to enjoy Colorado is to be a semiprofessional athlete. The **Eldorado Yoga Mountain Ashram** (2875 County Rd. 67, 303/249-1671, http://eldoradoyoga.org) is a gentle reminder that you can just be one with nature here. This special place offers drop-in yoga, meditation, and other classes. There is a family yoga class every Sunday and other family offerings on a seasonal basis as well.

Getting There

Eldorado Springs is about 9 miles (14.5 km) southwest of Boulder. To get here from Boulder, follow Broadway (Hwy. 93) south for about 6 miles (9.7 km) to Highway 170. Turn west on Highway 170 and drive 3 miles (4.8 km) to Eldorado Springs.

★ NEDERLAND

Funky is a word that sums up Nederland, a mountain town less than 20 miles (32 km) west of Boulder. Nederland initially came to be due to mining in the area; it has continued thanks to its location on the Peak to Peak Highway, a scenic byway that winds from Estes Park down to a suburb west of Denver. It's a prime spot for many outdoor adventures.

Just outside of Nederland is the Eldora Ski Resort for alpine skiing and the Brainard Lake Recreation Area, which offers many wonderful hiking and snowshoeing trails, depending on the season.

Sights

Nederland isn't exactly full of sights, but there is one place that's worth the drive up the canyon. **The Carousel of Happiness** (20 Lakeview Dr., 303/258-3457, www.carouselofhappiness.org, 11am-6pm Thurs.-Mon. winter, 10am-6pm Mon.-Thurs., 10am-8pm Sat.-Sun. spring-fall, $3) is made from so many dreams. Nederland resident Scott Harrison bought a used carousel, minus the animals, and taught himself how to carve wooden creatures. He spent years making 56 carousel animals; kids now squeal with delight as they ride them today. But he couldn't have pulled this off without the town's support; together they raised the funds to build a home for the carousel. Even if you don't have young kids, it's worth a visit to check out the one-of-a-kind carousel animals, such as an alpaca, a dolphin, and a dragon boat.

Festivals and Events

Ned (as locals call Nederland) has become known for its annual **Frozen Dead Guy Days** (http://frozendeadguydays.org, early

Mar.), held while the weather at 8,236 feet (2,510 m) is still wintry and cold. The annual event includes a parade through town, people dressed as though cryogenically frozen, coffin races, and other questionably tasteful activities.

It's a long story, but yes—there is a real frozen dead guy. Known simply as "Grandpa," Bredo Morstoel was cryogenically frozen (in a very amateur way) by his grandson, a Ned resident. Grandpa's body lies stored in a Tuff Shed (the kind used to store a lawn mower) on private property in town. Local filmmakers made a movie, *Grandpa's in the Tuff Shed,* that tells the whole story.

The **High Peaks Art Festival** (http://highpeaksartfestival.com, late June) is a weekend of making, judging, displaying, and selling artwork with activities for the whole family to enjoy. There are lots of booths with local crafts for sale, so plan to shop.

Sports and Recreation

Pack your hiking or skiing gear when you go to Ned because there are some beautiful places to explore.

HIKING

In summer, you can choose a fairly short hike or really challenge yourself with something longer at the **Brainard Lake Recreation Area** (Boulder Ranger District, 303/541-2500, www.fs.usda.gov, June-Oct., $10 per vehicle). As of 2021, you need reservations to hike here due to a significant increase in usage. Hikes to various lakes range 1-2 miles (1.6-3.2 km) one-way and reach elevations of more than 10,000 feet (3,000 m). There are picnic tables near the parking area and the lakes, so bring a lunch and relax after your hike. To get here, take Highway 72 north, then take a left on County Road 102.

In the greater **Indian Peaks Wilderness Area** (Boulder Ranger District, 303/541-2500, www.fs.usda.gov) surrounding Nederland are the **Lost Lake Trail** and the **Fourth of July Trail,** both moderate hikes. Lost Lake (elevation 9,800 feet/2,987 m) is 1.4 miles (2.2 km) one-way from the Hessie Trailhead; along the way you'll see and hear waterfalls crashing down the mountain. It's a longer hike of 2.6 miles (4.2 km) one-way to Diamond Lake (elevation 10,940 feet/3,335 m) on the Fourth of July Trail, which blooms with wildflowers in July and August. These trails are popular, so come early to avoid parking hassles.

To reach the Hessie Trailhead, take Highway 119 through Nederland and turn right at County Road 130. Stay right when the road forks for Eldora. To reach the Fourth of July Trailhead, drive 4 miles (6.4 km) past the Hessie Trailhead on a dirt road.

SKIING

A mere 21 miles (34 km) west from Boulder, the **Eldora Mountain Resort** (2861 Eldora Ski Rd., 303/440-8700, www.eldora.com) is where the University of Colorado ski team practices. Though these aren't the highest peaks or runs in the state, it's still a great place for a day on the slopes. Group and private lessons are available for downhill and cross-country skiing; their bunny hill for beginners is always popular. There is also a Nordic Center for cross-country skiers and snowshoers.

A casual restaurant on-site offers pizza, burgers, and chili, and beer is served in the Corona Bowl Bar. You can rent skis and boots for both alpine and cross-country skiing, and there are two shops that sell anything you forgot—snow pants, goggles, mittens. Here's a tip for a little free trail use: Look for signs for the Jenny Creek Trail, just to the east of the bunny slope, and start hiking up. (I'm a snowshoer, but I've seen telemark skiers on this trail, too.) This U.S. Forest Service trail is free, though you must stay on the trail and cannot access the ski slopes from here.

Cross-country skiers and snowshoers flock to **Brainard Lake Recreation Area** (303/541-2500, www.fs.usda.gov) in the winter. There is a large parking lot (with restrooms) where the gate closes the road in the off-season. Depending on conditions, you can snowshoe up this snow-covered road or go through the trees, while skiers can trek up the road. There is no trail use fee in the winter. To get here, take Highway 72 north, then take a left on County Road 102.

Food

Nederland represents a different time for dining out in Colorado, far different than Boulder. Here it's about tradition, locals, and familiarity, and not so much about farm-to-table ingredients and award-winning wines.

The **New Moon Bakery & Café** (1 W. 1st St., 303/258-3569, www.newmoonbakery.com, 7am-1pm Mon.-Fri., 7am-4pm Sat.-Sun., $10) is where locals go for a cup of "Ned-roast coffee" and a pastry before starting their day on the slopes or trails. Plan ahead and get a picnic lunch to take with you.

Salto Coffee Works (112 E. 2nd Ave., 303/258-3537, www.saltocoffeeworks.com, 8am-3pm daily, $5-10) is more than the name might lead you to believe. The simple menu harbors delicious breakfast and lunch items such as house-made granola, a fried egg with house-made pesto, or even duck tamales. There is also beer on tap. Check their online events calendar for live music, pizza nights, and other fun goings-on.

Who knows why it's irresistible to dine in a caboose? I don't know the answer, but **The Train Cars Coffee & Yogurt Company** (101 Hwy. 119, 303/258-2455, www.thetraincarscoffee.com, 6:30am-6:30pm Mon.-Fri., 6:30am-7pm Sat.-Sun., $5-10) is worth the stop for a sandwich, sweet, or coffee. The yogurt is just frozen yogurt, like dessert. The special treat here is not in the name; it's doughnuts in many flavors by the full or half dozen.

For more of a sit-down meal, try the **Crosscut Pizzeria & Taphouse** (4 E. 1st St., 303/258-3519, www.crosscutpizza.com, 2pm-8pm Mon.-Fri., 11:30am-7:45pm Sat.-Sun., $8-16), which is perfect for families after a day of skiing at Eldora, or just for grabbing a beer and a nibble with friends after a hike nearby.

Getting There

Nederland is 21 miles (34 km) west of Boulder. To get here from Boulder, take Highway 119 (Canyon Blvd.) west for 16 miles (26 km) into the mountains. Highway 119 travels west through Nederland to reach Eldora in 5 more miles (8 km).

Rocky Mountain National Park

Rocky Mountain National Park (970/586-1206, www.nps.gov/romo, $10-20 day pass) is 415 square miles of wilderness in north-central Colorado. It was designated a national park in 1915 by President Woodrow Wilson. It's an easy drive from Boulder, Denver, or Fort Collins. The scenery goes from elevations of 7,860 feet (2,395 m) above sea level to the highest point at 14,259 feet (4,346 m). All in all, there are 60 mountain peaks over 12,000 feet (3,600 m), and the Continental Divide runs north-south through the park.

The park is open year-round. As of 2020, there is a seasonal timed-entry reservation system to use the park from late May to October.

VISITORS CENTERS

There are four visitors centers at the park, plus an information center, a historic site, and a discovery center. For the hikes recommended in this book, you can either hike outside of the park and not bother with a visitors center or use the **Beaver Meadows Visitors Center** (year-round) or **Fall River Visitors Center** (spring-fall). Hours at all facilities are subject to seasonal changes, so always check the website for the latest conditions and restrictions.

Rocky Mountain National Park

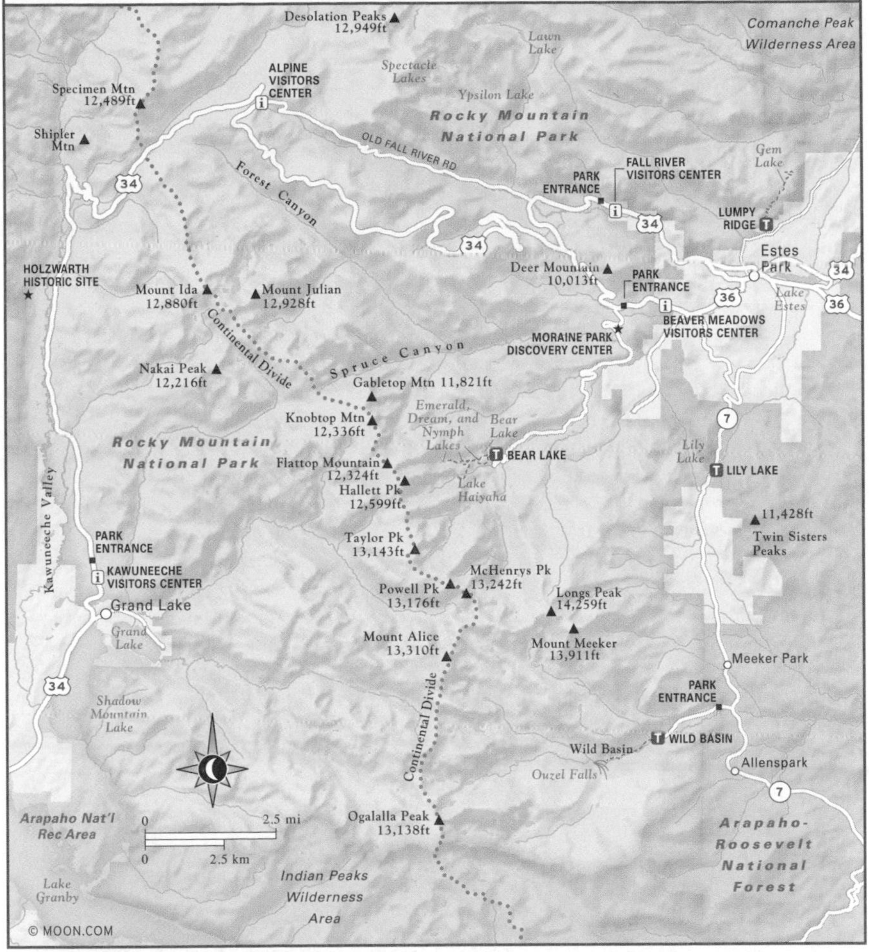

SIGHTS

If you can't spend time in the park for some reason, you can get a terrific view of it and Estes Park, the gateway town on the east side, from the **Estes Park Aerial Tramway** (970/475-4094, www.estestram.com, 9am-6pm daily Memorial Day-Labor Day, $14 adults, $12 seniors, $10 ages 6-11, free under age 6).

The park's visitors centers are worth your time and are often a highlight for young kids. On the east side, the **Beaver Meadows Visitors Center** (1000 Hwy. 36, 970/586-1206, www.nps.gov/romo, 8am-4:30pm daily mid-Oct.-mid-May, 8am-5pm daily mid-May-mid-June and early Sept.-mid-Oct., 8am-6pm daily mid-June-early Sept.) has a gift shop, a relief map of the park, a movie about the park, and helpful rangers on-site. The building itself is a National Historic Landmark.

For a more historic experience, head for the **Moraine Park Discovery Center** (Bear

Lake Rd., 1.5 mi/2.4 km from the Beaver Meadows Entrance Station, 970/586-8842, 9am-4:30pm daily Memorial Day-Labor Day), which was once part of a busy lodge for tourists. Today the two-story log building has interactive natural history exhibits, a short trail outside, and the requisite gift shop.

Nearby you can see the **William Allen White Cabins,** which house members of the park's artist-in-residence program. The cabins are named for a Pulitzer Prize-winning newspaper writer and editor who summered here between 1912 and 1943. These are not open to the public.

On the park's west side—accessible by Trail Ridge Road in the summer, or a few hours' drive around to Grand Lake the rest of the year—you will find the **Holzwarth Historic Site** (Hwy. 34, about 7.5 mi/12 km from the Grand Lake Entrance Station, summer only). This former vacation lodge from the 1920s gives you an interactive experience with hands-on activities.

If you are able to drive over Trail Ridge Road, you can stop at the **Alpine Visitors Center** (Trail Ridge Rd. and Old Fall River Rd., 970/586-1206, 9am-5pm daily summer, 10:30am-4:30pm daily spring and fall), the highest visitors center in the United States at 11,796 feet (3,595 m) elevation, where you can learn about the tundra surrounding this place.

RECREATION

TOP EXPERIENCE

★ Hiking

When you head to the park, make sure to be prepared for sun, changes in weather, altitude, and traffic. You may not always have cell phone coverage in the park, so don't rely on it, and bring maps. Bring plenty of fluids and adjust slowly to the altitude.

Before you even reach the park, you can go hiking. One of my favorites—especially if you are with little kids or just need to stretch your legs but not work out—is **Lily Lake.** There are two parking lots (be so careful crossing the road from one of them), restrooms, wheelchair access, and benches for resting during this easy little 0.8-mile (1.3-km) walk around the lake. You can extend your hike on adjoining trails (not wheelchair accessible). The trailhead is 6.3 miles (10.1 km) from the junction of Highways 7 and 36 in Estes Park.

The most popular trailhead in the park is

hiking in Rocky Mountain National Park

Bear Lake. You must get here early in the morning or take a shuttle bus into the park. Personally, I recommend bringing a picnic and arriving early so you can hike to as many lakes as possible along the way. Let's get real about the popularity: Parts of the trail have been asphalted to cope with heavy erosion. Still, it's awesome. You can do an easy 0.5-mile (0.8-km) walk around Bear Lake, but if you are able, head for **Nymph, Dream,** and **Emerald Lakes,** 3.65 miles (5.9 km) round-trip, gaining 605 feet (184 m) in elevation and a more moderate hiking experience.

In my opinion, a waterfall is the best payoff for hiking. **Ouzel Falls** is a moderate 5.4-mile (8.7-km) round-trip hike with an elevation gain of 950 feet (290 m). You start at the Wild Basin Trailhead, and if you don't have much time or stamina, you can see Copeland Falls in 0.3 miles (0.5 km) and then the Calypso Cascades in 1.8 miles (2.9 km) from the trailhead. It's out and back on the same trail.

If you are on the north side of Estes Park, head for the Lumpy Ridge Trailhead for an easy-to-moderate hike to **Gem Lake,** 4 miles (6.4 km) out and back. If you do this hike in summer, you should see lots of wildflowers. The lake itself is completely different than others suggested here; this onc sits in a granite bowl.

Horseback Riding

As long as you're having an adventure, why not see a national park while riding a horse? There are many stables within and outside the park boundaries for rides from 2 to 10 hours.

Sombrero Stables (970/577-6818, www.sombrero.com, $40-90) can get you partly up Long's Peak on horseback. They also offer rides in Estes Park with different themes such as a breakfast ride. Within the park boundaries, **Moraine Park Stables** (549 Fern Lake Rd., 970/586-2327, www.sombrero.com, mid-May-mid-Oct., $55-170) offers guided rides.

Rock Climbing

Depending on the hike you choose, you could be scrambling over some rocks. If you really want to climb rocks, though, you can do some bouldering (no ropes) at **Lake Haiyaha.** Park at Bear Lake, then follow trail signs to Lake Haiyaha and keep an eye out for Upper Chaps Canyon and Lower Chaos Canyon.

Other Activities

The park offers many possible activities beyond just hiking, horseback riding, and rock climbing. Check with rangers about seasonal options during your visit.

In the winter, you can go **snowshoeing** on many of the park's designated hiking trails to see frozen waterfalls and possibly wildlife, including elk, moose, and bighorn sheep. Ranger-led snowshoe walks (www.nps.gov/romo, free) are offered January-March, depending on conditions; reservations are required. Snowshoe rentals can be found in the communities of Estes Park and Grand Lake.

GETTING THERE AND AROUND

Rocky Mountain National Park is easy to get to from Boulder by taking 28th Street toward Lyons as it turns back into Highway 36 heading north. Once you reach Lyons, go left and through town to the stoplight where you can choose between taking Highway 36 (the faster way; 32 mi/52 km, 1 hour) or Highway 7 (55 mi/89 km, 1.5 hours). If you are aiming for Estes Park and trails that require entering the park via the Beaver Meadows Visitor Center, the Highway 36 route makes the most sense. However, some trails are found along Highway 7 as you drive toward Estes Park.

Fort Collins

Sights 180
Entertainment and Events 184
Shopping 190
Sports and Recreation 194
Food 199
Accommodations 203
Transportation and Services 204
Vicinity of Fort Collins . . 205

Fort Collins has its own unique personality, with a historic charm mixed with college energy, as well as a reputation for craft breweries and excellent cycling.

Located about 65 miles (105 km) north of Denver, Fort Collins is the fourth-largest city in Colorado. The town has consistently been named one of the best places to live in the United States by *Money* magazine, and the population is expanding steadily.

Beer aficionados will find a robust craft beer scene that is considered one of the best—if not *the* best—in the state. Yet even with one of Colorado's greatest concentrations of microbreweries, Fort Collins maintains a physically fit populace. The city was designed so that residents could easily cycle along a creek-side bike path, enjoy a meal

Highlights

Look for ★ to find recommended sights, activities, dining, and lodging.

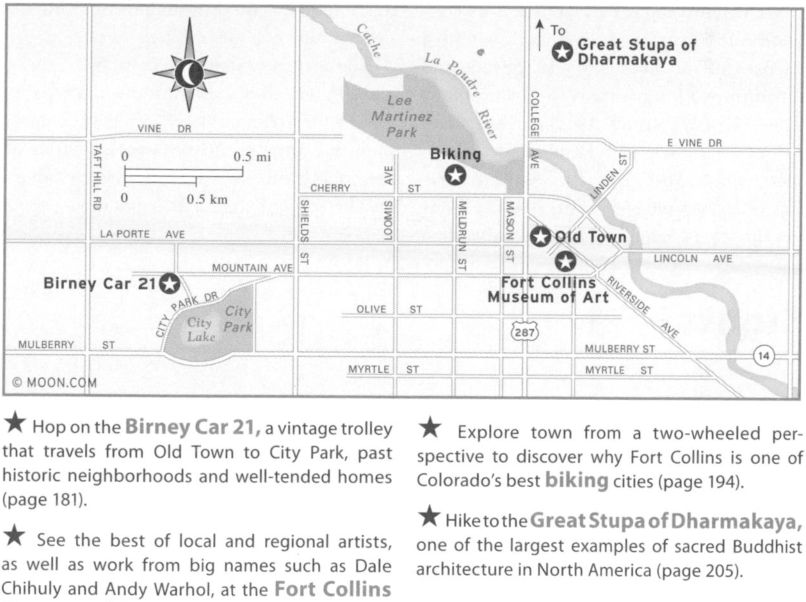

★ Hop on the **Birney Car 21,** a vintage trolley that travels from Old Town to City Park, past historic neighborhoods and well-tended homes (page 181).

★ See the best of local and regional artists, as well as work from big names such as Dale Chihuly and Andy Warhol, at the **Fort Collins Museum of Art** (page 183).

★ Stroll around the charming **Old Town** district, offering shops, eateries, and bars, all in an appealing pedestrian-friendly area (page 184).

★ Explore town from a two-wheeled perspective to discover why Fort Collins is one of Colorado's best **biking** cities (page 194).

★ Hike to the **Great Stupa of Dharmakaya,** one of the largest examples of sacred Buddhist architecture in North America (page 205).

outdoors, or take a leisurely walk from one point to the next. Visitors can stroll in the courtyards along College Avenue to shop, eat, or sip coffee or a cocktail in the city's Old Town neighborhood. The popularity of the Old Town area has led to new development on the fringes, with the River District to the north becoming home to new restaurants, bars, and other businesses. The Exchange, also just to the north, is one of the town's newest developments, partially constructed from recycled shipping containers to make for inviting breweries with patios, ice cream shops, and live music space.

The town's biggest draw, Colorado State University (CSU), was originally founded as an agricultural college; today it is known for its veterinary and forestry schools, and its campus offers gardens, art galleries, and a museum to explore.

What I love about Fort Collins is its connection to Disneyland. Fort Collins native Harper Goff did set design in Hollywood and ended up working with Walt Disney. Goff showed Disney pictures of his hometown, and Fort Collins, along with Disney's own childhood home in Missouri, served as the inspiration for Disneyland's Main Street, USA. Today you can see a portrait of Mr. Goff painted on the building currently housing the Crooked Stave Taproom (216 N. College Ave.) in Old Town.

PLANNING YOUR TIME

You can really explore at your own pace in Fort Collins, a small city with an ideal balance of culture and physical activity. Plan at least **one day,** with an **overnight** option.

Start with a hike in Lory State Park, less than 30 minutes from downtown. Return to Old Town for lunch at a craft brewery where you can sample the wares. To explore the town, hop on the Birney Car 21, a historic trolley car that goes past historic homes on a tree-lined street, all the way to City Park and back. Back in Old Town, visit the Fort Collins Museum of Art and then do a little shopping.

Spend the night at the Armstrong Hotel, Fort Collins's only historic hotel. Head down to the hotel's subterranean bar, Ace Gillett's Lounge, for cocktails and live music.

The next day, extend your visit by renting a bicycle and riding along the creek-side paths around the Colorado State University campus. Enjoy a foamy lunchtime beverage at one of this college town's many craft breweries, or go on a brew tour before heading home.

Sights

You can see quite a bit of Fort Collins in one day, depending on your pace. Just walking around Old Town puts you in proximity to some of the city's worthwhile sights, including one of the best sights—Old Town itself. The Colorado State University campus is a worthwhile stop, or opt for the Poudre Landmarks Foundation's **self-guided walking tour** (108 N. Meldrum St., 970/221-0533, http://poudrelandmarks.org), where you can learn about the original uses of many of the town's still-standing historic buildings. Tour highlights include Trimble Court in Old Town, the Hattie McDaniel house (McDaniel starred in the classic movie *Gone with the Wind*), the old post office that's now an art museum, the Armstrong Hotel, and a Carnegie library.

AVERY HOUSE

An early resident of Fort Collins, Frank Avery is credited with creating the city's

Previous: hiking above Horsetooth Reservoir; Old Town Fort Collins; Birney Car 21.

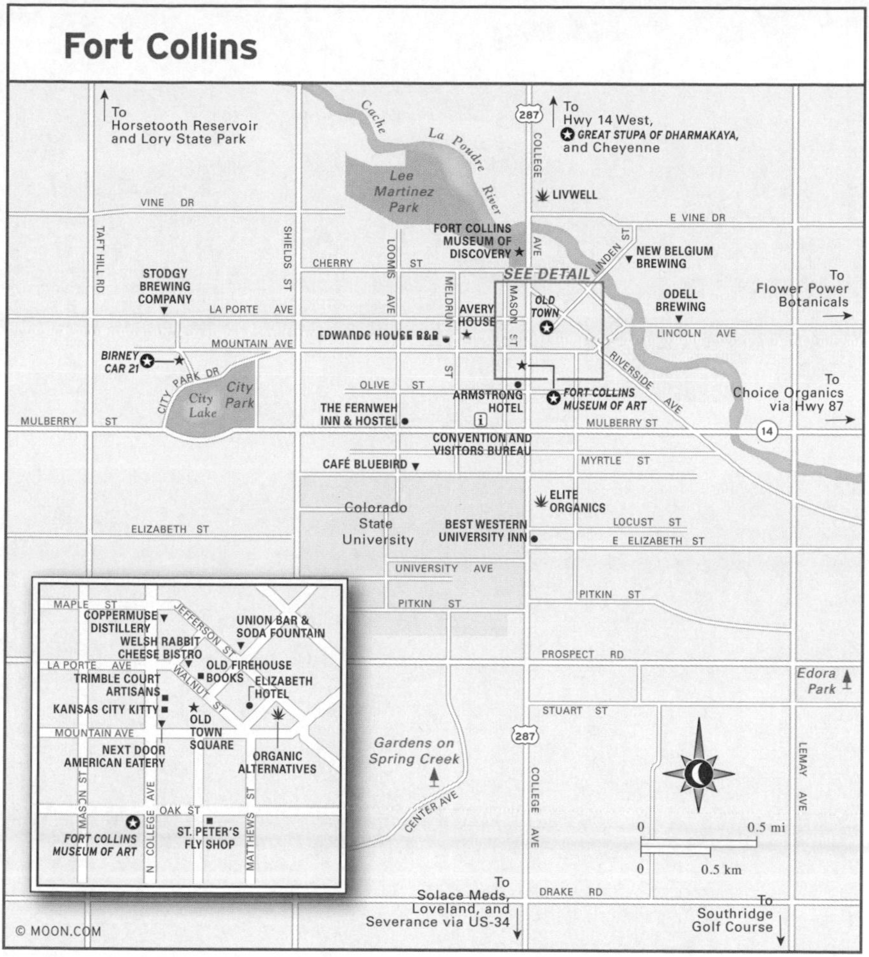

wide streets when he surveyed the town in 1873. Avery also founded the First National Bank and had a hand in the development of Fort Collins's agricultural enterprises. In 1879, Avery and his wife, Sarah, built a home for their family from locally quarried stone. Today the **Avery House** (328 W. Mountain Ave., 970/221-0533, http://poudrelandmarks.org, 1pm-4pm Sat.-Sun., free) is on the National Register of Historic Places and is open to the public for guided tours.

★ BIRNEY CAR 21

At one time there was a rail line from Fort Collins to Denver and Boulder, but it came to a halt in 1918 when transportation began to favor automobiles. In the 1980s, after many years of restoration, the Birney Car 21 came back to life. Today, locals and visitors alike can enjoy this 1.5-mile (2.4-km) trip through history. Riding on this little streetcar through Fort Collins's historic neighborhood reminded me of taking the streetcar in New Orleans.

The **Fort Collins Municipal Railway**

FORT COLLINS MUNICIPAL RAILWAY
21
21
21
21
1

2

3

4

Society (www.fortcollinstrolley.org, noon-4pm Sat.-Sun. May-Sept., $2 adults, $1 children and seniors, free under age 3) is an all-volunteer organization that runs the Birney Car 21. Boarding locations are at Howes Street and Mountain Avenue, Loomis Street and Mountain Avenue, Shields Street and Mountain Avenue, and City Park, at the tennis courts.

COLORADO STATE UNIVERSITY

Opened in 1879 as the Colorado Agricultural College, **Colorado State University** (970/491-6444, www.colostate.edu) is the flagship of the state university system. The school may be best known today for its veterinary medicine program, though it offers doctoral degrees in 40 fields of study. If you can time your visit right, you will be able to see the campus's **Trial Gardens** (www.flowertrials.colostate.edu, free) in full bloom. May to October, this display shows off the college's horticultural research.

The **Oval** is a large green space in the center of the campus, surrounded by American elm trees and the historic buildings of the school. It's more than just a favorite gathering place for students—President Barack Obama gave a campaign speech here.

The **Curfman Gallery** (Lory Student Center, http://lsc.colostate.edu, 10am-noon and 1pm-7pm Tues.-Wed., 10am-7pm Thurs., noon-6pm Fri.-Sat., free) shows off local artists' work as well as that of national and international artists. **The University Center for the Arts** (1400 Remington St., http://uca.colostate.edu), in the old high school, houses performance spaces and two museums, the **Gregory Allicar Museum of Art** (970/491-1989, www.artmuseum.colostate.edu, 10am-6pm Wed. and Fri.-Sat., 10am-7:30pm Thurs., 1pm-5pm Sun., free) and the **Avenir Museum of Design and Merchandising** (970/491-6648, http://avenir.colostate.edu, noon-4pm Tues.-Fri., free). You'll also find the Gustafson Gallery, Blackwell Gallery, and Lucile Hawks Gallery in this complex.

1: Birney Car 21 2: the historic Avery House 3: the Gardens on Spring Creek, lighted at night 4: Fort Collins Museum of Discovery

★ FORT COLLINS MUSEUM OF ART

In a historic post office building in the city's charming Old Town area is the **Fort Collins Museum of Art** (201 S. College Ave., 970/482-2787, http://moafc.org, 10am-5pm Wed.-Fri., noon-5pm Sat.-Sun., $1-5), which hosts an interesting variety of shows throughout the year. Past exhibits have included works by Marc Chagall, Ansel Adams, local artists, and themed group shows. Just outside of the building on the Oak Street Plaza is a sculpture, *Confluence,* by artist Lawrence Argent, who also created the *I See What You Mean* (aka the Big Blue Bear) sculpture in Denver.

FORT COLLINS MUSEUM OF DISCOVERY

The **Fort Collins Museum of Discovery** (408 Mason Court, 970/221-6738, www.fcmod.org, 10am-5pm Wed.-Sun., $12.50 adults, $9.50 seniors/students/children ages 3-12, free under age 3 or with membership) has a few exhibits that you won't find at the Denver Museum of Nature & Science. Exhibits on local wildlife include black-footed ferrets, while the histories of people and land are presented in a variety of formats, including photos, books, and videos. But what makes this museum different is the **Music & Sound Lab**—where you can not only learn about music but play music—and the **Otterbox Digital Dome Theater,** which shows a regular lineup of family-friendly movies that aren't your usual multiplex offers.

GARDENS ON SPRING CREEK

At the **Gardens on Spring Creek** (2145 Centre Ave., 970/416-2486, www.fcgov.com/gardens, 10am-5pm daily, $8-11, free for members), one of the city's lesser-known sights, visitors can stroll through a variety of gardens filled with primarily native plants. A

Public Art

The Fort Collins **Art in Public Places Program** (417 Magnolia Ave., 970/221-6735, www.fcgov.com/artspublic) turns ordinary objects into art. Through innovative programs like "pedestrian pavers" and "transformer cabinet murals," local artists are creating works of art throughout town. These public art sculptures are on display at the Colorado State University campus and around Old Town. Visit the website for a map of the artwork so you can take a self-guided tour—or just take your chances and hope to spy some while you are out and about.

real highlight is the children's garden, with colorful and interactive sculptures. Check the website for upcoming events and programs like yoga in the garden, summer tours, and farm-to-table garden dinners.

★ OLD TOWN

If you like Disneyland's Main Street, USA, then you are going to love Fort Collins—the theme park attraction was modeled on its downtown. The **Old Town** (www.downtownfortcollins.com) district contains 23 historic buildings, and it's bisected by broad and well-landscaped College Avenue, with public art and fountains arrayed alongside restaurant patios. Shops, galleries, a hotel, a museum, and brewpubs can all be found here. Old Town was listed on the National Register of Historic Places in 1978 and named a Preserve America city in 2005.

Entertainment and Events

Fort Collins has a college town vibe, evident at many of the downtown bars and at annual local festivals that emphasize beer. However, there is also a celebration of local music at both festivals and clubs. With a symphony orchestra, a professional dance company, and an opera, this town has a cultivated arts scene that appeals to many different audiences.

NIGHTLIFE

If you're staying in Old Town—and better yet, at the Armstrong Hotel—check out **Ace Gillett's Lounge** (239 S. College Ave., 970/449-4797, www.acegilletts.com, 4pm-11pm Thurs. and Sun., 4pm-midnight Fri.-Sat.), located under the Armstrong. There is music as well as fine dining and cocktails.

Elliot's Martini Bar (234 Linden St., 970/472-9802, www.elliotsmartini.com, 4:30pm-2am daily) offers a seasonally changing menu of classic and original martinis, including "dessertinis." Order an I Need a Minute, one of the bar's creative cocktails, or opt for a Naked in the Woods dessertini. Stop in on a Wednesday for specials on dirty martinis or come for a weekday happy hour (4pm-7:30pm) for $2 off martinis and tapas.

You've got to love the name of this place: **The Mayor of Old Town** (632 S. Mason St., 970/682-2410, http://themayorofoldtown.com, noon-10pm daily) is where you can enjoy a pint, a bite to eat, and sometimes live music. Try the stuffed pretzels and a flight of beer. Beer's not for you? They have limited wine and spirits, too.

Social (1 Old Town Square, 970/449-5606, www.socialfortcollins.com, 4pm-close daily) is the place for properly crafted cocktails, sommelier-selected wines, and charcuterie. Located underneath a shop at the entrance to Old Town Square, Social is designed with a soft yet modern industrial decor that keeps the focus on what they do best—quality food and drinks. Though there isn't a dress code, it tends toward a business-casual or cocktail-attire vibe.

The Forge Publick House (232 Walnut St., 970/682-2578, www.theforgepublickhouse.com, 2pm-midnight Wed.-Sat., 2pm-10pm Sun.-Tues.) is the antithesis of some of the well-known craft megabreweries in town. Off the beaten path, with an entrance in an alley, this one-room pub feels like a cozy den that is more like a typical bar. The dark wood, artwork, and lighting give it an Old World feel. They brag of their 18 rotating taps and grilled cheese sandwiches (not quite pairing, but close?).

For something different from the bar and music scene, the **Lyric** (1209 N. College Ave., 970/426-6767, http://lyriccinema.com, check website for showtimes) offers an alternative to the multiplex. This twin theater shows independent or foreign movies during the afternoon and evening, then shows cartoons. A large outdoor patio is also host to live music at this venue.

The Comedy Fort (167 N. College Ave., 970/232-9288, www.comedyfortcollins.com, check website for event calendar), a comedy club for 21 and up only, showcases regional talent and offers beer on tap for your entertainment and thirst needs.

Another option is **Comedy Brewers at Bas Bleu Theatre Company** (401 Pine St., 970/498-8949, www.basbleu.org/comedy-brewers, first Sun. monthly at 7pm). There's often a beer theme ("comedy six-pack" and "improv group at the top of their craft"), but it's still all about the laughs.

Washington's (132 Laporte Ave., 970/232-9525, www.washingtonsfoco.com) is a 900-person venue that has previously put on live shows by acts such as Yonder Mountain String Band, Trombone Shorty & Orleans Avenue, Devotchka, The Oh Hellos, and The Dirty Dozen Brass Band. This is one of a few local music venues supported by Bohemian Foundation (www.bohemianfoundation.org), which presents regular events such as Thursday Night Live (a free weekly summer concert series) and Bohemian Nights at NewWestFest (a free annual summer music festival) among the venues, including Washington's.

BREWERIES AND DISTILLERIES

In 2020, Colorado bars were newly allowed to sell drinks to go, such as 32- to 64-ounce "growlers," as a way for these businesses to stay afloat during closures to indoor dining (or sipping). It's not known how long this relaxed rule will continue, but it has been extended through 2026 so far.

Odell Brewing Company (800 Lincoln St., 970/498-9070, www.odellbrewing.com, taproom 11am-6pm Mon.-Tues., 11am-8pm Wed.-Sun.) has award-winning beers available for sampling. With food trucks to keep you snacking, it's easy for a summer afternoon to turn into evening on their large backyard patio. Check the website for tour information, and visit the Events page for live music nights.

Avuncular Bob's Beerhouse (830 S. College Ave., Suite 120, 970/484-2688, www.avuncularbobs.com, 3pm-8pm Tues.-Thurs., noon-8pm Fri.-Sat., noon-5pm Sun.) is all about fresh and local, with an emphasis on beers from northern Colorado on tap and locally sourced ingredients for their snacks and sandwiches. What does "avuncular" mean, anyway? You'll have to find out.

Coopersmith's Pub & Brewing (5 Old Town Square, 970/498-0483, http://coopersmithspub.com, noon-9pm Sun.-Thurs., noon-10pm Fri., 11am-10pm Sat., $8-20) has a full pub menu, billiards, and brewery tours (by appointment). Under one roof there are two restaurants and one brewery, so hours may vary depending on which one you end up in.

Coppermuse Distillery (244 N. College Ave., 970/999-6016, www.coppermuse.com, 4pm-8pm Thurs., 3pm-8pm Fri., noon-8pm Sat., noon-6pm Sun.) has a mission—to build upon Fort Collins's excellent craft brewing heritage and apply the same standards of quality to their distilling works. Coppermuse produces premium handcrafted spirits such as

1

2

3

Brew Tours and More

Fort Collins is proud to be Colorado's largest producer of beer. The city has come a long way since 1969, when it repealed Prohibition. Every brewery has its own claim to fame—the first microbrewery, the biggest, the most sustainable and eco-friendly, and other bragging rights. If you stop by for a pint, choose from this short list of creative possibilities.

Beer & Bike Tours (2451 Stanley Court, 970/201-1085, www.beerandbiketours.com, from $50): Drinking and riding can be a thing when you choose from several tours that stop at various breweries around town.

Magic Bus Tours (701 Aztec Dr., 970/420-0662, www.themagicbustours.com, $250 and up per group, reservations required): Hop on a Magic Bus and be driven from one brewery to the next, where you will get a tour of behind-the-scenes alecraft.

Extra Arts & Drafts (115 E. Mountain Ave., 970/893-2985, www.extraarts.com, cost varies by class or project) opened in 2021 as a place where people can craft as well as sip beer or other beverages. Maybe make a ceramic beer bottle? Needlepoint a pillow homage to your favorite ale?

Penrose Taphouse and Eatery (216 N. College Ave., 970/672-8400, www.penrosetaphouse.com, 11am-10pm Mon.-Wed., 11am-11pm Thurs.-Fri., 9am-11pm Sat., 9am-10pm Sun.) has the Beer It Forward program, which invites people to buy a beer for a friend, a teacher, or even a stranger, who then gets their name on the board at the restaurant. See your name? Show your ID and bottoms up! Penrose donates $1 for every name on the board to a local charity every quarter.

vodka, gin, rum, whiskey, and bourbon. Enjoy great bites and a comfy environment in the lively tasting room.

New Belgium Brewing Company (500 Linden St., 970/221-0524, www.newbelgium.com, 11am-8pm daily) is most likely the brewery you've heard of without ever having been to Fort Collins. The makers of Fat Tire and the creators of the Tour de Fat, New Belgium has set the bar high for other brewers. Come for live music, tours (11:30am-4:30pm Tues.-Sat., reservations recommended, free), tastings, and lots more beer-related fun.

Stodgy Brewing Company (1802 Laporte Ave., 970/232-9702, www.stodgybrewing.com, noon-8pm Sun.-Thurs., noon-9pm Fri., 11am-9pm Sat.) opened in 2021 with plenty of outdoor seating in the front yard (there is also indoor seating). Take one look at this place and you'll know it's got some history—it looks like a classic Western storefront. It was once a fireplace and stove store and sits next door to a (privately owned) log cabin. Enjoy a meat pie from Waltzing Kangaroo (available on Mondays) or a bite from whatever food truck is parked here while you sip on a lager (non-alcoholic beverages are also available).

NOCO Distillery (328 Link Lane #11, 970/414-7188, www.nocodistillery.com, 5pm-8pm Wed.-Thurs., 5pm-9pm Fri.-Sat.) has gorgeously bottled small-batch liquors and mixologists on staff to entertain and delight your booziest tastebuds. Can you say, "NoCo"? (It's short for Northern Colorado.) You'll need to because half the drinks here start with NOCO in the name. You might spot their rums, gins, or vodkas at other local bars too.

Crooked Stave Friends & Family Taproom (216 N. College Ave., 970/999-5856, www.crookedstave.com, noon-6pm Mon.-Thurs., noon-8pm Fri.-Sun.) offers their uniquely brewed ales (something about the yeast) in bottles and cans. It's part science/part drinking here, with aged oak and whiskey barrels, fruit flavors, and a process so complex they diagrammed it.

1: Odell Brewing Company **2:** Stodgy Brewing Company **3:** New Belgium Brewing Company

Tour de Fat

You saw this coming, right? Beer *and* bikes. The **Tour de Fat** (www.newbelgium.com, Sept.) started as a local event held by New Belgium Brewing Company in order to increase bicycle use in Fort Collins. It has since exploded into a national "rolling carnival of creativity" with music, beer, dance contests, and general wacky revelry. This costumed bicycle parade is free to participate in and attend. Funds raised through beer and merchandise sales benefit local charities. Tour de Fat events extend to 10 U.S. cities, where funds raised benefit nonprofits in each city.

CANNABIS DISPENSARIES

Marijuana dispensaries have popped up like weeds since it became legal to buy marijuana in Colorado. As a college town, Fort Collins has its fair share of dispensaries to choose from.

Choice Organics (813 Smithfield Dr., Unit B, 970/472-6337, www.choiceorganicsinc.com, 9am-8pm daily) prides itself on being first—the first Colorado dispensary to be licensed by the state in 2011 and the first retail cannabis store to open in Larimer County. The operation's longevity is evident thanks to its experienced budtenders and impressive selection of strains. Just off the highway a few miles from downtown, Choice Organics is perfectly situated for a pre-road trip pit stop, especially since there's ample parking for RVs, trucks, and trailers.

Across the street from the Colorado State University campus is **Elite Organics** (804 S. College Ave., 970/214-9889, http://eliteorganicscolorado.com, 9am-7:45pm Mon.-Sat., 10am-5:45pm Sun.), a hole-in-the-wall spot on the back side of Rock N' Robin's Smoke Shop (which doubles as Elite Organics' waiting room). Though it can be hard to find, it's worth the effort. Fans rave about the personal, homey vibe and all-natural flower.

Flower Power Botanicals (1308 Duff Dr., 970/672-8165, www.flowerpowerbotanicals.com, 8:15am-6:50pm daily) hints to its success in the name. Located in a strip mall east of downtown, Flower Power won't be winning any aesthetic points for its sparse, industrial ambience, but those in the know swear it boasts some of the most powerful buds available anywhere.

Spacious and welcoming, **LivWell** (900 N. College Ave., 970/484-8380, https://livwell.com, 8am-7:50pm daily), formerly Infinite Wellness Center, is north of downtown and is known for its ample selection, competitive prices, and a friendly rewards program.

Centrally located in Old Town Fort Collins, **Organic Alternatives** (346 E. Mountain Ave., 970/482-7100, www.organicalternatives.com, 10am-7pm Sun.-Wed., 10am-8pm Thurs.-Sat.) is about ambience and quality. The hardwood bar and ornate display shelves, salvaged from a former area music hall, make this swanky shop resemble a historical pharmacy. But the goods for sale are all cutting edge: top-shelf bud, edibles, concentrates, and everything in between.

South Fort Collins's lone retail pot shop, **Solace Meds** (301 Smokey St., 970/225-6337, www.solacemeds.com, 10am-8pm Mon.-Sat., 10am-7pm Sun.) prides itself on a huge selection of edibles, including its signature drinks: Canna Cappuccinos and Chai High Teas ("Colorado's Strongest Tea").

THE ARTS

The **Aggie Theatre** (204 S. College Ave., 970/482-8300, www.aggietheatre.com) is a tiny venue with big-name acts such as Reverend Horton Heat and Blues Traveler. It's a college town crowd here.

The **Lincoln Center** (417 W. Magnolia St., 970/221-6730, http://lctix.com) is home to a 1,180-seat performance hall and a 220-seat theater, as well as three galleries and an outdoor performance space and sculpture garden. This is where you will see **Opera Fort Collins Guild** performances (www.operafortcollins.org), including an annual Summer Soiree in the garden, and some of the **Fort Collins Symphony Orchestra** concerts (www.fcsymphony.org). The symphony also puts on a series of concerts called "Outside the Box," in which they perform at locales away from the center. This is also where you will see performances by **Canyon Concert Ballet** (www.ccballet.org), which puts on *The Nutcracker* each December and another classic ballet each spring. **Open Stage Theatre & Company** (www.openstage.com) is an award-winning theater group that produces about six shows a year—everything from Shakespeare to *The Rocky Horror Picture Show*—that can be seen at the center. There are also performances by touring theater companies and dance, music, and comedy groups.

Just when you think it's all happening at Lincoln Center, you discover **The Midtown Arts Center** (3750 S. Mason St., 970/225-2555, http://midtownartscenter.com) and its three separate performance spaces, including a Broadway-style dinner theater. In addition to dinner theater shows like *Oklahoma!* and *Sweeney Todd,* they also have an award-winning Young Audiences series with shows such as *The Cat in the Hat.*

Avogadro's Number (605 S. Mason St., 970/493-5555, www.avogadros.com) is a combination music venue, bar, and restaurant that is best known for bluegrass bands but also hosts burlesque, folk rock, and other genres. A night at "Avo's" is considered by many to be a quintessential Fort Collins experience.

You'll need a car—or plan to take the shuttle bus—to get to **The Mishawaka Amphitheatre** (13714 Poudre Canyon, Bellevue, 970/482-4420, www.themishawaka.com), but it's worth the drive to sit under the stars and dance the night away while a band plays on the riverfront stage. The on-site restaurant serves Odell's beer along with burgers and other bites.

FESTIVAL AND EVENTS

Once reserved just for "first Fridays," the city now suggests taking a **Gallery Walk** (http://downtownfortcollins.com) anytime, though the website has monthly themes to help focus your stroll. Head downtown and start wandering from place to place, taking in the town's paintings, photographs, and sculptures—all free unless you stop along the way for food and drinks.

Every third Friday of the month, **Foodie Walk Fort Collins** (http://downtownfortcollins.com, 5pm-8pm Fri.) offers an opportunity to nibble, walk, then nibble some more through specialty food shops such as Nuance Chocolate and The Welsh Rabbit Cheese Shop. Each event has a different theme, along with presentations and, of course, samples.

The **Larimer County Farmers Market** (200 S. Oak St., http://larimercountyfarmersmarket.colostate.edu, 9am-1pm Sat. May-mid-Oct.) starts in late spring each year and includes only Colorado- and Wyoming-grown, -raised, and -made products (now that you're this far north, the Wyoming state line is pretty close).

Spring

FoCoMX (http://focomx.focoma.org, Apr.) is about numbers: one weekend, more than 20 venues, and more than 200 bands. At the Fort Collins Music Experiment (FoCoMX, get it?), many local bands get a chance to win over new audiences as they rock out at places like the Aggie Theatre and the Fort Collins Museum of Discovery.

In spring, **Kids in the Park** (Spring Canyon Park, www.fcgov.com/recreation/kidsinthepark, May), previously known as Kites in the Park, draws kite fliers and builders from around the world. Not only is it spectacular to watch so many kites flying in the breeze, but you can also make kites and compete in kite flying during this one-day event.

Lace up for the **Colorado Marathon** (https://comarathon.com, early May) and enjoy the scenery. What's different about this run is that it is downhill. Begin the day early by shuttling up to the race start in Poudre Canyon. As the sun rises, descend more than 1,000 feet (300 m) in elevation to end in Old Town in 26.2 miles (42.2 km). This is a Boston Marathon qualifying run and includes a 10K and 5K.

Summer

If there isn't enough time to sample all the beers made in Fort Collins, you just might be able to squeeze it in during the weekend-long **Colorado Brewers' Festival** (Laporte Ave. and Mason St., http://downtownfortcollins.com, June). You can attend "Beer School" for tastings and demonstrations, listen to live music, eat great food, and, of course, drink more beer.

The weeklong **Larimer County Fair & Rodeo** (http://larimercountyfair.org, late July or early Aug.) harks back to the town's roots as an agricultural boomtown. The rodeo features roping, barrel racing, a horse show, and a lot of animals for the little ones to see (and smell and hear, too!), as well as carnival rides, food vendors, music, and an outdoor cinema night.

Bohemian Nights at NewWestFest (www.bohemiannights.org, Aug.) is a three-day free music festival held in Old Town. The emphasis is on the Colorado bands and musicians who play sets in between national headline acts like the Flobots.

Chances are that you can join a Tour de Fat celebration in a city near you, but this is where it started. **Tour de Fat** (Civic Center Park, www.newbelgium.com, Sept.) was created by the New Belgium Brewing Company to celebrate bike riding and to raise money through beer sales for nonprofit cycling clubs. This one-day event includes a parade of thousands of costumed people riding bikes through town.

Fall

Cuteness is on parade with the annual **Tour de Corgi** (https://tourdecorgi.org, first Sat. in Oct., free) as people either walk their funny little dogs or dress up as one. Check the website for the parade route and time.

Winter

Come December, you can celebrate with the **Downtown Festival of Lights** (www.visitfortcollins.com, Dec.) or the **Garden of Lights** (www.fcgov.com/gardens, Dec.). The Festival of Lights is spread out around the plazas and streets of Old Town and offers traditional Christmas displays. The Garden of Lights is held at the Gardens on Spring Creek (2145 Centre Ave.), with lights draped on plants and funny sculptures.

Shopping

The shops in Old Town are a fun mix of outdoor gear, hipster favorites, and local crafts. A handful of shops also have locations in Denver.

ARTS AND GIFTS

The **Center for Fine Art Photography** (400 N. College Ave., 970/224-1010, www.c4fap.org, 10am-6pm Tues.-Fri., 11am-5pm Sat.) is a real gem in the local arts scene, focused entirely on the art of photography. In addition to the changing exhibitions, there are photography workshops and portfolio reviews, and you can add them to your Gallery Walk. Exhibits might include local artists as well as international photographers.

Yes, it appears there are a lot of tchotchkes at **Trimble Court Artisans** (118 Trimble Court, 970/221-0051, www.trimblecourt.com, 10am-6pm Mon.-Sat., 11am-5pm Sun.), but they are the wares of local artists and

1: Nuance Chocolate **2:** The Welsh Rabbit Cheese Shop **3:** Trimble Court Artisans

CHOCOLATE
SMALL BATCH
NUANCE
CHOCOLATE
BEAN TO BAR
1

THE WELSH RABBIT
• CHEESE SHOP •
2

3

Trimble
Court
ARTISANS
ART & CRAFT
COOPERATIVE
OPEN

craftspeople. The shop is filled to the brim with pottery, photography, paintings, and all kinds of knickknacks for the home.

Blue Moose Art Gallery (4032 S. College Ave., 970/825-5704, www.bluemooseartgallery.com, 10am-4pm Tues.-Sat., 11am-4pm Sun.) displays and sells art—primarily made by Northern Colorado artists—but also lets you practice your artistic skills with on-site classes in watercolor painting, making objets d'art from clay, and more. It was voted best art gallery in NoCo (Northern Colorado) by *NoCo Style Magazine* in 2020.

Old Town Art & Framery (173 N. College Ave., 970/221-5105, www.oldtownartandframery.com, 11am-4pm Tues.-Wed. and Fri.-Sat.) specializes in art with a Western flair—from landscapes to barnyard critters—made by local and regional artists.

Makerfolk (144 N. College Ave., no phone number, www.makerfolk.com, 7am-3pm Sun.-Thurs., 7am-5pm Fri.-Sat.) offers a collection of locally made items including candles, T-shirts, jewelry, bath bombs, stationery, and a lot more.

BOOKSTORES

Old Firehouse Books (232 Walnut St., 970/484-7898, www.oldfirehousebooks.com, 10am-6pm daily) is a classic independent local bookstore with a rich selection of books for adults and kids with events to match. Come for story time on Tuesday morning, or plan to attend an author book signing and reading.

Bizarre Bazaar Books & Music (1014 S. College Ave., 970/484-1699, www.fortcollinsbazaar.com, 10am-8pm daily) is not just a bookstore; you can buy used hardbacks, paperbacks, and comic books, and even sheet music, posters, and magazines. If it's old school (VHS tapes, vinyl albums), you might find it or be able to sell it here. See if they're interested, and look for that hard-to-find item you've been searching for.

CLOTHING

This list just scratches the surface of the various boutiques in Fort Collins, which really rivals Cherry Creek North in Denver with the variety of styles, designers, and price range.

Fashion lovers should stop by **Kansas City Kitty** (136 N. College Ave., 970/482-5845, www.kckitty.com, 11am-6pm Tues.-Sat., 11am-5pm Sun-Mon.). They carry everything from Japanese denim brand One Green Elephant to local designers and Kansas City Kitty's own line.

Cira Ltd. (21 Old Town Square, 970/494-0410, www.ciralounge.com, 10am-7pm Mon.-Sat., 11am-5pm Sun.) sells fashions that appeal to college-age women who like to dress up on weekends in something sheer and slinky.

Solemates (172 N. College Ave., 970/472-1460, http://solematesinc.com, call for an appt.) has shoe lovers covered. Come here for the latest in heels, wedges, sandals, and boots from designers such as Kate Spade, Michael Kors, Frye, Diane von Furstenberg, and more. Of course, the perfect shoes need a matching handbag; fortunately Solemates also sells accessories.

Getting dressed for your next trip to Coachella? **Tula Boutique** (1 Old Town Square, 970/482-1953, https://shoptula.com, 10am-6pm Mon.-Sat., noon-5pm Sun.) has stylish—but pricey—loungewear (such as a Nili Lotan sweatshirt for $275, for example) for the occasion. Check their "outlet" section for deals, too.

Akinz (15 Old Town Square #132, 970/682-1750, https://akinz.com, 10am-5pm Mon.-Sat., noon-4pm Sun.) has exactly the hoodies, T-shirts, shorts, and beanies you need to don for hanging out at one of this city's brewpubs. Get a "Beer Makes Me Hoppy!" T-shirt and one of their made-in-house knit beanies. Everything is designed in-house and then screen-printed by hand right here. There is also a limited supply of baby and children's apparel, in addition to men's and women's.

CHILDREN'S TOYS AND CLOTHING

Even if you don't have kids, it's tempting to wander through **Clothes Pony and Dandelion Toys** (111 N. College Ave., 970/224-2866, www.clothespony.com, 10am-6pm Mon.-Thurs., 10am-7pm Fri.-Sat., 10am-5pm Sun.). The store is filled with the most adorable onesies, jammies, diaper bags, and stuffed animals. Familiar brands include Tea Collection, Brio, Petunia Pickle Bottom, and Toms.

OUTDOOR GEAR

Yes, there is an REI and the usual outdoor gear retailers at which to get your tent, sleeping bag, fishing rod, and more, but locals know to go to **Jax Mercantile** (1200 N. College Ave., 970/221-0544, www.jaxmercantile.com, 8am-8pm Mon.-Sat., 9am-6pm Sun.), which also has gear for ranching and hunting, not just camping and recreating. The store is locally owned and has multiple locations in greater Fort Collins and Boulder.

Gearage Outdoor Sports (119 E. Mountain Ave., 970/416-6803, http://gearageoutdoorsports.com, 11am-6pm Mon., 10am-6:30pm Tues.-Sat., 10am-6pm Sun.) is your affordable place for new and used outdoor gear, bike repairs, and bike rentals. The knowledgeable and friendly staff makes it even more appealing.

With more than disc golf Frisbees, **The Wright Life** (200 Linden St., 970/484-6932, www.wrightlife.com, 11am-6pm Mon.-Thurs., 10am-6pm Fri.-Sat., 10am-5pm Sun.) is a typical outdoor gear store in Old Town. That is, typical with lots of Frisbees, along with snowboard gear, skateboards, shoes, coats, and more.

Equestrians will find all that they—and their equines—need at **Happy Horse Tack Shop** (113 Peterson St., 970/484-4199, www.happyhorsetack.com, 11am-5pm Mon.-Sat.), in a cute old house. Beyond the gear there are saddle services, too.

SPECIALTY FOODS

The Cupboard (152 S. College Ave., 970/493-8585, http://thecupboard.net, 10am-6pm Mon.-Sat., 11am-5pm Sun.) is a large kitchen supply shop where you can sign up for cooking lessons with local chefs.

Nuance Chocolate (214 Pine St., 970/484-2330, www.nuancechocolate.com, 11am-7pm Mon.-Thurs., 11am-8pm Fri., 10am-8pm Sat., noon-4pm Sun.) is the chocoholic's answer to craft food. During pairing events you can learn what goes into making one delectable little truffle, eat chocolate, or sip a mug of hot chocolate. Everything is made from scratch in-house.

The Welsh Rabbit Cheese Shop (216 Pine St., 970/443-4027, www.thewelshrabbit.com, 10am-7pm Mon.-Thurs., 10am-8pm Fri.-Sat., 11am-4pm Sun.) is a cheese lover's paradise—locally made, flown in from Europe, just so long as it's cheese. Other kitchen staples sold here include mustard, preserves, butter, and more. Order a gift of cheese or walk around the corner and settle in for a meal at The Welsh Rabbit Cheese Bistro.

Sports and Recreation

You can enjoy Fort Collins by going for a bike ride or walk, or opt for a short drive into the foothills or to a local reservoir for wildflower hikes or boating. Horsetooth Reservoir, just outside of Fort Collins, provides boating activities, while the Cache La Poudre River makes this area a destination for white-water rafting.

BALLOONING

Float high above the Poudre Canyon and Fort Collins in a hot-air balloon with **Flights of Fancy** (970/581-5042, www.flightsoffancyllc.com, year-round, weather permitting, $230 pp). Each balloon ride is appropriate for groups up to four, but a second balloon is available if there are more in your party. Reservations are required.

★ BIKING

In 2018, *Bicycling Magazine* gave Fort Collins third place as the best city for bicycling in the nation. The city has a 310-mile (500-km) network of paths and bike lanes and a bike share program; in the nearby foothills of the Rocky Mountains are more miles of biking trails, or cyclists can head east for trails on the plains. Whether you are a mountain biker or a road cyclist, there is a path that will appeal to you.

Spring Creek Trail (www.fcgov.com/parks) offers 6.6 miles (10.6 km) of paved trail on relatively flat terrain that traverses the city from east to west. Start at the Poudre River Trail (near East Prospect Rd.) and ride west to Spring Canyon Park (2626 W. Horsetooth Rd.). This popular trail goes through the city, so you can lock up your bike and stop for lunch before you turn around. In spring, be mindful of runoff on this trail.

The **Poudre Trail** (www.fcgov.com/parks) is 12.3 miles (19.8 km) long. The trail follows the Cache La Poudre River, with one end at Lyons Park and the other at the Environmental Learning Center on the CSU campus. The trail travels from wooded areas to industrial areas. In spring, this path can become flooded and there might be detours.

Fossil Creek Trail (5381 S. Shields St. and Luther Lane, www.fcgov.com/parks), southwest of town, offers a paved riding experience for 8.5 miles (13.7 km) between the Cathy Fromme Prairie Natural Area and Spring Canyon Park (2626 W. Horsetooth Rd.).

Mountain Biking

Mountain bikers will surely prefer to get off the paved trails and over to **Lory State Park** (708 Lodgepole Dr., Bellevue, 970/493-1623, http://cpw.state.co.us, $4-9 daily). The **Corral Center Mountain Bike Park** (http://cpw.state.co.us) is a rare dirt jump and pump track within the state park; this former horse corral has miles of trails in a 70,000-square-foot bike park suitable for both beginner and advanced riders. The **Mill Creek Link Trail** is a mixed-use dirt trail in Lory State Park; though it is less than one mile long, it is considered difficult. It links to a similar trail called Mill Creek in the **Horsetooth Mountain Open Space** (County Rd. 38E, www.larimer.org, year-round), 4 miles (6.4 km) west of Fort Collins.

To reach Lory State Park from Fort Collins, take Highway 287 (College Ave.) north to County Road 54G. Make a left on Rist Canyon Road and turn left again on North County Road 23. After making a right on County Road 25G (Lodgepole Dr.), look ahead for parking.

Soapstone Prairie Natural Area (Rawhide Flats Rd., www.fcgov.com/naturalareas/soapstone, dawn-dusk daily Mar.-Nov.) is worth the trip thanks to its 28 square miles of prairie to explore. The Cheyenne Rim Trail, a shared-use single track, is the longest of the trails at nearly 12 miles (19 km). It's pretty, with views of the wide horizon and the sounds of native birds.

Soapstone Prairie Natural Area is 25 miles

Oh, the Things You Can Do . . . on Bikes

Just riding bikes isn't enough in this town. There is also the ongoing celebration of all things bike.

Bike-In Cinema is held every summer on the front lawn at New Belgium Brewing (500 Linden St.), with bikes, brews, and films shown outdoors. **Beer and Bike Tours** (2414 Stanley Court, 970/201-1085, www.beerandbiketours.com) has a variety of tours, some including breweries, others including whiskey, and one for the family with . . . root beer!

Some of these events serve as fund-raisers for **Bike Fort Collins** (http://bikefortcollins.org), a nonprofit that supports bicycle education and safety. They also advocate making Fort Collins a place that welcomes cycles on paths and roads.

(40 km) north of Fort Collins. Take I-25 north to Buckeye Road (exit 288) and turn left (west) to follow County Road 15. Drive north on County Road 15 and then onto Rawhide Flats Road to the entrance station.

Bike Rentals and Tours

Have a local give you a tour with **Front Range Guides** (Canby Way, 720/208-0152, www.frontrangerideguides.com, $159-219), where you can choose between half-day or full-day tours that include bike rental, helmet, snacks or lunch, an expert guide, and transportation to and from the trailhead.

Recycled Cycles (4031-A S. Mason St., 970/223-1969, www.recycled-cycles.com, 9am-8pm Mon.-Sat., 10am-6pm Sun., $20-25 per day) rents bikes, including children's models, and sells reconditioned bikes at discounted prices; they can also service your bike. A second location in the Lory Student Center (451 Isotope Dr., 970/491-9555, 9am-5pm Mon.-Fri.) on the CSU campus has different hours and inventory but the same concept.

BIRD-WATCHING

With more than 44 protected natural areas covering at least 41,000 acres around Fort Collins, the region offers some hot spots for birders. **Soapstone Prairie Natural Area** (Rawhide Flats Rd., www.fcgov.com/naturalareas/soapstone, dawn-dusk daily Mar.-Nov.) is one of the best areas. At this site, 25 miles (40 km) outside Fort Collins, more than 130 bird species have been spotted, including northern goshawks, white-tailed ptarmigans, mountain bluebirds, western tanagers, sandhill cranes, and burrowing owls. Take I-25 north from Fort Collins to Buckeye Road (exit 288) and turn left (west) to follow County Road 15. Drive north on County Road 15 and then onto Rawhide Flats Road to the entrance station.

The **Fort Collins Audubon Society** (www.fortcollinsaudubon.org) offers free birding field trips throughout the year. The Nature Conservancy's 1,700-acre **Phantom Canyon Preserve** (www.nature.org), 30 miles (48 km) northwest of Fort Collins, is home to more than 100 species. The preserve is open to the public through Nature Conservancy guided hikes and volunteer outings, which include birding hikes.

The **Environmental Learning Center** (2400 S. County Rd. 9, 970/491-1661, www.csuelc.org) on the CSU campus is an ideal setting for owls, hawks, waterfowl, and songbirds.

BOATING

It's been said that the only thing missing from Colorado is a beach (or an ocean); the local solution to this problem is **Horsetooth Reservoir** (County Rd. 38E, www.larimer.org, $9-18) west of Fort Collins. This 6.5-mile-long body of water is open to all kinds of water sports activities—water-skiing is very popular, Jet Skis are permitted, and there is a swimming beach. The reservoir is surrounded by public lands that offer hiking opportunities.

Horsetooth Reservoir is less than 10 miles

1

2

3

4

(16 km) from Fort Collins, about a 15-minute drive. From the intersection of Harmony and Taft Hill Roads, drive west onto County Road 38 to the entrance.

CLIMBING

Rock climbing and its close cousin, bouldering, are available in the Fort Collins area. The best source for information is **Northern Colorado Climbers Coalition** (970/682-0525, www.nococlimbing.org), a local nonprofit that sells books exclusively about rock climbing in the area and organizes rock climbing meet-ups and events. Check their Facebook page for more recent updates than what is found on their website.

Lory State Park (708 Lodgepole Dr., Bellevue, 970/493-1623, http://cpw.state.co.us, $4-9 daily) is your best bet for rock climbing, particularly on and near Arthur's Rock. There are bolted routes, so this does require some gear and technical knowledge. Park fees apply when inside the state park.

FISHING

There are plenty of fishing holes in and near Fort Collins, for all skill levels. Anglers can fish in designated natural areas in ponds, rivers, reservoirs, and creeks. Start by visiting the **City of Fort Collins** website (www.fcgov.com/naturalareas/fishing) for a list of areas, the fish stocked in each, and details on access. Depending on where you go, you might catch largemouth bass, yellow perch, common carp, or bluegill.

Horsetooth Reservoir (County Rd. 38E, www.larimer.org, $9-18), managed by Larimer County Parks Department, posts the latest fishing conditions on their website. Shoreline fishing and boat fishing are allowed. There are daily limits on the number of different types of fish that can be taken. The reservoir is stocked with rainbow and brown trout, walleye, smallmouth and largemouth bass, and panfish such as bluegill.

If you need to buy bait, get some friendly local advice, take a class, or hire a guide, visit **St. Peter's Fly Shop** (202 Remington St., 970/498-8968, www.stpetes.com, 9am-6pm Mon.-Sat. Apr.-Sept., 10am-6pm Mon.-Sat. Oct.-Mar.; 2008 E. Harmony Rd., 970/377-3785, 9am-6pm Mon.-Sat., 10am-4pm Sun. Apr.-Sept., 10am-6pm Tues.-Sat., 10am-4pm Sun. Oct.-Mar.), with two locations in Fort Collins. You'll find all the fishing gear you need and can opt for a half day or full day of guided angling.

GOLF

Fort Collins doesn't have quite the attraction for golfers that Colorado Springs does, but there are some beautiful and challenging courses with good mountain views. The City of Fort Collins operates three public golf courses: City Park Nine, Collindale, and Southridge. There are also public golf courses not operated by the city.

City Park Nine (411 S. Bryan Ave., 970/221-6650, www.fcgov.com/golf, $14-20) is a 9-hole par-36 course that has been here since 1940. The earliest tee times are 6:30am (mid-Apr.-mid-Sept.) and 9am (fall-winter).

Situated on 160 acres, **Collindale Golf Course** (1441 E. Horsetooth Rd., 970/221-6651, www.fcgov.com/golf, $26-37) is an 18-hole par-71 championship-length golf course that hosts the local U.S. Open qualifying every year.

Southridge Golf Course (5750 S. Lemay Ave., 970/416-2828, www.fcgov.com/golf, $26-37) is an 18-hole course on 128 acres. It has scenic views, is suitable for all skill levels, and is considered a great value for the quality of the course.

HIKING

There are many opportunities for head-clearing nature walks in the foothills near Fort Collins. A favorite local hiking trail is **Greyrock Mountain Trail** (www.fs.usda.gov, 7 mi/11.3 km round-trip, moderate-strenuous), which is about a 20-mile (32-km) drive outside town in the Poudre Canyon.

1: Horsetooth Reservoir **2:** mountain biker in Lory State Park **3:** fly-fishing near Fort Collins **4:** rafting on the Cache La Poudre

Atop the mountain: singing frogs, small lakes, and views to Wyoming! Get here early because this popular trail's parking lot fills up fast. To reach the trailhead, drive 11 miles (18 km) northwest on Highway 287, then turn left on Highway 14. Continue 9 more miles (14 km) to the parking lot.

Horsetooth Mountain Open Space (County Rd. 38E, www.larimer.org), 4 miles (6.4 km) west of Fort Collins via County Road 38E, offers popular hikes of moderate intensity and beautiful views, including the **Horsetooth Falls Trail** (1.2 mi/1.9 km one-way), which leads you to a waterfall, at its fullest in spring.

There are a dozen hiking trails (some mixed use, others pedestrian only) in **Lory State Park** (708 Lodgepole Dr., Bellevue, 970/493-1623, http://cpw.state.co.us), about 10 miles (16 km) west of Fort Collins. My favorite is the hiker-only **Arthur's Rock Trail** (1.7 mi/2.7 km one-way), an out-and-back trail that includes wildflowers in spring, a small waterfall, and a gurgling creek along part of the path. Oh, and there is a great view of Horsetooth Reservoir when you reach the summit. To reach Lory State Park from Fort Collins, take Highway 287 (College Ave.) north to County Road 54G. Make a left on Rist Canyon Road and turn left again on North County Road 23. After making a right on County Road 25G (Lodgepole Dr.), look ahead for parking.

The **Soapstone Prairie Natural Area** (Rawhide Flats Rd., www.fcgov.com/naturalareas/soapstone, dawn-dusk daily Mar.-Nov.), 25 miles (40 km) north of Fort Collins, offers 28 square miles of prairie. Bison were reintroduced here and roam within a giant fenced pasture. The area is also home to an archaeological site that dates to 10,000-12,000 years ago. The **Lindenmeier Overlook** (0.25 mi/0.4 km one-way) is a very short paved trail with benches and interpretive signs, making this a good introductory hike for young children. Bring your hat because this is an exposed area. Take I-25 north from Fort Collins to Buckeye Road (exit 288) and turn left (west) to follow County Road 15. Drive north on County Road 15 and then onto Rawhide Flats Road to the entrance station.

HORSEBACK RIDING

With so many mixed-use trails on the prairie, in the foothills, or creek-side, all you need is a horse and you can gallop away. **Beaver Meadow Stables** (100 Marmot Dr., Red Feather Lakes, 970/232-8326 or 970/231-1955, http://beavermeadowsstables.com, Memorial Day-early fall, $30-300) has everything from one-hour rides for the young'uns to full-day rides or even overnight trips. Rides are in the Roosevelt National Forest, west of Fort Collins.

Red Feather Lakes is less than one hour northwest of Fort Collins. Take Highway 287 north for 21 miles (34 km) to Livermore and then turn left onto County Road 74E (Red Feather Lakes Rd.). Drive 24 miles (39 km) until reaching Red Feather Lakes. Follow the road as it bends north and becomes Creedmore Lakes Road (County Rd. 73C); the road becomes a dirt road after 1 mile (1.6 km). Drive 3.3 miles (5.3 km) to the Beaver Meadows Ranch entryway.

Shiloh Guest Ranch (2720 Stove Prairie Rd., Bellevue, 970/295-4557), near Horsetooth Reservoir, offers hourly trail rides that go up into the mountains or out into rolling foothills amid wide-open vistas and beautiful scenery. This is described as a "small" experience with only six riders at a time.

RIVER RAFTING

White-water river rafting is a blast, and the **Cache La Poudre** (the only waterway in the state that is a federally designated Wild and Scenic River) has everything from Class I to Class IV rapids. It's served by plenty of experienced commercial outfitters who can take you on a wild ride.

Mountain Whitewater Descents (1329 N. Hwy. 287, 970/419-0917, www.raftmwd.com, hours vary) has a variety of options, including renting your own kayaks and canoes ($30-55 per day). Select your raft trip based on how fun (or scary) you want it to be. Raft trips ($70-365 pp) include rapids classes with enticing names like Splash and Plunge that give you an idea of what to expect.

A Wanderlust Adventure (4120 W. County Rd. 54G, LaPorte, 800/745-7238 or 970/482-1995, www.awanderlustadventure.com, mid-May-early Sept., $70-85 pp) offers two options for raft trips: Taste of Whitewater (beginner) and Blast of Whitewater (advanced). Either way, you're getting soaked.

Food

Many of the town's craft breweries double as restaurants serving both beer and food (see *Breweries and Distilleries* in the *Entertainment and Events* section), and most restaurants will have a local brew on tap. Many Front Range eateries have expanded here, so you might find yourself at the Fort Collins version of a Boulder or Denver establishment.

COFFEE AND TEA

In a town where many successful business owners have made their name with craft beer, it seems only natural for someone to fill the niche of craft coffee. Dedicated to that experience, **Harbinger Coffee** (505 S. Mason St., 847/274-2253, www.harbingercoffee.com, 7am-5pm daily) showcases some of the finest coffees from around the world and from fantastic roasters across the United States. They also serve tea, hot cocoa, and other beverages.

Happy Lucky's Teahouse (236 Walnut St., 970/689-3417, www.happyluckys.com, 10am-6pm daily) has a huge selection of teas to buy as gifts, learn how to brew, or just sip and hang out. The teahouse is next door to Old Firehouse Books.

The owners at **Mugs Coffee Lounge** (261 S. College Ave., 970/472-6847, www.mugscoffeelounge.com, 6:30am-5pm daily) want you to have an experience, not just a cup of joe to start your day. The concept is "community through coffee," and that happens in a few ways: sourcing and growing local ingredients and providing a free community space for meetings and gatherings. A full menu makes this your complete stop for breakfast or a hearty snack later in the day. There is another location, **Mugs @ the Oval** (306 W. Laurel St., 970/449-2265, 7am-5pm daily) by the CSU campus.

The **Bean Cycle** (144 N. College Ave., 970/221-2964, www.beancycleroasters.com, 7am-4pm Sun.-Thurs., 7am-7pm Fri.-Sat.) is a local favorite for lattes, espresso, and, of course, coffee. They emphasize locally sourced ingredients whenever possible. Also here is Makerfolk, a shop featuring handmade goods such as candles and jewelry.

It's more about the donuts than the coffee at **FoCo DoCo** (234 N. College Ave. Unit A1, 970/689-8978, www.focodoco.com, 7am-noon Mon., 7am-5pm Tues.-Thurs., 7am-7pm Fri., 8am-7pm Sat., 8am-5pm Sun.), aka Fort Collins Donut Company, in Old Town. There are your basic donuts like powdered sugar, and then there are the ones you wake up early for, like salted honey, Jitterbug (coffee glaze and chocolate-covered espresso beans), and Maple Tree Hugger (maple icing and cinnamon granola). And yes, there's coffee and lattes to wash down the donuts!

BREAKFAST

The **Silver Grill Café** (218 Walnut St., 970/484-4656, www.silvergrill.com, 7am-2pm daily, $4-9) is a local favorite for hearty and affordable breakfasts that start with giant cinnamon rolls. Also on the menu are omelets, breakfast burritos, steak and eggs, biscuits and gravy, and more.

★ **Café Bluebird** (524 W. Laurel St., 970/484-7755, www.cafebluebird.com, 7am-2pm daily, $10-12) might have a line out front for a weekend brunch, but it's worth the wait if you're hungry for one of their signature skillets. Kids will like the Mickey Mouse pancakes, even if most of the "kids" here are college students. Located close to the CSU campus, this place is popular with those who attend, work, and live at the school.

Also popular with the college crowd is **Butters** (1103 W. Elizabeth St., 970/797-2062, www.buttersbreakfast.com, 7am-1:30pm Mon.-Fri., 7am-2pm Sat.-Sun., $6.50-12), mainly for the From the Griddle section of the menu that goes beyond ordinary pancakes and waffles with dishes like a Pancake Roll (kind of like crepes, but a lot thicker), stuffed French toast, and Mama Mia Cakes made with sweet cream batter.

BISTRO

This is only slightly confusing: **The Welsh Rabbit Cheese Bistro** (200 Walnut St., 970/232-9521, www.thewelshrabbit.com, 11am-9pm Tues.-Thurs., 10am-10pm Fri.-Sat., $6-10) is where you can sit down and order various cheese plates with a glass of wine or a mug of beer. This should not be confused with The Welsh Rabbit Cheese Shop, which simply sells the cheese and other high-quality, locally sourced groceries—that's around the corner. Either one is delicious for cheese lovers.

Fox and the Crow (2601 S. Lemay Ave., 970/999-2229, www.thefoxandthecrow.net, 11am-7pm Tues.-Thurs., 11am-8pm Fri.-Sat., $7-10) is the perfect place to stop for a snack or a small meal. The emphasis is on cheese: cheese plate, grilled cheese, mac and cheese, plus great local beers. There is also a tasty selection of charcuterie. Stop here for your picnic supplies.

BURGERS AND HOT DOGS

Big Al's Burgers and Dogs (140 W. Mountain Ave., 970/232-9815, http://bigalsburgersanddogs.com, 11am-9pm daily, $4-7) is a locally owned and operated business specializing in Chicago-style hamburgers and hot dogs. They have mouthwateringly good burgers, hot dogs, fries, and milkshakes. Enjoy their original 60/40 Burger, made with 60 percent beef and 40 percent bacon, with a side of truffle fries.

COMFORT FOOD

Comfort food with a modern twist is found at **Restaurant 415** (415 S. Mason Ave., 970/407-0415, http://thefourfifteen.com, 11am-8pm Tues.-Thurs., 11am-9pm Fri.-Sat., 11am-8pm Sun., $4-15), where you can get salads, bowls, pizzas, and small plates. The menu offers many vegetarian options.

Old mixed with new, pie with wine—it's a different world over at **Ginger and Baker** market and bakery (359 Linden St., 970/223-7437, http://gingerandbaker.com, 11am-9pm Tues.-Fri., 9am-9pm Sat., 9am-6pm Sun., $11-24). Once the Northern Colorado Feeders Supply building, it's now a haven for pie lovers, wine lovers, and those who want to learn more about both in a teaching kitchen or tasting room. Ginger and Baker features breakfast all day, a full lunch and dinner menu, a rooftop bar, and a calendar of food-related events. Dine in or do takeout.

★ **Union Bar & Soda Fountain** (250 Jefferson St. 970/825-5558, www.unionbarsodafountain.com, 10am-10pm daily, $10-16) quickly became my go-to spot in Fort Collins for a post-hike meal or meeting up with friends. There's something for everyone on this menu with milkshakes and cocktails, breakfast and dinner, all tasty. If the weather is right, go for the patio and maybe a game of cornhole.

If you're in the mood for dressed-up comfort food, check out **The Emporium: An American Brasserie** (378 Walnut St., 970/493-0024, www.emporiumftcollins.com, 8am-11am and 4pm-9pm Wed., 4pm-9pm Thurs., 8am-11am and 4pm-10pm Fri., 8am-2pm and 4pm-10pm Sat., 8am-2pm Sun.) in the Elizabeth Hotel. Dig into shrimp and grits, pan-seared salmon, vegetable orecchiette, or meatloaf made from elk, beef, and pork.

LOCAVORE

★ **Next Door American Eatery** (100 N. College Ave., 970/568-8869, www.nextdooreatery.com, 11am-9pm Sun.-Thurs., 11am-10pm Fri.-Sat., $4-15) focuses on dishes made from ingredients sourced from local farms and ranches—just as it did in its previous incarnation, The Kitchen (it's still part of the same restaurant group). The menu is casual with sandwiches, quick bites, and bowls, all packed with flavor. Make it a date night at this posh spot. This is a cashless business, so bring your plastic to pay.

STEAKHOUSE

Much like John Elway in Denver, former Colorado State University Rams football coach Sonny Lubick is a local legend, celebrity, and namesake restaurant owner. **Sonny Lubick Steakhouse** (115 S. College Ave., 970/484-9200, www.sonnylubicksteakhouse.com, 4pm-9pm Sun.-Thurs., 4pm-10pm Fri.-Sat., $12-46) draws people in the mood for an upscale steak dinner—or those interested in the local football team.

AUSTRALIAN

Grab your mates and hunker down under with a few meat pies! The Australian accent and references are irresistible when trying **Waltzing Kangaroo** (1109 W. Elizabeth St., 970/568-8817, www.waltzingkangaroo.com, 11am-7pm Tues.-Sat., $5-8) and their traditional meat pies. The pies consist of either a gravy or sauce with chicken, steak, or lamb in a delicate pastry. The only thing missing is kangaroo or emu meat (yes, those are eaten in Australia). There's no indoor seating, so grab and go with a hot pie or get some frozen for later.

ITALIAN

Entrées at **Café Vino** (1200 S. College Ave., 970/212-3399, www.cafevino.com, 3pm-10pm Tues.-Sat., $6-18) are scrumptious, but what keeps people coming back are the tapas (bacon-wrapped dates) and desserts (toffee date cake). Enjoy an after-dinner caffeine boost and you'll get to taste Silver Canyon Coffee, a Colorado roaster. If beer isn't your thing, then you might appreciate the impressive wine list (they also offer wine tastings and wine menus).

RARE Italian (101 S. College Ave., 970/294-4544, www.rareitalian.com, 4pm-10pm Mon.-Thurs., 4pm-11pm Fri., 2pm-11pm Sat., 2pm-10pm Sun., $13-40) is part steakhouse, part delectable Italian dishes. The

a meat pie from Waltzing Kangaroo

pasta is made here, the pizzas are hand tossed, and gluten-free options are available. Come for happy hour to sample, or try the half servings at dinner if you're a small group.

KOREAN

It's fun when your meal can be an experience, as is the case at **Suh Sushi Korean BBQ** (165 E. Boardwalk Dr., 970/232-9435, www.suhbbq.com, 11am-8:30pm Wed.-Mon., $12-37), with the option of cooking the barbecue at your own table or sampling the *banchan* before your entrées arrive. Or just stick to the sushi, nigiri, and sashimi menus, which are also a draw for this place. And here's more fun: a selection of imported Japanese beers to sample.

LEBANESE

At **Yum Yum Social Club** (1300 Elizabeth St., 970/493-7937, http://eatmoreyumyum.com, 11am-9pm Tues.-Sat., noon-8pm Sun., $5-22), you'll find items like Lebanese pizza and Lebanese fries mixed in with traditional Middle Eastern fare such as gyros and shawarma.

MEXICAN

If you're looking for me, I might be at **Vatos Tacos + Tequila** (200 N. College Ave., 970/631-8533, https://vatostacosandtequila.com, 7am-9pm Mon.-Thurs., 7am-10pm Fri., 8am-10pm Sat., 8am-9pm Sun., $3-10), because like many people, I love street tacos. If tacos aren't your thing, there are also nachos, burritos, and enchiladas on the menu. This location is in Old Town so it's easy to walk to if you're in the area.

Nearby, burrito lovers will find their bliss at **Big Burrito City** (510 S. College Ave., 970/482-3303, www.bigcityburrito.com, 8am-9pm daily, $5-23), where the specialty is large stuffed and wrapped burritos with lots of choices. Seriously, lots. There are seven types of tortillas and ten fillings to choose from, not including salsas, picos, and extras. They are best known for the potato burrito, which seems like a sort of Mexican-Irish fusion to me?

THAI

Tararine Thai Cuisine (1401 Elizabeth St., 970/825-5951, www.tararinethaicuisine.com, 11am-2:30pm and 3:30pm-9pm Mon.-Fri., 11am-9pm Sat.-Sun., $6-11) will satisfy any curry craving with not just the usual red, green, *panang,* and *massaman* curries, but also a pumpkin and a pineapple curry too. Half of the menu consists of vegan options.

VIETNAMESE

For those craving pho, **Young's Café Vietnamese Cuisine** (3307 S. College Ave., 970/223-8000, http://youngscafe.com, 11am-9:30pm Sun.-Thurs., 11am-10pm Fri.-Sat., $8-38) will deliver and then some. Got a head cold coming on? Try one of their "flaming" soups for a cure. Most people just come for non-flaming rice paper wraps, a steaming bowl of pho, or fried rice with shrimp, chicken, beef, or tofu. The ambience means this can be a nice night out, not just a takeout on the couch kind of experience.

VEGETARIAN AND VEGAN

Tasty Harmony (130 S. Mason St., 970/689-3234, www.tastyharmony.com, 11am-8pm Tues.-Thurs., 11am-9pm Fri.-Sat., 11am-8pm Sun., $12-15) makes eating vegan fun and delicious. Menu items include silly names like Kentucky Fried Freedom, Heart of Provence, and the Ricky Bobby Wrap. It's a world of flavors with Thai, Mexican, and barbecue all on the menu in "mock" dishes.

Accommodations

There are plenty of chain hotels in Fort Collins, many close to I-25. For nonchain lodging, the most appealing options are found in and around Old Town; these have some historic characteristics and are in walkable communities.

For those looking for **marijuana-friendly rental properties** in the Fort Collins area, visit **Colorado Pot Guide** (www.coloradopotguide.com).

UNDER $150

The **Fernweh Inn & Hostel** (616 W. Mulberry St., 970/219-9493, www.fortcollinshostel.com, $79-129) is a cheery old house that has been converted into very affordable accommodations. Choose from a women-only shared bunk room, a coed bunk room, or two private rooms. Guests have 24-hour access to a communal kitchen, receive free parking, and are welcome to borrow a bike.

$150-250

Once the tallest building in Fort Collins, the ★ **Armstrong Hotel** (259 S. College Ave., 970/484-3883, www.thearmstronghotel.com, $159-339) has been renovated into a hip and historic lodging option in Old Town. The hotel's 43 rooms and suites have an eclectic mix of vintage and modern furnishings, set off by bright colors on the walls and in other accents. The central location makes it easy to walk to shops, restaurants, and the campus. Don't miss **Ace Gillett's Lounge,** the underground bar and restaurant at the hotel, where you can sip cocktails and listen to a little jazz music in the evening.

The **Edwards House Bed & Breakfast** (402 W. Mountain Ave., 970/493-9191, http://edwardshouse.com, $200-275) has eight rooms named after people who were significant to the history of Fort Collins. The updated decor reflects a more contemporary feel than the home's 1904 origins, but it's very comfortable, clean, and welcoming. The location—an easy walk to Old Town's amenities—can't be beat.

The **Best Western University Inn** (914 S. College Ave., 970/484-2984, www.bestwestern.com, $120-240) is in a prime place

Elizabeth Hotel

for those in town to attend a function on the CSU campus. Guests have access to an indoor pool and fitness center and receive complimentary daily breakfast.

The **Hilton Fort Collins** (425 W. Prospect Rd., 970/482-2626, www.hilton.com, $189-285) has more than 200 rooms and suites, many of which have a terrific view of the Rocky Mountains and were part of the hotel's multimillion-dollar refresh in 2017. Amenities include a pool, fitness center, and on-site restaurant. This hotel can be fun for families, but it also serves business travelers who need conference rooms, AV equipment, and printing services.

OVER $250

Located in Old Town, the **Elizabeth Hotel** (111 Chestnut St., 970/490-2600, www.theelizabethcolorado.com, $265-300) has a classic feel and artistic touches throughout. Got Marriott rewards? Use them here. Even if you're not a guest, pop in to the ground-floor Emporium Kitchen & Wine Market for a drink, a bite, or to buy some Colorado-made foods in the shop. Of the 164 rooms, three are expansive suites to indulge in for a special occasion. End the day at the top-floor Sunset Lounge, a swanky bar.

IN THE VICINITY

The ★ **Inn at Whiskey Belle Ranch** (2030 Cherokee Park Rd., Livermore, 970/482-0248, http://whiskeybelleranch.com, $175-195) is a working cattle ranch 22 miles (35 km) northwest of Fort Collins. Guests can experience a "true Western experience" by joining a cattle drive, fly-fishing, or going on a trail ride. It's part dude ranch, part bed-and-breakfast, and all appropriately elegant in a cattle ranch sort of way.

The Western feel can also be found 30 miles (48 km) south at the **Sylvan Dale Guest Ranch** (2939 N. County Rd. 31D, Loveland, 877/667-3999 or 970/667-3915, www.sylvandale.com, $138-468). These comfy cabins are suitable for a romantic weekend or a family gathering. Guests also can use the outdoor heated pool (summer only), tennis courts, and game room. Check their calendar for activities like the annual Native American week, cattle drive, cowgirl week, and more.

Transportation and Services

GETTING THERE AND AROUND

Car

From Denver, take I-25 north for 60 miles (97 km), then head west on Highway 14 for about 5 miles (8 km) to Fort Collins; the Prospect Road exit leads downtown. From Boulder, it's possible to take Highway 52 east to join I-25 north for 30 miles (48 mi) to Highway 14; also, I-287 leads north from Highway 52. Either drive can take about one hour.

Airport Transportation

From Denver International Airport, **Super Shuttle** (970/482-0505, www.supershuttle.com) offers service to Fort Collins, specifically the Colorado State University campus and a few hotels in the area.

Public Transit

Greyhound buses (www.greyhound.com, $10) stop at the Harmony Road Park & Ride (I-25 and Harmony Rd.) in Fort Collins en route to and from Denver daily. Within Fort Collins, the **Transfort Bus Service** (970/221-6620, www.ridetransfort.com, $1.25) offers multiple routes around town. Route 2 (Mon.-Sat.) visits the CSU campus, while Route 5 (Mon.-Sat.) serves downtown.

More tourist attraction than actual transportation, the antique Fort Collins Municipal Railway **trolley car** (1801 W. Mountain Ave., 970/224-5372, www.fortcollinstrolley.org, noon-5pm Sat.-Sun. May-Sept., $2) runs a 3-mile (4.8-km) round-trip between downtown and City Park on weekends in the summer months.

Amtrak trains do not serve Fort Collins.

INFORMATION AND SERVICES

The **Fort Collins Convention & Visitors Bureau** (19 Old Town Square, 970/232-3840 or 800/274-3678, www.visitftcollins.com, 8:30am-5pm Mon.-Fri., 11am-5pm Sat.-Sun.) has an online events calendar. You can request a free guide to the area as well.

The ***Fort Collins Coloradoan*** (www.coloradoan.com), the city's daily newspaper, is available online and in print. The ***Rocky Mountain Collegian*** (www.collegian.com) is a student-run daily or weekly newspaper. ***Fort Collins Magazine*** (www.ftcollinsmag.com) is a monthly glossy magazine that covers northern Colorado happenings.

Vicinity of Fort Collins

SHAMBHALA MOUNTAIN CENTER

The **Shambhala Mountain Center** (Red Feather Lakes, 4921 County Rd., Suite 68-C, 970/881-2184, www.shambhalamountain.org, usually 9am-6pm daily, $8-10) is not just for Buddhists or admirers of the Dalai Lama—anyone with an interest in religious architecture will enjoy a visit. Check the schedule for current retreats and events.

The 600-acre Shambhala Mountain Center is mostly wilderness, with 8 miles (13 km) of hiking trails, a garden, and access to the activities at nearby Red Feather Lakes. The center offers programs for children and those interested in yoga, meditation, massage, and Buddhism.

★ Great Stupa of Dharmakaya

Consecrated in a 10-day ceremony in 2001, the Great Stupa of Dharmakaya is one of the largest examples of sacred Buddhist architecture in North America. The word *stupa* refers to the 108-foot-tall building, which is painted white and other bright colors to symbolize the body of the Buddha. All around

Great Stupa of Dharmakaya

the building are other statues and mandalas, patterns that represent the universe. The interior of the Buddhist shrine houses a very large gold statue of the Buddha. Unlike typical stupas that are sealed shut, this one allows public visitation on the first floor, where pillows and chairs are available for peaceful meditation. The stupa holds the ashes of Chogyam Trungpa Rinpoche, a Tibetan exile who founded the Naropa University in Boulder and the Rocky Mountain Shambhala Center, where the shrine now sits.

Public tours (2pm Sat.-Sun.) are available, and group tours can be arranged in advance. The Great Stupa of Dharmakaya is sometimes closed for special events. After parking, head to the visitors center to register and get a map. It's a 20-minute hike up a gravel path to the stupa, which sits at more than 8,000 feet (2,400 m) above sea level. Bring water and wear comfortable shoes and sun protection.

Food

The Shambhala Mountain Center is used for many large conferences, and the dining facilities are set up to accommodate hundreds of people at one sitting. There are two indoor dining halls, an outdoor dining tent, and picnic tables outside. Three meals per day are included with lodging. If you're just visiting for the day, lunch (12:30pm-1:30pm, $10 pp) and dinner (5:30pm-6:30pm, hours and cost vary) are served.

Accommodations

Lodging at the Shambhala Mountain Center (reservations 888/788-7221) ranges from tents to luxurious suites. From June through September, **platform tents** ($79 d, $109 s) are available throughout the property; some are situated close to the dining halls and gift shop, while others are scattered higher in the trees and require a bit of a walk. Guests use shared public restrooms while staying in the tent sites.

Red Feather Lodge ($109) is a group of four cabins with a shared bathhouse that is removed from the core of the community but still within walking distance of the dining and meeting facilities. One cabin, Earth ($79), is set up like a dormitory; others have five double rooms each.

The rooms at **Ridgen Lodge** ($109) and **Shambhala Lodge** ($147-263) are more like traditional hotel rooms, with private baths in some (but not all) rooms, along with desks, public phones, and internet access.

Getting There

The center is an hour's drive west from Fort Collins and a 2.5-hour drive from Denver. From Fort Collins, take College Avenue (Hwy. 287) north for 3.4 miles (5.5 km). Turn right on North Shields Street to stay on Highway 287 for another 17 miles (27 km) until you reach County Road 74E (Red Feather Lakes Rd.). Turn left, and after 16 miles (26 km), take another left on County Road 68C (Boy Scout Rd.). Look for a blue-and-white sign for the center. Drive 5 miles (8 km; not all of the road is paved), then turn left at the entrance, where there is a large parking lot.

SHAMBHALA SHUTTLE

The **Shambhala Shuttle** (970/881-2184, ext. 235, travel@shambhalamountain.org, $88 round-trip) offers transportation between Fort Collins and the center. Pickup is from the Fort Collins Hilton at 2pm the day of scheduled programs. Reservations are required three weeks in advance and require careful timing for arrival and departure.

Colorado Springs

As the state's second-largest city, Colorado Springs has come into its own, with appealing sights, outdoor activities, restaurants, and nightlife.

Situated at 6,035 feet (1,839 m) above sea level (that's more than a mile high for those who are keeping score), Colorado Springs reaches into the foothills of the Rocky Mountains and boasts 300 days of sunshine per year. The scenic beauty of these mountains is what initially put Colorado Springs on the map, and some of the city's best attractions—such as Seven Falls and the Cheyenne Mountain Zoo with the Will Rogers Shrine—lie in these foothills.

The smaller metro population gives the city a more laid-back feel than Denver, but don't let that fool you into thinking that there isn't

Sights 209
Entertainment and Events 218
Shopping 223
Sports and Recreation 224
Food 229
Accommodations 234
Transportation and Services 237
Vicinity of Colorado Springs 238

Highlights

Look for ★ to find recommended sights, activities, dining, and lodging.

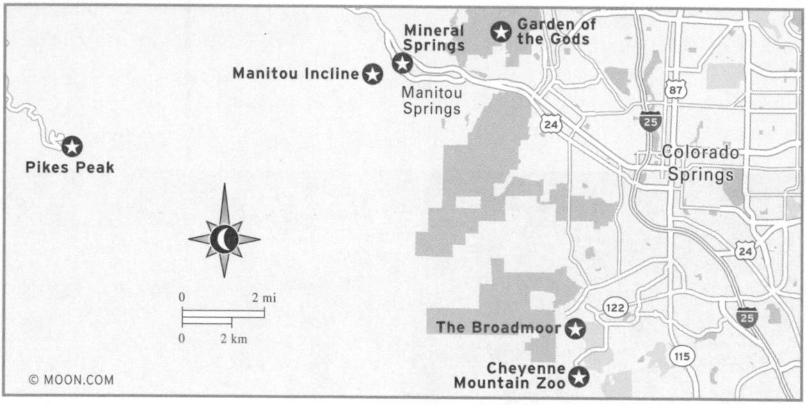

★ Feel like a celebrity at **The Broadmoor,** a family-friendly resort with incomparable service that is home to many of the city's best restaurants (page 209).

★ Hand-feed a giraffe herd at the unique **Cheyenne Mountain Zoo,** perched on a hillside overlooking Colorado Springs (page 211).

★ Roam the **Garden of the Gods**—whether you visit by foot or by horseback, in a car or on a mountain bike, the natural beauty of these red rocks will awe you (page 212).

★ Drink from Manitou Springs's **mineral springs**—their potentially healing waters trickle from decorative spigots and fountains around the historic town (page 239).

★ Hike, drive, or ride on a cog railway for epic views from the top of famed 14,115-foot (4,302-m) **Pikes Peak** (page 241).

★ Climb leftover railroad ties to the top of the **Manitou Incline**—the hike up this mountain is only 1 mile (1.6 km) long, but with a 40 percent grade (page 244).

much going on. Within the town are many subcultures: the military, cowboys and cowgirls, athletes in training, college students, and fundamentalist Christians. The military is the largest employer in Colorado Springs, as the Fort Carson United States Army base, the United States Air Force Academy, and the North American Aerospace Defense Command (NORAD) are all represented. Tourism and the high-tech industry also bring an estimated 5-6 million people to the area each year.

PLANNING YOUR TIME

It's not possible to see all of the sights in both Colorado Springs and Manitou Springs in one day, so it's best to plan a whole **weekend** to explore the area.

Spend the first day in Colorado Springs. Grab coffee and a bite at Ivywild, a former school turned farm-to-table collective of restaurants. Visit the Colorado Springs Fine Arts Center and peruse the current exhibits, or see a performance in their theater. If you are traveling with young children, the Cheyenne Mountain Zoo will be a hit—there is a large giraffe herd that visitors can feed. Families may prefer to spend their vacation at The Broadmoor, where they can take in a movie, bowl, swim, golf, play tennis, do a little boating, and dine out (or in)—all without leaving the premises.

The next day, head to Manitou Springs, enjoying a scenic drive through the Garden of the Gods en route. Once in Manitou Springs, walk around town sampling the mineral springs while window-shopping, and consider heading to the top of Pikes Peak.

Sights

★ THE BROADMOOR

The Broadmoor (1 Lake Ave., 719/577-5775 or 855/634-7711, www.broadmoor.com) is a five-star resort that is a destination in itself—not just a place to stay for the night. Set at the base of Cheyenne Mountain, the large, pink, Mediterranean-style hotel opened in 1918 and was meant to capture the luxury of Asian and European designs seen by owners Spencer Penrose and Julie Penrose in their travels. The numbers tell the story: There are 784 rooms and suites; 13 restaurants, cafés, and lounges; 5,000 acres, including three Wilderness Experience properties; six tennis courts (The Broadmoor is rated one of the top 10 tennis resorts in the country); championship golf courses; two swimming pools and a lap pool; and a Forbes Five-Star spa.

The Broadmoor also has an incredible collection of Western art. Sign up for a tour or, if the art inspires you, take a class or attend an art retreat with resident artist Patience Heyl (by appointment only). Falconry classes are another option. Historical tours and arts programs are available (even for nonguests) year-round by reservation.

COLORADO SPRINGS FINE ARTS CENTER

The **Colorado Springs Fine Arts Center** (30 W. Dale St., 719/634-5583, www.csfineartscenter.org, 10am-5pm Tues.-Sun., $8.50-10) is a wonderful little museum that has an impressive permanent collection (with art from John Singer Sargent, Fritz Scholder, and many other familiar names) and intriguing temporary exhibits. In the Lane Family Gallery, the hand-blown glass creations of artist Dale Chihuly are shown alongside Native American artworks—blankets and baskets—that influenced his work. Also look for Chihuly chandeliers elsewhere in the center.

Previous: hiking in Garden of the Gods; The Broadmoor; cog railway at Pikes Peak.

Colorado Springs

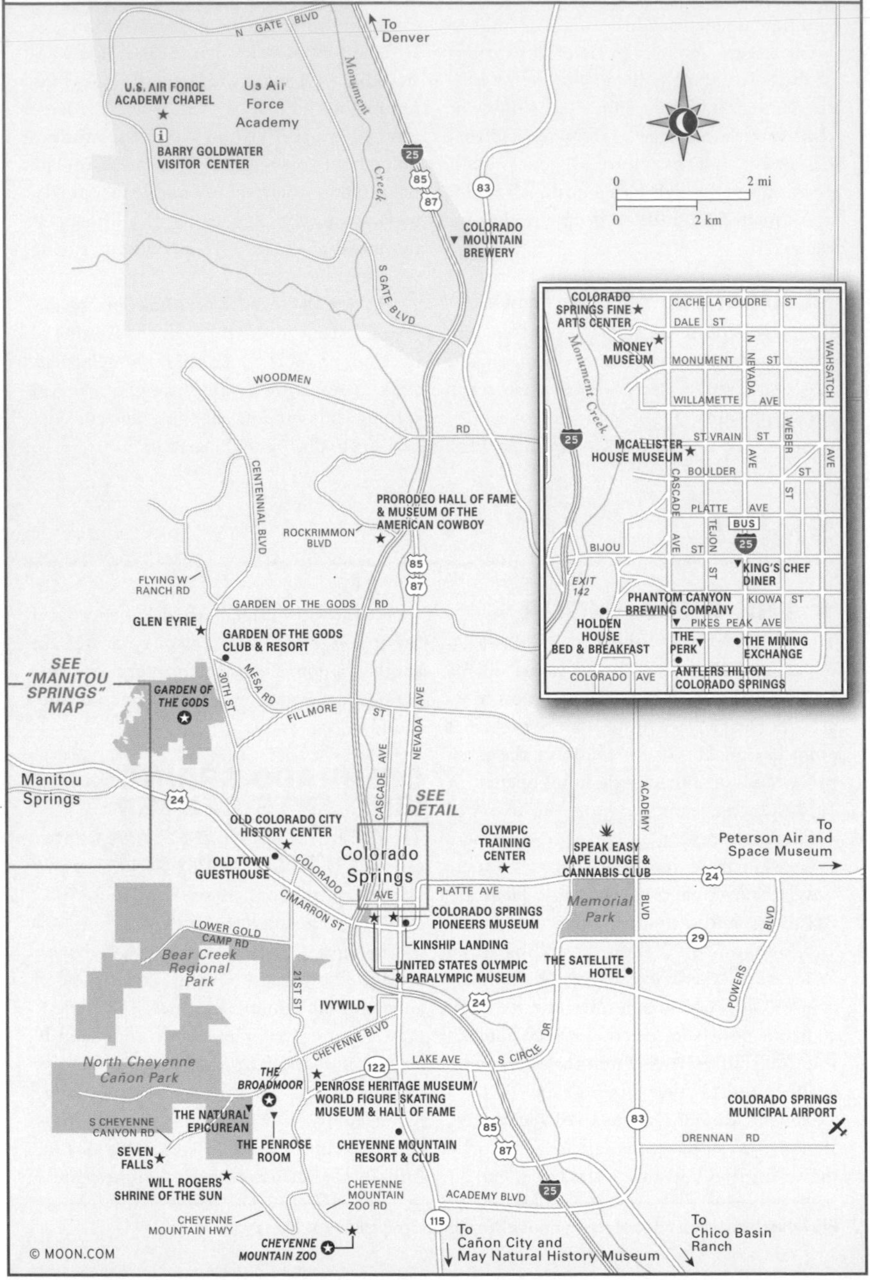
N GATE BLVD
To Denver
Monument Creek
U.S. AIR FORCE ACADEMY CHAPEL
Us Air Force Academy
BARRY GOLDWATER VISITOR CENTER
25
85
87
83
0
2 mi
0
2 km
COLORADO MOUNTAIN BREWERY
S GATE BLVD
WOODMEN RD
CENTENNIAL BLVD
PRORODEO HALL OF FAME & MUSEUM OF THE AMERICAN COWBOY
ROCKRIMMON BLVD
FLYING W RANCH RD
GARDEN OF THE GODS RD
GLEN EYRIE
GARDEN OF THE GODS CLUB & RESORT
SEE "MANITOU SPRINGS" MAP
GARDEN OF THE GODS
30TH ST
MESA RD
FILLMORE ST
CASCADE AVE
NEVADA AVE
Manitou Springs
24
SEE DETAIL
OLD COLORADO CITY HISTORY CENTER
OLD TOWN GUESTHOUSE
COLORADO AVE
Colorado Springs
CIMARRON ST
OLYMPIC TRAINING CENTER
PLATTE AVE
SPEAK EASY VAPE LOUNGE & CANNABIS CLUB
ACADEMY BLVD
To Peterson Air and Space Museum
Memorial Park
COLORADO SPRINGS PIONEERS MUSEUM
KINSHIP LANDING
UNITED STATES OLYMPIC & PARALYMPIC MUSEUM
LOWER GOLD CAMP RD
Bear Creek Regional Park
21ST ST
THE SATELLITE HOTEL
29
POWERS BLVD
IVYWILD
CHEYENNE BLVD
LAKE AVE
S CIRCLE DR
122
North Cheyenne Cañon Park
THE BROADMOOR
PENROSE HERITAGE MUSEUM/ WORLD FIGURE SKATING MUSEUM & HALL OF FAME
THE NATURAL EPICUREAN
THE PENROSE ROOM
S CHEYENNE CANYON RD
SEVEN FALLS
CHEYENNE MOUNTAIN RESORT & CLUB
COLORADO SPRINGS MUNICIPAL AIRPORT
DRENNAN RD
WILL ROGERS SHRINE OF THE SUN
CHEYENNE MOUNTAIN ZOO RD
ACADEMY BLVD
CHEYENNE MOUNTAIN HWY
115
CHEYENNE MOUNTAIN ZOO
To Cañon City and May Natural History Museum
To Chico Basin Ranch
© MOON.COM
COLORADO SPRINGS FINE ARTS CENTER
CACHE LA POUDRE ST
DALE ST
MONEY MUSEUM
MONUMENT ST
N NEVADA AVE
WAHSATCH AVE
WILLAMETTE AVE
ST VRAIN ST
WEBER ST
MCALLISTER HOUSE MUSEUM
BOULDER ST
CASCADE AVE
PLATTE AVE
TEJON ST
BUS 25
BIJOU ST
KING'S CHEF DINER
EXIT 142
PHANTOM CANYON BREWING COMPANY
KIOWA ST
HOLDEN HOUSE BED & BREAKFAST
PIKES PEAK AVE
THE PERK
THE MINING EXCHANGE
ANTLERS HILTON COLORADO SPRINGS
COLORADO AVE

The art deco building with Southwestern flair was designed in 1936 by Santa Fe architect John Gaw Meem. On the west end of the building are dining options with coffee and grab-and-go sandwiches and snacks (11am-3pm Thurs.-Sun.) or lunch on Friday in one of the dining rooms, which also offers pre-theater dining. Step into the Deco Lounge for a cocktail on First Fridays or before theater performances. The outdoor patio is a terrific place for a lunch with a view of Pikes Peak.

Group tours of the museum are available; advance reservations are required. Weekend tours (1pm-2pm, paid gallery admission required) don't require advance reservations.

★ CHEYENNE MOUNTAIN ZOO

What sets the **Cheyenne Mountain Zoo** (4250 Cheyenne Mountain Zoo Rd., 719/633-9925, www.cmzoo.org, 9am-5pm daily year-round, last admission 4pm; advance e-ticket purchase required) apart from other zoos is its elevation of 6,714 feet (2,046 m) and the large giraffe herd that lives and breeds here. The zoo's setting in the foothills beyond The Broadmoor gives the area a natural feel. There's the usual assortment of creatures—lions, elephants, meerkats, and a lot more but the giraffes are very popular, and the zoo sells special treats ($3-5) that can be fed directly to them by guests. There is also a **carousel** (9am-5pm daily May-Labor Day, 9am-5pm Sat.-Sun. Labor Day-May, $2) and an open-air chairlift **Sky Ride** (9am-5pm daily May-Labor Day, 10am-4pm Sat.-Sun. Labor Day-May, $5) that tours the entire zoo. Note that the Sky Ride sometimes closes for maintenance.

Tickets are $24 adults, $19 children 3-11, $22 over age 65, $16-21 military families, free under age 2. There are discounts for military and their family ($3 off regular rate).

Will Rogers Shrine of the Sun

Spencer Penrose, developer of The Broadmoor and the Pikes Peak Highway, was close friends with actor and humorist Will Rogers. In 1935, Penrose had begun construction of a tower overlooking the Cheyenne Mountain Zoo when he learned that Rogers had died in a plane crash. Penrose dedicated the tower as the **Will Rogers Shrine of the Sun** (719/578-5367, www.elpomar.org, 9am-4pm daily) to honor the memory of his friend.

The shrine is constructed from granite and bound by steel and cement—no wood or nails were used—and its unique design resembles a castle turret or stone fortress. On the lower level are the ashes of Spencer and Julie Penrose, housed in a chapel decorated with artwork that honors the couple's efforts to bring culture to Colorado Springs. The real draw, however, is the spectacular view from the top deck of the five-story shrine at 8,136 feet (2,480 m). (Acrophobes, just enjoy the zoo instead.)

Visitors must pay admission to the Cheyenne Mountain Zoo (4250 Cheyenne Mountain Zoo Rd., 719/633-9925, www.cmzoo.org) in order to visit the tower. The shrine is 1.4 miles (2.3 km) up a road within the zoo. Entrance fees to the zoo include access to the shrine.

COLORADO SPRINGS PIONEERS MUSEUM

Before even stepping inside the **Colorado Springs Pioneers Museum** (215 S. Tejon St., 719/385-5990, www.cspm.org, 10am-5pm Tues.-Sat., free), visitors are treated to a bit of local history: The museum is located in the restored El Paso County courthouse in the middle of Alamo Square Park in the heart of downtown. The museum is home to permanent collections that are uniquely local, such as a display of Van Briggle pottery and the former home (furnished, no less) of author Helen Hunt Jackson. Other exhibits tell the story of the city's prominent early creators, such as Spencer Penrose, and how early city leaders marketed the health benefits of this area to people suffering from tuberculosis.

TOP EXPERIENCE

★ GARDEN OF THE GODS

Before white settlers named it the Garden of the Gods, Native Americans made annual pilgrimages to these beautiful red rocks that stand so distinctly against the green mountain slopes just west of town. The **Garden of the Gods** (1805 N. 30th St., 719/634-6666, www.gardenofgods.com, 5am-11pm daily May-Oct., 5am-9pm daily Nov.-Apr., free) remains the top attraction around, with an estimated two million visitors each year.

Like many other sensational natural wonders in the area, Garden of the Gods has been tinkered with too much, and it has a heavy theme-park atmosphere that can be a big turnoff. There are bus tours, not one but three gift shops, and Native American dances for lunchtime entertainment. That said, you can take a number of easy hiking trails to escape the crowds (some trails also allow mountain biking and horseback riding) and appreciate the 1,350-acre park.

Stop in at the **Visitor and Nature Center** (8am-7pm daily Memorial Day-Labor Day, 9am-5pm daily Labor Day-Memorial Day) to learn more about the geology of the rocks and the plants and critters that dwell here. Visiting the park is free year-round, but there are fees for guided tours and special programs.

GLEN EYRIE

Glen Eyrie (3820 N. 30th St., 719/634-0808, reservations 719/265-7050, www.gleneyrie.org) is an English-style stone castle featuring 17 guest rooms, 24 fireplaces, two dining rooms, and four meeting rooms. The castle was built by General William Jackson Palmer, the founder of Colorado Springs, and is now owned by The Navigators, a Christian organization headquartered here. Tours of the Christian conference and retreat center (twice a day Mon.-Thurs., three times a day Fri.-Sat., once Sun., $12, reservations required) are offered, and tea (11am-3pm Wed.-Sat., $36 per person, reservations recommended) and overnight stays ($175-233) are also available.

MAY NATURAL HISTORY MUSEUM

The **May Natural History Museum** (710 Rock Creek Canyon, 719/576-0450, http://coloradospringsbugmuseum.com, 9am-6pm daily May-Sept., groups of 10 or more by appointment only Oct.-Apr., $8 adults, $7 seniors, $6 ages 6-12, free under age 6) has a lovely history all its own, as well as a stunning collection of preserved butterflies, moths, beetles, and other small creatures. The May Natural History Museum boasts that they have the "World's Largest Private Insect Collection," and who am I to doubt them? The bug collection is so spectacular, it's rumored that Walt Disney wanted it but was turned down. Look for the giant steel beetle replica in front of the museum, founded by James May in the 1940s as he put down roots for his traveling exhibition of insects collected from around the world. A big appeal of this place is how low-tech it is—it simply has the wow factor of freakishly large bugs.

MCALLISTER HOUSE MUSEUM

Given that there are castles to visit in this area, a small historic home may not seem worth the stop. However, the **McAllister House Museum** (423 N. Cascade Ave., 719/635-7925, http://mcallisterhouse.org, tours 10:30am, 12:30pm, 2:30pm Thurs.-Sat., by reservation only, $7 adults, $6 seniors, $3 ages 6-12, free under age 6) is an impressively preserved example of a family home built here when the town was known as "Fountain Colony" before being named Colorado Springs. Remember the three little pigs? This house of bricks was built in 1873 and was once surrounded by neighbors who built theirs with wood—now it's the only one of its vintage left standing. Plan 45 minutes for a docent-led tour to learn

1: The Broadmoor's infinity pool **2:** Garden of the Gods **3:** feeding the giraffes at Cheyenne Mountain Zoo **4:** Glen Eyrie castle

1

2

3

4

about Henry McAllister Jr., who served under General William Jackson Palmer, founder of Colorado Springs, and later moved west from Pennsylvania to work for General Palmer.

MONEY MUSEUM

At the American Numismatic Association's **Edward C. Rochette Money Museum** (818 N. Cascade Ave., 800/367-9723, www.money.org, 10:30am-5pm Tues.-Sat., $8 adults, $6 seniors and military, free under age 12) on the Colorado College campus, there is a monthly **Mini-Mint** demonstration (noon-4pm every 3rd Sat.) in addition to several fascinating and family-friendly exhibits about money. The Kids Zone is an interactive space for children to learn about money (shh! maybe a little math, too).

OLD COLORADO CITY HISTORY CENTER

Initially named El Dorado, Colorado City became the first permanent town in the Pikes Peak region. The story of the distinctive town that was later annexed by Colorado Springs is told at the **Old Colorado City History Center** (1 S. 24th St., 719/636-1225, www.occhs.org, 11am-4pm Tues.-Sat. May-Sept., 11am-4pm Thurs.-Sat. Oct.-mid-Dec., 11am-2pm Thurs.-Sat. mid-Dec.-early Apr., free). The remaining buildings of Colorado City, just northwest of downtown, are mainly home to tourist shops, restaurants, and bars, so it is worthwhile to learn more about the early life that went on here.

OLYMPIC TRAINING CENTER

Headquartered in Colorado Springs, the United States **Olympic Training Center** (1 Olympic Plaza, 719/866-4618, www.teamusa.org/csotc, call ahead for current hours, $12 adults, $10 seniors, $8 ages 5-12, free under age 5) is open for tours year-round. These guided one-hour tours include a video presentation and a glimpse of the facilities, which are home to swimming and shooting as well as gymnastics, fencing, weightlifting, tae kwon do, wrestling, modern pentathlon, and judo. Call ahead if you want to be there when you can actually see athletes training. Either way, save time for the gift shop so you can support Team USA.

PENROSE HERITAGE MUSEUM

Given that tourists and locals are still enjoying the places that Spencer Penrose created in Colorado Springs, it's not surprising that there is a place devoted just to learning about this visionary. The **Penrose Heritage Museum** (11 Lake Circle, 719/577-7065, www.elpomar.org, 10am-noon and 1pm-4pm Mon.-Sat., 1pm-4pm Sun., free, reservations required) showcases the auto collection of the Penrose family. Exhibits tell the story of how Penrose founded the Pikes Peak Hill Climb and the Pikes Peak Automobile Company as a way to give scenic tours of the area.

PETERSON AIR & SPACE MUSEUM

Colorado Springs is home to a few military bases, including Peterson Air Force Base in the southeast of the city. The **Peterson Air & Space Museum** (150 E. Ent Ave., Peterson AFB, 719/556-4915, http://petemuseum.org, 10am-4pm Tues.-Fri., free, nonmilitary must call base 24 hours in advance to request a pass) is on the base, which is the home of the 21st Space Wing, Air Force Space Command, United States Space Command, and the North American Aerospace Defense Command (NORAD). Visitors can tour outdoors to view vintage aircraft staged at various hangars and also go indoors and see missiles.

PRORODEO HALL OF FAME AND MUSEUM OF THE AMERICAN COWBOY

A reminder of Colorado's Western cowboy culture, the **ProRodeo Hall of Fame and Museum of the American Cowboy**

1: Money Museum **2:** May Natural History Museum **3:** Cadet Chapel at the United States Air Force Academy **4:** United States Olympic and Paralympic Museum

LIBRARY AND MUSEUM OF THE AMERICAN NUMISMATIC ASSOCIATION
Culture Art Science History
MONEY MUSEUM
Coins, Crowns & Conflict
1

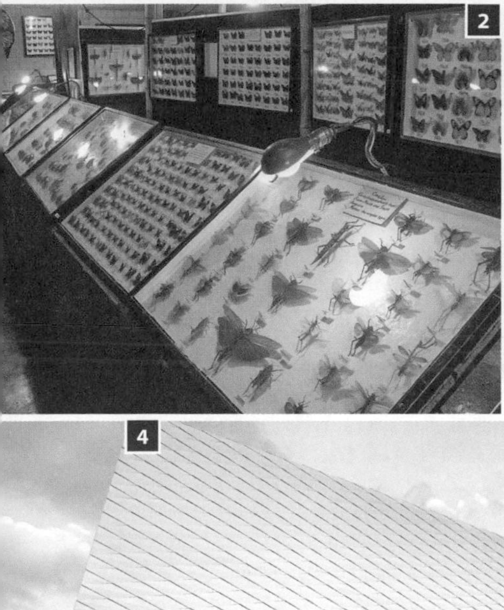
2

3

4
US OLYMPIC & PARALYMPIC MUSEUM

(101 Pro Rodeo Dr., 719/528-4764, www.prorodeohalloffame.com, 9am-5pm daily May-Aug., 9am-5pm Wed.-Sun. Sept.-Apr., $8 adults, $7 seniors, $6 military, $5 ages 6-12, free under age 5) is a unique place to learn about historic and modern rodeo cowboy (and cowgirl) culture, gear, and artwork. Tours begin with a 15-minute film about rodeo history. You can see dozens of saddles, costumes, and tributes to past rodeo champions and possibly a team roping event in their arena (check the event schedule).

SEVEN FALLS

A natural wonder, **Seven Falls** (2850 S. Cheyenne Canyon Rd., 855/923-7272, www.sevenfalls.com, 10am-6pm Fri.-Mon. late May-June, 10am-6pm Thurs.-Mon. July-Oct., 10am-6pm Fri.-Sun. Nov., $16.50 adults, $13.75 seniors and military, $10.50 ages 2-12, free under age 2) is now part of The Broadmoor, but it's been a tourist destination since the 1800s. The seven cascading waterfalls have been "enhanced" by different owners over the years with a road and stairway, lights, a viewing platform, an elevator, and now Restaurant 1858, a gold rush-themed restaurant featuring foods from the Old West. Note that this is a walking experience, and even if you don't go up the stairs to each of the falls, there is a walk of just under a mile from the parking area to the base of the falls. There is a tram ($2) available for those with mobility issues. The falls can be partially viewed from various points in the park, including at the base and from the viewing platform (accessible by elevator).

UNITED STATES AIR FORCE ACADEMY

Depending on the current U.S. security color code, visitors are generally welcome at the campus of the **United States Air Force Academy** (2346 Academy Dr., 719/333-2025, www.usafa.af.mil). One of the highlights is the **Cadet Chapel** (closed for extensive repairs until 2023), known for its boldly unique architecture and all-faiths worship model. Visitors are welcome to learn about the cadet experience during self-guided tours of the campus and at the **Barry Goldwater Visitor Center** (9am-5pm daily).

UNITED STATES OLYMPIC AND PARALYMPIC MUSEUM

The **United States Olympic and Paralympic Museum** (200 S. Sierra Madre St., 719/497-1234, https://usopm.org, 10am-5pm Sun.-Fri., 9am-6pm Sat., $25 adults, $20 seniors and military, $15 children ages 3-12) opened in 2020 and became an instant success as a popular attraction on the Front Range. The museum is accessible for people of all abilities and has interactive exhibits to explore, like being a skeleton driver. In addition to learning about athletes, you'll see exhibits about Olympic flames and medals. Plan a day here, with meals on offer at the on-site Flame Café, and be sure to hit the gift shop on your way out.

The museum includes a skybridge with mountain views to the west and access to **America the Beautiful Park** (126 Cimino Dr., 719/385-5940, http://parks.coloradosprings.gov) and its centerpiece, the sculptural **Julie Penrose Fountain,** below. The park has expansive grassy areas and a colorful playground.

WORLD FIGURE SKATING MUSEUM AND HALL OF FAME

During those years without a winter Olympics to watch, there is still a place to revel in the glory of one of the most popular winter sporting events—figure skating. The **World Figure Skating Museum and Hall of Fame** (20 1st St., 719/635-5200, www.worldskatingmuseum.org, 10am-4pm Tues.-Fri., $5 adults, $3 ages 6-12) showcases not just the big names of the sport but also the outfits they wore. Displays explain the physics of making those seemingly impossible spins. Don't miss the gift shop for your skating enthusiast back home.

1: Seven Falls **2:** the Julie Penrose Fountain
3: World Figure Skating Museum and Hall of Fame

1

2

3

Entertainment and Events

Colorado Springs is not the place one thinks of for a night of wild revelry, but make no mistake: There is plenty to do after dark here. The city's social calendar is filled with live music, annual events worth the trip, and plenty of bars and lounges. Since retail marijuana sales are prohibited in El Paso County, cannabis entrepreneurs have created social clubs: places for people to smoke the weed they bought outside the county (quite possibly in nearby Manitou Springs) inside the city.

NIGHTLIFE

Bars and Pubs

Just the entrance of **The Rabbit Hole** (101 N. Tejon St., 719/203-5072, www.rabbitholedinner.com, 4pm-11pm daily) lends an evening out a subversive feel as you descend stairs to enter this bar and restaurant. Once you put your lips to a flaming martini, you'll know this is no ordinary night on the town. The menu is just as full of surprises, with clever spins on comfort food, like bacon-wrapped rabbit meatloaf and truffle tricolor cauliflower mac and cheese.

Jack Quinn Irish Alehouse & Pub (21 S. Tejon St., 719/385-0766, www.jackquinnspub.com, 11am-10pm Sun.-Thurs., 11am-2am Fri.-Sat., brunch 11am-2pm Sat.-Sun., happy hour 3pm-6pm daily) has a loyal clientele who come back for tried-and-true Irish and Scottish whiskeys and ales. The menu never disappoints, with fried soda bread, Irish breakfast, fish-and-chips, and more. Come for live music or the Geeks Who Drink Pub Quiz (8pm Mon.).

Head over to Old Colorado City to sip brews on tap at **Alchemy** (2625 W. Colorado Ave., 719/471-0887, www.alchemypubcolorado.com, noon-8pm Mon.-Fri., brunch 9am-1pm Sat.-Sun.) and enjoy the classic pub atmosphere. Make a meal out of shared starters like untwisted pretzels or scotch quail eggs, but save room for traditional pub fare like Irish breakfast.

Oh so Colorado: a bar and a climbing gym combined. **The Ute & Yeti** (21 N. Nevada Ave., 719/634-0003, www.theuteandyeti.com, 4pm-10pm Tues.-Sat.) is a pub located inside **CityROCK Climbing Gym** (21 N. Nevada Ave., 719/634-9099, 6am-9:45pm Mon.-Fri., 9:30am-8pm Sat.-Sun.). It's all the things: climbing walls, a Geeks Who Drink trivia night, yoga classes, and a rotating tap beer list that includes many fine Colorado-born beers. You can get fresh salads, smoothies, flatbreads, and ramen bowls, too.

Brewpubs, Distilleries, and Taprooms

Trails End Taproom (3103 W. Colorado Ave., 719/428-0080, www.trailsendtaproom.com, 3pm-8pm Mon.-Tues., 3pm-10pm Wed., 3pm-9pm Thurs., 11am-10pm Fri.-Sat., noon-8pm Sun.) is Colorado's first self-pour taproom. Pay by the ounce, leave a tip that goes to local trail and humanitarian nonprofits, learn about local trails, and pour yourself craft beer, cider, or wine. Since they cater to outdoor enthusiasts, they know you need to carbo-load, too; check the menu for pizzas, sausages, and hearty snacks. There's a second location in Monument (252 Front St., 3pm-9pm Tues.-Thurs., 3pm-10pm Fri., noon-10pm Sat., noon-8pm Sun.) in a historic log cabin; Monument is about 20 miles (32 km) north of downtown Colorado Springs.

Founded in 2016, the **Goat Patch Brewing Company** (2727 N. Cascade Ave., Suite 127, 719/471-4628, www.goatpatchbrewing.com, noon-9pm Mon.-Thurs., noon-11pm Fri., 11am-11pm Sat., 11am-9pm Sun.) puts brew first, so check the events page for which local food trucks will be visiting if you're hungry. There are also events like yoga, live music, and trivia nights. Some of the more unique ales to sample include Goat Patch Punch, Purploid Sour Punch, and Black Chai Saison.

In the historic Cheyenne building is the **Phantom Canyon Brewing Company** (2 E. Pikes Peak Ave., 719/635-2800, www.phantomcanyon.com, 11am-last call daily), which offers a full floor of billiards in addition to the locally brewed beers. The menu incorporates beer into the dinner offerings.

Axe and the Oak Whiskey House (1604 S. Cascade Ave., 719/660-1624, www.axeandtheoak.com/whiskey-house, 4pm-10pm Tues.-Thurs., 4pm-1am Fri., 2pm-1am Sat.) was started by four friends who are passionate about spirits, namely whiskey. Part of the Ivywild School just southwest of downtown, this place is about having fun with friends—live music and games make a night out memorable. The drinks here are *local* because they make their own whiskey and then make cocktails from that whiskey. Can you say "exclusive"? The **Axe and the Oak Distillery** (4665 Town Center Dr., Ste. 140, 10am-4pm Mon.-Fri.) is on the east side of Colorado Springs; check the website for the latest information on tour availability.

Clubs

There's definitely a country-and-western scene in Colorado Springs. A good place to kick up your heels is **Cowboys** (25 N. Tejon St., 719/596-1212, www.cowboyscs.com, 7pm-close Wed., 7pm-close Fri.-Sat., no cover), which has live music and dancing (check the website calendar for lessons).

Comedy

Get ready to laugh at the **3E's Comedy Club** (1 S. Nevada Ave., 719/694-9911, www.3escomedy.com, 4pm-10pm Mon.-Thurs., 4pm-midnight Fri.-Sat.) when seeing comedians such as Jeremy Piven or Earthquake, or you make the jokes during a comedy class or open mic night. Ticket prices range depending on the act, usually $20-35.

LGBTQ Venues

Club Q (3430 N. Academy Blvd., 719/570-1429, http://clubqonline.com, 4pm-close Tues.-Sun.) serves the local LGBTQ population of Colorado Springs—as long as there is singing and dancing involved. Drag shows, karaoke, foam parties, ladies nights—it's a party all the time!

Opened in 2020, **ICONS** (3 E. Bijou St., 719/300-7863, www.icons-co.com, 4pm-midnight Tues.-Thurs., 4pm-1am Fri.-Sat., reservations may be required) is the city's only LGBTQ bar downtown—and it's a piano bar to boot. I'd come here just for the clever drink names: Ricky Martini, Berry Manilow, and Dolly Patron are just a few.

Wine Bar

Uva Wine Bar (1268 Interquest Pkwy., 719/598-1990, www.uvawinecoloradosprings.com, 4pm-9pm Wed.-Thurs., 4pm-10pm Fri., noon-10pm Sat.-Sun.) knows that not everyone drinks beer or ale or whiskey. This is a place for a fun wine tasting or a special date night out with a variety of wines to choose from by the glass or bottle and small plates of appetizers to nibble on.

CANNABIS SOCIAL CLUBS

Colorado Springs prohibits the sale of recreational marijuana, which means you'll have to head to nearby Manitou Springs to find pot shops. But Colorado Springs offers something Denver doesn't: private marijuana social clubs, which operate as civic organizations. Anyone age 21 or older who pays a membership fee can consume marijuana on the premises. Some take "donations" in exchange for products offered on-site, while others require you to BYOW (bring your own weed).

Speakeasy Vape Lounge & Cannabis Club (2508 E. Bijou St., 719/445-9083, http://speakeasy-vape-lounge-cannabis-club-sevl.business.site, 4pm-midnight Tues.-Sat., $5 daily membership fee, $25 monthly) sports a funky hip-hop vibe and prides itself on its well-stocked dab bar, where folks can sample a variety of high-THC concentrates using the in-house selection of dabbing pipes. Speakeasy also offers live music, not to mention stand-up comedy. Cannabis and live comedy—what could be better than that?

PERFORMING ARTS

The **Fine Arts Theatre School** (30 W. Dale St., 719/634-5581, www.csfineartscenter.org) performs a handful of comedies, musicals, and dramas each year. Some offerings, such as *Mary Poppins,* are for families. More experimental is the Rough Writers: A New Play Fest, a two-week-long festival held twice a year whereby people from around the world submit their work for readings. This is also one of the local venues where the **Veronika String Quartet** (http://veronikastringquartet.com) performs; the award-winning foursome is known worldwide, but this is their home.

The **Pikes Peak Center for the Performing Arts** (190 S. Cascade Ave., 719/576-2626, www.pikespeakcenter.com) is the place for the biggest acts in town. Previous shows include the blockbuster *Mythbusters,* Lyle Lovett & His Large Band, Todd Rundgren, and comedian Bill Maher. This is where you catch Broadway shows like *Les Misérables.* Centrally located, it is easy to access when staying downtown.

From fall to spring, the **Colorado Springs Philharmonic** (http://csphilharmonic.org) performs everything from Brahms to Disney's *Fantasia* at the Pikes Peak Center for the Performing Arts (190 S. Cascade Ave., 719/576-2626, www.pikespeakcenter.com) and the Ent Center for the Arts (5225 N. Nevada Ave., 719/255-3232, www.uccs.edu/entcenter) on the University of Colorado at Colorado Springs campus. They also offer concerts featuring music from well-known movies such as *Star Wars* or from rock legends like Pink Floyd.

Improv and kids seem to go together like peanut butter and jelly, so the geniuses behind the **Millibo Art Theatre** (1626 S. Tejon St., 719/465-6321, www.themat.org) combined the two. Performances include RIP Improv nights, Kids First performances (puppet shows, plays, or a circus), and a variety of touring shows for grown-ups.

Built in the 1960s as a United Artist Cinema 150 Cinerama Theater, the dome-roofed **Stargazers Theatre** (10 S. Parkside Dr., 719/476-2200, www.stargazerstheatre.com) is a 560-seat venue that showcases local music and film talents. Here you can catch the Flying W Wranglers, a classic cowboy band, and the Jake Loggins Band, a local blues group.

Theatreworks (1420 Austin Bluffs Pkwy., 719/255-3232, http://theatreworkscs.org) is a regional theater company that has its home in the Dusty Look Bon Vivant Theater at the Ent Center for the Arts on the University of Colorado at Colorado Springs campus. The company turns out seven plays a year with fresh takes on Shakespeare and Beckett alongside original works.

FESTIVALS AND EVENTS

Colorado Springs has quite a few fun events each year that are embraced by locals, but also welcome out-of-towners to join in the frivolity. The theme of these festivals is typically tied into the local history or something that is distinctly Colorado, like bighorn sheep or Pikes Peak.

Spring

Grab those binoculars and lace up your hiking boots in the hopes of seeing a flitting hummingbird during the **Cheyenne Cañon Hummingbird Experience** (http://cheyennecanon.org, May). Check out hummingbird-themed activities at the **Starsmore Visitor and Nature Center** (2120 S. Cheyenne Canyon Rd., 719/385-6086, http://coloradosprings.gov). Guided hikes with a leader from the Audubon Society, nature photography workshops, and bird banding are part of this weekend of fun for a whole family of birders. This festival is held

1: the Pikes Peak International Hill Climb, a road race to the top of the famous mountain **2:** cowboy culture at the annual Pikes Peak or Bust Rodeo

USE LOW GEAR
Red Bull
3
1

at&t
WORKPLACE
272 S. Academy Blvd.
Colorado Springs, CO 80910
719-574
Dodge
2

in conjunction with the **Pikes Peak Birding and Nature Festival** (http://pikespeakbirdingandnaturefestival.org, May).

Territory Days (http://shopoldcoloradocity.com, May) is held every Memorial Day—just as it has been for 40 years—in Old Colorado City. This popular three-day event features performances by Native American dancers in their traditional costumes as well as Wild West-style gunfight reenactments. There are more than 100 food and craft booths, live music, and kid-friendly areas for the whole family.

Summer

The **Pikes Peak International Hill Climb** (www.ppihc.com, June) is unlike any other auto race you will ever witness. Way back in 1901 two men drove up to the summit of Pikes Peak—in nine hours. Spencer Penrose, Colorado Springs's benefactor and champion, turned this carriage road into a highway and started the annual road race. The road to the top is now paved, and the race is open to motorcycles and automobiles who vie to make it to the peak first—in minutes, not hours—and collect the prize. Check the website for a full schedule of events.

Git yer buckaroos and buckarinas all saddled up for the **Pikes Peak or Bust Rodeo** (www.pikespeakorbust.org, July, $25-55), which has been going strong since 1940. The four-day event kicks off with a parade through town. Daily events show off the best of the best rodeo athletes in roping, steer wrestling, and bull riding. Yeehaw!

Not into auto racing? The **Pikes Peak Marathon** (www.pikespeakmarathon.org, Aug.) is for those who prefer to make it to the top on foot. Held since 1955, the marathon is for serious runners: to qualify you must have previously completed the Pikes Peak Ascent (occurs the same weekend) of 13 miles (21 km) and 7,815-foot (2,382-m) elevation gain, or have finished another marathon in under 5:45 in the past three years. Or . . . you can just take a shuttle bus to the top and cheer on those people.

Fall

The **Rocky Mountain Women's Film Festival** (http://rmwfilm.org, Nov.) features films—documentaries, narrative shorts, animated films—about women and by women in a special weekend of cinema celebration. Don't miss the opening night gala held at the Colorado Springs Fine Arts Center (30 W. Dale St., 719/634-5583, www.csfineartscenter.org). Centrally located screening rooms on the Colorado College campus (14 E. Cache La Poudre St.) make for a chance to explore downtown on foot.

Winter

Bighorn Sheep Day (www.visitcos.com, Feb.) takes place in the Garden of the Gods (1805 N. 30th St., 719/634-6666, www.gardenofgods.com, free), and there's a good chance you'll spy some bighorns through a high-powered telescope or your own binoculars. There are guided nature walks and shuttles to viewing areas.

Shopping

Colorado Springs is home to many independent shops that specialize in toys, women's fashions, books, souvenirs, and arts and crafts. You don't have to be staying at The Broadmoor to shop there, and it's worth the trip, whether you are looking for shoes or fossils.

You'll have to trek over to Manitou Springs to score at the dispensaries, which curiously also strive to have a "boutique vibe" and bragging rights to locally made (or grown, in this case) products.

SHOPPING DISTRICTS

Old Colorado City

Just northwest of downtown is historic **Old Colorado City** (W. Colorado Ave. from 24th St. to 27th St., 719/636-1225, www.shopoldcoloradocity.com), which was a town during the early gold rush days before Colorado Springs was developed. Now it's a few blocks of specialty shops, art galleries, and antiques stores mixed in with some restaurants and bars.

The **Michael Garman Museum & Gallery** (2418 W. Colorado Ave., 719/471-9391, www.michaelgarman.com, 10am-5:30pm daily) features the sculptures of Garman, as well as his Magic Town—a highly detailed miniature replica of a town. If there is such a thing as nostalgia art, then this is it.

Arati Artists Gallery (2425 W. Colorado Ave., 719/636-1901, www.aratiartists.com, noon-5pm Fri.-Sun. June-Aug.) is an artists' cooperative. The 20 member-artists not only create paintings, drawings, and sculptures but work as sales clerks in the gallery. Take home jewelry, pottery, or a painting that evokes your trip to Colorado Springs.

The Broadmoor

The shops at **The Broadmoor** (1 Lake Ave., 855/634-7711, www.broadmoor.com, hours vary by shop) are not what you expect—or at least not what I expected on my first visit. Yes, they have the requisite souvenir shop with postcards, T-shirts, and hats that have "The Broadmoor" stitched on them. Beyond that are boutiques with a solid inventory of books, shoes, men's and women's fashions, sports apparel, and jewelry that is in keeping with everything at this luxury resort—only the finest.

A personal fave is **Yarid's Shoes,** which squeezes shoes for men, women, and kids into a tiny space but still provides a good selection of casual and dressy from known designers like Stuart Weitzman and Tory Burch.

The Great Republic has a wonderful selection of U.S. flags, maps, and other Americana merchandise that you don't see in many mainstream shops. **Gibson's Gallery** is a lovely space filled with fossils, exotic stones, and artwork. (I loved the stories about stones found around the area.) The **Broadmoor Gallery** offers a small taste of the impressive art collection on display at the resort. In these shops, you can see paintings and sculptures evocative of the West by well-known artists.

BOOKS AND TOYS

Regularly voted "Best of" by locals, **Little Richard's Toystore** (342 N. Tejon St., 719/578-3072, 10am-6pm Mon.-Sat., 11am-5pm Sun.) and **Poor Richard's Books & Gifts** (320 N. Tejon St., 719/578-0012, www.poorrichardsdowntown.com, 9am-9pm daily) are designed for kids and readers who like to linger while they shop. The toy store sells plushy toys for infants and will continue to delight the kiddos right into their teen years with games, puzzles, science kits, dolls, and much more. The bookstore sells good-condition used books that are well organized into many categories for all interests.

CLOTHING

Downtown Colorado Springs has a few charming boutiques, primarily for women looking for the latest in a great-fitting pair of jeans or a sexy top, or seeking to discover local designers. The **Colorado Co-op** (315 N. Tejon St., 719/389-0696, http://coloradoco-op.com, 10am-6pm Mon.-Sat., noon-5pm Sun.) sells lesser-known designers alongside those you would find at your local Nordstrom, including dresses, jeans, stationery, and jewelry. **Eve's Revolution** (1312 W. Colorado Ave., 719/633-1357, www.evesrevolution.com, noon-5pm Mon.-Sat., noon-4pm Sun.) carries "emerging designers" (similar to those on ModCloth.com) with a few consignment items sprinkled in. If you're looking for a special flirty top or girlfriend gift, try **Terra Verde** (208 N. Tejon St., 719/444-8621, http://terraverdestyle.com, 10am-6pm Mon.-Sat., noon-5pm Sun.). The prices for everything from soap to jewelry to jeans and dresses are quite reasonable.

Inherent Clothier (123 N. Tejon St., 719/481-1038, https://inherentclothier.com, 11am-5pm Sun.-Tues., 11am-7pm Wed.-Sat.) has men's suits and what they describe as "casual wear," which is still pretty dressy for some guys (polo shirts, button downs, etc.). Inherent also has its own foundation, which is supported through a percentage of shop sales to benefit the mental health of men.

Sports and Recreation

Colorado Springs is as close to the mountains as people *think* Denver is; therefore it is possible to hike, run, and ride a bike right into the foothills from downtown. It is all closer here—the dramatic red rock formations of Garden of the Gods, Pikes Peak, the mountain creeks—and you're welcome to explore it. In a few places you have to earn your view, but you're always glad you made it to the top.

Although winters are fairly mild, the best seasons to get outside are fall, spring, and summer. Whenever pursuing any solo recreational activities, always tell someone else where you are headed and when you plan to return. It is possible to become lost or ill as a result of altitude sickness, even on a popular trail on a beautiful day.

Wildfires and floods may impact trail conditions. Contact the **U.S. Forest Service** (www.fs.fed.us) prior to your visit in order to ensure all trails and areas are open and accessible.

BALLOONING

Soar over Pikes Peak and Colorado Springs in a hot-air balloon ride with **Adventures Out West** (1680 S. 21st St., 888/501-5586, www.advoutwest.com, sunrise daily). Choose the daily (weather permitting) sunrise flight ($275 pp) or a private flight for two ($1,000).

BIKING

In town, you might want to try riding the **Santa Fe County Trail,** which crosses through Air Force Academy grounds and connects with the 16-mile (26-km) **Pikes Peak Greenway** (www.cospringstrails.com), part of the city's 118 miles (190 km) of urban bicycle trails. Northwest of Colorado Springs is **Ute Valley Park** (1705 Vindicator Dr., 719/385-5940, http://friendsofutevalleypark.com), a hidden gem of sandstone mesas with hiking and biking trails winding through prairie grasses.

An easy way to see Pikes Peak is to bike down the mountain—that's right, down *only.* **Challenge Unlimited** (204 S. 24th Ave., 800/798-5954 or 719/633-6399, www.pikespeakbybike.co, May-mid-Oct., weather permitting, $179-254) will meet you for breakfast and then drive you up Pikes Peak in their van before unloading the bikes and setting you free to roll down.

Pikes Peak Mountain Bike Tours (302

S. 25th St., 719/337-5311, www.bikepikespeak.com, $70-125) offers several options both on and off the peak. Your van ride up to the peak includes breakfast, the bike down, and lunch at the end. Their self-guided Bike Gold Camp tour follows an 1800s-era locomotive railway (not on the peak), which can also be combined with a horseback ride at The Broadmoor Stables.

Explore **Garden of the Gods Park** (1805 N. 30th St., 719/634-6666, www.gardenofgods.com) on a rented fat tire bike, electric bike, or BYOB—bring your own bike. There are guided bike tours available, or you can just guide yourself. The visitors center has trail maps and tips for mountain biking through the park, which involves sharing the road or trail with cars or hikers.

Bike Rentals

Bikes can be rented at **Criterium Bikes** (6150 Corporate Dr., 719/599-0149, www.criterium.com, 10am-7pm Mon.-Tues. and Thurs.-Sat., 10am-5pm Sun., $30-50). Electric bikes ($100 per day) and full-suspension mountain bikes ($60 per day) are also available in addition to mountain bikes.

If you're staying at **The Broadmoor** (855/634-7711, www.broadmoor.com, $45-85 for 2-4 hours, $159 pp guided rides), there are mountain bike rentals and guided mountain bike rides available. Call ahead for reservations for guided rides.

BIRD-WATCHING

The **Aiken Audubon Society** (http://aikenaudubon.com) is the Audubon chapter for the Pikes Peak Region; contact them for the latest information about local birding and guided hikes. **Pinello Ranch** (4940 S. Hwy. 85/87, http://coloradobirdingtrail.com, by appointment) has several ponds that attract nearly 300 bird species; the Aiken Audubon Society offers guided tours.

Chico Basin Ranch (22500 Peyton Hwy. S., Peyton, 719/683-7960, www.ranchlands.com), also called "The Chico," is a working cattle ranch that is also home to hundreds of bird species. In partnership with the Bird Conservancy of the Rockies (www.birdconservancy.org), there is bird banding here in the fall and spring. The ranch maintains a birding trail but asks that visitors check in first or that groups call ahead. Western meadowlarks, red-winged blackbirds, several kinds of sparrows, different species of waterfowl, and many more birds have been spotted here.

GOLF

Some of the area resorts have remarkable golf courses. **The Broadmoor** (1 Lake Ave., 855/634-7711, www.broadmoor.com/golf-courses, $85-275) has championship courses: West Course and East Course. The 18-hole West Course (year-round, weather permitting) is described as "challenging and rewarding." Jack Nicklaus won the U.S. Amateur championship on the links at The Broadmoor in 1959. When the East Course opened in 1918, it was the highest golf course in the United States at 6,400 feet (1,950 m) elevation (the newer West Course is 6,800 ft/2,050 m elevation). Today its expansive greens and tree-lined fairways make it one of the best in the country, if no longer the highest.

Cheyenne Mountain Resort & Club (3225 Broadmoor Valley Rd., 719/538-4095, www.cheyennemountain.com, $50-160) has an 18-hole Pete Dye-designed course along its 35-acre lake. Look into junior golf discounts and afternoon price specials.

Valley Hi Golf Course (610 S. Chelton Rd., 719/385-6917, http://parks.coloradosprings.gov, $10-38), owned by the city of Colorado Springs, is considered one of the best courses in the region. It's an 18-hole par-72 course with views of Pikes Peak and Cheyenne Mountain. There's also a 4-hole course for walkers only. The **Patty Jewett Course** (900 E. Espanola St., 719/385-6934, http://parks.coloradosprings.gov, $10-47) was built in the late 1800s and has both an 18-hole course and a 9-hole course to play. Advance reservations and payment are required.

HIKING

Pikes Peak

You can get to the top of Pikes Peak on your own two feet via the **Barr Trail** (www.barrtrail.net). This is no casual day hike—you are climbing 12 miles (19 km) and gaining almost 8,000 feet (2,400 m) in elevation. While this is not a technical climb, be prepared with the proper gear for the elements at 14,115 feet (4,302 m). Given that there also is a highway (used for an auto race) bringing people up to the summit (via bus and cog railway), it's a pretty busy spot and not a solitary jaunt in the wilderness. The 360-degree view, though, is breathtaking—as is the elevation!—and it's something to brag about to "bag" a fourteener. Trailhead parking can be found in Barr Lot (98 Hydro St., Manitou Springs). You can camp overnight at Barr Camp (www.barrcamp.com), about halfway to the summit, by making a reservation.

Garden of the Gods

Garden of the Gods (1805 N. 30th St., 719/634-6666, www.gardenofgods.com, 5am-11pm daily May-Oct., 5am-9pm daily Nov.-Apr.) has 15 miles (24 km) of hiking trails. Stop in at the visitors and nature center (8am-7pm daily Memorial Day-Labor Day, 9am-5pm daily Labor Day-Memorial Day) for maps of designated hiking, biking, and horseback riding areas. The center is also the meeting point for free guided nature walks (10am and 2pm daily). The easy **Garden of the Gods Loop** (4 mi/6.4 km) is family-friendly and allows leashed dogs; keep an eye out for cars where the trail crosses the road. For a short easy stroll, try the **Ridge Trail** (0.5-mi/0.8-km loop) or the **Perkins Central Garden Trail** (1.5-mi/2.4-km loop), which is wheelchair accessible. You'll be up close to rocks, but please mind the signs about climbing on them—it's tempting, but it's all-too-easy to get stuck up there.

Immediately south of the Garden of the Gods Visitor Center, you can walk around the **Rock Ledge Ranch Historic Site** (3105 Gateway Rd., 719/578-6777, http://rockledgeranch.com), which offers a living history program June-August (check the website for exact dates and times each year). On the National Register of Historic Places, the ranch shows life in this part of Colorado from the time of the Ute people to homesteading and farming.

North Cheyenne Cañon Park

North Cheyenne Cañon Park (719/633-5701, http://cheyennecanon.org, 5am-11pm daily May-Oct., 5am-9pm daily Nov.-Apr.) is a 1,600-acre park with natural waterfalls and wildlife (especially hummingbirds). The on-site **Starsmore Visitor and Nature Center** (2120 S. Cheyenne Canyon Rd., 719/385-6086, 9am-5pm daily June-Aug., 9am-3pm Tues.-Sat. Apr.-May and Sept.-Oct.) informs kids and adults with hands-on nature exhibits, a climbing wall, and a gift shop. This is a good place to pick up trail maps and find out more about the park. Nearby is the trailhead for the moderate **Columbine Trail**, which climbs up the canyon for 4 miles (6.4 km) one-way to **Helen Hunt Falls.** The falls are named after Helen Hunt Jackson, an author, poet, and Native American activist who came to Colorado Springs in 1873.

An easy hike to the Helen Hunt Falls starts at the **Helen Hunt Falls Visitor Center** (3440 N. Cheyenne Canyon Rd., 719/385-5701, http://coloradosprings.gov, 9am-5pm daily June-Aug.). The trail to the falls is less than 1 mile (1.6 km) long with minimal elevation gain, making it both family- and dog-friendly.

The **Seven Bridges Trail** (www.cospringstrails.com, 3 mi/4.8 km round-trip) includes a walk across seven wooden bridges and a 1,500-foot (455-m) elevation gain. Dogs are permitted on this moderate to difficult trail. To get here from Colorado Springs, go south on Nevada from I-25, then west on Cheyenne Boulevard. Drive 3 miles (4.8 km) before taking a right on Cheyenne Canyon

1: the unusual rocks at Paint Mines Interpretive Park, east of Colorado Springs **2:** rock climbing in Garden of the Gods **3:** horseback riding in Garden of the Gods

1

2

3

Road, where you will go 3.2 miles (5.1 km) to the trailhead parking lot.

Paint Mines Interpretive Park

It sounds counterintuitive to tell you to go east—away from the mountains—for a hike, but it's so worth it. One hour east of Colorado Springs (but still within El Paso County) is the **Paint Mines Interpretive Park** (29950 Paint Mines Rd., Calhan, 719/520-7529, www.elpasoco.com, 5am-11pm daily), a 750-acre park with dramatic white-and-yellow hoodoo rock formations as well as both Native American and ranching history. Come in the spring to see the wildflowers blooming on the prairie.

HORSEBACK RIDING

It's a truly Colorado experience to see this area on horseback. For a fun way to explore Garden of the Gods, contact **Academy Riding Stables** (719/633-5667, www.academyridingstables.com, 8:30am-4:30pm daily summer, $75-125) to make a reservation for a one- to two-hour ride in the summer. Fall to spring, check on availability and conditions for the 2.5-hour perimeter ride that skirts the 1,400 acres of the park. A whole family can enjoy this mode of travel and sightseeing—sometimes it's easier than bike riding with younger children.

Old Stage Riding Stables (6620 Old Stage Rd., www.comtnadventure.com, 719/448-0371, $60-120) offers everything from a 20-minute ride for peewees to a two-hour ride through the forest. There are also combo options with a Jeep ride one-way or bicycling one-way to minimize those saddle sores.

JEEP TOURS

Guess what? You can go up Pikes Peak or tour Garden of the Gods by Jeep! I know, it is amazing the number of ways to visit just these two places, so close to one another. **Adventures Out West** (888/501-5586, http://advoutwest.com/jeeps, $98 per adult, $68 per child under 12) offers a variety of options, including pairing a top-down Jeep tour with other adventures, like horseback riding.

Cheyenne Mountain Resort (719/538-4000, www.cheyennemountain.com) coordinates with **Colorado Jeep Tours** (719/275-6339, http://coloradojeeptours.com, $89-229) and others to get guests outside, seeing the mountains from a 4WD vehicle.

ROCK CLIMBING

It doesn't seem like it should be possible, given the fragile nature of the red sandstone formations in Garden of the Gods, but rock climbing is indeed allowed here. **Front Range Climbing Company** (719/632-5822 or 866/404-3721, www.frontrangeclimbing.com, $195-240) offers guided climbs and classes in Colorado Springs and other locations in the area. Note that prices vary depending on number of people participating.

The Broadmoor (855/634-7711, www.broadmoor.com, 9:30am and 1:30pm daily, $183-360 pp) has three climbing packages that take place in either Garden of the Gods or Cheyenne Canyon. There is a $49 "observance fee" for those who come along but do not climb.

Before you get to the actual rocks, try some walls—and even an indoor cave!—at **CityROCK** (21 N. Nevada Ave., 719/634-9099, www.climbcityrock.com, 6am-9:45pm Mon.-Fri., 9:30am-8pm Sat.-Sun., $15-20, plus equipment rental fees), which also has a casual café and pub with dozens of beers on tap in the same building.

SPAS

With so many resorts in Colorado Springs, there is a good chance your accommodations include a spa not far from your room.

Cheyenne Mountain Resort (3225 Broadmoor Valley Rd., 719/538-4095, www.cheyennemountain.com) has the Alluvia Spa and Wellness Retreat, with a large menu of massages, body scrubs, and nail treatments available.

You won't be surprised to learn that **The Broadmoor** (1 Lake Ave., 719/577-5770 or

866/686-3965, www.broadmoor.com/spa-treatments) has a decadent spa with a whole menu of treatments including facials (yes, also for men), hydrotherapy (the climate and altitude can be very drying), body massages, and polishes. Plan to arrive well before your appointment so you can take advantage of the waiting room, with beverages, light snacks, and a view of the East Golf Course.

Mateos Salon & Day Spa (5919 Delmonico Dr., 719/266-9295, http://mateosdayspa.com) has been voted the best in town by readers of the *Colorado Springs Gazette* for many years in a row. It's all about the ambience, relaxing with a cup of tea and maybe near a fireplace until you are treated to an unforgettable body care experience—whether that's hair color, pedicure, or massage.

ELKE (330 N. Nevada Ave., no phone, www.elkebeauty.com) debuted in 2021 with offers of massage treatments, nail care, and skin care. Describing the business as a "social self-care space" in a holistic beauty salon, ELKE states that all products used in treatments are non-toxic.

Food

Given that Colorado Springs is a large city, it is easy to forget the ranching and agriculture communities that surround it. But these close connections mean that many menus feature locally sourced ingredients. From The Broadmoor to a pay-what-you-can café, there are local farmers to thank for the fresh produce and other food served. This means that diners will be eating what's seasonally available—from lamb to herbs.

COFFEE AND TEA

Coffee shops aren't just for hitting on your way into the office in the morning. The **Coffee Exchange** (526 S. Tejon St., 719/635-0277, www.theexchangeontejon.com, 7am-7pm Mon.-Fri., 8am-7pm Sat.-Sun.) is ready with live music on Friday nights, when it becomes more of a bar. Breakfast and lunch are served all day with gluten-free options available.

There's a theme at **The Perk** (14 S. Tejon St., 719/635-1600, www.theperkdowntown.com, 6am-10pm Mon.-Thurs., 6am-11pm Fri., 7am-11pm Sat., 7am-9pm Sun.): local. Come to listen to the local music while sipping locally roasted coffee and noshing on locally baked breads and pastries. The Perk is locally owned and loved by those in need of a hot cup of coffee or tea and some free Wi-Fi.

Colorado Springs is home to dozens of evangelical Christian organizations. If this speaks to your interests, you can explore some Christianity with your coffee at **Café 225** (225 N. Weber St., 719/884-6225, www.first-pres.org), a venue for films, discussions, and other Christian events.

Switchback Coffee Roasters (330 N. Institute St., 719/345-2807, https://switchbackroasters.com, 6:30am-5pm Mon.-Fri., 7am-5pm Sat.-Sun.) has a café in the residential Shooks Run neighborhood, east of downtown. This local coffee roaster is all about the stories behind the beans for each cup o' joe. There's also a small food menu. Switchback has a second café location (909 E. Moreno Ave., 7am-3pm daily) in the Hillside neighborhood, southeast of downtown.

BREAKFAST AND LUNCH

With four locations in town, **Urban Egg: A Daytime Eatery** (28B S. Tejon St., 719/471-2311; 5262 N. Nevada Ave., Suite 100, 719/598-2969; 5925 Dublin Blvd., 791/591-7329; 9420 Briar Village Pt., 719/955-6650; www.urbaneggeatery.com, 7am-2pm Mon.-Fri., 7am-2:30pm Sat.-Sun., $9-19) is the city's go-to breakfast spot. Balance your day with a freshly squeezed juice made with Colorado honey before you dig into the stack of Bananas Foster pancakes. Gluten-free options are

Ivywild

A beautiful old elementary school has been turned into a "community marketplace" in Colorado Springs, just southwest of downtown. **Ivywild School** (1604 S. Cascade Ave., 719/368-6100, www.ivywildschool.com) is where the cool kids hang out as they flaunt their local roots. Under one roof you will find the **Bristol Brewery & Pub** (11am-10pm Mon.-Thurs., 11am-11pm Fri.-Sat., noon-10pm Sun.), the cleverly named cocktail and coffee bar **The Principal's Office** (11am-10pm Sun.-Thurs., 11am-midnight Fri.-Sat.), **Decent Pizza Co.** (4pm-9pm Mon-Thurs., 11am-9pm Fri.-Sun.), and three more restaurants, with offerings ranging from salads to burgers and empanadas. Ivywild also features a community garden, a live music venue, and artwork by children and local artists on display. Start the morning with a coffee and pastry or end the day with a brew and a bite.

available, along with—of course—many egg dishes.

Do you trust Guy Fieri, host of *Diners, Drive-ins, and Dives*? I kinda do, though I don't quite have his appetite for extra-spicy food. Fieri featured the ★ **King's Chef Diner** (110 E. Costilla Ave., 719/634-9135, www.kingschefdiner.com, 8am-2pm daily, $8-24) on his show, and he was right on. Voted a local favorite for years, this is the place for a green chili-smothered breakfast burrito. In fact, their Colorado Green Chili is sold in jars at markets throughout the state. Other menu items include sandwiches and eggs and incorporate ingredients from local ranches and farms. Depending on where you are staying, see if their second location (131 E. Bijou St., 719/636-5010) is closer to you.

Once in your life you should treat yourself to Sunday brunch at the **Lake Terrace at The Broadmoor** (1 Lake Ave., 866/381-8432 or 719/577-5771, www.broadmoor.com, 7am-11am Mon.-Sat., 9am-1:30pm Sun., Sun. brunch $17-52, free under age 4). Crepes, biscuits and gravy, eggs Benedict, omelets, pastries, fresh fruit, bacon, sausage—okay, I won't list the more than 150 food items on offer at this indulgent brunch feast, but it is a marvelous meal. Reservations are required, and attire is resort casual.

BREWPUBS

A sister brewpub to Denver's iconic LoDo Wynkoop Brewing Company, the **Phantom Canyon Brewing Company** (2 E. Pikes Peak Ave., 719/635-2800, www.phantomcanyon.com, 11am-9pm Sun.-Thurs., 11am-1am Fri.-Sat., $12-25) is located in a historic building downtown. They serve standard but dependably good pub food for lunch or dinner, with fresh beer on tap. The menu sometimes even incorporates beer into the dinner offerings—think amber ale battered fish and beer cheese soup.

If there was a category for Colorado food, the ★ **Colorado Mountain Brewery** (600 21st St., 719/466-8240, www.cmbrew.com, 11am-9pm Sun.-Thurs., 11am-10pm Fri.-Sat., $7-18) would be in it. Bison poppers, venison egg rolls, steak burgers named after Colorado peaks, and brisket soaked in their Ole 59er Amber Ale set this menu apart from other brewpubs. This location in the downtown area is set in a historic railroad roundhouse. There is a second location (1110 Interquest Pkwy., 719/434-5750, 11am-9pm Sun.-Thurs., 11am-10pm Fri.-Sat.) in north Colorado Springs. Both locations offer military and college student discounts.

COMFORT FOOD

Play at The Broadmoor (1 Lake Ave., 855/634-7711, www.broadmoor.com, hours vary, $6-28) is as close as the resort gets to a sports bar. The idea is in the name: There's a

1: the Golden Bee, one of The Broadmoor's popular restaurants **2:** Lake Terrace at The Broadmoor's Sunday brunch

1

2

restaurant on one side and a bowling alley on the other. Whether you order the popcorn appetizer, tacos, or pizza, it's playful food and a fun night out for families. Reserve a lane so you can enjoy a game with dessert.

Dog lovers who want to dine out with their pooches finally have a place to go in Colorado: **Pub Dog** (2207 Bott Ave., 719/375-0771, http://pubdogcolorado.com, 11am-9pm daily, $8-13 humans, $1.50-4 canines). The restaurant has a large patio and fenced-in turf area where dogs can play while people eat. People food is mostly pizza and sandwiches; the dog menu—well, it sounds a lot like the regular menu, with chicken soup and burgers.

FINE DINING

Start with the crème de la crème. ★ **The Penrose Room** (The Broadmoor, 1 Lake Ave., 855/634-7711, www.broadmoor.com, 6pm-9pm Tues.-Sat., tasting menu $90-240 pp) is Colorado's only five-star, five-diamond restaurant. Whether it's beets or beef, chances are good that your meal is fresh and local—maybe even sourced from The Broadmoor's own farm. Each dish has its own take, even if it's a classic like duck à l'orange, chateaubriand, or lamb loin. The tasting menu offers selections from the sommelier, and there is a selection of signature cocktails and wines by the glass. Note that there is a dress code—no denim allowed.

FOOD HALL

Food court meets bar meets . . . motorcycle museum? The **Tejon Eatery** (19 N. Tejon St., 719/653-3271, www.tejoneatery.com, 11am-8pm Wed.-Thurs., 11am-10pm Fri.-Sat., 11am-6pm Sun.) opened in 2021 with nine restaurants, two bars, and one **Rocky Mountain Motorcycle Museum** (upstairs from the food hall, 719/487-8005, www.themotorcyclemuseum.com, 11am-8pm Wed.-Sat., 11am-4pm Sun., free, guided tours by appt.) in 28,000 square feet of space downtown. The modern industrial design features picnic tables on the main floor and casual table and chair setups on the next level. Menus include ramen, mac and cheese, barbecue, ice cream, and lots of beer.

STEAKHOUSE

Another option for those special celebration dine-out nights is **Prime 25** (1605 S. Tejon St., 719/358-9822, www.prime25.com, 4pm-9pm Tues.-Fri., 5pm-10pm Sat.-Sun., $19-50), with seafood flown in daily, venison, duck, lamb, and, of course, very good steak. Note that they have special hours and menus for holidays, too. Cushy booths and modern fireplace elements make for a glamorous feel.

ASIAN

Colorado Springs isn't exactly known for its ethnic fare, but now there's a dedicated ramen shop, **Rooster's House of Ramen** (323 N. Tejon St., 719/578-3031, https://cosramen.com, 11am-10pm Tues.-Thurs., 11am-11pm Fri.-Sat., noon-7pm Sun., $8-14) with steaming bowls of savory broth and noodles. For Food Network fans, note that chef Mark has been on *Chopped* and *Cooks v. Cons*.

BRITISH

Located just outside the main building of The Broadmoor is a classic English-style pub, the **Golden Bee** (1 Lake Ave., 719/577-5776, www.broadmoor.com, 11:30am-1am daily, $11-21). Bangers and mash, Scottish salmon, and lamb burger are all featured on a menu enhanced by English and Irish drafts. Fans collect the restaurant's golden bee patches—tiny little decals that are locally stitched with a variety of themes. Join the sing-along that starts at 9:30pm nightly.

FUSION

It's not every day you see a fusion of Hawaiian and Mexican food, and it's even more surprising to find it in Colorado Springs. **La'au's Taco Shop** (830 N. Tejon St., Suite 110, 719/578-5228, http://laaustacoshop.com, 11am-8pm Tues.-Sat., $7-10) masterfully blends these flavors in tacos, burritos, and salads. What makes it Hawaiian is the addition of pineapple, mango, and green papaya spiced up with jalapeños. Don't miss the *huli-huli* chicken, marinated in peanut butter and miso.

Colorado is one of the Four Corners states, and that connection inspired a restaurant here. **Four by Brother Luck** (321 N. Tejon St., 719/434-2741, www.fourbybrotherluck.com, 10am-9pm Sun.-Thurs., 11am-10pm Fri.-Sat., $23-29) draws on the influences of "Western European, Spanish Colonial, Native American, and Latin American cuisine." This translates to offerings such as Ute Tribe Blue Cornbread, Confit Rabbit Pot Pie, and Green Chile Poutine. Another Food Network alum who has bragging rights from a winning appearance on *Beat Bobby Flay* and *Chopped* heads up this unique restaurant.

ITALIAN

For truly authentic Italian food, **Ristorante de Lago** (1 Lake Ave., 855/634-7711, www.broadmoor.com, 7am-11am and 5:30pm-10pm daily, $16-36) is the place—they have some of their ingredients flown in from the home country. Not only do you get to know the story behind your mozzarella, but you also learn about the cows and trees of Italy, where generations of families have made the same delicious cheeses and oils.

There is such a nostalgic charm to **Fargo's Pizza** (2910 E. Platte Ave., 719/473-5540, www.fargospizza.com, 11am-9pm Sun.-Thurs., 11am-11pm Fri.-Sat., $4-22)—housed in a historic two-story 500-seat building—that eating almost seems beside the point. This Wild West Italian version of Denver's Casa Bonita restaurant includes a full arcade for family entertainment. The thin-crust pizza is pretty tasty, and there is a large salad bar.

JAMAICAN

Craving that curried goat you tried on vacation? **Dainty's Jamaican Kitchen** (302 E. Platte Ave., www.facebook.com/DaintysKitchen, 11am-5pm Mon., 11am-7pm Tues.-Sat., $7-18) serves not only curried goat, but also fried plantains, jerk pork, oxtail, and other Caribbean delights.

LATIN AMERICAN

There is no such thing as too many tacos. **T-Byrd's Tacos & Tequila** (26 E. Kiowa St., 719/375-3376, www.tbyrdstacos.com, 11am-10pm Mon. and Wed.-Thurs., 11am-midnight Tues. and Fri.-Sat., brunch 10am-3pm Sun., $4-8) agrees and offers several mouthwatering ones to choose from: Aguacate Frito (that's fried avocado) and Pescado Frito (Colorado trout) with some seasonal surprises.

VEGETARIAN

At The Broadmoor's ★ **Natural Epicurean** (1 Lake Ave., 855/634-7711, www.broadmoor.com, 6am-4pm daily, $7-25), the food is almost too pretty to eat. Get a green smoothie, delectable soup, or any vegetarian, vegan, or gluten-free seasonal salad, soup, or entrée for lunch or dinner. The restaurant's "living wall" of plants and a patio garden are reminders that you are eating what grows here.

Does 50 percent vegetarian appeal to vegetarians? **TAPAteria** (2607 W. Colorado Ave., 719/471-8272, www.tapateria.com, 11:30am-close Mon.-Sat., 1pm-close Sun., $3-9) must be on to something because their menu is 100 percent gluten-free, 50 percent vegetarian, and 25 percent vegan small plates, including meat and seafood. There is a full wine list to accompany these Spanish goodies, too.

Accommodations

When it comes to accommodations in Colorado Springs, The Broadmoor is the ultimate destination. Yet there are many lodging options for different styles and budgets between downtown Colorado Springs and throughout Manitou Springs. And, like The Broadmoor, it seems every hotel or inn has an interesting history behind it—or at least an enviable view to take in.

For marijuana-friendly rental properties in the Colorado Springs area, check out www.coloradopotguide.com as well as the listings below.

UNDER $150

The Satellite Hotel (411 Lakewood Circle, 719/596-6800 or 800/423-8409, http://satellitehotel.net, $90-120) is a hybrid hotel that has been half converted into apartments and condominiums. Many of the rooms in this 14-story hotel feature sliding glass doors with views of the mountains. There is an outdoor pool for use in the summer.

Situated between all good things in both Colorado Springs and Manitou Springs is the family-owned **Buffalo Lodge Bicycle Resort** (2 El Paso Blvd., 719/634-2851, http://bicycleresort.com, $149-209). The 1919 former hunting lodge has been turned into a haven for cyclists in the area, and you can just ride on two wheels over to the Garden of the Gods and other sights.

Located in the heart of downtown, **Kinship Landing** (415 S. Nevada Ave., 719/203-9309, www.kinshiplanding.com, $55-245) offers a variety of lodging options, from affordable shared bunkhouse rooms to more expensive private bedrooms. There's even a glamping-style option: For $20 a night, you can sleep in a tent on a fourth-story deck. Just like when camping, you get mountain views! Unlike camping, you get a private full bathroom with soft towels. (You'll need to bring your own camping gear.) The hotel also has a full restaurant and bar on-site.

$150-250

Before there was Airbnb there were places like the **Holden House Bed & Breakfast Inn** (1102 W. Pikes Peak Ave., 719/471-3980 or 888/565-3980, www.holdenhouse.com, $175-195) that make guests feel like they are staying over at a friend of a friend's place. Isabel Holden is credited with building this home in 1902, which has since been restored to offer all the modern amenities, such as refrigerators, free Wi-Fi, and flat-screen TVs. Today the six guest rooms of Holden House include the Victorian home next door.

In downtown Colorado Springs, the **Antlers Hilton Colorado Springs** (4 S. Cascade Ave., 719/955-5600, www.antlers.com, $179-369) is popular with business travelers, but it is also a convenient location for seeing the sights. The original Antlers Hotel was built within a few years of General Palmer founding the city of Colorado Springs; the hotel's name was derived from the general's large collection of deer and elk antlers that was housed here. After the original hotel burned down, the Antlers was rebuilt in 1901 and then again in 1967 (that is the hotel where guests stay today). West-side rooms have views of Pikes Peak, and guests can dine at the Antlers Grille for breakfast, enjoy Italian fare at Sportivo Primo, or head to the Piccadilly Bar.

The **Old Town Guesthouse** (115 S. 26th St., 719/632-9194 or 888/375-4210, www.oldtown-guesthouse.com, $195-285) is in Old Colorado City. Despite the name, this is a new building (1997 meets 1859), and their most popular room is one that "exceeds ADA requirements." Nearly every room has a view of Pikes Peak, a fireplace, a personal hot tub—and a waterbed ("waveless flotation

1: Kinship Landing **2:** a suite at The Broadmoor

1

2

mattresses"). Yes, that's a throwback to yet another era. Your total comfort is the goal—after a good soak while taking in the view, you can drift off to dreamland.

OVER $250

For that prime downtown location, stay at ★ **The Mining Exchange** (8 S. Nevada Ave., 719/323-2000, www.wyndham.com, $250-350), a Wyndham Grand Hotel. This building was constructed in 1902 as the stock exchange for the area's 20th-century mining companies. Guests will see the original bank vault in the lobby. Upstairs rooms resemble cool downtown lofts with high ceilings, exposed brick walls, and modern amenities such as flat-screen TVs and baths with dual showerheads. This 117-room hotel also has a wonderful restaurant, Springs Orleans, and the Stratton Lobby Bar offers pub-style food to go with cocktails.

★ **The Broadmoor** (1 Lake Ave., 719/577-5775 or 855/634-7711, www.broadmoor.com, year-round) is a five-star resort that has been expanding its accommodations. Guests can choose from rooms ($280-400) and suites ($750-1,000) in the hotel spread out along Cheyenne Lake, cottages ($750-1,000), and the all-inclusive The Ranch at Emerald Valley or Cloud Camp.

Open since 2013 for seasonal stays in summer only, **The Ranch at Emerald Valley** ($1,270-1,700 all-inclusive) is a newer addition to The Broadmoor. It includes 10 perfectly appointed cabins surrounded by Pike National Forest and sitting at over 8,000 feet (2,400 m) elevation. Meals are served in the Grand Lodge and days are spent hiking, riding bikes, fishing, and just soaking up the scenery. It's not quite "glamping" (glamorous camping that gets people outdoors with nary an inconvenience), but it's close—modern luxury meets the great outdoors.

On the historic site of founder Spencer Penrose's Cheyenne Lodge is **Cloud Camp** ($1,000-1,250 all-inclusive). Perched at 9,200 feet (2,800 m) elevation, it contains a mix of lodge accommodations and cabins for couples or groups. Just getting here from The Broadmoor is an adventure. Jeep or mule? Neither? You can hike in with a guide—in three hours. Cloud Camp is only available seasonally.

The most rustic of The Broadmoor's outlying "Wilderness Experience" accommodations is among the newest. **Broadmoor Fishing Camp** ($975) debuted in 2015 on the Tarryall River. Guests of The Broadmoor have day-use access to this private camp, where fly-fishing, horseback riding, and hiking are all available. Seven cottages can accommodate overnight stays with a communal lodge nearby for meals.

★ **Cheyenne Mountain Resort & Club** (3225 Broadmoor Valley Rd., 719/538-4000, www.cheyennemountain.com, $199-515) might be the closest competition to The Broadmoor. In fact, the four-diamond resort has many of the same amenities found at The Broadmoor: Spread out across 217 acres, the grounds include a private 35-acre lake that has its own beach, as well as tennis courts, a golf course, three restaurants, and three outdoor pools. Yet it's a different vibe altogether, and the decor is more contemporary. Still, it's all about the amenities, even if it's not possible to take advantage of them all in one stay. Once here, it's hard to take yourself away from just sitting on a deck and gazing at Cheyenne Mountain while the sun goes down. Go kayaking, sailing, or paddleboarding on the beautiful lake, or take lessons on the Pete Dye-designed golf course.

Garden of the Gods Club & Resort (3320 Mesa Rd., 719/632-5541, www.gardenofthegodsclub.com, $300-900) was once a playground for Hollywood luminaries such as John Wayne and Walt Disney. Rooms feature spectacular views of the park's jutting red rocks. In addition to an infinity pool and a recreation pool, amenities include a seasonal splash park for families, tennis courts, and adult and junior golf programs at the 27-hole golf course.

Chico Basin Ranch (22500 Peyton Hwy. S., 719/683-7960, www.ranchlands.com, starting at $332 pp per night all-inclusive with three-night minimum) is a working cattle ranch 30 miles (48 km) southeast of the city, but still part of Colorado Springs. While this is a family-run ranch, it is owned by the Colorado State Land Board and managed by Ranchlands, and what it offers is unique. Lakes and creeks on the property attract wildlife, and hunting and fishing are allowed on the property. The all-inclusive deal includes meals and activities. Rooms are in a historical adobe building with double beds or bunks.

Transportation and Services

AIR

The **Colorado Springs Airport** (COS, 7770 Milton E. Proby Pkwy., 719/550-1900, http://coloradosprings.gov/flycos) offers flights on American Airlines, Delta, Frontier, and United to 15 destinations, some of them only seasonally. There is transportation to rental car agencies as well as check-in counters for those agencies at baggage claim. Some hotels offer shuttle service to and from the airport; check the airport website. The airport is about 10 miles (16 km) east of Colorado Springs, accessible via I-25. There is a small art collection in the airport to look at as you queue up in various lines.

Airport Transportation

Ground transportation options from the Colorado Springs Airport include limos, taxis, shuttles, and buses. **Groome Transportation** (719/687-3456, https://groometransportation.com) offers shuttle service to and from Colorado Springs Airport, as well as a shuttle to the Denver airport. For taxi service, contact **Pikes Peak Cab** (719/888-900, https://pikespeakcabllc.com) or **zTrip** (previously Yellow Cab, 719/777-7777, www.ztrip.com).

CAR

Unless you are going straight to a resort or plan to stay in Manitou Springs, you might want a car so that you can visit local attractions from downtown Colorado Springs. Colorado Springs is just over an hour's drive from Denver, and many people make a day trip from the Mile High City.

To reach Colorado Springs from Denver, take I-25 south for about 70 miles (113 km) and look for signs to the various sights or downtown. **Groome Transportation** (719/687-3456, https://groometransportation.com) offers shuttle service to and from Denver in small passenger vans.

Car Rental

Car rental agencies are available at the **Colorado Springs Airport** (7770 Milton E. Proby Pkwy., 719/550-1900, http://coloradosprings.gov/flycos) and include most of the major companies, including **Budget** (719/596-2751) and **Enterprise** (800/736-8222).

PUBLIC TRANSIT

Greyhound buses (120 S. Weber St., 719/635-1505, www.greyhound.com, 8am-9pm daily, $15-29) serve Colorado Springs from Denver daily. **Mountain Metropolitan Transit** (http://coloradosprings.gov/mountain-metro, $0.85-1.75) is a citywide bus service that serves as Colorado Springs's public transportation option. Route 3 provides service to Manitou Springs, while Route 2 gets you to Garden of the Gods.

Amtrak trains do not serve Colorado Springs.

INFORMATION AND SERVICES

Stop by the **Experience Colorado Springs at Pikes Peak Visitor Center** (515 S. Cascade Ave., 719/635-7506, www.visitcos.com, 8:30am-5pm Mon.-Fri. winter,

10:30am-5:30pm daily summer) for maps and brochures of the area. The **Colorado Springs Gazette** (www.gazette.com) is the city's main newspaper, with listings of the latest local happenings. There is also the alternative weekly the **Independent** (www.csindy.com).

In an emergency, dial 911 for immediate assistance. **Memorial Hospital Central** (1400 E. Boulder St., 719/365-5000, www.uchealth.org) offers many services, including emergency, trauma, and pediatrics. Penrose-St. Francis Health Services includes **Penrose Hospital** (2222 N. Nevada Ave., 719/776-5000, www.centura.org) and **St. Francis Medical Center** (6001 E. Woodmen Rd., 719/571-1000, www.centura.org) and include an urgent care facility.

Vicinity of Colorado Springs

MANITOU SPRINGS

Manitou Springs is a charming town with its own identity, but it's so close to Colorado Springs that one could walk between the two—if you had the time for a 6-mile (9.7-km) one-way jaunt. But where downtown Colorado Springs feels very much like a city with office buildings, large hotels, and a campus, Manitou Springs is a walkable town of quaint shops, restaurants, inns, and a creek running through it.

It's been called a "Hippie Mayberry," and the town is certainly an appealing blend of historical allure and New Age trappings. Manitou Springs is also the gateway to Pikes Peak, as well as the Garden of the Gods. On a clear day, the view from Pike's 14,115-foot (4,302-m) peak is incredible—and even inspired the lyrics for *America the Beautiful.*

Cave of the Winds Mountain Park

If you have ever been curious about caves, but too timid to crawl around in the dark, then maybe **Cave of the Winds Mountain Park** (Hwy. 24, 719/685-5444, http://caveofthewinds.com, 9am-9pm daily summer, 10am-5pm daily winter, $15-45, free under age 5, prices vary by tour) is just right. Guided tours of the cave are well lit with wide walkways and handrails, and visitors can clearly see stalagmites, stalactites, and limestone caverns. The Discovery Tour takes 45 minutes and is offered every 30 minutes. The Lantern Tour is for the slightly more adventurous spelunker and takes twice as long, with some stooping and less light. Overall, it can be a fun experience for school-age children. For another type of adventure, try their via ferrata climbing route or zip lines.

Cave of the Winds was "discovered" by two brothers in the late 1800s. Today, it is a tourist trap—an enormous gift shop cleverly conceals the cave entrance. There is a pretty incredible view of the canyons below from the gift shop deck, which is equipped with binoculars. Cave of the Winds is about a five-minute drive from Manitou Springs.

Manitou Cliff Dwellings Preserve and Museums

Right off the bat, you should know that the **Manitou Cliff Dwellings** (Hwy. 24, 719/685-5242, www.cliffdwellingsmuseum.com, 9am-5pm daily May-Aug., 9am-4:30pm daily March-Apr. and Sept.-Oct., 9am-4pm daily Nov., 10am-4pm daily Dec.-Feb., $12 adults, $9 seniors, $7.50 children, free under age 4) were relocated from somewhere else, and some of the buildings are reproductions. The good news is that this lack of authenticity means more access to the entire site, unlike truly preserved cliff dwellings in southwestern Colorado. There are self-guided tours of the site and a lack of Do Not Touch signs, as the effort here is to educate people about Native American cultures. There is a large gift shop and snack bar on-site.

Manitou Springs

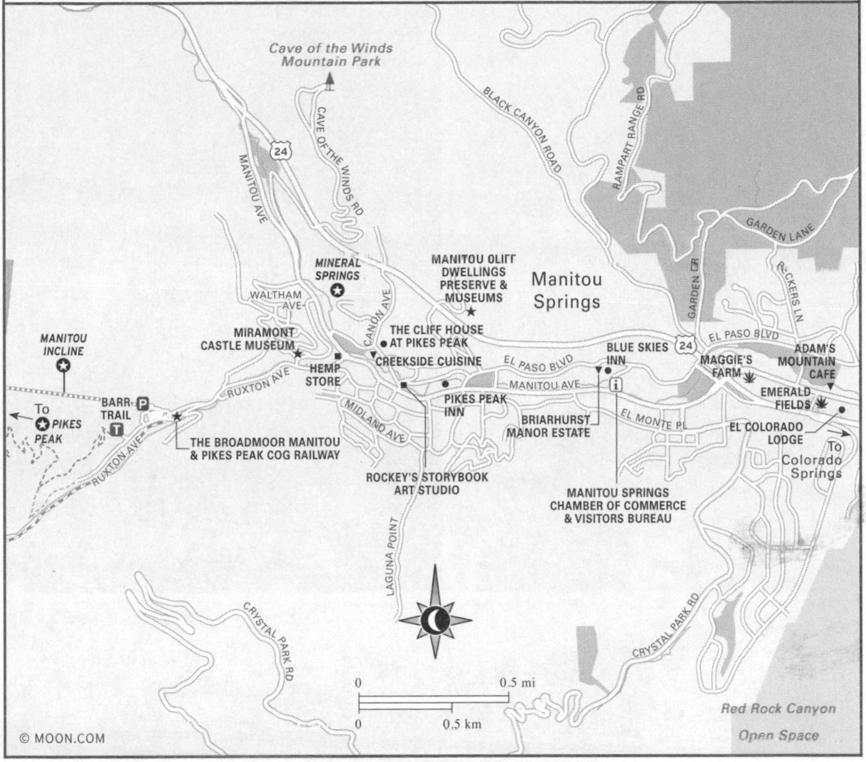

★ Mineral Springs

Some of the best attractions in Manitou Springs are the springs themselves, conveniently available in decorative fountains located around the historic downtown. The water that fills the springs begins its journey as snowmelt from Pikes Peak. It then filters into the ground and becomes mineralized before resurfacing via cavernous limestone where it develops its effervescence—all over hundreds of years. The Native Americans who lived in this area drank from these unique mineral springs in order to heal themselves; they considered them medicinal as well as spiritual. As this area became settled in the late 1800s, the water was marketed as having healing properties in order to attract visitors.

Today, unique artistic fountains are installed around town so that visitors can sample the waters while learning a bit of their history. Stop in at the **Manitou Springs Chamber of Commerce and Visitors Bureau** (354 Manitou Ave., 719/685-5089 or 800/642-2567, www.manitousprings.org, 8:30am-5pm Mon.-Fri., 9am-4pm Sat.-Sun., free), where you will be given a small plastic souvenir cup for sampling the springwater (or just bring your own water bottle), a map of the various springs, and a detailed list of the health benefits of the mineral springwater. I'm not sure why or how, but the water at each of the springs has a completely different taste, some far less palatable than others.

1

2

3

Saratoga of the West

The first settlement in these parts was Colorado City (now part of Colorado Springs), founded in 1859. Not only was the scenery an attraction, but the high altitude and dry climate were believed to have healing effects for people with tuberculosis. In 1871, the city of Colorado Springs was founded by General William Jackson Palmer. Palmer and Dr. William A. Bell came to the area after reading explorers' accounts of the healing waters found at the base of Pikes Peak. Together the two men founded the town of Manitou Springs, envisioning a spa resort here. Palmer had already founded the Denver & Rio Grande Railroad; in 1881, a railroad spur brought people to the new town.

Many of the hotels in Manitou Springs that still stand today hosted guests in the 1890s, when it was dubbed "Saratoga of the West" after Saratoga, New York, also known for its mineral springs.

★ Pikes Peak

Pikes Peak (www.springsgov.com) is not only the state's most famous "fourteener" (a mountain peak that stands over 14,000 ft/4,200 m high); it is the second-most visited peak in the world. Over the years, people seem to have come up with every conceivable way to experience or ascend this mountain (all for a fee, unless you are fit enough to hike up). The 360-degree panorama from the top is simply spectacular.

If you aren't hiking or biking, try **The Broadmoor Manitou & Pikes Peak Cog Railway** (515 Ruxton Ave., 719/685-5401, www.cograilway.com, $48-68, schedule changes seasonally). This very scenic ride might be the best way to get to the top of a fourteener in Colorado. It's popular, so book tickets as far in advance as possible. The historic cog railway reopened in 2021 after a couple years' worth of extensive renovations. At the same time, the Pikes Peak Visitor Center on the top of the mountain was redone to offer more food options (yes, the famous doughnuts are still here!) so you can linger at 14,115 feet (4,302 m) above sea level.

There is also bus service to the top via **Gray Line** (719/465-1871, http://pikespeaktour.com, departs 8am, 9am, 1pm, and 2pm daily May-Sept., 9am and 1:30pm daily Oct.-Memorial Day, $35-65), which takes four hours round-trip and includes a visit to the gift shop and facilities on the summit.

Pikes Peak also has its own toll road—19 miles (31 km) of curvy mountain driving that is paved for only about half the distance; the last 9 miles (14.5 km) are gravel. Every summer, the **Pikes Peak International Hill Climb** (719/685-4400, www.ppihc.com, June) takes place on this seemingly dangerous road.

The **Barr Trail** is the route for hikers to get to the peak, and this inspires an annual event with the Pikes Peak Marathon in August.

Miramont Castle Museum

Tucked into the town's historic district is a large castle that was constructed as a private home for a French priest and his mother in 1895. **Miramont Castle Museum** (9 Capitol Hill Ave., 719/685-1011, www.miramontcastle.org, 10am-4pm Tues.-Sun., $12 adults, $11 seniors, $8 children ages 4-12, free under age 3 and for active duty firefighters and military) is an amalgam of architectural styles with 46 oddly shaped rooms. The castle has had many uses over the years—sanitarium, apartments—and is now filled with furniture and curiosities of the Victorian era.

1: the mineral springs at Manitou Springs **2:** cog railway at Pikes Peak **3:** Manitou Cliff Dwellings

1

2

3

Entertainment and Events

Old-fashioned theater fun is found at the Iron Springs **Chateau Historic Melodrama Theatre** (444 Ruxton Ave., 719/685-5104, http://ironspringschateau.com). While the concept of vaudeville ("Cheer the hero; boo the villain!") is not new, the plays are unique, with titles such as *Panic on Pikes Peak*. This is dinner theater, so no need to dine out first.

If you haven't already noticed, they do things differently in Manitou Springs. The self-named "Manitoids" like to get in the Halloween spirit of late October with . . . coffin races in memory of poor Emma Crawford, an early resident who came to the area to cure her tuberculosis (after a recovery, she succumbed to the illness). Crawford was buried on Red Mountain, as she requested, but when a rainstorm flooded the area, her empty coffin washed down the slopes. It's believed she haunts the mountain. The **Emma Crawford Coffin Races** (http://manitousprings.org) take place the Saturday before Halloween.

It's the classic love-hate relationship with fruitcake during the **Manitou Springs Great Fruitcake Toss** (www.visitcos.com/fruitcake-toss) in January. First, contestants toss or fling or sling their own fruitcakes or one "rented" for this purpose; there is then a judging that factors in important details like distance. Kids, families, teams, and individuals are all invited to give it a go in this competition. Next, there is a local baking competition for the best fruitcake. People get very creative with both their tossing implements and their fruitcake recipes.

Shopping

Shopping in Manitou Springs means the usual tourist candy stores, T-shirt shops, and art galleries. But then things get more interesting, with themed stores. There is the **Hemp Store** (2 Ruxton Ave., 719/685-1189, www.toddshempstore.com, 11am-6pm daily), with a variety of items made from the fiber.

Not a store, but worth a look, is **Rockey's Storybook Art Studio** (10-12 Cañon Ave., 719/685-9076, www.rockeyartmuseum.org, hours vary), where artist and local legend C. H. Rockey lived and worked; though Rockey passed away in 2019, his artworks remain on display. In addition to an intricately illustrated storybook, you'll see the artist's landscapes, townscapes, portraits, fantasy scenes, sculptures, and furniture, and have a chance to buy posters, postcards, and other souvenirs to bring back home.

CANNABIS SUPPLIES

Manitou Springs (or elsewhere outside El Paso County) is the only place to go for local recreational marijuana dispensaries. **Maggie's Farm** (141 Manitou Ave., 719/685-1655, www.maggiesfarmmarijuana.com, 8am-11:45pm daily) has won several Best of Colorado Springs awards for its offerings—possibly in part because it was the only game in town for a while. That doesn't mean its offerings aren't top notch, if a bit pricey. True to its name, Maggie's Farm sells only all-natural marijuana grown in the great outdoors on high-altitude farms.

An offshoot of an operation that launched in the Denver area several years ago, **Emerald Fields** (27 Manitou Ave., 719/375-0554, www.emeraldfields.com, 8am-11pm daily) opened to challenge Maggie's Farm's longtime Manitou Springs monopoly. The 3,000-square-foot space has an upscale boutique vibe, with attendants on hand to answer any questions.

Sports and Recreation

Manitou Springs is really in the foothills. No matter where you are in town, you can stroll and see the sights or enjoy a bit of nature on a trail, by foot, or on two wheels.

1: Manitou Incline **2:** Miramont Castle Museum
3: Pikes Peak as seen from Colorado Springs

RING THE PEAK TRAIL

You can start—and stop—a hike on the **Ring the Peak Trail** (Crags and Horsethief Park Trails, 615 County Rd. 62, www.ringthepeaktrail.org) that partially encircles Pikes Peak, though it is not a full ring yet. Added together, the Ring offers 63 miles (101 km) of trails, so it makes sense to just do a section and double back. No matter how much of the ring you choose to hike, you'll see a less traveled part of famed Pikes Peak.

★ MANITOU INCLINE

Where a cable car once crept up the side of the mountain, today people creep up the old rail ties on the **Manitou Incline** (7 Hydro St., www.manitouincline.com, free reservations required). This is a serious hike! In 1 mile (1.6 km), you will climb over 2,000 vertical feet (600 m)—from about 6,500 feet (2,000 m) to more than 8,500 feet (2,600 m)—and there is a very steep 68 percent grade in some spots. Depending upon your fitness level, it can take 1-3 hours to get to the top—unless you're a professional athlete like Olympic champion speed skater Apolo Ohno, and then apparently you can just run up there in less than 20 minutes. The views are amazing from the top.

Food

Adam's Mountain Café (26 Manitou Ave., 719/685-1430, https://adamsmountaincafe.com, lunch 8am-3pm daily, dinner 5pm-9pm Tues.-Sat. May-Sept., lunch 8am-3pm Tues.-Sun., dinner 5pm-9pm Tues.-Sat. Oct.-Apr., $8-22) is a homey-feeling restaurant with lots of vegetarian options. Note that it's a ways off the beaten path in town.

The Cliff House at Pikes Peak (306 Cañon Ave., 719/685-3000 or 888/212-7000, www.thecliffhouse.com, 6:30am-10:30am, 11:30am-2:30pm, and 5:30pm-9pm daily, $20-35) is open for breakfast, lunch, and dinner with a separate (cheaper) Veranda menu available in the summer months for dining outside. The restaurant has received the 4 Diamond Award in Fine Dining from AAA.

A fine-dining option is the **Briarhurst Manor Estate** (404 Manitou Ave., 719/685-1864 or 877/685-1448, www.briarhurst.com, 5pm-8:30pm Wed.-Sun., $29-47), which was the home of Manitou Springs's founder, Dr. William Bell. The pink sandstone Tudor-style house is open for dinner nightly; entrées feature Colorado lamb and deer.

Accommodations

UNDER $150

Pikes Peak Inn (626 Manitou Ave., 719/685-5616 or 800/664-2704, www.pikespeakinn.com, $90-160) is a real bargain, but it feels like a much pricier lodging with its clean updated rooms decorated to evoke the West. You can walk to many of the sights in downtown Manitou Springs.

El Colorado Lodge (23 Manitou Ave., 719/685-5485 or 800/782-2246, www.elcoloradolodge.com, $120-200) isn't a lodge at all, but a group of historical adobe cabins that are both family-friendly (pool, hot tub, and on-site playground) and pet-friendly. The cabins range in size and amenities—some have kitchens or fireplaces—and can sleep up to eight people or only two.

$150-250

Sometimes a bed-and-breakfast crosses the line from quaint to kitsch. This is the case at the **Blue Skies Inn** (402 Manitou Ave., 719/685-3899 or 800/398-7949, www.blueskiesinn.com, $175-250). The theme is fun (there is a Blue Skies room with images of blue skies painted on the walls), and there is a variety of whimsical rooms—one room is Indian Rock Art, another room is Morning Glory. Beyond the canopied beds and coordinating tile, each room has a gas or electric fireplace, and some have jetted tubs large enough for two. The inn is next to a creek, and the owners spend time gardening, so there are lots of flowers in bloom in spring and summer.

For a small town, Manitou Springs has a lot of lodgings. The best in town has to be ★ **The Cliff House at Pikes Peak** (306 Cañon Ave.,

719/785-1000, www.thecliffhouse.com, $215-450), right in the heart of the action. The Cliff House began as a stop for miners, but then became popular with those who came for Manitou Springs's famous "healing waters." Such notable guests as Clark Gable and Theodore Roosevelt laid their heads here. The in-house restaurants, the award-winning Dining Room and the Red Mountain Bar and Grill, offer sophisticated contemporary cuisine.

Transportation and Services

To get to Manitou Springs from Denver, take I-25 south just past the exit for downtown Colorado Springs and exit on Cimarron Street (which becomes Hwy. 24) or Colorado Avenue. The drive takes about 1.25 hours from downtown Denver, but try to time your trip to avoid rush-hour gridlock in Colorado Springs.

To get to Manitou Springs from Boulder, take Highway 36 east to Denver, then drive south on I-25 through Denver to Colorado Springs. Once in Colorado Springs, take the exit for Manitou Springs.

In the summer, you can catch a free **shuttle** (www.springsgov.com) in Manitou Springs that will take you around town. The **Manitou Springs Chamber of Commerce and Visitors Bureau** (354 Manitou Ave., 719/685-5089 or 800/642-2567, www.manitousprings.org, 8:30am-5pm Mon.-Fri., 9am-4pm Sat.-Sun.) has more brochures than you will ever need and helpful staff to answer questions and make suggestions. Take Highway 24 to Manitou Avenue; the visitors center is on your right before entering town.

Background

The Landscape.........246
History 248
Government and
Economy 252

The Landscape

Colorado is divided by the Rocky Mountains, with the largest concentration of cities and people to the east in what is called the Front Range. The 14,000-foot peaks of the Rockies frame the Front Range cities of Denver, Boulder, Fort Collins, and Colorado Springs. The largest of these cities, Denver, is on the high plains about 12 miles (19 km) east of the foothills. Despite an elevation of 1 mile (5,280 ft/1,609 m) above sea level, this is the flatter part of the state. Denver is a little bit of both mountains and plains, and the topography of the core neighborhoods

Floods and Fire

For all the talk of Denver being so arid, water has dramatically shaped the city.

As the first settlements at the confluence of Cherry Creek and the Platte River were being built, Native Americans warned the newcomers that flooding was a risk. But before they could be proved right, a fire broke out in 1863 when drunken revelers knocked over a lamp. The simple wood-frame structures were engulfed in flames and most of the city's business district was lost. Though precious supplies were gone, the buildings were quickly rebuilt—this time with brick.

Brick, however, was no help a year later, when Cherry Creek became a raging torrent of water after heavy spring rains. Lives, buildings, livestock, and much more were lost, but people kept rebuilding, even in the floodplain. There were many more floods until the 1950s, when the Army Corps of Engineers built the Cherry Creek Dam.

In 1965, the relatively tame South Platte River became swollen with rainwater and crashed through bridges and property, causing $300 million in damage. The floodwaters were full of the refuse that residents freely dumped in the river, including items as big as refrigerators. This disaster led to the Platte Redevelopment Committee, which, over the next decade, turned the waterways into a greenbelt and a growing source of civic pride.

varies greatly from floodplains to hills overlooking the city and everything in between.

Shaped by the beauty that lies to the west in the Rocky Mountains, Denver, Boulder, Colorado Springs, and Fort Collins each have a natural appeal of their own. All of these elements combine to make Colorado an attractive place to visit and explore, and you can have the best of both worlds—urban cities and the great outdoors.

GEOGRAPHY AND CLIMATE

While the word *plains* suggests flatland or lowland, in reality the land is more dynamic, with the plains east of Denver at an even higher elevation than that of the city. This causes the waters of Cherry Creek to flow northwest, unlike rivers that run south and east from the mountains. From a different perspective, Denver is at the western edge of the plains, not the eastern side of the mountains. Boulder, Fort Collins, and Colorado Springs lie closer to the foothills; in some places, folks can just walk out the door and start hiking.

Lush isn't a word used to describe any of these cities on the Front Range. Rivers and creeks run through each city, with numerous reservoirs on the outskirts, but still, this is an arid place, a high desert climate, with minimal precipitation: The average annual rainfall in Denver is 15.47 inches (39.3 cm), and the average annual snowfall is 59.6 inches (151.4 cm). Summers are dry and can be quite hot—though statistics put the average high at 88.1°F (31.2°C) in July, it frequently climbs into the 100s (over 37.8°C). Denver has more annual days of sunshine than coastal places like San Diego; typically, a couple of inches of snowfall will melt off within a few days.

Winters can be quite chilly, with average January lows at 16.9°F (-8.4°C), but snowfall varies significantly. Some years, there's little snow all season, but every few years, it seems like the city is paralyzed by a blizzard. Because those blizzards garner a lot of national headlines, people mistakenly believe that Denver has severe storms every winter. It's a paradox for officials: The rarity of such snowstorms can mean there aren't enough plows and staff on hand, yet such emergencies do happen. It can be bad publicity for the city but is usually good news for the ski resorts.

Previous: Garden of the Gods.

ENVIRONMENTAL ISSUES

Growth is a double-edged sword for the Front Range cities, and always has been for Denver, resulting in two prominent environmental issues: air pollution and water use.

Since Denver's earliest days, there have been struggles to divert enough clean water to supply the city—and now the greater metro area, which consists of seven counties. There first needs to be a certain amount of precipitation at the highest points in the mountains, where rivers and streams are fed by rain and snow each year. Most of the rivers head west from the Continental Divide, and what is flowing east doesn't simply end in Denver, but keeps heading south through other parched states to the distant ocean. One source of water is brought "uphill" over the Continental Divide to provide water to Denver and its suburbs. Water laws and rights are complicated issues that have become more prominent during drought years. There are mandatory water-use rules and water "police" who fine people for watering their grass at the wrong time. The strict hit-them-in-the-wallet restrictions have decreased water use by billions of gallons, but as growth continues amid the naturally arid conditions, conservation efforts are an ongoing part of life in Denver and elsewhere on the Front Range.

While taking fewer showers or living with a yellow lawn turned out to be acceptable conservation measures for residents, helping to reduce air pollution and the city's notorious "brown cloud" is another challenge.

Once upon a time, Denver had a streetcar system that was done away with to make way for the almighty automobile. As the population boomed between 1960 and 1980, the number of cars on the freshly built highways and roads also exploded. It wasn't until the 1980s that auto emission tests became mandatory. Cars weren't the only source contributing to the smog (or "smaze," as some called it), and trash burning was prohibited. Coal-burning power plants have had to cut their emissions, and wood-burning fireplaces are nearly obsolete, with restrictions on days that they can be used. The fact that Denver lies in a river basin between the plains and the mountains means that the fine particles of pollution—whether from road sand or carbon monoxide emissions or smoke—are going to settle in the air in this low spot.

The brown cloud is not gone, and it can obscure views from the city or of the city itself when approaching it, but there is more and more emphasis on alternative transportation in Denver and beyond to possibly reduce the haze and pollution. Residents and visitors alike are encouraged to ride bikes, take the light rail trains or buses, or simply walk instead of driving. The city often struggles to stay in compliance with Environmental Protection Agency standards and has to keep finding ways to reduce air pollution.

History

It is speculated that Europeans first came through what is now Colorado in the 1500s, and that the search for riches of silver and gold began in the 1700s. The Louisiana Purchase of 1803 meant that the land east of the Continental Divide and north of the Arkansas River was transferred to the United States. Exploratory parties were sent out, and by the 1850s prospectors were making their way west into the Colorado Territory. Supply towns were built, along with railroads, and the growth paved the way for Colorado to become a state in 1876.

DENVER

Denver is that rare city that was not built up along a road, railroad, or navigable body of water. There is evidence that people had used the area as a hunting ground as long as 11,000 years ago. The Laramie Treaty of 1851 had conceded this land to the Arapaho and Cheyenne nations, but that agreement was pretty much ignored when prospectors found flecks of gold in the Platte River in 1858. (Other whites had come through this stretch prior to the gold discovery, only to categorize it as a "desolate wasteland" and keep on going.) Though there wasn't really a fortune to be found in the waters near the confluence of Cherry Creek and the Platte River, prospectors set up their town on the banks of the two waterways. General William Larimer of Kansas put some sticks on a nearby hill to make his claim, which later became Denver.

There were initially three towns, but in 1859, a shared barrel of whiskey was all it took for the two smaller towns to be convinced to become part of Denver. Even the naming of the city was a bit of a bumble: Local leaders strove to impress territorial governor James Denver, who lived in Kansas, by naming the city after him, but he had already retired and never came to Denver.

As the first Denver City was established with cabins and tents set up at what is now Confluence Park, Native Americans were edged out—often in violent and bloody confrontations. The new settlers and the Cheyenne and Arapaho people clashed, and a new treaty was drawn up in 1861 that gave Denver to the United States.

In those early years, Denver was the Wild West, with saloons, brothels, and lawlessness. The city established itself as a supply center for the thousands flocking to the newest gold discoveries in the nearby mountains, and the mountains' harsh winters sometimes drove people back to the more hospitable Denver weather; people also came to Colorado, and specifically Denver, as well as other cities like Manitou Springs to the south, seeking a cure for tuberculosis. The town weathered devastating fires and floods, but there were always those optimists who saw the potential for Denver to be more than a dusty frontier town.

The population in Denver was only 3,500 in 1866, when it was among the Front Range cities competing to be the territory's capital. For a brief time the city of Golden held the honor, but in 1867 Denver finagled its way into becoming the territorial capital, and it retained the title when Colorado achieved statehood in 1876. Denver officially became Colorado's capital in 1881.

Railroads are what truly cemented Denver's place on the map. Hundreds of trains a day were passing through here in the late 19th century, many loaded with supplies for mining towns. The beaux arts-style Union Station was erected in 1914 and is the city's only remaining train depot, but train museums show off old locomotives and fancy passenger cars and give a more in-depth telling of how railroads shaped Denver and many cities in the West.

Denver's citizens learned about building a city the hard way. Fire destroyed most of the town's early wood-frame buildings, while floods wiped out structures and took lives. Cyclical economic downturns also affected the city. But the miners making their fortunes in the mountains continued to invest in Denver, and by the turn of the 20th century the population was over 100,000, and grand theaters and hotels were built to meet the needs of the city. When the silver boom crashed, Denver slumped into a depression along with the rest of the country; agriculture and food processing kept the economy going. When the Dust Bowl years came along about 1930 and the Great Depression hit, Denver was brought to its knees. That frontier "can-do" spirit prevailed, and the New Deal meant improvements in parks, trails, and roads that brought tourists to the area.

World War II also changed economic fortunes for Denver. Because the city was considered an unlikely place to be bombed, Buckley Air Force Base, the Rocky Mountain Arsenal, and other military installations were built here and created more jobs. Over time, federal scientific, research, and technological facilities also established themselves in the greater Denver area.

After World War II, oil and gas businesses took interest in Denver for its location near energy fields and thus began the upward growth of the city's downtown skyscrapers. As boom-and-bust cycles continued, the city grew and shrank again, but now it is clear how those booms have led to Denver's current moment as a darling city to live in and visit. Mayor Federico Peña, Denver's first Latino mayor, was elected in 1983 and is credited with getting Denver International Airport funded (that's why you drive on Peña Boulevard coming and going from DIA), getting a tax approved to fund the building of Coors Field (home of the Colorado Rockies baseball team), and getting the Scientific and Cultural Facilities District tax approved by voters. Next up in 1991 was Wellington Webb, the city's first black mayor, and he too had a long-term vision for his hometown as he oversaw development of many of today's urban playgrounds, like Commons Park.

Today Denver's population is over 700,000, and the greater metro area, which includes seven counties, is at nearly three million. The boom is here.

BOULDER

The Southern Arapaho people were the first to live in the Boulder area. Utes, Cheyenne, and other Native Americans would visit and were also drawn to the region for its natural beauty. In the 1850s European settlers arrived seeking gold, and by 1859 the town of Boulder was created (though it wasn't incorporated until 1871) as a supply center for miners headed into the nearby mountains to dig out their fortunes. As the town established itself with a school, railroad service, and other basic necessities, the University of Colorado was able to get its start here in 1876.

As Boulder developed a local economy, it began a lifelong cycle of seasonal population fluxes. In its first few years, the University of Colorado had a tiny enrollment of less than 100 students; today, around 30,000 students pour into Boulder at the beginning of each school year. After Chautauqua Park was built in 1898, Boulder developed a reputation as a summer retreat, drawing a few thousand visitors each year. With the influx of students and vacationers, and easy access via the railroad, Boulder began to develop a tourism industry.

Yet Boulder did not rely solely on tourists to keep the economy going. In the 1950s the town became the home of the National Bureau of Standards' Radio Propagation Laboratory—and that got the ball rolling on federal government and scientific organizations basing themselves here. Rocky Flats, a nuclear weapons manufacturing facility, was built south of Boulder; Ball Aerospace was founded here; and Boulder became the headquarters for the National Center for Atmospheric Research. Since then, IBM and many other tech businesses have set up shop.

As business and organizations attracted new residents, city leaders maintained an emphasis on preserving the natural beauty of Boulder as it grew. Restrictions on building heights were put in place, sanitation lines were brought into the mountains, and green space was preserved.

Today, Boulder sits in a nest flanked by the dramatic rising mountains on one side and open space on the other. This combination of intellectualism, physical fitness, and business savvy surrounded by gorgeous scenery is what makes Boulder so appealing to the 105,000 people calling it home as of 2020.

COLORADO SPRINGS

There are a few funny misunderstandings in the story of how the city of Colorado Springs came to be. Take the name of Pikes Peak, the 14,115-foot (4,302 m) peak to the west of the city. Explorer Zebulon M. Pike did make it to the area in November 1806 and attempted to hike the mountain, but snow and hunger turned him and his party back; the peak and national forest are thus named after him for his "discovery" of the peak, not for his summiting of it. Of course, the high mountain peak—along with the sculptural red rocks, cascading waterfalls, and mineral springs that attract visitors to Colorado Springs

Preserving Historic Buildings

By the 1960s, there was growing concern among preservationists about the demolition of many historic homes, buildings, and neighborhoods within Colorado's towns. These protests were led in large part by Dana Crawford and other like-minded women, such as future congresswoman Patricia Schroeder, who took on developers' plans to tear down all of Denver's Larimer Square. The Daniels and Fisher Tower on 16th Street was saved, but many other buildings were lost to the wrecking ball. The original town of Auraria, founded at the same time as Denver and eventually incorporated into the city, was demolished even though it was a historic Latino enclave. The land—about 20 city blocks—was used to make way for the Auraria college campus.

In 1970, the organization **Historic Denver** (www.historicdenver.org) was formed, and the Molly Brown House was successfully saved and restored. This was just the first of many important preservation projects in Denver, and the stories of many of those salvaged edifices are found in Historic Denver's series of small paperback books. The books serve as neighborhood guides or thematic tours of landmarks such as churches. Places like the Molly Brown House Museum and the Colorado History Museum sell the books.

Another preservationist managed to save that most valuable asset: the mountain view. Helen Millet Arndt, founder of the Denver Landmark Preservation Committee, conducted a survey that revealed that locals thought the mountain backdrop was what made their city special. In 1968, city council passed the Mountain View Preservation ordinance, thanks to Arndt and her supporters. This has prevented building that might obstruct the mountain view from the state capitol and numerous city parks.

today—drew Native Americans to the region hundreds of years before Pike and his party set eyes on the area.

After the California gold rush was exhausted in 1859, miners (called "Fifty-niners") turned their attention to Colorado. They aimed for Pikes Peak—some even going so far as to paint the mountain's name on their covered wagons—but gold was actually discovered 85 miles (137 km) north of the mountain, close to what is now Denver. A significant gold mine was discovered on the western slope of Pikes Peak in 1891, and the Cripple Creek Gold Camp was created.

The discovery of gold created a population explosion in Colorado Springs, as the area became known, resulting in a "city of millionaires." Much of that money was poured into making the area more attractive for tourism. After Spencer Penrose earned his first million in the Cripple Creek mine (as well as in mines in Utah), he established The Broadmoor, the Cheyenne Mountain Zoo, and the Pikes Peak Highway.

During World War II, military bases were established in Colorado Springs. This industry became an important cog in the local economy. Today, Colorado Springs is home to six major military installations: U.S. Army base Fort Carson, the U.S. Air Force Academy, Peterson Air Force Base, the U.S. Space Command, Schriever Air Force Base, and the North American Aerospace Defense Command (NORAD).

In 2020, the population of Colorado Springs was tallied at close to 490,000 and the greater metropolitan population was close to 670,000 (compare that to the metro area population of Denver at 2.7 million). Yet in many ways, Colorado Springs still feels like an up-and-coming metropolis when compared to the more bustling Denver, and that's a good thing for vacationers.

FORT COLLINS

Like many Western towns and cities, Fort Collins's history has to do with water. In 1862, Camp Collins started as a military outpost built on the Overland Trail and situated along the Cache La Poudre River (so named because

French Canadian fur traders hid their gunpowder here). In 1864, it was relocated after a flood to the current location of Old Town Fort Collins.

Soon, settlers began to arrive, and Camp Collins ceased being a fort. By the time the railroad arrived in 1877, the former camp had become a town with a hotel, a general store, a post office, and a school. Colorado Agricultural & Mining College built its first classroom here in 1879; in 1957, the institution became Colorado State University.

Water remained an important aspect of the town's economy, as a combination of farming and ranching began to put Fort Collins on the map. Farmers grew sugar beets, which then were fed to sheep, which were then slaughtered. (At one point, Fort Collins was referred to as "the lamb-feeding capital of the world.") Economic times changed, and by the 1960s the university became the primary economic engine of the city.

Even as Fort Collins grew and expanded, preservationists worked to maintain the original buildings and character in the city. Thanks to the combination of outdoor life and good jobs, the town has been named one of the best places to live and one of the best places to retire in the United States. Unfortunately, flooding has continued to be a part of life in Fort Collins, with both Spring Creek and the Cache La Poudre sometimes overflowing their banks. As of 2020, the population of Fort Collins was 174,000 citizens, with a metro population of 337,000.

Government and Economy

Colorado's economic history is one of struggle and reinvention, as the state has weathered dramatic ups and downs through the years. Fortune seekers, entrepreneurs, thinkers, leaders, and visionaries have long come to Colorado to better themselves or make this place better for others.

The economic sectors that shaped Colorado remain important even as new industries add to the bottom line. In mid-2015, the University of Colorado Leeds School of Business found that the state economy was outpacing the U.S. economy—and tourism is a huge part of that. Investing in the arts is also paying off in Colorado. The Colorado Business Committee for the Arts found that the arts generated $1.9 billion of total economic activity in the Denver metro area's seven counties, which include Boulder, in 2017.

Tourism has been breaking records, and again, outpacing national averages. In 2019, 86.9 million visitors spent $24.2 billion in Colorado. Some of those tourism dollars can be attributed to the legalization of recreational marijuana. The Colorado Department of Revenue reported $2 billion in marijuana sales in 2020, and that doesn't factor in money spent on lodging, dining, beer, and more.

Essentials

Transportation

Transportation 253
Conduct and
Customs 256
Travel Tips 259

GETTING THERE AND AROUND

Air

Denver International Airport (DEN, 303/342-2000, www.flydenver.com), known locally as DIA, is the fifth-busiest airport in the country. The airport's distinctive white-peaked roof has become a symbol of the city—and copied in smaller versions. The airport is 25 miles (40 km) from downtown Denver, and like most airports these days, it's a mall of sorts, too (look for local favorite Root Down). In addition to the shops and restaurants, the airport offers free Wi-Fi

Coronavirus and the Front Range

At the time of writing in fall 2021, the coronavirus pandemic had significantly impacted the United States, including Colorado, and the situation was constantly changing. Be mindful of the evolving situation when planning your trip.

BEFORE YOU GO

- Check local websites (listed below) for updated **local restrictions** and the **overall health status** of destinations in this area.
- If you plan to fly, check with your airline as well as the **Centers for Disease Control and Prevention** (www.cdc.gov) for updated **recommendations** and **requirements.**

RESOURCES

- **State of Colorado:** Colorado Department of Public Health & Environment (https://cdphe.colorado.gov), Colorado State Parks (http://cpw.state.co.us)
- **Denver:** Denver Department of Public Health & Environment (www.denvergov.org/Government/Agencies-Departments-Offices/Public-Health-Environment)
- **Boulder:** Boulder County Public Health (www.bouldercounty.org/departments/public-health)
- **Fort Collins:** Larimer County Department of Health and Environment (www.larimer.org/health)
- **Colorado Springs:** El Paso County Public Health (www.elpasocountyhealth.org)
- **National Park Service:** Rocky Mountain National Park (www.nps.gov/romo)

(303/342-7275 for technical support) and has a **U.S. Post Office** (Level 6, Jeppesen Terminal, Mon.-Sat.), a **USO Center** (303/342-6880), a Jewish and Christian Interfaith Chapel, and an Islamic Masjid, all open 24 hours. Security wait lines can be miserable; try the line leading to Concourse A, then take the elevator to the trains to reach other concourses. Be sure to note your baggage claim number and location, as there are baggage claim carousels on both sides of the terminal, east and west.

DIA is served by most major domestic airlines. **Frontier** (801/401-9000, www.frontierairlines.com), which maintains a hub in Denver, is a low-cost carrier. **Southwest** (800/435-9792, www.southwest.com) has provided some good low-airfare competition, and legacy carriers **United** (800/864-8331, www.united.com) and **American** (800/433-7300, www.aa.com) have many flights daily to and from DIA. International airlines that serve DIA include Aeroméxico, Air Canada, Air France, British Airways, Icelandair, and Lufthansa.

The **Colorado Springs Airport** (COS, 7770 Milton E. Proby Pkwy., Colorado Springs, 719/550-1900, http://flycos.coloradosprings.gov) offers daily nonstop flights to 15 destinations on American, Delta, Frontier, and United.

AIRPORT TRANSPORTATION

It's typically a $55 flat rate to take a cab between DIA and downtown Denver. The **RTD Bus** (303/299-6000, www.rtd-denver.com, $10.50 one-way) is the cheapest transportation.

Previous: Denver's Union Station.

Shuttle vans are available at the airport to take passengers directly to destinations like Vail, Estes Park, and Boulder, and directly to downtown Denver hotels. **Epic Mountain Express** (970/754-7433 or 800/525-6363, www.epicmountainexpress.com) goes to Vail, Aspen, Keystone, Breckenridge, and other ski towns for $49-309; **Estes Park Shuttle** (970/586-5151, www.estesparkshuttle.com) costs $95 round-trip between the airport and Estes Park; and **Super Shuttle** (303/370-1300 or 800/258-3826, www.supershuttle.com) offers door-to-door service with discounts for ride shares. Contact the airport's **Ground Transportation Information Office** (Level 5, Jeppesen Terminal, 303/342-4059, 6:30am-11:30pm daily) for additional information about services.

There are 12 rental car companies based at DIA, and each provides free shuttle service to its rental lot. The rental car agencies also have service counters in the Jeppesen Terminal, Level 5.

There is short- and long-term **parking** at DIA, and it can fill up fast, so leave time for walking in from the economy lots or taking a shuttle from those located off-site. The closest garage parking is $28 per day or $5 per hour, and uncovered parking lots that are still within walking distance of the terminal cost $17 per day or $5 per hour. The west-side parking lots seem to fill up faster than the east side. There are cheaper parking lots that require shuttle bus service to reach, and those cost $8 per day or $2 per hour.

Train

Amtrak (800/872-7245, www.amtrak.com) has arrivals and departures on the California Zephyr route at Denver's **Union Station** (1701 Wynkoop St., 303/592-6712, http://unionstationindenver.com), but there is no further service to Boulder, Fort Collins, or Colorado Springs.

RTD (303/299-6000, www.rtd-denver.com) light rail trains travel from the Denver suburbs to downtown and are packed at rush hour. Regional routes provide service from Denver to Golden, Boulder, and Nederland.

Bus

Greyhound (800/231-2222, www.greyhound.com) runs its service through Denver's **Union Station** (1701 Wynkoop St., 303/592-6712). It also provides service to Fort Collins and Colorado Springs from Denver.

To get around Denver, its suburbs, and other Front Range cities, use **RTD** (1600 Blake St., 303/299-6000, www.rtd-denver.com). The main bus terminal is in the LoDo neighborhood of Denver, behind Union Station; you can pick up schedules for just about every route. RTD provides bus service to and from the airport, Boulder, and many other towns in the greater metro area. City and regional buses are almost always equipped with bike racks in front.

Groome Transportation (719/687-3456, www.groometransportation.com, from $50 pp one-way) provides bus service from DIA to Colorado Springs, Castle Rock, and Monument, south of Denver.

Car

No matter where you are coming from by car, you'll end up on I-70 (east-west across the state) or I-25 (north-south across the state) to get to Denver, Colorado Springs, Fort Collins, and even Boulder. The most unpredictable part of the drive can be I-70 in the mountains, where icy roads, traffic accidents, and rock- and snowslides have all closed the road at one time or another.

Like most midsize to large cities, Denver is plagued by gridlock on the highways that circle much of the city. Light rail trains do not do much to alleviate the rush hour congestion, even though the trains are standing-room-only during those times. Rush hour congestion makes driving from Denver to Fort Collins and Colorado Springs a real challenge. Highway 36 into Boulder added an express lane for those carpooling or willing to pay a fee to travel faster; otherwise it's clogged with traffic, too. Fortunately, it is possible to get around Denver on foot, bicycle, bus, or light rail, with limited expense and hassle.

Check **road conditions** (dial 511 or 303/639-1111, or check www.cotrip.org or www.cdot.gov), especially when driving in winter in the mountains. I find the Twitter account from co.trip.org very helpful during road closures around Colorado.

CAR RENTALS

There are major car rental agencies at the Denver airport (DEN, 303/342-2000, www.flydenver.com) and in downtown Denver, including **Avis** (1900 Broadway, 303/839-1280, www.avis.com, 7am-6pm Mon.-Fri., 8am-3pm Sat., 9am-3pm Sun.), **Enterprise** (2255 Broadway, 303/293-8644, www.enterprise.com, 7am-6pm Mon.-Fri., 8am-4pm Sat.-Sun.), and **Budget** (1980 Broadway, 303/292-9341, www.budget.com, 7am-6pm Mon.-Fri., 8am-2pm Sat., 10am-2pm Sun.).

Car rental agencies are also available at the Colorado Springs Airport (COS, 7770 Milton E. Proby Pkwy., 719/550-1900, http://flycos.coloradosprings.gov) and include **Budget** (719/597-1271) and **Enterprise** (719/591-6644).

Taxis

In the Denver metro area and the Front Range cities, it's almost impossible to walk out to the street and hail a cab. Most hotel entrances will be home to a small fleet of cabs waiting for a fare. Otherwise, it's better to call and wait for the taxi to show up.

Metro Transportation (303/333-3333, https://metrotransportationdenver.com) is Denver's largest taxi company; **Yellow Cab** (303/777-7777, www.denveryellowcab.com) has some hybrid vehicles. In Colorado Springs, try **zTrip** (719/777-7777, www.ztrip.com).

Rideshare companies Lyft and Uber both operate in Colorado.

Biking

Colorado, and especially Denver, is increasingly accommodating to bicyclists, as two-wheeled transportation gets more support as an environmentally friendly alternative to cars. Try **Lyft Bikes** (www.lyft.com) in Denver; **Boulder B-cycle** (http://boulder.bcycle.com) in Boulder has e-bikes; and **PikeRide** (http://downtowncs.com) in Colorado Springs offers rental rides. Many city streets have bicycle lanes, biking paths are common, and city and regional buses (say, those going to Boulder) have bike racks on the front so people can pedal to the bus stop, ride, and then pedal on home or to the office.

Learn about bicycle ordinances, find bike maps, and get riding tips at www.denvergov.org/bikeprogram, or check out www.bikedenver.org, a bicycling advocacy group's blog. The **Denver Bicycle Touring Club** (www.dbtc.org) organizes group rides for members throughout Denver.

Conduct and Customs

GENERAL ETIQUETTE

Don't be surprised at how friendly people are in Colorado, with total strangers smiling and saying hello as they pass on the street. This is also common when out walking or hiking in the mountains, where it's considered normal behavior for people to greet each other with a simple, "Hi, how's it going?" as they pass one another on a trail. It's a great icebreaker for the next question, "How much farther to the top?"

On busy urban pedestrian and bike paths, it is customary for faster bicyclists to shout, "On your left!" (or something similar) as they approach slower cyclists or pedestrians from behind. Some paths are designated for only cyclists or pedestrians, and others are shared use.

Throughout many popular sights in downtown Denver, such as Civic Center Park and along the 16th Street Mall, there are often unhoused people panhandling. As in other cities, this is a complex issue with no ready solutions on the horizons. Back in 2012, the city approved a "camping ban" intended to allow law enforcement to evict anyone caught sleeping in a public place. How and when the law was enforced became controversial and it is now tied up in the courts.

BUSINESS HOURS

Most shops open at 10am Monday-Saturday, but not until noon on Sunday; closing time is usually 5pm to 7pm. Local art galleries tend to close on Sunday-Monday.

Many restaurants also take Monday off, but hours frequently change. Typical kitchen closing time in Denver restaurants is about 10pm, and bars close up by 2am or earlier. If a restaurant has a bar, there is often a late-night menu. Some bars prefer not to specify their closing times so that they can close early on a slow night or extend hours on a busier night.

SMOKING

The Colorado Clean Indoor Air Act bans smoking indoors in public places throughout the state. The Denver City Council has passed more specific ordinances, such as banning smoking outside hospitals. It is not uncommon to see signs outside some buildings asking smokers to stand a certain distance from a building entrance or exit. More common is the sight of restaurant and bar patios—or simply sidewalks in front of these establishments—filled with smokers in any kind of weather. The lone exception is cigar bars, such as the Churchill Bar in The Brown Palace Hotel, where cigar smoking is permitted. There are also designated smoking areas inside the Denver International Airport.

TIPS FOR CANNABIS CONSUMERS

While Colorado might have been first to regulate and sell recreational marijuana, the state is far from a cannabis free-for-all. Following are some tips to keep you safe and on the right side of the law.

Purchasing

Colorado visitors age 21 or older are allowed to *purchase* up to 0.25 ounce at a time from a retail marijuana shop; you may *possess* up to 1 ounce of cannabis in total. What this means is that you cannot purchase the 1-ounce allotment in one place. (Colorado residents may purchase their total 1-ounce allotment in a single store visit.) Typically, you need cash to purchase cannabis products, and ATMs are conveniently on-site in dispensaries.

The cannabis sold in stores has been cultivated into varying degrees of potency. At the high end are "dabs," chemically extracted marijuana concentrates that can boast three to four times the psychoactive punch of raw cannabis. On the low end are marijuana edibles, which may seem like a consumer-friendly way to try cannabis but can take up to several quantities to produce any effect. For expert advice, seek out a knowledgeable "budtender" at the retail dispensary of your choice and ask them to guide you through your first purchase.

Safety

Colorado has set the legal limit of THC (tetrahydrocannabinol) for drivers at 5 nanograms per milliliter of blood. Marijuana impairment can vary widely depending upon a person's metabolism; some users may retain high THC levels in their blood yet not feel impaired, while others may have very low levels and be unsafe to drive. The best advice is to let someone else do the driving. Fortunately, many cannabis tour companies offer this service, such as **Colorado Cannabis Tours** (303/420-8687, www.coloradocannabistours.com) and **My 420 Tours** (855/694-2086, www.my420tours.com). Both are located in the Denver area.

Colorado law forbids driving with open containers of marijuana in your vehicle. Since it's up to law enforcement to determine

A Glossary of Cannabis Terms

- **Buds:** A slang term for marijuana, and why people who work at retail marijuana shops and medical dispensaries are known as "budtenders." A marijuana plant's dried buds are the parts that are consumed medically or recreationally. Other common names for cannabis include herb, flower, and, of course, pot and weed.
- **Concentrates:** An extremely potent form of marijuana produced by chemically extracting the psychoactive components of the marijuana plant. Dabs, as concentrates are also known, can come in several different forms: shatter (flat, clear, and solid), budder (opaque and creamy), and oil (a sticky liquid). Concentrates can be consumed in a variety of ways, most prominently via specially designed "oil rigs."
- **Edibles:** Marijuana-infused food products. According to Colorado law, edibles can pack a maximum of 100 milligrams of THC per package and must be broken up into 10-milligram sections. Edible marijuana metabolizes much slower than smoked or vaporized kinds; it might take several hours to take effect.
- ***Indica:*** One of the two main species of marijuana. Known for a relaxing and calming body high (aka "couch lock"), *indica* is best used at night before going to bed.
- ***Sativa:*** The second main species of marijuana, associated with a more energetic and cerebral high. Many prefer *sativa* for use during the day.
- **Topicals:** Cannabis-infused lotions and creams. These products are believed to help relieve muscle pain but aren't associated with the typical marijuana "high." Some companies produce transdermal skin patches and sublingual tinctures placed under the tongue that are purported to have both psychoactive and medicinal effects.
- **Vaporizers:** Products that vaporize, rather than combust, cannabis, allowing users to consume marijuana without smoking it. Most large and expensive at-home vaporizer machines have given way to portable vaporizers or "vape pens"—small, discreet devices that, depending on the product, can be used with marijuana concentrates or flowers.

what exactly entails an "open container," it's best to transport any marijuana in its original childproof container inside the trunk of your vehicle.

Use and Consumption

Colorado may have legalized adult possession of marijuana, but *public consumption* is still illegal. That means you may partake in Colorado residences and hotel rooms when and where permitted, and in a handful of communities that host private marijuana clubs. Public consumption by any means—including marijuana vape pens and edibles—is illegal in public spaces such as bars, clubs, theaters, restaurants, and most venues. Fines for public consumption can run $999.

Legal Concerns

The purchase and possession of marijuana may be legal within Colorado, but the laws change when traveling beyond the state line. Airline travel is federally regulated, which means your legally obtained cannabis becomes a federal crime as soon as you board the plane home. (Colorado airports have installed marijuana disposal bins; it's best to use them.) So while it may be tempting to bring home a souvenir of your adventures, it's not worth the risk.

Travel Tips

WHAT TO PACK

Colorado dresses casual, so don't worry about bringing formal wear unless you are coming for a black-tie event. Even The Brown Palace's stately Palace Arms restaurant in Denver has given up its jacket-and-tie policy, though an evening gown and tuxedo would not look out of place. Jeans, slacks, T-shirts, and sandals are all worn to four-star restaurants.

Finally, a place to acceptably wear that bolo tie! Denver and a couple of other Western cities are about the only places I've seen officials—governors, mayors, and the like—donning cowboy boots, hats, and decorative bolo ties for work. If you've got one, throw it in the suitcase and drive up to The Fort in Morrison for a Western dinner like no other.

You can easily buy the basics—hat, sunscreen, sunglasses, good walking or hiking shoes, thermal underwear—needed for any season in every neighborhood. A small backpack or other tote bag is handy to have for carrying extra water, sunscreen, and snacks on sightseeing walks or if you choose to hike in the nearby foothills.

VISITOR INFORMATION

The official State of Colorado website (www.colorado.gov) has a lot of helpful information, a place to ask questions, and resources for tourism, government, education, and more. The **Colorado Tourism Office** (www.colorado.com) has Colorado Welcome Centers at roadside spots around the state. The closest to Denver is in Morrison at Red Rocks Amphitheatre. You can also order a free vacation guide from the website.

Visit Denver (1555 California St., Suite 300, Denver, 800/233-6837, www.denver.org), the Convention & Visitors Bureau, has a public visitors center where you can pick up bags full of brochures and maps and ask lots of questions. They also have a visitors center at Denver International Airport.

Area Codes and Time Zones

There are three area codes used throughout the greater Denver metro area: 303, 720, and 983. The area code in Colorado Springs is 719, and the area code in Fort Collins is 970. Always dial the entire 10-digit phone number, including the area code, even for local calls.

Colorado follows daylight saving time, so it is either on mountain standard time or mountain daylight time.

Newspapers and Periodicals

The ***Denver Post*** (www.denverpost.com) continues to print a daily newspaper, but there are regular layoffs and it has become steadily thinner. Go online to read ***The Colorado Sun*** (https://coloradosun.com), a news outlet started in 2018 by many reporters and editors from the former *Rocky Mountain News*.

Even though the physical size of the alternative weekly, ***Westword*** (www.westword.com), also keeps shrinking, the voice is still big and strong, thanks largely to longtime editor Patricia Calhoun, who knows Denver inside out. *Westword* magazine is free and can be picked up at businesses all over town. The weekly event listings can be really helpful when looking for something fun to do.

The monthly ***5280 Magazine*** (pronounced "fifty-two eighty," www.5280.com) is a glossy magazine that has a mix of serious news, restaurant reviews, and very popular "Best Of" issues on topics from food to doctors.

Boulder has ***The Daily Camera*** newspaper (www.dailycamera.com), Colorado Springs has the ***Colorado Springs Gazette*** (https://gazette.com), and Fort Collins has ***The Coloradoan*** (www.coloradoan.com). ***NoCo Style*** (https://nocostyle.com) is a fun magazine for the Northern Colorado scene, and ***Colorado Springs Magazine*** (www.coloradospringsmag.com) covers all things millennial and more in its glossy pages.

Maps

There are maps of downtown available for free at the shuttle bus stops on each block of the 16th Street Mall. **Visit Denver** (www.denver.org) has maps of area attractions and accommodations available for download from the website. You can also find maps, atlases, and gazetteers at any **Tattered Cover Book Store** location (www.tatteredcover.com), or at office supply stores.

VISAS AND OFFICIALDOM

To enter the United States, visitors from other countries must have a valid passport and a visa, except for Canada, Bermuda, and countries eligible for the U.S. government's Visa Waiver Program. This program allows tourists from many countries to visit without a visa for up to 90 days. To check if your country is on the list, go to http://travel.state.gov. To qualify, you must apply online with the Electronic System for Travel Authorization at www.cbp.gov and hold a return ticket to your country of origin dated less than 90 days from your date of entry. Even with a waiver, you still need to bring your passport and present it at the port of entry.

HEALTH AND SAFETY

Whether staying in Denver, Boulder, Fort Collins, or Colorado Springs or venturing up into the mountains, prevention is the key to warding off a few common local illnesses.

The altitude affects everyone differently, and increases can be subtle, especially when driving or even hiking. Mild symptoms of fatigue, dizziness, headache, nausea, and nosebleeds can develop into a more serious illness. It's best to drink extra water and rest frequently. The body eventually acclimates to the decreased oxygen.

You're simply closer to the sun at high altitudes, so sunscreen (for lips too) is a must, and hats and sunglasses are generally a good idea for adults and kids. Even on overcast days or on snowy slopes, you can get sunburned.

Bring your own water or water purification tablets with you while hiking, because you risk getting giardia from drinking infected river or lake water. This intestinal illness causes nausea, cramps, and diarrhea.

For medical or fire emergencies, or to reach the police in an emergency, dial **911.** For issues that are not life-threatening, contact the **Denver Police/Fire/Paramedics Communication Center** (720/913-2000), the **Rocky Mountain Poison and Drug Center** (303/739-1123 or 800/222-1222), or **Metro Denver Crimestoppers** (720/913-7867).

Leave No Trace

The city of Denver has a **Keep Denver Beautiful** plan (311 hotline, 311@ci.denver.co.us, www.denvergov.org) that promotes the message to not litter, period—this includes anything from cigarette butts to food wrappers and drink containers. Littering is illegal and fines can add up to $1,000.

While Denver's laws apply to city streets as well as parks and bike paths, there are additional rules and customs to follow once you set off to explore the mountains.

For starters, always stay on designated trails or pathways to minimize your impact on the natural areas that make the area so appealing in the first place. You may even see signs that read Closed for Restoration in areas that have been trampled by heavy use. These designated trails—whether they are mere dirt footpaths or paved with concrete or asphalt—will also prevent you from getting lost. As people try to explore true wilderness more and more, either by going out of bounds on a ski mountain or breaking their own trail on a summer hike, officials are becoming less patient and understanding because of the high cost of search and rescue. For this same reason, it's a good idea to always let someone know where you are headed when you go out for a run, bike ride, or hike.

Even if you are just going on a short day hike in the foothills, remember to "pack out what you pack in" and don't leave *any* waste. In some places, even city parks in the foothills of Boulder, you will find special garbage cans that are designed to keep animals (particularly bears) out, but otherwise you need to be prepared to carry out all garbage.

Because of the dry conditions, especially along the Front Range, be extremely cautious about making campfires. During intense drought seasons, fires of any kind are banned, so it's best to check with park rangers on the latest conditions and warnings in the specific park you are visiting. If fires are not banned, still use caution and only build a fire in an established campfire ring, and be sure to put out the fire completely before leaving.

For more information, visit the **Leave No Trace Center** (303/442-8222, www.lnt.org).

Wildlife

Wildlife and people interact more and more in the foothill communities, where mountain lions, bears, deer, and elk will just show up in backyards and even on busy town streets. This is just a reminder that you should never feed wildlife—whether in the confines of a national park or in someone's backyard. State and national park visitors centers always have helpful information about how to react when you encounter wildlife, which is species-specific and depends on mating seasons. Use special care if you are with small children or dogs when hiking, as they are easier prey for hungry wildlife.

Wildlife and pets, especially dogs, are not a good mix. Be sure to verify if dogs are even allowed at the park you are visiting and what the leash laws are.

ACCESS FOR TRAVELERS WITH DISABILITIES

Many trails and facilities in **Colorado State Parks** (303/866-3437, http://cpw.state.co.us) are designed for and welcome people in wheelchairs. Nature lovers in Denver can enjoy most of the **Denver Botanic Gardens** (1005 York St., 720/865-3500, www.botanicgardens.org) on the facility's wide, smooth concrete pathways. The gardens also have complimentary wheelchairs available.

There is a theater group in Denver called the **Physically Handicapped Actors and Musical Artists League** (PHAMALY, 303/575-0005, www.phamaly.org) that performs a few times a year in the Denver area and at the Denver Center for the Performing Arts. The group was formed in 1989, when physically disabled acting students became frustrated with the lack of parts available to them.

Five companies offer wheelchair transportation service from Denver International Airport and elsewhere around Denver. RTD's **Access-a-Ride** (303/292-6560, www.rtd-denver.com) is for people who cannot board a wheelchair-equipped bus. Metro and regional RTD buses—including the free shuttles on the 16th Street Mall—are wheelchair accessible. Both **Metro Taxi** (303/333-3333, www.metrotransportationdenver.com) and **Yellow Cab** (303/777-7777, www.denveryellowcab.com) have wheelchair-accessible vehicles available for passengers.

TRAVELING WITH CHILDREN

There are many fun attractions and things to do with young kids in Colorado, but it's a good idea to ask about age limits at local museums and hotels. For example, Denver's Kirkland Museum does not allow any children under the age of 13 with or without an adult, and children ages 13-17 must be accompanied by an adult. While the Molly Brown House Museum in Denver states that children are welcome, they are asked not to touch *anything,* which is hardly fun for a toddler. (Grown-ups have to follow the same rules.)

Of course, the Children's Museum of Denver is a perfect place to play with kids, newborn through age eight, and the Platte Valley Trolley, which makes a stop outside the museum, is fun for adults and children. The Denver Art Museum has built a variety of child-friendly activities into its permanent exhibits, as well as a small make-your-own-art area. At the Denver Museum of Nature & Science, kids can watch an IMAX movie on the enormous screen, see the stars and planets at the Gates Planetarium, watch volunteers clean off dinosaur bones, step inside replicas of original Native American homes, or pretend to be astronauts. The Denver Zoo appeals to children of any age who like animals. Check ahead to see what's on the schedule for families and kids at the History Colorado Center and the Denver Public Library, where there are different themes monthly.

Some of the best parks with playgrounds for kids include Washington Park, Cheesman Park, and City Park, and there is a playground at the Children's Museum. City Park also has paddleboats in the summer. In the winter, there is sledding at Commons Park.

Sometimes kids just like to be outside where they can run free, such as at the Denver Botanic Gardens and Commons Park, where there aren't any playgrounds.

Visit **Denver's Family Guide** (www.denverkids.com) to find coupons for various classes and attractions, or pick up ***Colorado Parent Magazine*** (www.coloradoparent.com) to get information on local classes and events.

LGBTQ TRAVELERS

Denver is a fairly supportive place for gay, lesbian, bisexual, and transgender people, with many organizations, events, and businesses geared toward this population. In 2008, anti-discrimination laws were expanded to protect against discrimination based on sexual orientation in the workplace and beyond.

For more information on the local LGBTQ scene, check out the **Colorado LGBTQ Chamber of Commerce** (http://colgbtqcc.org) or **The Center** (www.lgbtqcolorado.org), which puts on the annual two-day Pridefest event. ***Out Front Colorado*** (www.outfrontmagazine.com) is a free weekly paper available all over the city.

TRAVELERS OF COLOR

Though the population of the Front Range is diversifying, it remains predominantly white. Of the region's four major cities, the Denver metro area is the most diverse.

In Denver, 80.9% of the population identify as white (54.9% non-Hispanic white), 29.3% Hispanic, 9.8% Black, and 4.1% Asian. The percentages are smaller for members of other groups, including American Indian/Native Alaskan and Native Hawaiian/Pacific Islander.

In Boulder, 90% of the population identify as white (77.4% non-Hispanic white), 14% Hispanic, 5% Asian, and 1.2% Black.

In Fort Collins, 88.3% of the population identify as white (79.6% non-Hispanic White), 11.6% Hispanic, 3.5% Asian, and 1.6% Black.

In Colorado Springs, 78.5% of the population identify as white (68.6% non-Hispanic white), 17.6% Hispanic, 6.5% Black, and 2.9% Asian.

Denver's diverse communities have infused the city with their cultural influences and celebrations. The Black American West Museum & Heritage Center and the Blair-Caldwell African American Research Library in the historic Five Points neighborhood offer a chance to learn more about Black history in Colorado. A visit to the Museo de las Americas in the Santa Fe Arts District can be followed by taking in a performance at Su Teatro Cultural and Performing Arts Center. The city's Cinco de Mayo festival is one of the largest in the country. Each June, the Cherry Blossom Festival in downtown's Sakura Square celebrates Japanese American culture, and in July the Dragon Boat Festival at Sloan's Lake highlights Asian American and Pacific Islander communities with food, dance, and of course boat races.

Visit Denver has put together several resources that showcase the city's diversity (www.denver.org/about-denver/diverse-denver), including webpages titled Denver's African American Culture and Hispanic Denver.

If you're looking for businesses owned by

members of the BIPOC community in the Denver area, consult these resources: **Denver Little Black Book** (https://denverblackpages.com), **Colorado Hispanic Chamber of Commerce** (www.hispanicchamberdenver.com/business-directory), **Asian Chamber of Commerce Colorado** (www.acccolorado.org), and **Rocky Mountain Indian Chamber of Commerce** (https://rmicc.org).

TRAVELING WITH PETS

While Denver is quite pet friendly, there is less love in the public sector. In most public places, dogs are required to be on a leash, and there are fines for not complying with this rule. For a list of off-leash dog parks in Denver and other Colorado cities, visit **Dog Parks in Denver** (www.dogparksindenver.com), which includes detailed directions, hours, and rules. Owners are required to clean up after their dogs; Dogipot receptacles are conveniently located near popular parks and walkways for disposing of those little plastic baggies.

There is a small enclosed area for pet exercise at Denver International Airport (www.flydenver.com), but keep in mind it is off the main terminal, and travelers must go through security again to get back to their concourse.

ALTERNATIVE LODGING

Short-term rentals in private residences are widely available in Denver and other cities along the Front Range. For years, short-term rentals were illegal in Denver, but there was no enforcement and they were widespread. In late 2017, a law was passed to require licensure and limit these rentals to the owner's primary residence, such as a carriage house, mother-in-law apartment, etc. This change led to a decrease in people renting out second homes in the area. There is increased enforcement of the new law, with fines and penalties for those who rent out properties that aren't their primary residence. In general, rates on these types of rentals are competitive with local hotels and, as in other cities, you trade some perks, such as complimentary breakfast or fitness facilities, when you rent privately.

Resources

Suggested Reading

HISTORY

Abbott, Carl, Stephen J. Leonard, and Thomas J. Noel. *Colorado: A History of the Centennial State*, 4th ed. Denver, CO: University Press of Colorado, 2005. Tom Noel, a history professor at the University of Colorado at Denver, is nicknamed "Dr. Colorado" for his bottomless well of knowledge of all things Denver and Colorado.

Brosnan, Kathleen A. *Uniting Mountain and Plain: Urbanization, Law and Environmental Change along the Front Range*. Albuquerque, NM: University of New Mexico Press, 2002. This was the first book by University of Houston professor Kathleen Brosnan, who specializes in environmental and Western history.

Garnsey, Georgia, and Mary Motian-Meadows. *The Murals of Colorado: Walls that Speak*. Denver, CO: Bower House Books, 2012. Learn about Colorado history through colorful murals.

Goodstein, Phil. *Denver in Our Time: A People's History of the Mile High City*. Denver, CO: New Social Publications, 1999. Goodstein has written several books about Denver, most with a specific neighborhood or topic focus, but this one gives a more general overview.

Leonard, Stephen J., and Thomas J. Noel. *Denver: Mining Camp to Metropolis*. Denver, CO: University Press of Colorado, 1989. A precursor to the larger *Colorado: A History of the Centennial State* by the same authors, and just as packed with facts.

Noel, Thomas J., and Cathleen M. Norman. *A Pikes Peak Partnership: The Penroses and the Tutts*. Denver, CO: University Press of Colorado, 2001. The story of two families and the development of Colorado Springs and the Pikes Peak area, including Spencer Penrose, the man behind The Broadmoor.

Sprague, Marshall. *Colorado: A Bicentennial History*. New York: W. W. Norton, 1976. A brief history of the state of Colorado.

Stephens, Ronald J., and La Wanna M. Larson. *African Americans of Denver (Images of America: Colorado)*. Mount Pleasant, SC: Arcadia Publishing, 2008. Learn more about the African Americans who came to Denver and Colorado and their impact on the city and state through the years. Author La Wanna M. Larson is the curator of Denver's Black American West Museum.

Wyckoff, William. *Creating Colorado: The Making of a Western American Landscape, 1860-1940*. New Haven, CT: Yale University Press, 1999. Montana State University geography professor Wyckoff includes maps and historical photographs to illustrate his unique environmental telling of Colorado history.

TRAVEL AND RECREATION GUIDES

Berman, Joshua. *Moon Colorado Camping,* 6th ed. Berkeley, CA: Avalon Travel, 2020. Go beyond the skyscrapers of downtown Denver and get out under the stars for a few nights in a tent with the handy maps and insightful descriptions found in this book.

English, Erin. *Moon Rocky Mountain National Park,* 2nd ed. Berkeley, CA: Avalon Travel, 2020. Plan a whole trip to this national park just an hour's drive from Denver.

Fielder, John. *John Fielder's Best of Colorado.* Boulder, CO: Westcliffe Publishers, 2002. John Fielder is a local photographer whose images make this hefty guidebook as interesting to look at as it is to read.

Irwin, Pamela, with David Irwin. *Colorado's Best Wildflower Hikes, Volume I: The Front Range.* Boulder, CO: Westcliffe Publishers, 1998. These wildflower hikes invite people of any fitness level to hike with a purpose.

Sink, Mindy. *60 Hikes within 60 Miles of Denver and Boulder,* 3rd ed. Birmingham, AL: Menasha Ridge Press, 2020. Find hiking trails for all levels within a one-hour drive of Denver and Boulder.

Internet Resources

COLORADO

Bicycle Colorado

www.bicyclecolorado.org

This website offers free online cycling maps and also sells printed copies.

bikepaths.com

www.bikepaths.com

A great selection of less-traveled trails, a calories-burned calculator, and a list of regional cycling events. The creator of the site has moved out of Colorado, but much of the information remains valuable.

Colorado Tourism Office

www.colorado.com

Whether you are a resident in search of a "daycation" or coming for a longer stay, be sure to check out this site for vacation ideas and travel values.

The Passport Program

www.thepassportprogram.com

For about $20, this passport gets you 2-for-1 drinks at participating bars and restaurants during the summer months. Passports are available for Denver, Boulder, Fort Collins, and Colorado Springs.

Pikes Peak Country Attractions

www.pikes-peak.com/blog

Want to explore the outdoors around Colorado Springs but aren't sure where to go? Check this blog for ideas.

State of Colorado

www.colorado.gov

What isn't on this website? You can get a hunting or fishing license, learn about avalanche conditions, view maps, buy a state park pass, and much more.

DENVER

Bike Denver

www.denvergov.org/bikeprogram

These websites portray bicycling not just as a sport but as a movement and a way of life. Each includes general information about advocacy for bicycling in Denver, ordinances, and maps.

City of Denver
www.denvergov.org
The city's website is fairly easy to navigate and includes helpful options like the 311 option for city services and signing up for street-sweeping-day parking alerts. Look for the Bike Maps link to plan a two-wheeled excursion or route.

Denver Beer Trail
www.denver.org/restaurants/denver-bars-clubs/denver-beer-trail
Sure, it's kind of a gimmick, but how else are you going to choose which brewery to go to first? This map breaks down your options by neighborhood so you can walk, scooter, or bike between each brewpub easily.

Denver Infill
www.denverinfill.com
Find out how Denver is growing *in* with infill projects where there were once industrial sites or parking lots.

Denver She Wrote
http://denvershewrote.com
Kimberly Irwin has one of my favorite local Instagram accounts, where she shares the latest places she has eaten a wonderful meal or stayed overnight around Denver.

Eat Drink Denver
www.denver.org/restaurants/denver-dining
Visit Denver's guide to the latest in eating and drinking in the Mile High City.

Eater Denver
www.denver.eater.com
Keeping up with the hottest restaurants in Denver and Boulder is a monthly sport. Stay tuned to this site for the places that are coming, going, and still worth it.

5280
www.5280.com
The monthly *5280 Magazine* has in-depth articles, plus regular "Top of the Town" issues with lists of favorite restaurants and more in Denver.

Gabby Gourmet
www.gabbygourmet.com
A radio show food critic now has a website with reviews, photos, and "find of the month" restaurant listings.

Greenprint Denver
www.denvergov.org/sustainability
An interesting look at the whole concept of a "sustainable city" and what plans are in the works to make Denver more "green."

Metro Denver Economic Development Corporation
www.metrodenver.org
An affiliate of the Denver Metro Chamber of Commerce, the Metro Denver EDC has a lot of statistical data for the seven-county area. Request a *Denver Relocation Guide* if you are a newcomer or are considering relocating to the area.

Regional Transportation District
www.rtd-denver.com
Not only can you find bus and light rail schedules and fare information, but the Regional Transportation District (RTD) website also has a trip-planning feature to help you figure out your mass-transit route.

Visit Denver
www.denver.org
This Convention & Visitors Bureau website is designed for tourists, locals, and yes, conventioneers. The site is loaded with facts, and it can help with finding hotels, restaurants, and upcoming events.

Westword
www.westword.com
Find out about the latest events around town and check out the annual Best Of lists, as well as restaurant reviews.

BOULDER

Downtown Boulder

www.boulderdowntown.com/blog

Handy and insightful content for both locals and tourists on what to do if you're in town for an Ironman competition or looking for deals on a sidewalk sale.

COLORADO SPRINGS

City of Colorado Springs

http://coloradosprings.gov

The official website of the city of Colorado Springs, with maps, business listings, and transportation information.

FORT COLLINS

Fort Collins Magazine

http://fortcollinsmag.com

It's the 5280 of Fort Collins, with articles on local happenings and how national issues are being felt locally.

Visit Fort Collins

www.visitftcollins.com/category/fort-collins-blog

On the official website for the city, the blog is regularly updated with seasonal travel tips for this area.

CANNABIS TOURISM

City of Denver Marijuana Information

www.denvergov.org/Government/Departments/Marijuana-Information

It's legal, but you need to know the laws about buying and using marijuana within the city of Denver.

Colorado Pot Guide

www.coloradopotguide.com

Touted as a practical guide for the marijuana enthusiast visiting Colorado.

Leafly

www.leafly.com

Information on strains of marijuana and the ability to search where to buy locally.

Weedmaps

www.weedmaps.com

Just look for the little green leaf to find a dispensary near you.

Index

A

Academy Riding Stables: 21, 228
accessibility: 261
Aggie Theatre: 188
air travel: 253-255
Ale House: 69
Alpine Visitors Center: 176
American Museum of Western Art: 29
America the Beautiful Park: 216
Anne U. White Trail: 158
aquatic park: 131
area codes: 259
Armstrong Hotel: 22, 203
Arthur's Rock Trail: 198
Art in Public Places Program: 184
art tours, Denver: 37
Auraria Campus: 38-39
auto travel: 255-256
Avenir Museum of Design and Merchandising: 183
Avery Brewing: 19, 145
Avery House: 180-181
Avogadro's Number: 22, 189
Avuncular Bob's Beerhouse: 185
Axe and the Oak Distillery: 219
Axe and the Oak Whiskey House: 219

B

Ball Arena: 76
Barr Trail: 226, 241
Barry Goldwater Visitor Center: 216
Bear Lake: 177
Beaver Meadows Visitors Center: 174, 175
beer/breweries: general discussion 19; Boulder 145; Colorado Springs 218-219, 230; Denver 12, 65-66, 68-69, 80-81, 130, 132; Fort Collins 185, 187, 188, 190, 195
Beer Spa, The: 19, 66
bicycling: general discussion 20, 21, 256; Boulder 154, 156, 170; Colorado Springs 224-225; Denver 39, 42, 57, 92-93, 94, 97, 98, 131, 133; Fort Collins 188, 190, 194-195
Biennial of the Americas: 81
Bierstadt Lagerhaus: 19, 65
Big Blue Bear: 18, 29
Bighorn Sheep Day: 222
birds/bird-watching: Boulder 154, 169; Colorado Springs 220, 222, 225, 226; Denver 39, 53; Fort Collins 194, 195
Birney Car 21: 181, 183
Black American West Museum & Heritage Center: 29-30, 32
Black Cat Farm: 161
Black Project Spontaneous & Wild Ales: 66
Blair-Caldwell African American Research Library: 58, 78
Blossoms of Light: 82
Bluebird Theater: 29, 63
boating: Denver 97, 98; Fort Collins 195, 197
Boettcher Concert Hall: 73
Bohemian Nights at NewWestFest: 190
BolderBOULDER: 148
botanical gardens: 47
Boulder: 136-168; maps 138, 141
Boulder Ballet: 148
Boulder Canyon: 21, 158
Boulder County Farmers Market: 18, 140, 141
Boulder Creek: 149, 154, 159
Boulder Creek Bike Path: 20, 154
Boulder Creek Festival: 149
Boulder Flatirons: 20, 157, 158
Boulder History Museum: 140
Boulder International Fringe Festival: 149
Boulder Museum of Contemporary Art: 140-141
Boulder Reservoir: 159
Boulder Theater: 148
Boulder, vicinity of: 169-174; map 170
Bradford Washburn American Mountaineering Museum: 127-128
Brainard Lake Recreation Area: 21, 173
Bristol Brewery & Pub: 19, 230
Broadmoor, The: 23, 209, 223, 236
Broadmoor Manitou & Pikes Peak Cog Railway, The: 241
Brown Palace Hotel, The: 32
Buff, The: 22, 160
Buffalo Bill Museum and Grave: 128
Bug Theatre: 76, 77
Buntport Theater: 74
business hours: 257
bus travel: 255
Byers-Evans House: 33

C

Cache La Poudre: 21, 198
Cadet Chapel: 216
cannabis/cannabis dispensaries: general discussion 257-258; Boulder 145, 147; Colorado Springs 219-220, 243; Denver 69-71; Fort Collins 188

Canyon Concert Ballet: 189
Capitol Hill: 29, 45-49, 51-53; map 48-49
Carousel of Happiness: 172
car travel: 255-256
Cathedral Basilica of the Immaculate Conception: 45-46
Cattail Ponds at the Boulder County Fairgrounds: 156
Cave of the Winds Mountain Park: 238
Celestial Seasonings: 141
Celtic on Market, The: 66
Centennial Gardens Park: 28, 39, 42
Center for Colorado Women's History: 33
Center for Visual Art: 74
Challenge Unlimited: 224
Chateau Historic Melodrama Theatre: 243
Chautauqua: 18, 20, 141, 143, 154, 157
Cheesman Park: 97
Cherry Creek Arts Festival: 78
Cherry Creek Bike Path: 20, 94
Cherryvale Trail: 158
Cheyenne Cañon Hummingbird Experience: 220
Cheyenne Mountain Zoo: 211
Chico Basin Ranch: 225
children, traveling with: 261-262
Children's Museum of Denver: 42
City and County Building: 34
City Park: 29, 45-49, 51-53, 78; map 48-49
Civic Center Park: 17, 33-35
Clear Creek History Park: 128
Clear Creek Whitewater Park: 21, 131
Cleo Parker Robinson Dance: 73
climate: 247
climbing: general discussion 20-21; Boulder 153, 157, 158-159, 169, 177; Colorado Springs 218, 226, 228; Denver 94; Fort Collins 197
Clyfford Still Museum: 35
Colfax Marathon: 81
color, travelers of: 262-263
Colorado Avalanche (hockey): 95
Colorado Ballet: 75
Colorado Brewers' Festival: 190
Colorado MahlerFest: 149
Colorado Marathon: 189-190
Colorado Mountain Brewery: 230
Colorado Mountain School: 158
Colorado Music Festival: 149
Colorado Rockies (baseball): 95
Colorado School of Mines: 128-129
Colorado Shakespeare Festival: 22, 143, 149
Colorado Springs: 207-238; map 210
Colorado Springs, vicinity of: 238-245
Colorado Springs Fine Arts Center: 23, 209, 211
Colorado Springs Philharmonic: 220
Colorado Springs Pioneers Museum: 211
Colorado State Capitol: 17, 34, 46-47
Colorado State University: 183
Colorado Symphony Orchestra: 73
Colorado Veterans Memorial: 34
Columbine Trail: 226
Comedy Brewers at Bas Bleu Theatre Company: 185
Comedy Fort, The: 185
Comedy Works: 75
Commons Park: 18, 28, 42, 95
Conference on World Affairs: 143, 149
Confluence Park: 93, 94
Coopersmith's Pub & Brewing: 185
Coors Brewing Company: 19, 130
Coors Field: 17, 28, 42, 44
Coppermuse Distillery: 185
Corner Bar, The: 22, 144
coronavirus: 254
Corral Center Mountain Bike Park: 194
country-and-western clubs: Colorado Springs 219; Denver 62-63
Crawford Hotel: 17, 121
Crooked Stave Friends & Family Taproom: 187
cross-country skiing: general discussion 21; Boulder 173; Denver 133
Curfman Gallery: 183
Curtis Park: 29

D

Dairy Center for the Arts: 148
David Cook Fine Art: 75
Denver: 24-127; maps 26-27, 30, 34, 40-41, 48-49
Denver Art Museum: 17, 28, 35, 37
Denver Arts Week: 81
Denver Beer Company: 68
Denver Beer Trail: 19, 65
Denver Beer Week: 19, 80
Denver Botanic Gardens: 17, 47
Denver Broncos (football): 29, 95
Denver Center for the Performing Arts (DCPA): 72
Denver Chalk Art Festival: 78
Denver Cherry Blossom Festival: 78
Denver Cinco de Mayo celebration: 77
Denver International Airport: 17, 124-125, 253-255
Denver International Film Festival: 81
Denver March Powwow: 77
Denver Museum of Nature & Science: 29, 46, 47, 51
Denver Nuggets (basketball): 95
Denver Performing Arts Complex (DPAC): 72
Denver Pridefest: 78
Denver Public Library: 18, 37-38
Denver Skatepark: 95
Denver St. Patrick's Day Parade: 77
Denver Zoo: 29, 46, 52
Dikeou Collection: 32
disabilities, travelers with: 261
distilleries: Boulder 145; Colorado Springs 219; Denver 68; Fort Collins 185, 187

DNVR Bar, The: 68
Doors Open Denver: 80
Downtown Boulder Fall Fest: 149
Downtown Denver: 29-30, 32-33; map 30
Downtown Festival of Lights: 190
Dragon Boat Festival: 80, 97
Dream Lake: 177
Dushanbe Teahouse: 18, 143, 159

E

Eben G. Fine Park: 154
economy: 252
Edward C. Rochette Money Museum: 214
1830s Rendezvous and Spanish Colonial Art Market: 80
Eldorado Canyon State Park: 169-170, 172
Eldorado Canyon Trail: 170
Eldorado Springs: 169-170, 172
Eldorado Springs Pool: 172
Eldora Mountain Resort: 21, 173
Elizabeth Hotel: 22, 204
Ellie Caulkins Opera House: 72
Emerald Lake: 177
Emma Crawford Coffin Races: 243
Emmanuel Gallery: 39
Emporium, The: 22, 200
environmental issues: 248
Environmental Learning Center: 195
Estes Park Aerial Tramway: 175
etiquette: 256-257
eTown: 148

F

Fair Winds Hot Air Balloon Flights: 21, 154
Fall River Visitors Center: 174
Ferril Lake: 97
Fillmore Auditorium: 76
Fine Arts Theatre School: 220
First Bite: Boulder Restaurant Week: 150, 159
fish/fishing: Boulder 156, 159, 169; Denver 97, 98; Fort Collins 197
Fiske Planetarium: 144
5 Green Boxes: 17, 91, 121
Five Points: 29, 78
Flagstaff Mountain: 20, 157
Flagstaff Nature Center: 157
Flatirons: 20, 157, 158
FoCoMX: 189
food halls: 106
Foodie Walk Fort Collins: 189
food/restaurants: 12
Foothills Art Center: 129-130
Fort, The: 114
Fort Collins: 178-205; map 181
Fort Collins Gallery Walk: 189
Fort Collins Museum of Art: 22, 183
Fort Collins Museum of Discovery: 183
Fort Collins Symphony Orchestra: 189
Fossil Creek Trail: 194
Fourth of July Trail: 173
420: 147
Fowler Trail: 169
Fox Theatre, The: 148
Frasca: 18, 162
free admission days: 51
Frozen Dead Guy Days: 22, 172

G

Garden of Lights: 190
Garden of the Gods: 11, 20, 21, 22, 212, 226
Garden of the Gods Loop: 226
Garden of the Gods Park: 225
Gardens on Spring Creek: 183-184
Garner Galleria Theatre: 72
Gem Lake: 177
geography: 247
Glen Eyrie: 212
Goat Patch Brewing Company: 218
Golda Meir House: 39
Golden: 127-133; map 129
Golden City Brewery: 132
Golden Gate Canyon State Park: 131
Golden History Center: 130
Golden Triangle: 28, 33-35, 37-38; map 34
golf: Colorado Springs 225; Denver 97, 131; Fort Collins 197
government: 252
Grand Illumination: 82
Grasmere Lake: 98
Grawlix, The: 76
Great American Beer Festival: 19, 80-81
Great Divide Brewing Company: 19, 68
Greater Denver: 53-55, 57; map 54-55
Great Stupa of Dharmakaya: 205-206
Greek Theatre: 34
Greenbelt Plateau Trail: 154
Gregory Allicar Museum of Art: 183
Gregory Canyon: 157
Greyrock Mountain Trail: 197

H

health and safety: 254, 260-261
health clubs: 93
Helen Bonfils Theatre Complex: 72
Helen Hunt Falls: 226
Heritage Center: 144
Highlands: 28, 63-65; map 64
Highlands Square Street Fair: 78
High Peaks Art Festival: 173
hiking: general discussion 20; Boulder 13, 141,

156-158, 169-170, 172, 173, 176-177; Colorado Springs 226, 228, 241, 244; Denver 53, 98, 130-131, 133; Fort Collins 195, 197-198
history: 248-252
History Colorado Center: 18, 38
Holzwarth Historic Site: 176
horseback riding: general discussion 21; Boulder 154, 158, 170, 177; Colorado Springs 225, 226, 228; Denver 133; Fort Collins 198
Horsetooth Falls Trail: 198
Horsetooth Mountain Open Space: 194, 198
Horsetooth Reservoir: 195, 197
hot-air balloons: general discussion 21; Boulder 154; Colorado Springs 224; Fort Collins 194
Hotel Boulderado: 18, 167

IJK

ice-skating: 93, 133
Indian Market and Ceremonial Dance: 77
Indian Peaks Wilderness Area: 173
Institute for Western American Art: 35
itineraries: 17-23
Ivywild: 230
Jeep tours: 228
Jones Theatre: 72
Julie Penrose Fountain: 216
Juneteenth (Denver): 78
kayaking/rafting: general discussion 21; Boulder 159; Denver 93, 94-95, 98, 131; Fort Collins 198-199
Kids in the Park: 189
Kilstrom Theatre: 72
Kirkland Museum of Fine & Decorative Art: 38
Kitchen, The (Boulder): 18, 160
Kitchen, The (Denver): 17, 103

L

Lake Haiyaha: 177
Larimer County Fair & Rodeo: 190
Larimer County Farmers Market: 189
Larimer Square: 44
Leave No Trace: 260-261
Levitt Pavilion Denver: 76
LGBTQ travelers: 262
License No. 1: 22, 144
Lily Lake (Rocky Mountain National Park): 176
Lily Pond (Washington Park): 98
Lincoln Center: 188
Lincoln Park: 28, 33-35, 37-38; map 34
Lindenmeier Overlook: 198
Little Man Ice Cream: 18, 29, 112
lodging, alternative: 263
LoDo (Lower Downtown): 28, 38-42, 44-45; map 40-41
LoHi (Lower Highlands): 28, 65, 111
Lookout Mountain Nature Center and Preserve: 130
Lory State Park: 20, 21, 194, 197, 198
Lost Lake Trail: 173
Loveland: 134
Lucile's Creole Café: 18, 160

M

Manitou Cliff Dwellings: 238
Manitou Incline: 20, 244
Manitou Springs: 23, 238-239, 241, 243-245; map 239
Manitou Springs Great Fruitcake Toss: 243
maps and tourist information: 260
Matthews/Winters Park: 130
May Natural History Museum: 212
McAllister House Museum: 212, 214
Meow Wolf: 71
Mercantile: 17, 104, 121
Midtown Arts Center: 189
Mile High Spirits: 68
Mill Creek Link Trail: 194
Millennium Bridge: 18, 44
Millibo Art Theatre: 220
mineral springs: 239
Mines Museum of Earth Science: 129
Mining Exchange, The: 23, 236
Miramont Castle Museum: 241
Mishawaka Amphitheatre: 189
Mission Ballroom, The: 73
Molly Brown House Museum: 52-53
Moraine Park Discovery Center: 175
Mountain Sun Pub & Brewery: 18, 19, 145
Mt. Sanitas Trail: 157-158
Museo de las Americas: 73
Museum of Contemporary Art Denver: 28, 44-45
Music & Sound Lab: 183

N

National Ballpark Museum: 45
National Center for Atmospheric Research: 143
National Western Stock Show: 82
NCAR Trailhead: 158
Nederland: 22, 172-174
New Belgium Brewing Company: 19, 22, 187
newspapers and periodicals: 259
910 Arts: 74
Ninth Street Historic Park: 39
NOCO Distillery: 187
North Cheyenne Cañon Park: 226
Nymph Lake: 177

O

Odell Brewing Company: 19, 185
Ogden Theatre: 29, 76-77

Old Capitol Grill & Smokehouse: 19, 131
Old Colorado City History Center: 214
Old Town Fort Collins: 22, 184
Olympic Training Center: 214
Open Stage Theatre & Company: 189
Opera Colorado: 72
Opera Fort Collins Guild: 189
Otterbox Digital Dome Theater: 183
Our Mutual Friend Brewing Company: 65
Ouzel Falls: 177
Oval, the: 183

P

packing tips: 259
Paint Mines Interpretive Park: 228
Paramount Theatre: 73
parks and gardens: Boulder 141, 143, 154; Colorado Springs 212, 216, 224, 225, 226, 228, 238; Denver 33-35, 39, 42, 46, 53, 57, 93-94, 97-98, 130-131; Fort Collins 183-184, 194
passports: 260
Pearl Street Mall: 22, 144, 150-151, 153
Penrose Heritage Museum: 214
Penrose Taphouse and Eatery: 187
Perkins Central Garden Trail: 226
Peterson Air & Space Museum: 23, 214
pets, traveling with: 263
Phantom Canyon Brewing Company: 19, 219, 230
Phantom Canyon Preserve: 195
Pikes Peak: 20, 23, 226, 241
Pikes Peak Birding and Nature Festival: 222
Pikes Peak Center for the Performing Arts: 220
Pikes Peak Greenway: 224
Pikes Peak International Hill Climb: 222, 241
Pikes Peak Marathon: 222, 241
Pikes Peak or Bust Rodeo: 222
Pinello Ranch: 225
Pints Pub: 66
planning tips: 14-16
Platte River Greenway: 94
Platte River Valley: 28, 38-42, 44-45; map 40-41
Polar Bear Plunge: 150
Ponti, The: 17, 101
Poudre Trail: 194
Pour House on Market: 68
ProRodeo Hall of Fame and Museum of the American Cowboy: 23, 214, 216

QR

Rabbit Hole, The: 23, 218
rafting: *see* kayaking/rafting
Rattlesnake Gulch Trail: 170
Rawhide Trail: 130
Red Rocks Amphitheatre: 12, 20, 53, 57
Red Rocks/Dakota Ridge: 130
Red Rocks Park: 53, 98
Renegade Brewing Company: 66
rental cars: 256
Ridge Trail: 226
Ring the Peak Trail: 244
RiNo (River North Art District): 29, 57, 58
Robischon Gallery: 75
Rock Ledge Ranch Historic Site: 226
Rocky Mountain Arsenal National Wildlife Refuge: 53
Rocky Mountain Motorcycle Museum: 232
Rocky Mountain National Park: 13, 21, 174-177; map 175
Rocky Mountain Quilt Museum: 130
Rocky Mountain Women's Film Festival: 222
Root Down: 18, 29, 111
Royal Arch: 157
running/jogging: Boulder 136, 139, 148, 153, 158, 165, 169; Colorado Springs 222, 241; Denver 29, 39, 46, 81, 94, 97; Fort Collins 189-190

S

safety: 254, 257-258, 260-261
Sandlot Brewery: 19, 68
Santa Fe County Trail: 224
scenic drive: 172
Scott Carpenter Park: 154, 159
Seven Bridges Trail: 226
Seven Falls: 216
Shambhala Mountain Center: 205-206
Silent Film Festival: 149
Singleton Theatre: 72
16th Street Mall: 28, 32, 58, 73
Ska Street Brewstillery: 145
skateboarding: 95
skiing/snowboarding: general discussion 21; Boulder 173-174; Denver 133, 134
Skyline Park: 93
sledding: 95
Sloan's Lake Park: 97
Smith Lake: 98
smoking: 257
Snooze: 18, 103, 104, 121
snowshoeing: 21, 172, 173, 177
Soapstone Prairie Natural Area: 194, 195, 198
SoBo (South Broadway): 28, 33-35, 37-38; map 34
Sombrero Stables: 21, 177
Sommers Bausch Observatory: 144
South Boulder Creek on Walker Ranch Open Space: 156
South Mesa Trail: 172
Space Gallery: 74
spas: Boulder 159; Colorado Springs 228-229; Denver 93, 98, 133
spectator sports: Colorado Springs 222; Denver 95; Fort Collins 190

Spring Creek Trail: 20, 22, 194
Spruce Farm & Fish: 22, 162
Stargazers Theatre: 220
Starsmore Visitor and Nature Center: 220, 226
state parks: Boulder 169-170, 172; Denver 131; Fort Collins 194, 197, 198
St. Cajetan's: 39
St. Elizabeth's Church: 39
Stodgy Brewing Company: 187
Strange Craft Beer: 66
Streamside Trail: 169
Summit Music Hall: 61
Su Teatro Cultural and Performing Arts Center: 74
swimming: Boulder 159, 172; Fort Collins 195
Switch on the Holidays: 150

T

Taste of Colorado, A: 80
Tattered Cover Book Store: 17, 88, 121
taxi travel: 256
Temple Hoyne Buell Theatre: 73
tennis: 98
Territory Days: 222
Theatreworks: 220
3E's Comedy Club: 219
time zone: 259
Tivoli Student Union: 39
Tour de Corgi: 190
Tour de Fat: 21, 188, 190
Trails End Taproom: 218
train travel: 255
transportation: 253-256
travelers of color: 262-263
Trial Gardens: 183
TRVE Brewing Company: 66
Tulip Fairy and Elf Festival: 149

U

Uhl's Brewing: 145
Underground Music Showcase: 80
Union Station: 17, 28, 45, 104
United States Air Force Academy: 216
United States Mint at Denver: 32-33
United States Olympic and Paralympic Museum: 22-23, 216
University Center for the Arts: 183
University Memorial Center: 144
University of Colorado: 22, 143-144
University of Colorado Museum of Natural History: 144
Upslope Brewing Company: 145
Ute Valley Park: 224

VWXYZ

Valmont Bike Park: 156
Veronika String Quartet: 220
Vida Ellison Gallery: 37
visas: 260
visitor information: 259-260
Voorhies Memorial: 34
Walden Ponds Wildlife Habitat: 156
Walker Fine Art: 74
Wally Toevs at Walden Ponds: 156
Walter Orr Roberts Weather Trail: 158
Washington Park: 97-98
waterfalls: Boulder 173, 177; Colorado Springs 216, 226; Fort Collins 198
weather: 247
Western Art Gallery: 37
White Ranch Open Space Park: 20, 130
wildlife/wildlife-watching: general discussion 261; Boulder 154, 156-157, 158, 170, 172, 177; Colorado Springs 222, 226; Denver 53, 131; *see also* birds/bird-watching
Wild Provisions Beer Project: 145
William Allen White Cabins: 176
William Havu Gallery: 74
Williams & Graham: 18, 29, 65
Will Rogers Shrine of the Sun: 211
Winter Park Resort: 21, 133-134
Wolf Theatre: 72
Wonderbound: 75
World Figure Skating Museum and Hall of Fame: 23, 216
Wynkoop Brewing Company: 17, 19, 68
yoga: 172
Zoo Lights: 52, 82
zoos and animal parks: Colorado Springs 211; Denver 52

List of Maps

Front Map
Denver, Boulder & Colorado Springs: 4-5

Discover Denver, Boulder & Colorado Springs
chapter divisions map: 14

Denver
Denver: 26–27
Downtown Denver: 30
Golden Triangle, Lincoln Park, and SoBo: 34
LoDo and Platte River Valley: 40–41
Capitol Hill and City Park: 48–49
Greater Denver: 54–55
Highlands: 64
Golden: 129

Boulder
Boulder: 138
Downtown Boulder: 141
Vicinity of Boulder: 170
Rocky Mountain National Park: 175

Fort Collins
Fort Collins: 181

Colorado Springs
Colorado Springs: 210
Manitou Springs: 239

Photo Credits

All photos © Mindy Sink except: Title page photo: courtesy VISIT DENVER; page 2 courtesy VISIT DENVER; page 3 © Nikki A. Rae Photography/courtesy VISIT DENVER; page 6 © (top left) Rich Grant/Boulder CVB; (top right) courtesy VISIT DENVER; (bottom) courtesy VISITCOS; page 7 (top) courtesy VisitCOS; (bottom left) © Nikki A. Rae Photography/courtesy VISIT DENVER; (bottom right) © Steve Crecelius/courtesy VISIT DENVER; page 8 © (top) Linda Mohammad; page 9 © (top) Gnagel | Dreamstime.com; (bottom left) Denise Chambers/Boulder CVB; page 10 © Mdenhof | Dreamstime.com; page 12 © (top) courtesy The Beer Spa; (middle) Sepavo | Dreamstime.com; (bottom) Arinahabich08 | Dreamstime.com; page 13 © Haveseen | Dreamstime.com; page 15 © (bottom) Stephen Collector/Boulder CVB; page 16 © Gaylon Wampler Photography/courtesy VISITCOS; page 17 © (left) Scott Dressel Martin/courtesy VISIT DENVER; (right), SoGnar Creative Division/VISIT DENVER; page 18 © (bottom) Boulder CVB; page 22 (left) courtesy VisitCOS; (right) courtesy VISITCOS; page 23 © (bottom) © Kevin Syms/VisitCOS; page 24 © Evan Semón/courtesy VISIT DENVER; page 25 (top left) courtesy VISIT DENVER; page 31 © (top) Steve Crecllus/courtesy VISIT DENVER; (left middle) courtesy VISIT DENVER; (right middle) Bryce Boyer/courtesy VISIT DENVER; (bottom) courtesy VISIT DENVER; page 36 © (top) Cantelow | Dreamstime.com; (left middle) © Rebecca Todd/courtesy VISIT DENVER; (right middle)Carol M. Mighsmith/Library of Congress, LC-DIG-highsm- 48771; (bottom) Jeff Wells/courtesy VISIT DENVER; page 43 (top) courtesy VISIT DENVER; (bottom) © Stan Obert/courtesy VISIT DENVER; page 50 © (top) Scott Dressel-Martin/courtesy VISIT DENVER; (left middle) Bryce Boyer/courtesy VISIT DENVER; (right middle) © Rebecca Todd/courtesy VISIT DENVER; (bottom) © Evan Semón/courtesy VISIT DENVER; page 56 (top) courtesy VISIT DENVER; (left middle) © Nikki A Rae/Courtesy VISIT DENVER; (right middle) © Rocky Mountain Arsenal Visitor Center/Curtis Lewis/courtesy VISIT DENVER; (bottom) Joseph Rouse | Dreamstime.com; page 63 courtesy VISIT DENVER; page 67 © (top left) Evan Semón/courtesy VISIT DENVER; (top right) Evan Semón/courtesy VISIT DENVER; (bottom left) courtesy The Beer Spa; (bottom right) © Evan Semón/courtesy VISIT DENVER; page 72 © Kennedy Cottrell/Courtesy Meow Wolf; page 79 (top) courtesy VISIT DENVER; (left middle) © Rebecca Todd/courtesy VISIT DENVER; (right middle) courtesy VISIT DENVER; (bottom) © Evan Semón/courtesy VISIT DENVER; page 81 © courtesy VISIT DENVER; page 86 (top) courtesy VISIT DENVER; (bottom) © Kit Anderson; page 96 (left middle) courtesy VISIT DENVER; (bottom) courtesy VISIT DENVER; page 103 © Ashley Davis Tilly/courtesy VISIT DENVER; page 106 © Nikki A. Rae Photography/courtesy VISIT DENVER; page 110 (top left) courtesy VISIT DENVER; (top right) courtesy VISIT DENVER; (bottom) courtesy VISIT DENVER; page 118 (top) © D'Arcy Leck/courtesy VISIT DENVER; (left middle) courtesy VISIT DENVER; (right middle) courtesy VISIT DENVER; (bottom) courtesy VISIT DENVER; page 120 © Andeck Photo/courtesy VISIT DENVER; page 128 courtesy VISIT DENVER; page 135 © (top) Arinahabich08 | Dreamstime.com; page 136 courtesy Boulder CVB; page 137 © (top left) Linda Mohammad; (top right) courtesy Boulder CVB; page 140 courtesy Boulder CVB; page 142 (top right) courtesy Celestial Seasonings/Boulder CVB; (bottom) courtesy Boulder CVB page 146 © (top) Denise Chambers/Boulder CVB; (left middle) Bdingman | Dreamstime.com; (right middle) Denise Chambers/Boulder CVB; (bottom) Casey Cass/University of Colorado; page 152 (top) courtesy Boulder CVB; page 155 © (top) courtesy Boulder CVB; (left middle)courtesy GO Boulder; (right middle) courtesy Boulder CVB / Stephen Collector; (bottom) courtesy Boulder CVB; page 163 © (top) Kitleong | Dreamstime.com; page 169 © Sparty1711 | Dreamstime.com; page 171 © (top) Celin Serbo/Boulder CVB; (bottom) Sparty1711 | Dreamstime.com; page 176 © Haveseen | Dreamstime.com; page 178 © AJ Cohen; page 179 © (top left) Marekuliasz | Dreamstime.com; page 182 © (top) Ryan Burke/courtesy Visit Fort Collins; (left middle) Marekuliasz | Dreamstime.com; (right middle) courtesy Visit Fort Collins; (bottom) Richard Haro/Visit Fort Collins; page 186 © (top left) courtesy Visit Fort Collins; (bottom) Richard Haro/Visit Fort Collins; page 196 © (top) Indigojoey | Dreamstime.com; (left middle) Marekuliasz | Dreamstime.com; (right middle) Ryan Burke/Visit Fort Collins; (bottom) Richard Haro/Visit Fort Collins; page 203 © The Elizabeth Hotel; page 205 © mavrick/123RF; page 207 courtesy VISIT DENVER; page 208 © (top left) The Broadmoor/courtesy VISIT DENVER; (top right) courtesy VISITCOS; page 213 (top) courtesy VISITCOS; (left middle) Andreykr | Dreamstime.com; (right middle)courtesy VISITCOS; page 215 © (top) courtesy VISITCOS; (left middle) courtesy VISITCOS; (right middle)courtesy VISITCOS; (bottom) courtesy VISITCOS; page 217 © (top left) Kevin Syms/courtesy VISIT DENVER; (bottom) courtesy VISITCOS; page 221 © (top) courtesy VISITCOS; (bottom) courtesy VISITCOS; page 227 © (top left) courtesy VISITCOS; (top right) courtesy VISITCOS; (bottom) courtesy VISITCOS; page 231 © (top) courtesy VISITCOS; (bottom) courtesy VISITCOS; page 235 © (top) courtesy VISITCOS; (bottom) courtesy VISITCOS; page 240 © (top left) courtesy VISITCOS; (top right) courtesy VISITCOS; (bottom) courtesy VISITCOS; page 242 © (top left) Jakeschimetz | Dreamstime.com; (top right) courtesy VISITCOS; (bottom) courtesy VISITCOS; page 246 © Fotoeye75 | Dreamstime.com; page 253 courtesy VISIT DENVER

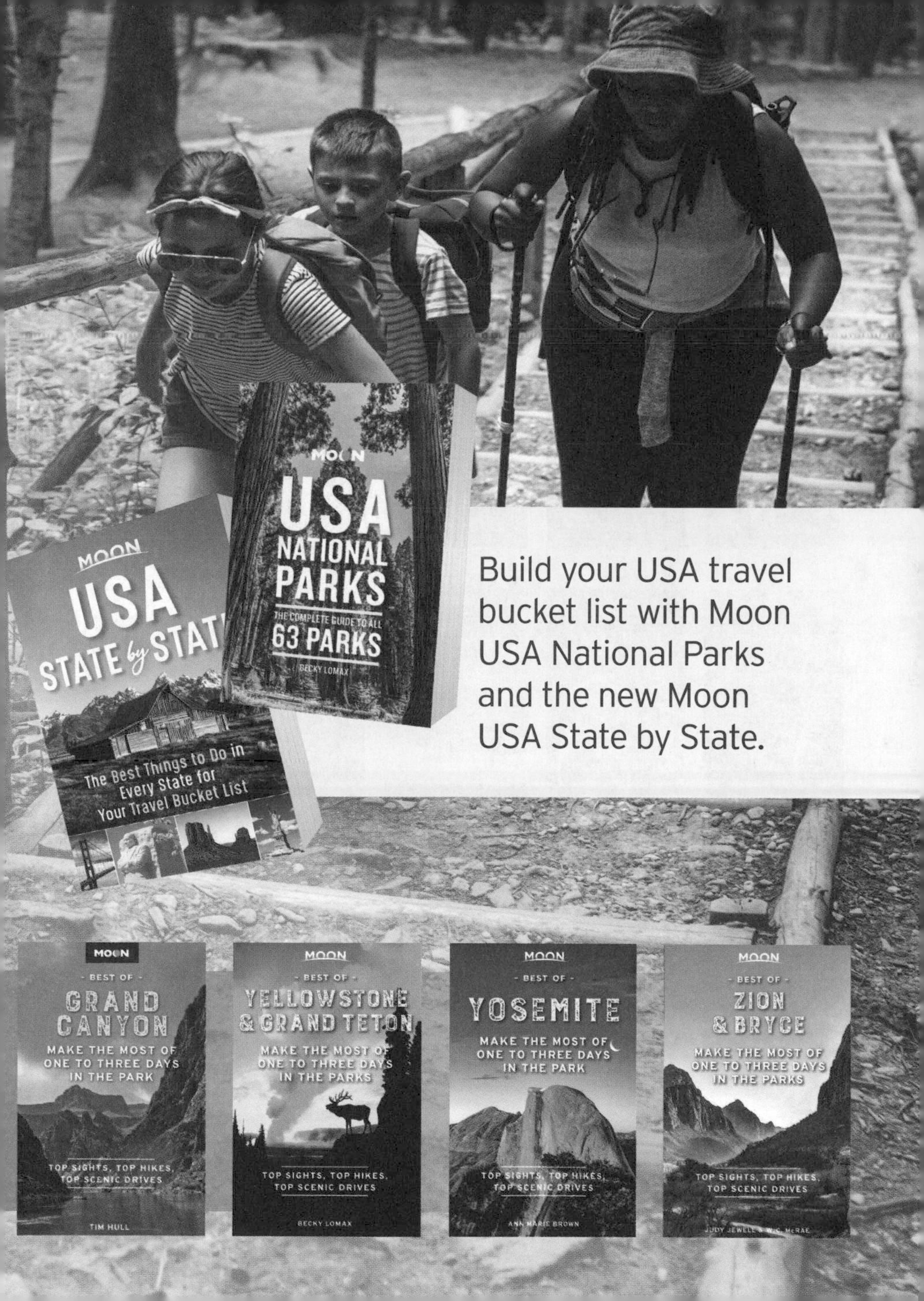
MOON
USA
NATIONAL
PARKS
THE COMPLETE GUIDE TO ALL
63 PARKS
BECKY LOMAX
MOON
USA
STATE by STATE
The Best Things to Do in
Every State for
Your Travel Bucket List
Build your USA travel bucket list with Moon USA National Parks and the new Moon USA State by State.
MOON
- BEST OF -
GRAND CANYON
MAKE THE MOST OF ONE TO THREE DAYS IN THE PARK
TOP SIGHTS, TOP HIKES, TOP SCENIC DRIVES
TIM HULL
MOON
- BEST OF -
YELLOWSTONE & GRAND TETON
MAKE THE MOST OF ONE TO THREE DAYS IN THE PARKS
TOP SIGHTS, TOP HIKES, TOP SCENIC DRIVES
BECKY LOMAX
MOON
- BEST OF -
YOSEMITE
MAKE THE MOST OF ONE TO THREE DAYS IN THE PARK
TOP SIGHTS, TOP HIKES, TOP SCENIC DRIVES
ANN MARIE BROWN
MOON
- BEST OF -
ZION & BRYCE
MAKE THE MOST OF ONE TO THREE DAYS IN THE PARKS
TOP SIGHTS, TOP HIKES, TOP SCENIC DRIVES
JUDY JEWELL & W.C. MCRAE

MOON
Drive & Hike Appalachian Trail
Timothy Malcolm
MOON
Baseball Road Trips
Timothy Malcolm
The complete guide to all the ballparks, with beer, bites, and sights nearby
MOON
Blue Ridge Parkway Road Trip
With Shenandoah & Great Smoky Mountains National Parks
Jason Frye
MOON
California Road Trip
Stuart Thornton
MOON
Nashville to New Orleans Road Trip
Margaret Littman
MOON
New England Road Trip
Seaside spots, majestic mountains & fall foliage, cozy getaways
Miles Howard
MOON
Northern California Road Trips
Stuart Thornton & Kayla Anderson
MOON
Oregon Trail Road Trip
Katrina Emery
MOON
Pacific Coast Highway Road Trip
California, Oregon & Washington
Ian Anderson
MOON
Drive & Hike Pacific Crest Trail
Caroline Hinchliff
MOON
Pacific Northwest Road Trip
Allison Williams
MOON
Route 66 Road Trip
Jessica Dunham
MOON
South Florida & the Keys Road Trip
Jason Ferguson
MOON
Southern California Road Trips
Ian Anderson
MOON
Southwest Road Trip
Tim Hull
MOON
U.S. & Canadian Rocky Mountains Road Trip
Becky Lomax
MOON
U.S. Civil Rights Trail
A traveler's guide to the people, places, and events that made the movement
MOON
Yellowstone to Glacier National Park Road Trip
Carter G. Walker
MOON
Road Trip USA
MOON
the Open Road
50 Best Road Trips in the USA
From Weekend Getaways to Cross-Country Adventures
Jessica Dunham

MAP SYMBOLS

- Highway
- Primary Road
- Secondary Road
- Unpaved Road
- Trail
- Ferry
- Railroad
- Pedestrian Walkway
- Stairs
- City/Town
- State Capital
- National Capital
- Highlight
- Point of Interest
- Accommodation
- Restaurant/Bar
- Other Location
- Information Center
- Parking Area
- Church
- Winery/Vineyard
- Trailhead
- Camping
- Train Station
- International Airport
- Regional Airport
- Park
- Golf Course
- Unique Feature
- Unique Feature Hydro
- Waterfall
- Mountain
- Ski Area
- Glacier

CONVERSION TABLES

°C = (°F - 32) / 1.8
°F = (°C x 1.8) + 32
1 inch = 2.54 centimeters (cm)
1 foot = 0.304 meters (m)
1 yard = 0.914 meters
1 mile = 1.6093 kilometers (km)
1 km = 0.6214 miles
1 fathom = 1.8288 m
1 chain = 20.1168 m
1 furlong = 201.168 m
1 acre = 0.4047 hectares
1 sq km = 100 hectares
1 sq mile = 2.59 square km
1 ounce = 28.35 grams
1 pound = 0.4536 kilograms
1 short ton = 0.90718 metric ton
1 short ton = 2,000 pounds
1 long ton = 1.016 metric tons
1 long ton = 2,240 pounds
1 metric ton = 1,000 kilograms
1 quart = 0.94635 liters
1 US gallon = 3.7854 liters
1 Imperial gallon = 4.5459 liters
1 nautical mile = 1.852 km

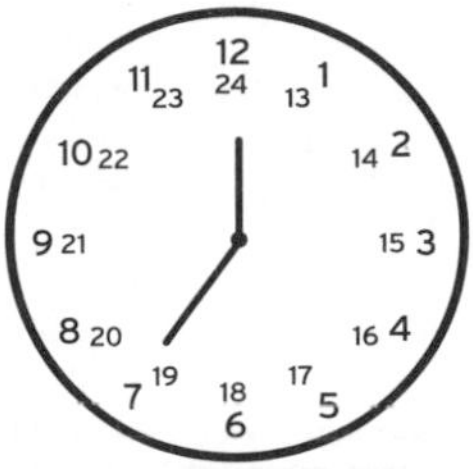

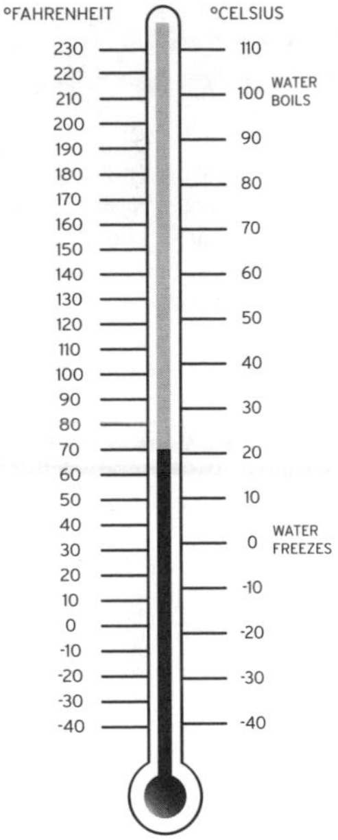

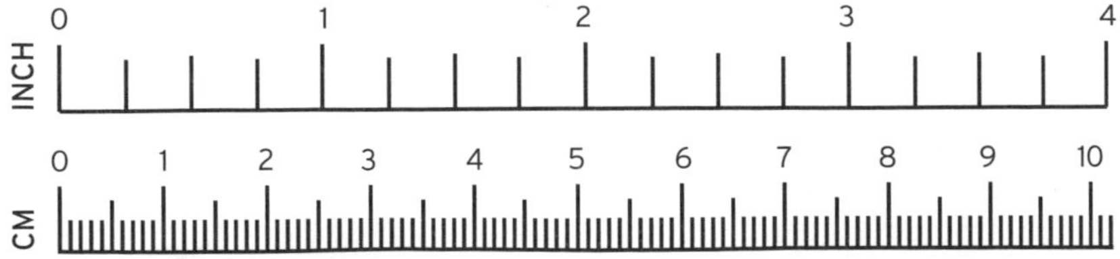

MOON DENVER, BOULDER & COLORADO SPRINGS
Avalon Travel
Hachette Book Group
1700 Fourth Street
Berkeley, CA 94710, USA
www.moon.com

Editor and Series Manager: Kathryn Ettinger
Acquiring Editor: Nikki Ioakimedes
Copy Editor: Deana Shields
Graphics Coordinator: Ravina Schneider
Production Coordinator: Ravina Schneider
Cover Design: Toni Tajima
Map Editor: John Culp
Cartographers: Brian Shotwell and John Culp
Indexer: Greg Jewett

ISBN-13: 978-1-64049-600-2

Printing History
1st Edition — 2016
3rd Edition — August 2022
5 4 3 2 1

Front cover photo: sunrise over Boulder © Dfikar | Dreamstime.com
Back cover photo: mule deer in Rocky Mountain Arsenal National Wildlife Refuge © Jdebordphoto | Dreamstime.com

Printed in Malaysia for Imago